BETWEEN THEATER
AND ANTHROPOLOGY

BETWEEN THEATER & ANTHROPOLOGY

RICHARD SCHECHNER

FOREWORD BY VICTOR TURNER

UNIVERSITY OF PENNSYLVANIA PRESS • PHILADELPHIA

Frontispiece: From Squat Theatre's *Mr. Dead and Mrs. Free.* Photo by Roe DiBona.

Cover photo: A Yaqui Deer Dancer demonstrating the dance at a conference sponsored by the Wenner-Gren Foundation for Anthropological Research, New Pascua, Arizona, 1981.

I rehearse and revise, then revise again and again. Thus there are many "originals" for each of the chapters of this book. Usually there are changes from one version to another. Everything in the book has been thoroughly revised for it.

Chapter 1, "Points of Contact," was written first for the Wenner-Gren Foundation for Anthropological Research International Symposium on Theater and Ritual, 1982. It also appeared in *South Asian Anthropologist* (Ranchi, India) 4, 1 (1983), in a special issue honoring Victor Turner.

Chapter 2, "Restoration of Behavior," was written first for the Wenner-Gren Symposium on Cultural Frames and Reflections, 1977. It was first published in *Studies in Visual Communication* 7, 3 (1981). An abridged version was included in *A Crack in the Mirror,* ed. Jay Ruby (Philadelphia: University of Pennsylvania Press, 1982). Still another version is in my own *Performative Circumstances from the Avant Garde to Ramlila* (Calcutta: Seagull Books, 1983).

Chapter 3, "Performers and Spectators Transported and Transformed," began as a lecture given at the Walker Art Center in Minneapolis in 1979. A version was printed as "Ritual in/of/and Theatre" in *New Wilderness Newsletter* 9 (1980). Another version was printed in the *Kenyon Review,* 3, 4 (1981).

Chapter 4, "Ramlila of Ramnagar," appeared in the *National Centre for the Performing Arts Quarterly Journal* (Bombay) 11, 3/4 (1982). An earlier version, co-authored with Linda Hess, appeared in *The Drama Review,* 21, 3 (1977).

Chapter 5, "Performer Training Interculturally," was published in French as "Défense et illustration de la formation 'mécanique' " in *La Grande Réplique,* (Montreal) 10 (1981). Another version was part of the *Canadian Theatre Review* 35 (1982), a special issue devoted to training.

Chapter 6, "Playing with Genet's *Balcony,*" was presented at a Colloquium on Theory of Drama and Performance at the University of Toronto in 1980. It was published in *Modern Drama* 25, 1 (1982).

Chapter 7, "News, Sex, and Performance Theory," was a paper I delivered to a conference on "innovation/renovation" in Racine and Milwaukee in 1981. An abridged version was printed in *Innovation/Renovation: New Perspectives on the Humanities,* ed. Ihab and Sally Hassan (Madison: University of Wisconsin Press, 1983).

I thank all the editors, organizers, and patrons for giving me the various stages necessary to think on my feet and revise in my study.

Design by Adrianne Onderdonk Dudden

Library of Congress Cataloging in Publication Data

Schechner, Richard, 1934–
  Between theater and anthropology.

  Bibliography: p.
  Includes index.
  1. Theater.   2. Anthropology.   I. Title.
  PN2041.A57S33   1985   792'.01   84–5197
  ISBN 0–8122–1225–8 (paper)

Printed in the United States of America

10 9 8 7 6 5

To Carol Martin

CONTENTS

For an anthropologist (working in several cultures, "posttribal," "peasant," and "urban-industrial"), it was both theoretically illuminating and personally rewarding to meet Richard Schechner, whose life has been dedicated to organizing and understanding performances. My own field experience had forced me to pay special attention not only to institutionalized performances, such as rituals and ceremonies, but also to what Erving Goffman calls the (dramatic) "presentation of self in everyday life." My own self was now presented with an experimentalist in performing. I learned from him that all performance is "restored behavior," that the fire of meaning breaks out from rubbing together the hard and soft firesticks of the past (usually embodied in traditional images, forms, and meanings) and present of social and individual experience. Anthropologists usually see and hear but try not to interfere with the life they immerse themselves in among initially "alien" cultural milieus. Inevitably, like all scientists, their modes of observation *do* set up disturbing ripples in the "fields" of social relations they "observe," but on the whole they try to be discreet. A director like Schechner is committed by his role to "interference." If he happens also to be fascinated by theory, he tries to infer from the results of his interference in all the components and relations of theater certain conclusions about the nature and structure of the whole theatrical process, indeed about the whole cultural performative process, of which his professional speciality is an outstanding species.

A theatrical impresario, versed in and open toward sociological and psychological theories, clearly has available to him, as does any social scientist with complementary interests, a laboratory of performative experiments normally inaccessible to field anthropologists, who can look and stare but seldom change or experiment with the cultural performances they encounter. Almost by chance, though we had read snatches of each other's publications, Schechner and I met a few hours before Clifford Geertz's 1977 Trilling Lecture (for which I was a commentator) in New York, poured out our ideas on and to one another, and began a relationship that has had me performing ethnographic texts of rituals and "social dramas" with drama as well as anthropology students in New York, and Schechner giving lectures on Indian folk and Japanese traditional theater to anthropological and other "academic" audiences in the United States and elsewhere.

Schechner opened up for my study a new world of performative techniques. Anthropologists, by their training, are not qualified to investigate the training of actors in ritual, ritualized theatre, and more secular types of cultural performance—how they prepare for the public events, how they transmit performative knowledge, how they dress, mask, and apply cosmetics, their personal "shtick," that is, attention-getting devices unique to each performer. Anthropologists are more concerned with *stasis* than with *dynamis,* with texts, institutions, types, protocols, "wiring," custom, and so on than with the *how* of performance, the shifting, evanescent, yet sometimes utterly memorable relationships that develop unpredictably among actors, audience, text, and the other situational variables discussed by Schechner in this book. Schechner also brought to my attention the indigenous theorizings of non-Western theater, themselves rooted in religious and ethical world views unfamiliar to the tradition deriving from Athens-Rome-Jerusalem, which encompasses our Euro-American outlooks and articulates the texts, scenarios, mise-en-scènes, training, and symbolic codes of our familiar cultural performances from film, telescreen, to stage. In this book he goes into great detail, in inter- and cross-cultural terms, as to how ritual and theatrical traditions become enfleshed in performance and in their dynamic incarnation act as a reflexive metacommentary on the life of their times, feeding on it and assigning meaning to its decisive public and cumulative private events.

I hope that anthropologists will not turn away from Schechner's fundamental contribution to the understanding of performance because he writes in a vivid style, with many allusions to his personal experiences. What he is offering is a prodigious gift to those of us who have so often been afraid to dip our toes in the waters of life—for fear of contamination by what seems to be a polluted stream. Schechner is a practiced diver, and he brings up for us many treasures as well as dead men's bones. He might just be the catalyst anthropologists need to get them thinking about what Dilthey called "lived-through experience." This is not to deny the venerable past and the founding ancestors but to bring the discipline back into touch with the bodily as well as mental life of humankind. Actors are deeply aware of how the human body can be made by costume, cosmetics, and stylization a matrix of living meaning, at once epitomizing and evaluating the social life of the times. Schechner has given us many instruments for operating cognizantly on the living body of historical humankind. We have much to thank him for.

ACKNOWLEDGMENTS

A book like this is written by one person but the ideas expressed are nurtured by a group: colleagues, artists, friends, research assistants, students; deans, foundation officials, government workers. Many whose names I will never know: the people who keep the railroads running in India, telephone operators, helpful strangers. Some people belong to several categories. I want to thank them all, even those I forget to thank.

I want to thank my dear friend Victor Turner who died on 18 December 1983. Victor was a great, just, and generous man. During many hours of conversation, in seminars and workshops, at conferences and meetings, in his home and mine, we shared ideas and visions, jokes and songs, lore and theories. See you someday in Glasgow, Victor.

Thanks to Carol Martin who read the essays in this book with a constructive, critical editorial eye.

Michael Kirby is a close friend whose opposing viewpoints keep me alert, as I hope mine do him.

Edith Turner, Barbara Kirshenblatt-Gimblett, Barbara Myerhoff, Jerome Rothenberg, Jerzy Grotowski, Herbert Blau, and Brian Sutton-Smith have each enriched me with their work, friendship, and talk.

Brooks McNamara, Marcia Siegel, and Kate Davy—colleagues in the Department of Performance Studies, Tisch School of the Arts, New York University—have helped me develop many of my theories in courses, seminars, and faculty discussions.

David Oppenheim, dean of the Tisch School, has always been warmly supportive.

Dan Sandford and Cathy J. Sharp made life easier by running an efficient, and pleasant, departmental office.

Thanks also to the many students, performers, and other performance artists and scholars who have worked with me in workshops, rehearsals, productions, classes, seminars, and conferences: these people and these gatherings are the soil of my thinking.

Sally Harrison not only typed the manuscript but, as a performance theorist, made many helpful suggestions. Lita Osmundsen and Willa Appel of the Wenner-Gren Foundation for Anthropological Research supported my work and made possible a gathering of performing artists and scholars from around the world to consider some of the ideas discussed in this book.

Grants and fellowships from Guggenheim, Fulbright, Smithsonian, and the Social Science Research Council have all made my research in America and overseas possible.

My son Samuel, who was born when work on this book began, has been a source of constant delight and inspiration.

BETWEEN THEATER
AND ANTHROPOLOGY

1
POINTS OF CONTACT
BETWEEN ANTHROPOLOGICAL
AND THEATRICAL THOUGHT

Whether practitioners and scholars of either discipline like it or not, there are points of contact between anthropology and theater; and there are likely to be more coming. These points of contact are at present selective—only a little of anthropology touches a little of theater. But quantity is not the only, or even the decisive, measure of conceptual fertility. This mixing will, I think, be fruitful. Clifford Geertz writes that "in recent years there has been an enormous amount of genre mixing in social science, as in intellectual life generally" (1980, 165). He goes on to specify the "drama analogy" as one of the major trends in anthropological thinking. That analogy has been developed most thoroughly and thoughtfully by Victor Turner, who saw social conflict following the structure of drama and adapting its subjunctive "as if" mood. Turner's work fits nicely with that of Erving Goffman, who, at the level of scene and "character" (who is being, or pretending to be, who), found theater everywhere in everyday life.

But what about contacts being made from the other direction, from the various performing arts? These are the contacts I know something about from my work as a theater director. And these are the ones I will concentrate on here.

To what degree are performers of rituals—the deer dancers of the Arizona Yaqui or the Korean shamans (to name just two groups about whom I have direct information)—aware of the performing-arts aspects of their sacred work? Also, what about large-scale performative events that cannot really be easily classified as belonging to either ritual or theater or politics? I mean performances like the Ramlilas of northern India (see chapter 4) and the Ta'Ziyeh passion plays of Iran. Is contact a one-way or even a two-way operation? Some anthropologists, Turner foremost among them, began "performing anthropology" (Turner and Turner 1982); and some theater people, Peter Brook, Jerzy Grotowski, and Eugenio Barba especially, explored what Barba calls "theatre anthropology" (Barba 1980, 1981, 1982a). Before looking at these concrete examples, I will discuss each of six points of contact.

Transformation of Being and/or Consciousness

Either permanently as in initiation rites or temporarily as in aesthetic theater and trance dancing, performers—and sometimes spectators too—are changed by the activity of performing. How is a permanent transformation or a tempo-rary transportation achieved? Is Olivier playing Othello different than a Noh actor performing the mask of Benkei or a Balinese sanghyang dancer in trance? Is there any real difference in meaning among the various terms different cultures have devised to describe what performers do? Can the transformation of consciousness during performance be measured at the level of brain activity?

While watching the deer dance of the Arizona Yaqui in November 1981, I wondered if the figure I saw was a man and a deer simultaneously (plate 1); or, to say it in a way a performer might understand, whether putting on the deer mask made the man "not a man" and "not a deer" but somewhere in between. The top of his head (man's/deer's), with its horns and deer mask, is a deer; the bottom of his head below the white cloth, with its man's eyes, nose, and mouth, is a man. The white cloth the dancer keeps adjusting is the physicalization of the impossibility of a complete transformation into the deer. At the moments when the dancer is "not himself" and yet "not not himself," his own identity, and that of the deer, is locatable only in the liminal areas of "characterization," "representation," "imitation," "transportation," and "transformation" (see chapter 3). All of these words say that performers can't really say who they are. Unique among animals, humans carry and express multiple and ambivalent identities simultaneously.

Those of the Yaqui watching the deer dance feel that a being from the *huya aniya* ("flower world"), the world of wild, free beings, has temporarily entered the human world—not exactly a captured being but one who has agreed to visit. This is not so different from what the Balinese feel about the gods and spirits who "descend" to possess dancers in trance. However it may be conceptually, the techniques of "getting there," of preparing the performer to perform, are much the same for the deer dancer as for the Balinese trance dancer or for an actor playing a role in New York: observation, practice, imitation, correction, repetition.

At the same time, it must be noted that when an "outsider" learns the deer dance, or a version of it, the Yaqui themselves regard this dancing very differently than they do their own deer dancing. The Mexican Ballet Folklorico has a number called "Deer Dance." Anselmo Valencia, ritual leader of the Yaqui of New Pascua, Arizona, says this about the Ballet Folklorico:

Valencia: The people that brought this Mexican company together were practicing the various cultural dances in many parts of Mexico—anyone can learn the dance, and they did. So they brought out a very broad imitation of the deer dance.

Question: How did that make the Yaquis who saw it, and who knew how to dance the deer, feel?

Valencia: Very, very discouraged. In fact, one of the young men that became a deer dancer was in training at that time for the military and he saw the dance in Mexico. He was very discouraged and he said: "You know, they are just making fools of the Yaquis." I told him, don't look at it that way. Look at it as a play. There's nothing religious about it, nothing Indian about it. It is for the non-Indian population. It's not a Yaqui performance.

Question: Are things different in the Folklorico from the dance we saw yesterday?

Valencia: Everything is different. The deer head is different, the gait is different. It doesn't harm us, it frustrates us. So our people stopped doing it. It's frustrating to have somebody else say, "I'm doing a Yaqui thing," when the Yaquis know that it is not. [1981, 4]

Valencia also told of old deer songs that were recorded and sold. The old songs had been "very good for hundreds and hundreds of years," but "recording the mysteries of such deer songs took spiritual powers away from the songs" and the people stopped singing them.

Valencia: If a hundred songs were recorded, and a hundred songs were sold, I think that we would not use them anymore. It's not the condition of "freshness." You have to be a Yaqui, or at least an Indian, to understand how the mysteries of that song— the words, the purpose of it, the spiritual purpose of it—to understand that the spiritual benefits of the song are withdrawn if the song is commercialized. [1981, 4–5]

At present, largely due to Valencia's leadership, the songs and the dances are being restored to the Yaqui. The point to note is that such performances do not have an independent life: they are related to the audience that hears them, the spectators who see them. The force of the performance is in the very specific relationship between performers and those-for-whom-the-performance-exists. When the consumer audience comes in, the "spiritual powers" depart.

The transformations of being that compose performance reality evidence themselves in all kinds of anachronisms and strange, incongruous combinations that reflect the liminal qualities of performance. That the deer singer's water drum sits in a modern metal cooking pot, straight from the kitchen right next door to the dance ramada (plate 2), is not only a question of modernization, of making do (which performers are famous for around the world), but an example of transformative doubling. The kitchen pot is analogous to the dancer and the singers: the pot does not stop being itself even as it serves to evoke the flower world of the deer songs. Both pot and performers are "not themselves" and "not not themselves." Pot and performers link two realms of experience, the only two realms performance ever deals with: the world of contingent existence as ordinary objects and persons and the world of transcendent existence as magical implements, gods, demons, characters. It isn't that a performer stops being himself or herself when he or she becomes another—multiple selves coexist in an unresolved dialectical tension. Just as a puppet does not stop being "dead" when it is animated, so the performer does not stop being, at some level, his ordinary self when he is possessed by a god or playing the role of Ophelia. Even Stanislavski—whose work supported the most systematic naturalism—said:

Never lose yourself on the stage. Always act in your own person, as an artist. You can never get away from yourself. The moment you lose yourself on the stage marks the departure from truly living your part and the beginning of exaggerated false acting. [1946, 167]

The Balinese say that a person who injures himself while in trance is faking.

The beauty of "performance consciousness" is that it activates alternatives: "this" and "that" are both operative simultaneously. In ordinary life people live out destinies—everything appears predetermined: there is scant chance to say "Cut, take it again." But performance consciousness is subjunctive, full of alternatives and potentiality. During rehearsals especially, alternatives are kept alive, the work is intentionally unsettled. This celebration of contingency—a true, if temporary, triumph over death and destiny—describes even ritual performances, especially those rituals conducted by old masters whose ability to improvise is not denied them.

This same performative principle applies to Noh drama and is visible there in the mask that is too small for the actor's face—too small, that is, if the mask is intended to cover the whole face (as it does in Ramlila). In Noh,

1. A Yaqui Deer Dancer at New Pascua, Arizona, 1981. Photo by Richard Schechner.

2. The gourd water drum resting on its metal pot near the rasper and the upturned deer mask. Photo by Richard Schechner.

below the delicate white mask of the young female the spectator sees the thick, dark jowls of the mature male performer. The extreme formality of Noh leaves no doubt that this double exposure is no accident. Why is part of the main actor's face left showing—thereby undercutting the very illusion the mask and costume create? Is not the delight of Noh increased by the knowledge of the incomplete transformation achieved?

Zeami, instructing the Noh shite in the fifteenth century on how to train and perform, emphasizes the dialectical tension between *tai* and *yu*, literally "what is seen by the mind" (tai) and "what is seen by the eyes" (yu). Recently, Tatsuro Ishii has investigated the later writings of Zeami where these ideas are expressed.

Zeami does not explicitly define tai and yu in a modern sense, but tai can be interpreted as a fundamental texture in acting dependent on the mind of a performer, and yu is the outer, visual manifestation. . . . Copy tai, and it will become yu. If one copies yu it will become a false tai, and one will not be able to have either tai or yu. . . . The idea of tai and yu reminds us of another clearcut axiom concerning acting given in [Zeami's] *Kakyo:* "Move your mind a hundred percent and your body seventy percent." [1982, 8–9]

As with many instructions given the actor—in Euro-American traditions as well as Asian—an apparently simple statement is actually, in practice, complex. For the tai of Noh may be said to reside in the mask, which is plainly visible but not materially of the actor, and the yu of Noh is in the fleshy jowl revealed behind the mask but mostly concealed by it. The work of the shite is to make wholly manifest the tai of the mask: this is done not just by wearing the mask or by actively animating it but by surrendering to it, by abolishing one's own yu. This kind of work is not so different from what Grotowski—influenced by Asian forms, especially yoga and Kathakali—urged on his performers.

To the average actor the theatre is first and foremost *himself*, and not what he is able to achieve by means of his artistic technique. . . . Such an attitude breeds the impudence and self-satisfaction which enable him to present acts that demand no special knowledge, that are banal and commonplace. . . . The actor who undertakes an act of self-penetration, who reveals himself and sacrifices the innermost part of himself— the most painful, that which is not intended for the eyes of the world—must be able to manifest the least impulse. He must be able to express, through sound and movement, those impulses which waver on the borderline between dream and reality. [1968, 29, 35]

Both Grotowski and Zeami demand of actors years of training. Obtaining the means to manifest tai is equivalent to what Grotowski calls the actor's "sacrifice [of] the innermost part of himself."

In both these cases the actor undergoes profound, even permanent, changes in consciousness. It is very important to note, with regard to the state of Euro-American culture in the late twentieth century, that while Zeami's program has been in place for more than four hundred years, being passed on from father to son among several families of Noh shite, Grotowski's "poor theatre" phase, producing masterful productions like *The Constant Prince, Akropolis,* and *Apocolypsis cum Figuris,* lasted barely ten years, until about 1969. It was as if Grotowski's project could not find the means of continuing because the personal consciousness it evoked and required on a continuous basis was too demanding, his rigorous system of training not compatible with Euro-American individualism-narcissism.

Brecht, like Zeami, Stanislavski, and Grotowski, emphasizes the creative possibilities of the incomplete and problematic kind of transformation that the performer undertakes.

The actor [Brecht says] does not allow himself to become completely transformed on the stage into the character he is portraying. He is not Lear, Harpagon, Schweik; he shows them. He reproduces their remarks as authentically as he can; he puts forward their way of behaving to the best of his abilities and knowledge of men; but he never tries to persuade himself (and thereby others) that this amounts to a complete transformation. [1964, 137]

The distance between the character and the performer allows a commentary to be inserted; for Brecht this was most often a political commentary, but it could also be—as it is for postmodern dancers and performance artists—an aesthetic or personal commentary. Brecht found the kind of acting he wanted in Chinese theater. Pointing out the difficulties European actors have in "becoming" their roles night after night, Brecht says, "These problems are unknown to the Chinese performer, for he rejects complete conversion. He limits himself from the start to simply quoting the character played. But with what art he does this!" (1964, 94). Thus Brecht, like the other master performers-directors, emphasizes techniques necessary for this kind of acting: acting where the transformation of consciousness is not only intentionally incomplete but also revealed as such to the spectators, who delight in the unresolved dialectic.

Needless to say, this is not the only kind of acting. Stanislavski's work, especially as it was elaborated on in America, forms the basis of a naturalism that attempts to hide all artifice. This is the dominant style in American films and television. If not dominant, it is strongly present in American theater. And there are numerous places where by means of trance, masks for the face and body, or other performative techniques a total transformation of consciousness is intended. These transformations are for the most part temporary—I call them "transportations" (see chapter 3). Interestingly enough, the more mature, skilled, and respected the performer, the more likely she or he is to practice an incomplete or unresolved transformation.

A corollary issue that may upon full investigation prove to be the key to the problem of transformation of consciousness is exactly what it is that is expected of the audience. Are they to watch from a distance and judge, as Brecht wanted his audiences to do? Or are they meant to be swept up into the performance, responding with such intensity—as at some of the churches I've attended in New York City—that during the peak of the service everyone, or nearly everyone, is performing? Between these extremes almost every other kind of audience deportment and participation can find its place. All along the continuum, different kinds of attention are required of the spectators—and different kinds of transformations of consciousness within the performers. Thus there are several varieties of transformed consciousness involved: among individual performers, among the performing group, among the audience as individuals and as a group—and between these entities.

Intensity of Performance

In all kinds of performances a certain definite threshold is crossed. And if it isn't, the performance fails. When I was directing The Performance Group (1967–80), bad reviews sometimes combined with bad weather and lack of advertising money so that very few people showed up at the theater. On several occasions the members of TPG debated just before a scheduled performance whether indeed the "show must go on." As a rule of thumb, we decided that if the performers outnumbered the audience we'd cancel. Because unless there were enough spectators to animate the theater—an environmental theater, mind you, wherein performers are aware of the audience, where space is shared and brought to life by the interaction between performers and spectators—the show itself would lack living yeast and fail to rise. No theater performance functions detached from its audience. Of course, theater and dance (whether aesthetic or ritual) that need audience participation are more dependent on the audience than events where the spectator's role is that of passive recipient. But even when apparently passive, as at a concert of classical music or a performance of Racine, a full house eager to see this performance, to attend the work of this particular artist, literally lifts a cast of players, propels, and sustains them.

Spectators are very aware of the moment when a performance takes off. A "presence" is manifest, something has "happened." The performers have touched or moved the audience, and some kind of collaboration, collective special theatrical life, is born. This intensity of performance—and I, person-ally, don't think the same kind of thing can happen in films or television, whose forte is to affect people individually but not to generate collective energies—has been called "flow" by Mihaly Csikszentmihalyi (1975, 35–36).

Performances gather their energies almost as if time and rhythm were concrete, physical, pliable things. Time and rhythm can be used in the same way as text, props, costumes, and the bodies of the performers and audience. A great performance modulates intervals of sound and silence, the increasing and decreasing density of events temporally, spatially, emotionally, and kinesthetically. These elements are woven into a complicated yet apparently inevitable (experienced as simple) pattern. This "flow" occurs even in perfor-mances that do not build to a climax the way a Pentecostal church service does or the way a performance of *Death of a Salesman* or *Macbeth* might. For example, the whirling dervishes of Turkey, or the whirling postmodern dances of Laura Dean, or the excruciatingly slow movements, extruded over a period of hours, of Robert Wilson's *Deafman Glance* or *Einstein on the Beach* each develop patterns of accumulating, if not accelerating, intensities. In fact, dancer Trisha Brown calls some of her most powerful works "accumula-tions." "The accumulation is an additive procedure where movement 1 is presented; start over. Movement 1; 2 is added and start over. 1, 2; 3 is added and start over, etc., until the dance ends" (1975, 29).

Performances like Dean's, Brown's, and the dervishes' do not rise to a climax; the accumulation-repetition lifts performers, and often spectators too, into ecstatic trance. In an accumulation, as in repetitious music such as Philip Glass's, the spectator's mind tunes in to subtle variations that would not be detectable in a structure where attention is directed to narrative or melodic development. Several times I've organized "all-night dances" to show the power of accumulation and repetition. Groups of from eight to twenty-five persons danced in a simple counterclockwise circle from four to eight hours. Why counterclockwise? It may have to do with left-brain/right-brain differ-ences. Each time I've participated in this kind of dance I've had, and others too have had, a trancelike experience, an experience of total flow where for varying periods the sense of me as an individual, the amount of time passing, the awareness of the environment I was in (outdoors in a field and inside a gymnasium, to name two) were abolished. What was left were a vaguely recollectable sense of moving in the circle and the feel of other persons, the other bodies, to either side of me. This kind of experience is one I describe as "total low intensity," as distinct from what happened to me in the Pentecostal church or at a pig-kill festival in the highlands of Papua New Guinea where I experienced "total high intensity" (see Schechner 1977, 63–98). In both cases my sense of me as Richard Schechner dissolved. Total low intensity is trophotropic: heart rate decreases, as does blood pressure; the pupils are constricted, the EEG is synchronized. There is a tendency toward trance or sleepiness. Total high intensity is ergotropic: heart rate increases, as does blood pressure; the pupils are dilated, the EEG is desynchronized. There is a high level of excitement and arousal. For a full discussion of these states see Lex 1979.

Understanding "intensity of performance" is finding out how a performance builds, accumulates, or uses monotony; how it draws participants in or intentionally shuts them out; how space is designed or managed; how the scenario or script is used—in short, a detailed examination of the whole performance text. Even more, it is an examination of the experiences and actions of all participants, from the director to the child sleeping in the audience.

The deer dance at New Pascua seemed to follow an eight-phase intensity pattern. The dance moved from a slow start to a very fast finish of high intensity followed by an abrupt breaking off and starting again. This pattern is analogous to the jo-ha-kyu of Japanese aesthetics.

The expression of jo-ha-kyu represents the three phases into which all the actions of an actor are subdivided. The first phase is determined by the opposition between force which tends to increase and another which holds back (jo = to withhold); the second phase (ha = to break) occurs in the moment in which one is liberated from this force, until one arrives at the third phase (kyu = rapidity) in which the action reaches its culmination, using up all of its force to suddenly stop as if face to face with an obstacle, a new resistance. . . . The three phases of jo-ha-kyu impregnate the atoms, the cells, the entire organism of Japanese performance. They apply to every one of an actor's actions, to each of his gestures, to respiration, to the music, to each theatrical scene, to each play in the composition of a Noh day. It is a kind of code of life which runs through all the levels of organization of the theatre. [Barba 1982a, 22]

In the deer dance I saw in 1981, I recorded the following phases. (1) The interlude, or cool down/warm up occurred both before the dancing and after, forming a kind of background of ordinariness from which the extraordinary features of the dancing arose. During the interlude everybody relaxed. There was a lot of talking, smoking, drinking coffee, moving around. (2) Young Pascolas begin dancing, without masks, accompanied by two old men playing a violin and a harp. Pascolas are Yaqui ritual clowns. Often they wear animal or demon masks—but never a deer mask. Pascolas interact with spectators, making fun of them (as they did of me). Yaqui and scholars agree that Pascolas are ancient, maybe older than the deer dance, but Pascola music is made with European instruments. The water drum, raspers, whistle, and skin drum of the deer dance are Native American. As the young Pascolas dance, only a few Yaqui watch (the scholars were rapt: professional observers). This phase of the dancing was also a kind of public training session. Later, after the deer dance was over, two less skilled dancers danced in a practice session. Valencia confirmed that practice does happen this way, in public as well as in private rehearsals. Pascola and deer dance both alternately and together. The dancing and music show the layering of Native American and Euro-American elements. Pascola is both older and newer than deer. (3) To the beating of the skin drum and blowing of the whistle, the deer dancer begins to put on his mask. The young Pascolas dance with their masks on, but the deer does not dance. There is a mixture of music from violin, harp, skin drum, and whistle. (4) Water drum and raspers begin to play music; the violin and harp stop playing. (5) The deer, masked, dances while at the other end of the ramada the old Pascolas, masked, dance. Here there is a kind of confrontation between the deer's "flower world"—naively natural—and something more part-demonic–part-human represented by the Pascolas. During this phase the deer singers sing, the water drums and raspers are sounded, the deer shakes his rattle. Some who wish to see mimetic drama in the deer dance feel that this phase includes a suggestion of the deer being hunted. (6) The oldest, most senior, Pascola dances. The tempo is faster. This is the "full dance" and includes direct confrontation between deer and Pascola as the Pascola moves from his end of the ramada into the deer's territory. Here, certainly, mimetic action can be detected by those looking for it. Music is supplied only by the deer's instruments: water drums, raspers, skin drum, whistle. The harpist is smoking at the back of the ramada; the violinist stands and watches but with a studied detachment. (7) The Pascola withdraws to the back end of the ramada. The deer dances solo. When the Pascola leaves, the skin drum and whistle stop, but deer singing, water drums, and raspers continue. It appears that this is the oldest, deepest, most "essentially deer" section. (8) All stop. This stopping occurs suddenly—just an end to the song, and that's it. There is talk in the ramada. The deer removes the mask. Pascola dancers wander. Violin and harp start to tune up for another eight-phased round. Phase 8 = phase 1.

This eight-phased pattern of deer dancing is, as I noted, like the Japanese jo-ha-kyu pattern described by Zeami many centuries ago. There is no question here of diffusion. What we have is my application of a Japanese theory of aesthetics to a native American genre. Anthropologists may bridle at this. They require the participant observer to "see with a native eye" and maybe even "feel with a native heart." But one must be very careful that such requirements do not merely sugar-coat arrogance. Who is to determine what the native eye sees or the native heart feels? I prefer to let the "natives" speak for themselves. For my part, I acknowledge that I am seeing with my own eyes. I also invite others to see me and my culture with their eyes. We are then in a position to exchange our views.

Using aesthetics interculturally relates directly to social theory. For example, Turner's four-part "social drama"—breach, crisis, redressive action, reintegration (or schism)—is derived from the Greco-European model of drama. But, as Turner says, sometimes a phase of a social drama seethes for years and years; sometimes there is no resolution even after a climactic series of events. Great excitement is followed by a sudden breaking off or ceasing of turmoil; it is not that everything has been resolved as at the end of *Hamlet*. If Turner had used the jo-ha-kyu model, he might have seen the long festering as jo, the sudden eruption of crisis as ha, and the rapid rise to a climax as kyu. Then, either the crisis is resolved through redressive action (as Turner calls it) or it subsides into another long jo. This pattern does not suit all social dramas, but neither does Turner's four-phase Greco-European scheme. It may be that some social dramas are better looked at in Japanese aesthetic terms than in Greco-European ones, for some social dramas do not resolve themselves but pass from a climax, a kyu, into a new slow phase, jo. It may be that jo-ha-kyu, in some circumstances, is a subset of Turner's redressive action phase.

There are a number of "basic" performance theories originating in different cultures. Each of these might be used singly or in combination as a lens through which to focus both social and aesthetic systems. As Beverly Stoeltje of the University of Texas told me when we discussed these ideas in April 1983, "I have this image of a kaleidoscope of aesthetic systems which can be turned upon any bit of data, producing different perspectives." A true intercultural perspective is actually a multiplicity of perspectives. Where do these performance theories come from? Is it axiomatic that social life precedes theatrical life? That is of course the Platonic-Aristotelian idea: art imitates life. But maybe the Hindu-Sanskrit view as expressed in the *Natyasastra* is more appropriate to these postmodern, reflexive times. Theater and ordinary life are a möbius strip, each turning into the other.

Audience-Performer Interactions

At Brooklyn's Institutional Church of God in Christ on a Sunday late in August 1982, a group of visiting anthropologists and scholars were welcomed by the pastor of the church, Bishop Carl E. Williams. These outsiders were part of an International Symposium on Ritual and Theatre.[1] Attendance at Institutional was part of a nine-day program that included, in addition to the usual papers and panels, a smorgasbord of performances, including Squat Theatre,[2] an experimental group; *A Chorus Line*, the Broadway hit; ceremonies conducted by Korean shamans; Kutiyattam, a Sanskrit theater from

Kerala, India; Noh; and a music, dance, and drama group from Nigeria (modern but with many traditional African elements). Obviously, participants received contrasting performative messages.

The Korean shamans and the pastor, deacons, and congregation at the Institutional Church requested, demanded, needed just about everyone present to participate. People got up out of their seats, moved freely in the space, sang and danced in the aisles (at the church) and in a large circle (with the shamans). It was striking how similar the Korean ceremony was to the black church service—although, again, there was no question of diffusion or mutual influencing. In both performances people achieved joy, even ecstasy, by singing and dancing. In each ritual a charismatic leader (the chief shaman, a powerful slim woman, Mme Kim, in her fifties; Bishop Williams, a huge God-the-Father man with powerful hands) was the focus of the ceremony. Strong music made dancing a necessity: the Korean drummers, the black church choirs, gospel singers, and congregation driven by piano, drums, tambourines, and organ. Mme Kim shared food with everyone, got people out of their seats to dance in circles, performed knife-blade walking on her bare feet. The congregation at Institutional participated by hand-clapping and waving, by shouting and dancing. In both services collecting money and displaying it were key features. The success of the services was known to all by the quantity of money, the intensity of participation, the sheer number of people dancing, singing, clapping, swaying. A turning point at Institutional came when not only regular members of the congregation but visiting anthropologists and theater people lined up to have Bishop Williams lay hands on them. At that moment the line between participants and visitors partly and triumphantly dissolved. The visitor who went deepest into trance when she was touched was a Korean scholar of shamanism (residing for some years in America). From her own culture she knew what was expected of her in Brooklyn, although these two cultures—Korean, Afro-American—had not previously interacted.

We need to know more about audience-performer interactions. What happens when performances tour, playing to audiences that know nothing of the social or religious contexts of what they are experiencing? Certainly Mme Kim found it a bit baffling to be shamanizing for people who didn't speak Korean or need her services. On the other hand, I felt at home at Institutional. There, members of the church urged us to return, which I've done. The Christians are proselytizers. But it made a difference that the audience was the one who "toured"—if only to Brooklyn. No doubt touring audiences are changing performances everywhere. It is more than the results of tourism. It is also a function of people who are truly serious about their theatergoing. These days audiences in New Delhi, Nairobi, or New York include people who, fifty years ago, would not "belong" to any of those places. Audiences are increasingly sophisticated and cosmopolitan. Changes in the audience lead to changes in the performances.

Michelle Anderson describes the three forms of vodun she researched recently in Haiti: a ritual/social form for Haitians "only" (though she was there), a social/theatrical form for Haitians and tourists, and a theatrical/ commercial form for tourists "only" (though some Haitians studying these different kinds of events were there). Anderson says these three forms taken together compose "authentic" vodun.

Nansoucri represents the voodoo which has had the least exposure to recent non-Haitian influences. Mariani has had the most exposure, and vividly exemplifies adaptation to these influences. . . . Voodoo at Jacmel is most revealing of the three; it embodies the very process of re-arrangement, of the stage of distortion, of liminality, that voodoo must continuously pass through—in one way or another—on its way to, but never reaching, an appropriately responsive or "finished" form. Living ritual, like living theatre, is never finished. [1982, 99]

What makes these changes—what keeps vodun "living"—is the changing audience. And that's what could kill it too, for there is only so much change that a genre can absorb before it is no longer itself.

The Whole Performance Sequence

Generally, scholars have paid attention to the show, not to the whole seven-part sequence of training, workshops, rehearsals, warm-ups, performance, cool-down, and aftermath. Theater people have investigated training, rehearsals, and performances but have slighted workshops, warm-up, cool-down, and aftermath. Just as the phases of the public performance itself make a system, so the whole "performance sequence" makes a larger, more inclusive system. In some genres and cultures, one or the other of the parts of the sequence is emphasized.

In Noh, for example, the extensive training of the shite traditionally starts when he is five years old. This training, from the very beginning, consists of learning parts of actual Noh performances. Some aspects of the performances—the way the feet move, the placement of the spine, the style of chanting—are constant from role to role. In learning the specifics of this or that role, the neophyte also learns the basic principles of Noh. Slowly, the learner accumulates enough concrete information to perform simple roles.

In his *Kyui*, Zeami outlines nine levels of acting, divided into three groups (see also chapter 5). Zeami advises the young actor to begin with the middle three levels. "The mark of surface design [naturalism, sheer imitation] is considered the first gateway on the path of study of the nine levels" (Zeami, in Nearman 1978, 314). After the performer masters the middle levels he scales the highest three levels. Only after learning these does he descend to the first three levels, the most primitive and gross roles. These roles, says Zeami, require a skill that only a master shite can provide: the ability to balance the grotesqueness of a role with the subtlety of how it is performed. Only after a shite has mastered the sublimity of the highest three levels is he equipped to descend to the lowest roles. This is still another aspect of incomplete transformation: In roles of the lowest levels the mask is gross while the partly revealed face behind it is sublime. Zeami, sadly, notes that "even today [the fifteenth century] in our art, there are fellows who treat the lower three levels as the first gateway to the study of the Way and perform accordingly. This is not the proper route" (1978, 330).

Zeami's secrets of training were kept in the Kanze family—passed down through the generations largely through oral transmission—until this century. These teachings form the core of the Kanze performance style. Such an emphasis on detailed training has made rehearsals and workshops in the Euro-American sense unnecessary in Noh. In a traditional Noh performance—still widely adhered to today—the shite summons the other groups of performers, all of whom have practiced separately—the drummers, flute player, *waki* (second role, unmasked), and *kyogen* (interlude)—and explains to them what he intends to do in the performance. He may point out or even demonstrate some *mai* (dance movement) if he is planning anything unusual. But the only time the whole Noh will be done is during the performance itself. The shite and chorus compose one performative unit, the waki another, the drummers another, and so on. That these radically separate groups of specialists can, during performance itself, work together as a superb ensemble shows Western theater people that there is more than one way to skin a cat.

Sometimes, as in classical Indian theater, preparations before a performance are very important. This seems to have been true in India from the very start. The *Natyasastra* devotes all of chapter 5 to "the preliminaries of a play." These include playing drums and stringed instruments as a way of telling the public that the performance is to begin; doing various rituals honoring the gods; performing special kinds of introductory dances; and making circumambulations of the stage. Today, were all these preliminaries performed, they would take several hours; usually they are much abbreviated. Before the onstage preliminaries, there are those in the green room. In Kutiyattam (the most ancient surviving Indian form, dating back at least to the tenth century) putting on the costume and applying the ornate makeup to the body and face take at least two hours; ditto for Kathakali. Each day before Ramlila, the boys who play the main roles rehearse for two hours and spend another two getting into costumes and makeup. But the men who play roles they've performed annually for years hardly rehearse at all. By way of contrast, Actors' Equity, the American actors' union, has a rule requiring actors to be at the theater one-half hour before curtain. Some actors come in earlier, but many do not. Jazz musicians tune up on stage with the audience present. Squat Theatre does not rehearse, train, or warm up. Members discuss the exact procedures of the performance, construct its physical environment, and wait for actual performances before doing what they have planned. This method, they say, gives each night's performance freshness (see Schechner 1978).

Discussing the cool-down from performances is more difficult because documentation is scant. The cool-down ought to be investigated from the point of view of both performers and spectators. The spectators, having experienced the performance, have been affected by it. After Ramlila of Ramnagar the boys who play Rama, Sita, and Rama's brothers are carried back to where they live for the month of performances. Except when performing their feet are never permitted to touch the ground while they wear their full regalia. Once their costumes are removed, they eat a special meal rich with whole milk, yogurt, fruit, nuts, and sweets. Soon enough they are asleep. More ordinary performers remove their costumes, eat, and socialize; some recite prayers or go to a temple for puja. There is no prescribed behavior that everyone follows. The audience also breaks into several parties. Many go straight home by the most efficient means. I don't know what they do. A few have rented rooms in Ramnagar for the Ramlila month. These nemis—faithful, wholly devoted spectators—may read the *Ramcharitmanas*, sing devotional songs, or in other ways continue their worship of Rama. A number of people gather in front of small shrines on the road back to the center of Ramnagar and chant kirtans with sadhus whose singing fills the night. Many spectators board rowboats for the thirty-minute voyage across the Ganga back to Varanasi. While on the sacred river they sing songs about Rama, Sita, and Hanuman. These activities keep the day's lila firmly in heart and mind.

In Bali it is just as important to get a dancer out of trance as to put him in. Smoke is inhaled, holy water sprinkled, and sometimes a chicken is sacrificed. At Institutional and other trance-inducing churches, black or white, when a brother or sister "falls out" (goes into trance) a group of friends and relatives gathers around, keeps the trancer from falling or in any way injuring himself or others, and accompanies him back to his seat. There, often, the trancer is fanned, has his brow mopped: the heat of the religious ecstasy is reduced. I've experimented with cool-down exercises—group breathing, the passing of water, some quiet talking about the performance (nothing critical, more in the way of individuals sharing experiences).

In theaters around the world, performers after a show eat, drink, talk, and celebrate. A newcomer to actors wonders how so much energy is left for these after-the-theater bouts. But truly these activities don't come "after" but are "part of" the performance and should be studied as such. In many cultures, taking food and drink, sharing memories of what happened, is either a concluding part of the performance or part of after-the-performance ceremonies. It appears that a wholehearted performance literally "empties" the performers, and one way they restore themselves (or are restored) to ordinary life is by being refilled with food and drink, sacred or profane. Or, conversely, the performance so fills performers with energy and excitement that they need time to let it all out in exuberant sociality.

Aftermath is even less systematically discussed than cool-down. The aftermath is the long-term consequences or follow-through of a performance. Aftermath includes the changes in status or being that result from an initiatory performance; or the slow merging of performer with a role he plays for decades (see chapter 3); or the reviews and criticism that so deeply influence some performances and performers; or theorizing and scholarship—such as this book. At the distance of reviews, criticism, theory, and scholarship careers are built not in the arts and rituals of performing but in commenting on performances. Of course, aftermath feeds back into performing—and the theories of practitioners such as Brecht, Stanislavski, and Zeami for examples are especially instrumental.

In limiting their investigations mostly to what happens during the performance itself, scholars are following modern Euro-American theatrical convention: You don't go backstage unless you're part of the show. The history of the development of the Western playhouse has been to reposition an event that was largely open, outdoors, and public into one that is closed, indoors, and private.

As I noted earlier, the seven phases of performances—training, workshop, rehearsal, warm-ups or preparations immediately before performing, the performance itself, cool-down, and aftermath—are not emphasized equally in all cultures. Traditional performances—the Mass, Purim speils, Noh, and so on—usually demand training but very little rehearsal. It's obvious: If you play the same role over and over again, as in Ramlila, or if there is an orderly, predictable progression of roles that lie before you over the years, as in Noh, the idea of figuring out what to do beforehand is unnecessary—doubly unnecessary if the mise-en-scène is fixed by tradition. But in cultures, like the Euro-American, where "originality" is prized (so prized that works are praised simply for being "new"), rehearsals are often more important than training.

Most American actors look forward to the time when they are "finished" training. Lip service is paid to lifelong training, but in fact only a small fraction of actors continue training after leaving acting school. Dancers are more likely to keep training—probably because a dancer without a flexible body is washed up. But how many dancers are really "in" their training. If a dancer could keep her body fit without training, would she still train? On the other hand, most performers enjoy rehearsals. That's where "creative work" gets done. Characterizations are built, choreography invented or learned, the many elements that compose a performance are tried out. How different from Noh. In Euro-American theater it is not so important that an artist be shaped to conform to a particular set of performative expectations already laid down by tradition. It is more important that the artist's "instrument" (= body and soul) be able to flexibly adapt to this or that temporary grouping of people and with them swiftly and efficiently release feelings and, along with the choreographer or director, invent or call upon a stock of movements, gestures, voices, and emotions. If this is accomplished, maybe audiences will believe that this temporary group is an "ensemble."

Since around 1960, and especially in experimental theater and dance, a situation has arisen where both script and mise-en-scène are "researched" and composed in a special performative phase between training and rehearsal called workshop. In theater that comes from workshop, there is no preexistent script—or there are too many scripts ("materials" or "sources"). The words do not determine everything else but are knitted into a performance text consisting of many braided strands: lighting, costumes, scenography, iconography (the arrangement of the performers in space), theater architecture, music, and so on. There are also many workshops that do not lead to public performances. Skills as diverse as t'ai chi or mask making are learned. Or, as in the "paratheatrical" work of Grotowski and others, an intense personal experience occurs. This kind of work borders on the "human potential movement," a movement that has taken a lot of its technique from theater, dance, and music.

Looking at the whole seven-phase performance sequence, I find a pattern analogous to initiation rites. A performance involves a separation, a transition, and an incorporation (Van Gennep [1908] 1960). Each of these phases is carefully marked. In initiations people are transformed permanently, whereas in most performances the transformations are temporary (transportations). Like initiations, performances "make" one person into another. Unlike initiations, performances usually see to it that the performer gets his own self back. To use Van Gennep's categories, training, workshop, rehearsal, and warm-ups are preliminary, rites of separation. The performance itself is liminal, analogous to the rites of transition. Cool-down and aftermath are postliminal, rites of incorporation. These phases of the ritual process may be applied to performance in another way too.

When workshops and rehearsals are used together, they constitute a model of the ritual process (see also chapters 2 and 6). Workshops, which deconstruct ordinary experience, are like rites of separation and transition while rehearsals, which build up, or construct, new cultural items, are like rites of transition and incorporation. Workshops and rehearsals converge on the process of transition. One of the advantages for performance theorists of Turner's talmud on Van Gennep is the extremely suggestive flexibility of the ritual process as Turner interprets it.

Transmission of Performance Knowledge

What is "performance knowledge"? For too long, in theater at least, performance knowledge has been identified with knowing the great dramatic texts (from Aeschylus through Shakespeare to Ibsen, Chekhov, Pirandello, and Brecht and on to Beckett). What performers and directors did was acknowledged but segregated. Then, in the sixties, came a time of the ascendancy of the practical—in America a number of "conservatory schools" of theater were formed. Students there learn the crafts of the stage but little literature and less theory. But performance knowledge is integrative.

Patrice Pavis in his *Languages of the Stage* identifies six kinds of texts used in the theater:

1. *Dramatic text:* the text composed by the author that the director is responsible for staging. . . .

2. *Theatrical text:* the text in a concrete situation of enunciation in a concrete area before an audience.

3. *Performance:* the ensemble of stage systems used, including the text, considered prior to the examination of the production of meaning through their interrelationships.

4. *Mise-en-scène:* the interrelationship of the systems of performance, particularly . . . the link between text and performance.

5. *Theatre event:* the totality of the unfolding production of the *mise-en-scène* and of its reception by the public, and the exchanges between the two.

6. *Performance text:* the mise-en-scène of a reading and any possible account made of this reading by the spectator. [1982, 160]

This kind of separating out of the different kinds of performance codes is necessary if we are ever to comprehend performance interculturally and theoretically. I do not agree entirely with Pavis's distinctions—I use "performance text" to mean all that happens during a performance both onstage and off, including audience participation. Usually only what happens onstage can be transmitted by a master to a neophyte; and these actions make up most of what is taught during training. I emphatically agree with Pavis that a detailed descriptive terminology needs to be developed.

This is so because it is by now very clear that a performance is much different and more complex than the "staging of a playtext." Both historically in terms of the origins of performance and interculturally in terms of the performances now going on, the staging of written texts comprises but a small fraction of the world's theater activity. Speaking of what might have been the world's earliest theater, the events occurring within the paleolithic caves of southwest Europe, I wrote in 1973:

We know nothing of the "scripts" used by the dancer-shamans of the paleolithic temple-theatres. . . . I say "scripts," which mean something that pre-exists any given enactment, which acts as a blueprint for the enactment, and which persists from enactment to enactment. Extrapolating from the existing evidence and modern experience, I assume that the dancing [in the caves] took a persistent (or "traditional") shape which was kept from one instance to another; that this shape was known by the dancers and by the spectators (if there were any), and that the shape was taught by one group of dancers to another. Most probably this teaching was not formal, but through imitation. However, a case could be made that the inaccessibility of the caves indicates an esoteric cult, and that the "secrets" of the cult would be definitely and formally transmitted. . . .

However, the performance is merely implicit or potential in the script; it is not until much later that power is . . . absorbed into the written word. To conceive of these very ancient performances—some as far back as 25,000 years ago—one has to imagine absolutely non-literate cultures; unliterate is probably a better word. Drawings and sculptings, which in the modern world are associated with "signs" and "symbols" (word-likeness), are in paleolithic times associated with doings (theatre-likeness). Thus, the "scripts" I am talking about are patterns of doing, not modes of symbolization separate from doing. Even talking is not fundamentally configured (words-as-written) but sounded (words-as-breath and vocal tone). Ultimately, long after writing was invented, drama arose as a specialized form of scripting. The potential manifestation that had previously been encoded in a pattern of doings was now encoded in a pattern of written words. The dramas of the Greeks, as Aristotle points out, continued to be codes for the transmission of action, but action no longer meant a specific, concrete way of moving/singing—it was understood "abstractly" or metaphorically, as a movement in the lives of people. Historically speaking, in the West, drama detached itself from doing; communication replaced manifestation. [1973a, 6–7]

Thus dramatic literature arose at specific places in specific historical circumstances. Nonliterary, non-written-down theater continues to thrive. Sometimes, as in Noh and Kathakali, an extensive theatrical literature exists but is learned as part of its actual use in performance.

Performance knowledge belongs to oral traditions. How such traditions are passed on in various cultures and in different genres is of great importance. Some surprising parallels exist, for example, between the way professional sports in America and traditional performances in Asia are coached and taught. Sports are fine examples of nonverbal performance—dramatic and kinesthetic yet not "dance" or "theater" in the classical, modern, or postmodern sense. The coaches of sports teams are usually former players. They personally give their "secrets" to younger players. Older players, even when they can't play anymore are respected for their records; participants and fans alike delight in anecdotes about the old great ones. Some of these ancestors are enshrined in "halls of fame," and some are kept on as coaches or in the front office. This is not so different from what happens to the most respected performers of Ramlila, Noh, Kathakali, Korean dance, and so on throughout Asia. Old performers teach, some are designated "living national treasures," and roles are set aside for them to play.

Elsewhere I have discussed the problem of transmission of performance knowledge as it applies to the American avant-garde (see Schechner 1982*b*). When theater people know more about how rituals and traditional performances are transmitted the problem will be less intractable. Some progress is being made. Western theater and dance workers by the hundreds have studied Asian and African performance techniques. I know mostly about those who have gone to India, Japan, and Indonesia. What's important about these contacts is not the direct taking of Asian ways—these imitations can be embarrassing—but the adaptation to American circumstances of underlying patterns, the very thought of performance: the master-disciple relationship; the direct manipulation of the body as a means of transmitting performance knowledge; respect for "body learning" as distinct from "head learning"; also, a regard for the performance text as a braiding of various performance "languages," none of which can always claim primacy. ("Languages" is in quotation marks because I am suspicious of the linguistic model as applied to performance. I think Aristotle was closer to being right when he identified "action" [*praxis*] at the core of performance: a very dense, dynamic system of shifting valences and twisting helixes. If performance theorists are in need of a guiding metaphor, we are more likely to find it in particle physics or biology than in linguistics.)

Of course the roads East-West/South-North are crowded with traffic going both ways. Hundreds of Africans, Asians, and Latin Americans have come to Europe and America to study performance. At first these people mostly worked in the Euro-American mainstream, and they brought back to their cultures versions of modern Western theater and dance and music. But, more recently, many non-Westerners have participated in experimental perform-ance. This has led to the development of intercultural companies and a marvelously complicated exchange of techniques and concepts that can no longer be easily located as belonging to this culture or that one. This dialogue relating modern, traditional, and postmodern elements even takes place within single nations. A conference held in Calcutta in 1983 focused on the relationship between Indian classical dance-drama genres and the modern theater. Actors, dancers, musicians, and scholars assembled from all over the world. Theater director Mohan Agashe of Pune, India, pointed out that the relationship among genres and cultures within India itself cannot simply be one of taking this dance step, that rhythm, or that story but must be some-thing more like metabolism where deep learning takes place, eventuating in artistic works that may not at all look like what they have come from. Euro-American theater is full of examples of the metabolic process Agashe is talking about. The puppets of Mabou Mines's *Shaggy Dog Animation* combine Japa-nese bunraku with Euro-American vaudeville puppetry as typified by Edgar Bergen's Charlie McCarthy. The masks of Islene Pindar's *Night Shadows* were crafted by Balinese artists for her Balinese-American Dance Company. These masks reflect Balinese interpretations of an American choreographer's ideas—an American who has studied in Bali. John Emigh's *Little Red Riding Shawl* uses Balinese topeng masks and movements in telling a story very much in the American vein. In Emigh's production of Brecht's *Caucasian Chalk Circle*, the basic dramaturgy (as well as the masks) reflects his work in Bali. Ron Jenkins studied clowning at the Barnum and Bailey Clown College and in Bali, where he actually performed with a Balinese troupe. In his *One Horse Show* Jenkins integrated his experiences in such a way that the surface appears very American but the underlying patterns combine cultures. Julie Taymor's masks for not only her own shows but also Liz Swados's *Haggadah* are similarly metabolized from Taymor's experiences in Java. Phillip Zarrilli teaches the Indian martial art kalarippayatt as basic performer training. There is a good model for this: many years ago much of kalarippayatt was taken into the training regime of Kathakali. Zarrilli also uses kalarippayatt in his own productions. When he and I collaborated on *Richard's Lear* in 1982, kalarippayatt was not only an essential part of the training but also important in the staging of two fight scenes. The list goes on. Some work is more wholly metabolized than others. My point is that these new kinds of performances also call into existence new means of training, which means new ways and means of transmitting performance knowledge—new to the West but not new to Asia or Africa.

Techniques of transmission of performance knowledge are a strong basis for exchange among theater people and anthropologists. Theater people know about training; it is expected that teachers of theater be able also to practice it, which means that the teachers have been trained as actors, directors, scenographers, costumers, et cetera. Anthropologists are trained observers; and some anthropologists—not enough, but a growing number—also participate in the cultures they observe. Theater people can help anthropologists identify what to look for in a training or performance situation; and anthropologists can help theater people see performances within the context of specific social systems.

How Are Performances Generated and Evaluated?

Evaluation runs from totally subjective statements like "I enjoyed that" to detailed semiotic analysis; from a teacher's pointing out what was useful in even a failed performance to the enthusiastic response of a sophisticated spectator—or the confused response of an ignorant spectator. In Asian performances the evaluation of a performance is actually part of the performance itself. Before the days of newspaper critics there were patrons. A performance of Noh or Kathakali is supposed to be as good as those seeing it "deserve." A person who sponsors, or even attends, a Noh drama is supposed to have considerable knowledge about it. The connoisseur knows what he is being offered and can react appropriately. The comparison to Americans' attitude toward sports is again instructive. Spectators at sports know the rules of the game, and its finer points of play. They know the players and their records; they know each team's history; they debate management decisions from on-field strategy to finances. In short, every aspect of the game, its playing, and its players comes under the heat of informed opinion. Excellence is applauded, bad play booed. Sports spectators are connoisseurs. If theater were to attract such an audience, things would get better quick.

How can a "good" performance be distinguished from a "bad" one? Are there two sets of criteria, one for inside the culture and one for outside? Or are there four sets: inside the culture by the professionals who also make performances; inside by ordinary audiences; outside the culture by visiting professionals; outside by ordinary audiences? Who has the "right" to make evaluations: only people in a culture, only professionals who practice the art in question, only professional critics? Is there a difference between criticism and interpretation? (Has Clifford Geertz studied, interpreted, criticized, or reviewed the Balinese cockfight?) Most artists scoff at critics but accept their praise. These same professionals welcome the criticism of fellow performers when offered in private. What is resented is the public nature of critics' opinions and the power these opinions have to advance or extinguish careers. Who is the evaluation for: those doing, those attending, those who might attend? Newspaper reviews are mainly consumer guides. Scholarly journals vary wildly in quality, and they come out months after a performance happens. The lack of immediate, critical, but non-consumer-oriented discussion hurts the performing arts badly.

The only really effective criticism is that backed up by more practice. During each night's performance of anything I direct, I make notes which are then shared the next day with the performers. The notes always demand rehearsal, which is a continuous process. Slowly, over months or even years, some productions achieve a fineness through a process of doing, seeing, evaluating, criticizing, and redoing.

Conclusions

These six points of contact need to be broadened and deepened. Anthropological and theatrical methods are converging. An increasing number of people in both disciplines are crossing boundaries. Grotowski, Brook, Barba, Turner, Turnbull, and others are working specifically and concretely in ways that are intercultural and interdisciplinary.

Since 1970, Brook has directed his International Center for Theater Research in Paris. His company includes performers from Africa, Asia, Europe, and the Americas. His field trips have taken him and his group to all these continents exchanging techniques and research material for a variety of productions ranging from *The Ik* (based on Colin Turnbull's *Mountain People*), *L'Os* (based on an African tale by Birago Diop), and *The Conference of the Birds* (based on a Sufi story) to the not-yet-finished version of the *Mahabharata*.

For three months in 1972–73 Brook's troupe traveled to villages in Algeria, Niger, Nigeria, Dahomey, and Mali (plate 3). What they did was simple enough. They entered a village, spread out their "performance rug"— something to define the place where they performed—and showed some improvisations. After the improvisations, Brook's people talked with the villagers. The performance was "influenced, second-by-second, by the presence of the people, the place, the time of day, the light—all of those reflected themselves in the best performances" (1973, 41). Brook describes his group's method of working and the core idea of the trip as follows:

One would come to a village where such a thing had never happened. We'd see the chief of the village and, through some interpreter, perhaps just a child from the village, I would talk to the chief and explain in a very few words the fact that a group of people, from different parts of the world, had set out to discover if a human contact could be made through this particular form called theatre. . . . It was an event that was always welcomed, and always taken directly on its own terms for what it was. [1973, 43]

But were there actual exchanges? Or was the trip more a chance for Brook's group to explore improvisatory acting techniques while enjoying local hospitality?

Once we sat in Agades [Niger] in a small hut all afternoon, singing. We and the African group sang, and suddenly we found that we were hitting exactly the same language of sound. Well, we understood theirs and they understood ours, and something quite electrifying happened because, out of all sorts of different songs, one suddenly came upon this common area. [1973, 45]

Another time Brook's group was camping in a forest. Children appeared and told them that in a nearby village there was a celebration going on. The actors went.

We were made very welcome and sat there, in total darkness, under the trees, just seeing these moving shadows dancing and singing. And after a couple of hours they suddenly said to us: the boys say that this is what you do, too. Now you must sing for us. So we had to improvise a song for them. And this was perhaps one of the best works of the whole journey. [1973, 45]

It is not always so idyllic. Brook—and others doing similar work—has been accused of acting arrogantly, even imperialistically.

But this having been said, I still sympathize with Brook's fundamental impulse (sometimes imperfectly carried through), which is also the impulse of Jerzy Grotowski, Eugenio Barba, and Victor and Edith Turner, as well as others, both Euro-Americans and non-Westerners:

Our work is based on the fact that some of the deepest aspects of human experience can reveal themselves through sounds and movement of the human body in a way that strikes an identical chord in any observer, whatever his cultural . . . conditioning. [Brook, 1973, 50]

As Brook observes, "the body as such becomes a working source." Whether grounded in neurobiology or in universally recognized displays of emotions, the affective aspects of theater are less in need of translation than literature.

Barba, founder-director of the Odin Teatret in Denmark (plate 4) and a man long associated with Grotowski, is currently developing his International School of Theatre Anthropology (ISTA; see chapter 5). ISTA involves training, exchange of techniques, seminars, films, and a "team of scientific

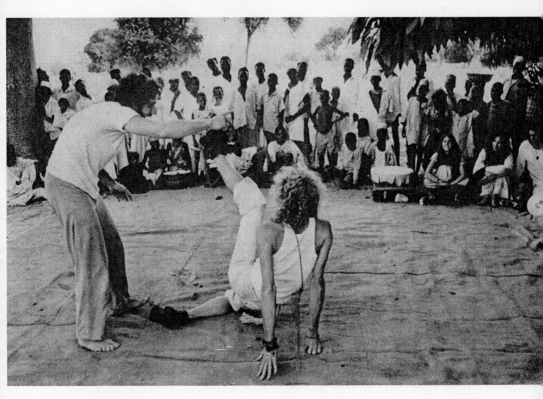

3. Peter Brook's company performing an improvisation in an African village. Photo by Ellen Mark.

collaborators." Two sessions of the school have met for several months each in 1980 and 1981, and more are planned. Aside from student participants and members of the Odin, totaling around sixty persons, teachers came from India, Bali (plate 5), Japan, Sweden, Denmark, and China. Barba describes ISTA and its goals as follows:

Theatre anthropology is the study of the biological and cultural behavior of man in a theatrical situation, that is to say, of man presenting and using his physical and mental presence in accordance with laws differing from those of daily life.

Laws exist that govern the particular use of the actor's body, i.e., his technique. Certain biological factors (weight, balance, displacement of weight/being off-balance, the opposition between weight and spinal column, the way of using the eyes) make it possible to achieve "pre-expressive" organic tensions. These tensions determine a change in the quality of our energies, causing our body to "come alive," thereby attracting the attention of observers long before the intervention of any personal expression. [1981, 2]

Different actors, in different places and times, in spite of the stylistic forms specific to their traditions, have used some principles which they have in common with actors from other traditions. To trace these "recurrent principles" is the first task of theatre anthropology. The "recurrent principles" are not proof of a "science of the theatre," nor of a few universal laws. They are particularly good "bits of advice," "information," which are very likely to be useful to theatrical practice. . . . The "bits of good advice" are particular in this way: they can be followed or ignored. They are not inviolate

4. Eugenio Barba, *right*, works with kyogen actor Kosuka Namura during a session of the International School of Theater Anthropology. Photo by Nicola Savarese.

5. Jas, a young Balinese dancer, demonstrating her walking technique at ISTA. Photo by Nicola Savarese.

6. A Papua New Guinea Tubuan initiand approaches for outdoor rites in the "performed ethnography" staged at the University of Virginia by Mimi George under the guidance of Victor and Edith Turner. Photo by Pamela Freese.

laws. Rather—and this is perhaps the best way to use them—one respects them so as to be able to break and overcome them. [1982a, 5]

Barba, in his own way, is extending Grotowski's work of developing actor training and mise-en-scène.

Turner did for anthropology what Barba is doing for theater. Turner's work spans several decades and covers vast conceptual areas. From the sixties he was interested in ritual-as-performance and more recently in what he called "performing ethnography" (plate 6). Collaborating with his wife, Edith, Turner has

been experimenting with the performance of ethnography to aid students' understanding of how people in other cultures experience the richness of their social existence, what the moral pressures are upon them, what kinds of pleasures they expect to receive as a reward for following certain patterns of action, and how they express joy, grief, deference, and affection, in accordance with cultural expectations. At the University of Virginia, with anthropology students, and at New York University, with drama students, we've taken descriptions of strips of behavior from "other cultures" and asked students to make "playscripts" from them. Then we set up workshops— really "playshops"—in which the students try to get kinetic understanding of the "other" sociocultural groups. Often we selected either social dramas—from our own and other ceremonies—or ritual dramas (puberty rites, marriage ceremonies, potlatches, etc.), and asked the students to put them in a "play frame"—to relate what they are doing to the ethnographic knowledge they are increasingly in need of, to make the scripts they use "make sense." This motivates them to study the anthropological monographs—and exposes gaps in those monographs in so far as these seem to depart from the logic of the dramatic action and interaction they have themselves purported to describe. The actor's "inside view," engendered in and through performance, becomes a powerful critique of how ritual and ceremonial structures are cognitively represented. [Turner and Turner 1982, 33–34]

Over the past several years the Turners staged with their students a typical Virginia marriage, the midwinter ceremony of the Mohawk of Canada, an Ndembu girl's puberty rite, and the *hamatsa* dance of the sacred winter ceremonials of the Kwakiutl.

From all this experience the Turners came to several interesting conclusions. They are against staging rituals and myths because these "have their source and raison d'être in the ceaseless flow of social life" and should not willy-nilly be ripped from their contexts (1982, 47–48).

Our recommendation, then, is this: If we attempt to perform ethnography, let us not begin with such apparently "exotic" and "bizarre" cultural phenomena as rituals and myths. Such an emphasis may only encourage prejudice, since it stresses the "otherness of the other." Let us focus first on what all people share, the social drama form, from which emerge all types of cultural performance, which, in their turn, subtly stylize the contours of social interaction in everyday life. [1982, 48]

The Turners go on to say how important rehearsals are, as well as the sharing of the particular foods associated with the culture being studied. Of course they also emphasize the aftermath: "At least one session should be allocated to a close review of all aspects of the performance seen in retrospect" (1982, 48). This is one way the "field work" of the performed ethnography gets "written up" in the more cognitive language of academic discourse (the seminar, the term paper).

It would be good to see some of Barba's ideas joined with those of the Turners. I mean: How about emphasizing not only the cognitive and experiential aspects of the ethnographies enacted but also the kinesthetic—how the body is handled, held, restrained, released? This would put into the bodies of the student performers a living sense of what it is to move "as if" one were the other. And this would then involve the performers not only in rehearsals but in training. At the symposium in New York in August 1982 I noted the reluctance of some anthropologists to participate in the workshops that were part of the program. In early September I had the experience of working directly with Noh shite Takabayashi Koji who, along with several other Noh artists, came from the New York symposium to Cornell University where they offered a three-day workshop. Doing the movements of Noh concretely— even for such a brief period—told me more in my body than pages of reading.

What's more, when I returned to the reading, to concepts like jo-ha-kyu or ko-shi, I had a firmer sense of what these concepts were. It is this kind of in-the-body work that brings the Turners and Barba together.

Other anthropologists have taken to drama. At the University of Chicago McKim Marriott stages a "game" with one of his classes through which they act out the social world of the Indian caste system as it might operate in a village. Marriott also staged in May 1982 a Hindi folkplay, *Rup-Basant* (which he translated into English) as part of his class on South Asia. The audience played the role of Indian villagers. Marriott reports concerning this experience:

Actors were encouraged to rewrite their parts and test them on the audience's responses, the audience being by now rather learned about some things Indian, and including the critical instructor [Mariott], who was most attending to realistic body language, Hindu style. This was fun for nearly everybody, made each session a surprise, and gave opportunities to convey a great deal of gutsy cultural information. [1982, n.p.]

Colin Turnbull not only worked with Peter Brook on adapting his *Mountain People* into *The Ik* but has continued at George Washington University to explore the relationship between anthropology and drama (see Garner and Turnbull 1979). Grotowski has long been interested in intercultural performance. His Polish Laboratory Theater was among the first to metabolize non-European influences. Grotowski has been to Asia several times beginning in 1956. He has also worked with aesthetic and ritual performers from Haiti, Mexico, India, and elsewhere. Grotowski's intercultural work—including his latest project, "objective drama"—is discussed in chapter 5. All of these experiments, and more not mentioned, are harbingers. The six "points of contact" are highly charged nodes attracting people from anthropology and theater. Around these nodes—what Turner would call a "liminoid" field—is being formed something in-between and postmodern.

But why these specific six points of contact and not others? These specific points may not exhaust what could be defined, but they do mark out a very concrete and coherent field that is of deep interest to performance theorists. Who performers are, how they achieve their temporary or permanent transformations, what role the audience plays—these are the key questions not about dramatic literature but about the living performance event when looked at from the viewpoint of the human beings involved in the performance. Other questions could be developed that would concentrate on scenography, uses of space, costumes, props and implements of performance, and the various layerings of technology from puppets to holography. But anthropology, as the name implies, has focused on human action; and although these other questions are important, and clearly derive from human action, I am proposing points of contact that can be taken up now, and that seem to me to be central. The remaining three points—the whole performance sequence, the transmission of performance knowledge, and evaluations—are harder to categorize. They constitute particular areas of difficulty within the world I live in as a theater director. In a sense, I am looking for help in understanding these processes—a holistic grasp of the subject of performance, the concrete means by which nonliterary, nonlinear knowledge is passed on, and the relationship between artists and ritualists and the societies-at-large they inhabit.

I turn to anthropology, not as to a problem-solving science but because I sense a convergence of paradigms. Just as theater is anthropologizing itself, so anthropology is being theatricalized. This convergence is the historical occasion for all kinds of exchanges. The convergence of anthropology and theater is part of a larger intellectual movement where the understanding of human behavior is changing from quantifiable differences between cause and effect, past and present, form and content, et cetera (and the linear modes of analyses that explicate such a world view) to an emphasis on the deconstruction/reconstruction of actualities: the processes of framing, editing, and rehearsing; the making and manipulating of strips of behavior—what I call "restored behavior."

In each chapter of this book I deal with one or more aspects of these points of contact. I turn the problems they evoke over and over. I am far from "solving" any problem. In fact, my aim is closer to one of deep meditation: a consideration of the talmudic complexity and multivocality of this, that, and another permutation of the performance paradigm. We accept our species as sapiens and fabricans: ones who think and make. We are in the process of learning how humans are also ludens and performans: ones who play and perform.

NOTES TO CHAPTER 1

¹The symposium was held in New York, August 23–31, 1982. It was sponsored by the Wenner-Gren Foundation for Anthropological Research in association with the American Theatre Association, the Asian Cultural Council, the Asia Society, the International Theatre Institute, and the Tisch School of the Arts, New York University. The symposium brought theater practictioners from Asia, Africa, and Euro-America together with theater scholars and anthropologists. Sessions included demonstrations of training and performance techniques as well as theoretical and historical discussions. In Calcutta, India, January 2–11, 1983, a similar conference studying the relationship between traditional Indian dance and modern theater was held. Delegates from Asia, Euro-America, Latin America, and the Middle East attended. Performances and discussions were augmented by many demonstrations of various training, workshop, and rehearsal techniques. For a summary of the meeting in Calcutta, see Martin and Schechner 1983.

²Squat's techniques, themes, and unique use of the street outside its theater is discussed in Schechner 1978, 1982*b*, and chap. 7, herein; Shank and Shank 1978; and Shank 1982, 179–89.

2

RESTORATION OF BEHAVIOR

Restored behavior is living behavior treated as a film director treats a strip of film. These strips of behavior[1] can be rearranged or reconstructed; they are independent of the causal systems (social, psychological, technological) that brought them into existence. They have a life of their own. The original "truth" or "source" of the behavior may be lost, ignored, or contradicted—even while this truth or source is apparently being honored and observed. How the strip of behavior was made, found, or developed may be unknown or concealed; elaborated; distorted by myth and tradition. Originating as a process, used in the process of rehearsal to make a new process, a performance, the strips of behavior are not themselves process but things, items, "material." Restored behavior can be of long duration as in some dramas and rituals or of short duration as in some gestures, dances, and mantras.

Restored behavior is used in all kinds of performances from shamanism and exorcism to trance, from ritual to aesthetic dance and theater, from initiation rites to social dramas, from psychoanalysis to psychodrama and transactional analysis. In fact, restored behavior is the main characteristic of performance. The practitioners of all these arts, rites, and healings assume that some behaviors—organized sequences of events, scripted actions, known texts, scored movements—exist separate from the performers who "do" these behaviors. Because the behavior is separate from those who are behaving, the behavior can be stored, transmitted, manipulated, transformed. The performers get in touch with, recover, remember, or even invent these strips of behavior and then rebehave according to these strips, either by being absorbed into them (playing the role, going into trance) or by existing side by side with them (Brecht's *Verfremdungseffekt*). The work of restoration is carried on in rehearsals and/or in the transmission of behavior from master to novice. Understanding what happens during training, rehearsals, and workshops— investigating the subjunctive mood that is the medium of these operations— is the surest way to link aesthetic and ritual performance.

Restored behavior is "out there," distant from "me." It is separate and therefore can be "worked on," changed, even though it has "already happened." Restored behavior includes a vast range of actions. It can be "me" at another time/psychological state as in the psychoanalytic abreaction; or it can exist in a nonordinary sphere of sociocultural reality as does the Passion of Christ or the reenactment in Bali of the struggle between Rangda and Barong; or it can be marked off by aesthetic convention as in drama and dance; or it can be the special kind of behavior "expected" of someone participating in a traditional ritual—the bravery, for example, of a Gahuku boy in Papua New Guinea during his initiation, shedding no tears when jagged leaves slice the inside of his nostrils; or the shyness of an American "blushing bride" at her wedding, even though she and her groom have lived together for two years.

Restored behavior is symbolic and reflexive: not empty but loaded behavior multivocally broadcasting significances. These difficult terms express a single principle: The self can act in/as another; the social or transindividual self is a role or set of roles. Symbolic and reflexive behavior is the hardening into theater of social, religious, aesthetic, medical, and educational process. Performance means: never for the first time. It means: for the second to the *n*th time. Performance is "twice-behaved behavior."

Neither painting, sculpting, nor writing shows actual behavior as it is being behaved. But thousands of years before movies rituals were made from strips of restored behavior: action and stasis coexisted in the same event. What comfort flowed from ritual performances. People, ancestors, and gods participated in simultaneously having been, being, and becoming. These strips of behavior were replayed many times. Mnemonic devices insured that the performances were "right"—transmitted across many generations with few ͺl variations. Even now, the terror of the first night is not the presence ublic but knowing that mistakes are no longer forgiven. s constancy of transmission is all the more astonishing because restored behavior involves choices. Animals repeat themselves, and so do the cycles of the moon. But an actor can say no to any action. This question of choice is not easy. Some ethologists and brain specialists argue that there is no significant difference—no difference of any kind—between animal and human behavior. But at least there is an "illusion of choice," a feeling that one has a choice. And this is enough. Even the shaman who is called, the trancer falling into trance, and the wholly trained performer whose performance text is second nature give over or resist, and there is suspicion of the ones who too easily say yes or prematurely say no. There is a continuum from the not-much-choice of ritual to the lots-of-choice of aesthetic theater. It is the function of rehearsals in aesthetic theater to narrow the choices or at least to make clear the rules of improvisation. Rehearsals function to build a score, and this score is a "ritual by contract": fixed behavior that everyone participating agrees to do.

Restored behavior can be put on the way a mask or costume is. Its shape can be seen from the outside, and changed. That's what theater directors, councils of bishops, master performers, and great shamans do: change performance scores. A score can change because it is not a "natural event" but a model of individual and collective human choice. A score exists, as Turner says (1982a, 82–84), in the subjunctive mood, in what Stanislavski called the "as if." Existing as "second nature," restored behavior is always subject to revision. This "secondness" combines negativity and subjunctivity.

e

Put in personal terms, restored behavior is "me behaving as if I am someone else" or "as if I am 'beside myself,' or 'not myself,' " as when in trance. But this "someone else" may also be "me in another state of feeling/being," as if there were multiple "me's" in each person. The difference between performing myself—acting out a dream, reexperiencing a childhood trauma, showing you what I did yesterday—and more formal "presentations of self" (see Goffman 1959)—is a difference of degree, not kind. There is also a continuum linking the ways of presenting the self to the ways of presenting others: acting in dramas, dances, and rituals. The same can be said for "social actions" and "cultural performances": events whose origins can't be located in individuals, if they can be located at all. These events when acted out are linked in a feedback loop with the actions of individuals. Thus, what people in northern Hindi-speaking India see acted out in Ramlila tells them how to act in their daily lives; and how they act in their daily lives affects the staging of the Ramlila. Mythic enactments are often regarded as exemplary models. But the ordinary life of the people is expressed in the staging, gestures, details of costume, and scenic structures of Ramlila (and other folk performances).

Sometimes collective events are attributed to "persons" whose existence is somewhere between history and fiction: the Books of Moses, the *Iliad* and *Odyssey* of Homer, the *Mahabharata* of Vyas. Sometimes these actions and stories belong anonymously to folklore, legend, myth. And sometimes they are "original," or at least attributable to individuals: the *Hamlet* of Shakespeare, the *Ramcharitmanas* of Tulsidas, the *Oedipus* of Sophocles. But what these authors really authored was not the tale itself but a version of something. It's hard to say exactly what qualifies a work to belong to, and come from, a collective. Restored behavior offers to both individuals and groups the chance to rebecome what they once were—or even, and most often, to rebecome what they never were but wish to have been or wish to become.

The restoration of behavior model (figures 2.1, 2.2, 2.3, 2.4) is processual, describing emergent performances from the point of view of rehearsal. Figure 2.1 shows restored behavior as either a projection of "my particular self" ($1 \rightarrow 2$), or a restoration of a historically verifiable past ($1 \rightarrow 3 \rightarrow 4$), or—most often—a restoration of a past that never was ($1 \rightarrow 5_a \rightarrow 5_b$). For example, interesting as the data may be, the "historical Richard III" is not as important to someone preparing a production of Shakespeare's play as the logic of Shakespeare's

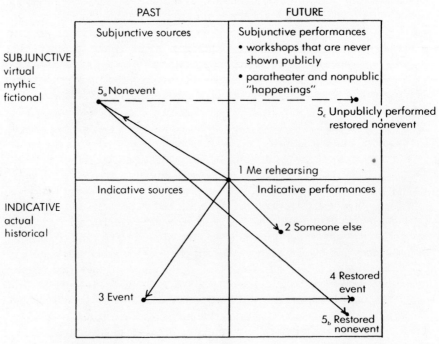

Figure 2.1

text: the Richard of Shakespeare's imagination. Figures 2.2, 2.3, and 2.4 elaborate the basic idea; I will discuss these elaborations later. A corollary to the basic thesis is that most performances—even those that apparently are simple $1 \rightarrow 2$ displacements or $1 \rightarrow 3 \rightarrow 4$ re-creations—are, or swiftly become, $1 \rightarrow 5_a \rightarrow 5_b$. For it is this "performative bundle"—where the project-to-be, 5_b, governs what from the past is selected or invented (and projected backward into the past), 5_a—that is the most stable and prevalent performative circumstance. In a very real way the future—the project coming into existence through the process of rehearsal—determines the past: what will be kept from earlier rehearsals or from the "source materials." This situation is as true for ritual performances as for aesthetic theater. Even where there are no rehearsals in the Euro-American sense, analogous processes occur.

Figure 2.1 is drawn from the temporal perspective of rehearsal and from the psychological perspective of an individual performer. "Me" (1) is a person rehearsing for a performance to be: 2, 4, or 5_b. What precedes the performance—both temporally and conceptually—is either nothing that can be definitely identified, as when a person gets into a mood, or some definite antecedent event(s). This event will either be historically verifiable (3), or not (5_a). If it is not, it can be either a legendary event, a fiction (as in many plays), or—as will be explained—the projection backward in time of the proposed event-to-be. Or, to put it another way, rehearsals make it necessary to think of the future in such a way as to create a past. Figure 2.1 is divided into quadrants in order to indicate mood as well as temporality. The upper left

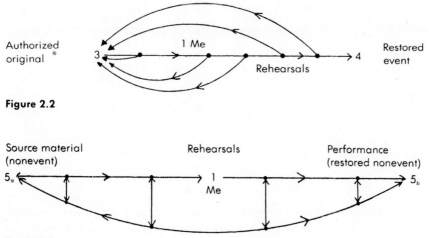

Authorized original

3

1 Me

Rehearsals

4

Restored event

Figure 2.2

Source material (nonevent)

5_a

Rehearsals

1 Me

Performance (restored nonevent)

5_b

Figure 2.3

quadrant contains mythic, legendary, or fictional events. The mood is subjunctive. In Turner's words:

Here cognitive schemata that give sense and order to everyday life no longer apply, but are, as it were, suspended—in ritual symbolism perhaps even shown as destroyed or dissolved. . . . Clearly, the liminal space-time "pod" created by ritual action, or today by certain kinds of reflexively ritualized theatre, is potentially perilous. [1982*a*, 84]

This past is one that is always in the process of transformation, just as a papal council can redefine Christ's actions or a great twentieth-century Noh performer can introduce new variations into a fifteenth-century mise-en-scène of Zeami's.

The lower left quadrant—that of the actual/indicative past—is history understood as an arrangement of facts. Of course, any arrangement is conventionalized and conditioned by particular world and/or political views. Events are always rising from the lower left to the upper left: today's indica-

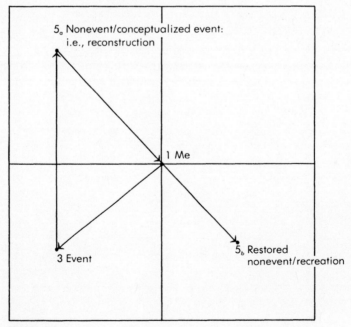

Figure 2.4

tive becomes tomorrow's subjunctive. That's one of the ways human experience is recycled.

The lower right quadrant—the future/indicative—is the actual performance-to-be-enacted. It is indicative because it actually happens. It is in the future because the figure is conceived from the temporal perspective of a sequence of rehearsals in progress: in figures 2.2 and 2.3, "me" is moving along with rehearsals from the left to the right.

There is nothing in the upper right quadrant—the future/subjunctive—because performances are always actually performed. But one might place some workshops and Grotowski's paratheater there, as a sequence $1 \rightarrow 5_a \rightarrow 5_c$. Paratheater and workshops are preparations and process implying performances that never-will-be. The paratheatrical work goes along "as if" there might be a performance, an end to the process; but the process doesn't end, it has no logical finality, it simply stops. There is no performance at point 5_c.

In $1 \rightarrow 2$ I become someone else, or myself in another state of being, or mood, so "unlike me" that I appear to be "beside myself" or "possessed by another." There is little rehearsal for this kind of performance, sometimes none. From birth, people are immersed in the kind of social performative actions that are sufficient preparations for entering trance. Watching children, infants even, at a black church or in Bali reveals a continuous training by osmosis. The displacement of $1 \rightarrow 2$ may be slight, as in some mood changes, or very strong, as in some trances. But in either case there is little appeal to either an actual or a subjunctive past. "Something happens" and the person (performer) is no longer himself. This kind of performance, because it is so close to "natural behavior" (maybe extraordinary from the outside but expected from within the culture)—either by surrender to strong outside forces, as in possession, or by giving in to moods within oneself—can be very powerful. It can happen to anyone, suddenly, and such instant performative behavior is regarded as evidence of the strength of the force possessing the subject. The performer does not seem to be "acting." A genuine if temporary transformation (a transportation) takes place. Most $1 \rightarrow 2$ performances are solos, even if these solos happen simultaneously in the same space. The astonishing thing about Balinese sanghyang trance dancing is that each dancer has by her/himself so incarnated the collective score that solo dances cohere into group performances. Upon recovering from the trance, dancers are often unaware that others were dancing; sometimes they don't remember their own dancing. I've seen similar meshing of solo performing into an ensemble several times at the Institutional Church in Brooklyn. As the gospel singing reached a climax more than a dozen women, men, and children "fell out" into the aisles. People watched them closely, grabbing them if they became too violent, preventing them from knocking against the chairs, calming them down when the singing subsided. The same kind of assistance is offered to trance dancers in Bali and elsewhere. The event in Brooklyn is very neatly organized. The singers whose gospel fired the trance dancing were definitely not in trance. They were the "transporters" propelling the dancers into trance. The dancers depended upon their friends to keep the dancing safe. The others in the church—potentially trance dancers but for the time being either more or less involved in the action—filled out a continuum from cool spectators to nearly wholly entranced clappers, foot stompers, and shouters. Each trance dancer was dancing in trance alone, but the whole group was dancing together, the whole church was rocking with collective performative energy. Peter Adair's film of a snake-handling, white, fundamentalist Christian sect in West Virginia, *The Holy Ghost People*, shows the same thing.

In 1 → 3 → 4 an event from some other place or past is restored—a "living newspaper" or a diorama at the American Museum of Natural History. Strictly speaking, dioramas are restored environments, not behaviors. But increasingly action is being added to the environments. Later I will discuss "restored villages" and "theme parks" where fact and fancy are freely mixed. Some zoos, however, try their best to make their displays genuine replicas of the wild. Reacting to the vanishing wilderness, zoo keepers are creating "breeding parks."

In the breeding park near Front Royal, Virginia, the attempt to keep an authentic and pristine environment is such that all visitors except breeders, veterinarians, and ethologists are excluded. At the San Diego Wild Animal Park in the lovely hills thirty miles northeast of the city, there is a combination of authenticity and local cultural values (shtick). Those riding the monorail around the 600-acre display are repeatedly reminded by the tour guide of the authenticity of the park. The brochure all visitors get begins:

Join us here . . . to contemplate the wild animals of the world and nature's wilderness . . . to strengthen a commitment to wildlife conservation throughout the world . . . and to strive toward man's own survival through the preservation of nature.

Of course, there are adjacent to the monorail "wild preserve" a number of food stands, souvenir stores, and theaters offereing animal shows (trained birds, a petting pen, etc.). Also, the park features nightly concerts of jazz, bluegrass, calypso, and "big band sounds." There is a McDonald's. This same brochure invites the more spendy visitors to "Join us for a tempting 10-ounce Delmonico steak dinner at Thorn Tree Terrace each evening, and take a new

Caravan Tour into the preserve." Oh, well. But what interested me most was when I asked the monorail guide what the lions "roaming free" ate? Special food pellets packed with everything nutritious. Why not some of the wildebeests running across the fence from the lions? Well, I was told, although there is no shortage of wildebeests and lions do hunt them back in Africa, it would take too much space and, maybe, it wouldn't be so nice for the monorail visitors to witness such suppers. In this way, $1 \rightarrow 3 \rightarrow 4$ is transformed by specific cultural values into $1 \rightarrow 5_a \rightarrow 5_b$. The whole tone of the Wild Animal Park is of peaceful cohabitation. The hunting behavior of carnivores, though known, is not seen. The 5_a that the park restores is consistent with current California notions of how best "to contemplate . . . nature's wilderness."

Many traditional performances are $1 \rightarrow 3 \rightarrow 4$. So are performances that are kept in repertory according to a strict adherence to the original score. When the Moscow Art Theatre visited New York in the mid-sixties, it claimed to present Chekhov according to Stanislavski's original mise-en-scènes. When I saw several plays of Brecht at the Berlin Ensemble in 1969 I was told that Brecht's Modelbuchs—his detailed photo accounts of his mise-en-scènes—were followed. Classical ballets have been passed on through generations of dancers. But even the strictest attempts at $1 \rightarrow 3 \rightarrow 4$ frequently are in fact examples of $1 \rightarrow 5_a \rightarrow 5_b$. $1 \rightarrow 3 \rightarrow 4$ is very unstable, simply because even if human memory can be improved upon by the use of film or exact notation a performance always happens within several contexts, and these are not easily controllable. The social circumstances change—as is obvious when you think of Stanislavski's productions at the turn of the century and the Moscow Art Theater today. Even the bodies of performers— what they are supposed to look like, how they are supposed to move, what they think and believe—change radically over relatively brief periods of time, not to mention the reactions, feelings, and moods of the audience. Performances that were once current, even avant-garde, soon become period pieces. These kinds of contextual changes are not measurable by Labanotation.[2] The difference between $1 \rightarrow 3 \rightarrow 4$ and $1 \rightarrow 5_a \rightarrow 5_b$ is shown in figure 2.2. In $1 \rightarrow 3 \rightarrow 4$ there is an event (3) that is always referred back to. This event serves as model and corrective. If during a rehearsal of one of Brecht's plays, according to his authorized mise-en-scène, it is suspected that some gesture is not being performed as Brecht intended it, the gesture is checked back against the Modelbuch (and other documentary evidence). What the Modelbuch says goes. It is the authority. All details are checked against an "authorized original." Many rituals follow this pattern. This is not to say that rituals—and Brecht's mise-en-scènes—do not change. They change in two ways: first, by a slow slippage made inevitable by changing historical circumstances; second, through "official revisions" made by the owners-heirs of the "authorized original." In either case, it is my view that $1 \rightarrow 3 \rightarrow 4$ is very unstable: it is always becoming $1 \rightarrow 5_a \rightarrow 5_b$.

Noh drama is a very good example of a performance genre that is both $1 \rightarrow 3 \rightarrow 4$ and $1 \rightarrow 5_a \rightarrow 5_b$ simultaneously and consciously. The whole score of a Noh play—its mise-en-scène, music, text, costuming, masking—is transmitted within several schools or families from one generation to the next with only minor variations. In this sense, Noh—at least since the Meiji Restoration of the nineteenth century—is a clear example of $1 \rightarrow 3 \rightarrow 4$. During his lifetime a Noh shite (the main actor, literally the "doer," the one who wears the mask) moves from one role to another in a progression; the accumulation of roles equals a full career. He accepts the score of the role he approaches and leaves behind the score of the role he has just played. Only the greatest masters of Noh dare change a score. These changes are taught by the shite to his disciples: the changes become part of the score. The roles, and their place within the total performance text, and the performance texts themselves as steps along the progression of Noh plays that compose a lifetime of performing make up a complicated but decipherable system. But each individual Noh performance also includes surprises. The groups who come together to do a Noh play are made of members of different families, each with its own traditions, its own "secrets." The shite and chorus work together; the waki, kyogen, flutist, and drummers work separately. That is, if a Noh play is done according to the tradition the ensemble does not gather until a few days before the performance. Then no rehearsals occur; instead, the shite outlines his plans. True to its Zen aspect, a Noh drama staged traditionally occurs only once, finding in the absolute immediacy of the meeting among all its constituent players its essence. Like the Zen archer, the shite and his colleagues either hit the mark or they don't.

During the performance—through subtle signals issued by the shite to the musicians and others—variations occur: routines are repeated or cut, emphases changed, tempos accelerated or slowed. Even the selection of what costume and mask to wear sometimes depends on the shite's opinion regarding the mood of this audience assembled now. The shite gauges the mood of the audience by watching them assemble or by seeing how they react to the first plays of a full Noh program that may include five Noh and four comic kyogen plays and take seven hours or more. Those Noh performers made into a "company" for foreign tours, where they repeat the same plays over and over, performing with the same players, complain of boredom and the lack of creative opportunity. Optimally, then, each performance of Noh, and every variation during a performance, is the leading edge of a long tradition formed during Kanami's and Zeami's time in the fourteenth and fifteenth centuries, almost extinguished by the mid-nineteenth, and flourishing again now. This leading edge is both $1 \rightarrow 3 \rightarrow 4$ and $1 \rightarrow 5_a \rightarrow 5_b$.

Some contemporary experimental theater in New York also combines $1 \rightarrow 3 \rightarrow 4$ and $1 \rightarrow 5_a \rightarrow 5_b$, but in a way that suggests the configuration $1 \rightarrow 3 \rightarrow 5_b$: the restoration in a subjunctive mood of a past that is demonstrably factual. In *Rumstick Road* of the Wooster Group, actual sound tapes of Spalding Gray interviewing his father, grandmother, and mother's psychiatrist are played as part of a reminiscence that presents Gray's state of mind regarding his mother's life and suicide. Techniques used in *Rumstick Road*—dancelike movements, direct address to the audience, a progression of events organized according to associational rather than linear narrative conventions, performers sometimes playing themselves and sometimes playing characters—all are well established in experimental Euro-American theater. But the core documents used in *Rumstick Road*—the audiotapes, letters and photographs that Gray found in his father's house—are used "raw," as is. Robert Wilson in his work with Raymond Andrews, a deaf boy, and Christopher Knowles, a brain-damaged boy (or one unusually tuned to experience, depending on one's view of the matter), similarly introduces "raw" material and behaviors into highly "artified" performances. Squat Theatre—with the back wall of its stage actually being a window directly facing busy Twenty-third Street in Manhattan—also combines the raw, the unrehearsed or untreated, with the highly refined (or processed). Of course, what's raw from one perspective may be refined from another. How can Twenty-third Street be raw nature, or maybe it is raw human nature—or is that a contradiction in terms? (For more on this problem, see chapter 7 and Schechner 1982*b*.)

Just as interesting as Noh or experimental performance in regard to the relationship between $1 \rightarrow 3 \rightarrow 4$ and $1 \rightarrow 5_a \rightarrow 5_b$ types of restored behavior is Shaker dancing. Carol Martin in her 1979 paper, *"The Shakers:* Sources and Restoration," introduced me to the complexities of the Shaker story. The Shakers were a religious sect who migrated from England to America in 1774. Since Shakers do not marry, their numbers depend entirely on conversions. As of 1983 there were only six surviving Shakers, all of them aged. But around the time of the Civil War there were about six thousand. Shaker ritual included song and dance (plate 7). Originally these were done by and for the Shakers themselves. But according to Suzanne Youngerman:

as Shakerism grew, the religion and the social organization it engendered became less ecstatic and more rigid and institutionalized. The dances and songs, which were the main form of worship, also changed from involuntary ecstatic and convulsive movements with glossolalia occurring during spells of altered states of consciousness to disciplined choreographed marches with symbolic steps, gestures, and floor plans.

7. Shakers dancing, based on a color lithograph of Anthony Imbert, ca. 1826. Photo courtesy of the New York Public Library.

8. Doris Humphrey's *The Shakers* as danced in 1938. Photo by Barbara Morgan.

These rituals became elaborate and fixed dance "exercises." A steady stream of tourists came to the Shaker communities to watch these spectacles. [1978, 95]

The Shakers had stopped dancing by 1931 when Doris Humphrey, one of the pioneers of American modern dance, choreographed *The Shakers* (plate 8). Working from pictures and research materials but never having seen any Shakers dancing, Humphrey in her dance was able to actualize something of Shaker culture. Youngerman says: "Humphrey's choreography embodies a wide range of Shaker culture incorporating many direct references to actual Shaker dances" (1978, 96). Dance scholar Marcia Siegel told me that after *The Shakers* people regarded Humphrey as an authority on Shakers; she received letters concerning them and her advice was solicited. But it wasn't until 1955 that Humphrey even met a Shaker.

Humphrey's dance was in the repertory of the José Limon Dance Company where I saw it performed in 1979 and 1981. The Limon company is the inheritor of Humphrey's approach to dance. The dance is also Labanotated, which means other companies can dance Humphrey's dance much the way orchestras can play a Beethoven symphony. In fact, in 1979 the Humphrey dance was performed by the Louisville Ballet at Shakertown, a

9. "Shaker Service" as reconstructed/restored by the Liberty Assembly. Copyright © 1983 by the Liberty Assembly.

reconstructed Shaker village at Pleasant Hill, Kentucky. This is certainly not the only example of an aesthetic dance being a main way of physically re/membering (= putting back together what time has dis/membered) an extinct behavior. Shakers dancing is $1 \rightarrow 3 \rightarrow 4$; Humphrey's *Shakers* is $1 \rightarrow 5_a \rightarrow 5_b$.

Dance scholar Dorothy Rubin suggests another "route" around the model depicted in figure 2.1. I have shown Rubin's route in figure 2.4. Rubin worked on what she calls "recreating" seventeenth-century English masque dances. Data concerning these dances are incomplete, yet there is some information available. What the "recreations" do is use what historical information there is (3), to build a model of what the masque dances might have been (5_a), and then to perform these (5_b).

Since we are recreating and not merely reconstructing or restoring, I propose that the continuum start at the "me," move through the primary sources concerning the actual event, 3, progress to the "reconstruction"—i.e., primary sources + educated guesses to fill in the gaps, 5_a, flow through the "me," 1, (all decisions made both in reconstructing and rehearsing), and culminate at the "recreation," 5_b. [Rubin 1982, 10]

I like Rubin's variation of the model. Not only does it yield important processual information, but it demonstrates the flexibility of the model itself.

The Shaker story continues. Figures 2.1 and 2.4 illuminate it. Robin Evanchuk visited a few surviving Shakers in 1962 and again in 1975. These people had long since stopped dancing. By using their memories and the memories of people who knew Shakers and by drawing on the research of Edward Deming Andrews,[3] Evanchuk reconstructed the "authentic" dances. As of 1977 three groups had "learned and presented this reconstruction," including her own group, the Liberty Assembly (plate 9). Evanchuk is always bringing in new dancers. This requires orientation and rehearsal.

During the teaching sessions, the dancers must overcome their fear of appearing ridiculous due to the strangeness of movements and the intense emotion. In addition to a strong orientation, I find that constant repetition of the movements, which allows the dancers to gradually become familiar with them, tends to lessen their embarrassment and moves the emphasis from how the dancers feel to concern for how the Shakers themselves felt when they were involved in the exercises. [Evanchuk 1977–78, 22]

Thus we have three different but related performance traditions: the Shakers themselves (now gone), an art dance choreographed by Humphrey that is still performed by the Limon company and others, and an "authentic" reconstruction of Shaker dancing by Evanchuk. Of the first of these traditions— Shaker dancing in the nineteenth century—I can say nothing, but I guess that it was of the $1 \to 2$ or $1 \to 3 \to 4$ type, soon becoming $1 \to 5_a \to 5_b$ as tourists visited the Shakers to watch them dance. This same conversion of a performance genre from something focused inward on a community to something broadcast outward to tourists is widespread; I've seen it in India and Bali. Clearly Humphrey's *Shakers* is $1 \to 5_a \to 5_b$. But Evanchuk always refers back to 3, an "authorized original." If after some rehearsals she finds her dancers departing from the original, she corrects them. Still it is hard to categorize the Evanchuk restoration as $1 \to 3 \to 4$. She works by referring back to an authorized original, but she also states that it is her wish to restore not just Shaker dances but Shaker feelings as well: the fervor, joy and ecstasy that go with the dancing. Humphrey doesn't call her dance an ethnographic reconstruction, and Evanchuk doesn't call her work art. But Humphrey achieved something other than fiction; anthropologist Youngerman thinks Humphrey's dance comes close to expressing the heart of the sect. Youngerman reports that

one of the last two Shaker brothers, Ricardo Belden, then 87 years old, saw the 1955 reconstructure of *The Shakers* at Connecticut College and reportedly was "enthralled" by the performance. He later wrote to Humphrey offering to come to New London the following summer to teach Shaker dances. What greater tribute could there be? [1978, 106]

Evanchuk used the notes of this same Ricardo Belden. It would seem to me that Evanchuk's reconstructions are actually $1 \to 5_a \to 5_b$, evolving out of $1 \to 3 \to 4$ or Rubin's $1 \to 3 \to 5_a \to 5_b$. The determining factor is whether or not a performance is based on previous performances. In cultures where performances are transmitted orally, is not the process of transmission very much like Humphrey's process in making *The Shakers*? The authority in such cultures rests not with "data" or "documented" earlier performances but with "respected persons" who themselves, in their very bodies, carry the necessary performance knowledge. The original is not fixed, as in Evanchuk's notes (or, ironically enough, in the Labanotated *Shakers*), nor is it in quasi-literary texts; it is in bodies that pass on not only the "original" but their own particular incarnation/interpretation of that original.

$1 \to 5_a \to 5_b$ is a performance based on previous performances. The totality of all those previous performances as incorporated in the oral tradition may be called the "original." The people possessing the latest version of the original often presume (falsely) that it has come down unchanged over many generations. Unlike a specific performance text of Brecht's or a particular Labanotated dance of Humphrey, the Evanchuk reconstruction of Shaker dancing is founded on her own construction of what Shaker dancing was. This construction is based on several sources, including the memories of surviving Shakers. Evanchuk says she is restoring "authentic" Shaker dances. I ask: Which dances, performed on which occasions, before what audiences, with what dancers? Humphrey's original *Shakers* is $1 \rightarrow 5_a \rightarrow 5_b$, while new productions following the Labanotated score of that original are $1 \rightarrow 3 \rightarrow 4$. The Evanchuk "authentic" Shaker dancing is more likely to be $1 \rightarrow 5_a \rightarrow 5_b$, for the original Evanchuk is looking at is not "an" original at all but a bundle of performances—and nonperformances (documents, memories, etc.)—conventionally labeled "an" original.

But even where there is "an" original—as in Brecht, the Moscow Art Theatre Chekhovs, and Humphrey's *Shakers*—contextual and historical circumstances make even the exact replication of a scored/notated original different than the original. Hard as it may be for some scholars to swallow, performance originals disappear as fast as they are made. No notation, no reconstruction, no film or videotape recording can keep them. What they lose first and most importantly is their immediacy, their existence in a specific space and context. Media recording abolishes these almost totally. Restorations are immediate, and they exist in time/space as wholes; but the occasion is different, the world view is different, the audience is different, and the performers are different. One of the chief jobs challenging performance scholars is the making of a vocabulary and methodology that deal with performance in its immediacy and evanescence. Even now, most discourse on the subject has been adapted from considerations of literature—where the argument can be made that originals exist and persist. Not so with performances, where the closest one can get to an original is the "most recent performance of . . . ." Technically the Moscow Art Theatre productions of Chekhov, the Berlin Ensemble productions of Brecht, and the Limon company's production of *The Shakers* are $1 \rightarrow 3 \rightarrow 4$. But in actuality—in the immediacy of their being performed now—all these performances are $1 \rightarrow 5_a \rightarrow 5_b$.

Other examples of $1 \rightarrow 5_a \rightarrow 5_b$ are theater when the mise-en-scène is developed during rehearsals; ethnographic films shot in the field and edited at home; modern versions of "ancient forms," whether or not labeled "neoclassical" or "restorations" or "recreations"; and rituals that actualize,[4] commemorate, or dramatize myths or old stories (though probably it's the other way around; myths follow, are word versions of, elaborations based on, rituals). In $1 \rightarrow 5_a \rightarrow 5_b$ the event to be restored either has been forgotten, never was, or is overlaid with so much secondary stuff that its actuality-in-history is lost. History so-called is not "what happened" but what has been constructed out of events, memories, records: all shaped by the world view of whoever—individually or collectively—is encoding (and performing) history. To "make history" is not to do something but to do something with what has been done.

History is not what happened but what is encoded and transmitted. Performance is not merely a selection from data arranged and interpreted; it is behavior itself and carries in itself kernels of originality, making it the subject for further interpretation, the source of further study.

$1 \to 3 \to 4$ is unstable due to the difficulty of "fit." It is not possible to "get back to" what was. 4 can never match 3. As I noted, performers' bodies are different, audiences are different, performative contexts are different. $1 \to 5_a \to 5_b$ replaces $1 \to 3 \to 4$ because rehearsals (or whatever preparatory steps are followed) conflate the past, present, and future. The work of rehearsals is to "re-present" a past for the future (performance-to-be). Performers repeat yesterday's work at today's rehearsal on behalf of the future "presentation." This synchronic aspect of $1 \to 5_a \to 5_b$ is shown in figure 2.3, suggested to me by Barbara Kirshenblatt-Gimblett. Figure 2.3 shows that the pastness of 5_a is focused through the prism of "today's rehearsals" and projected forward to the project-to-be, 5_b. It is always this project-to-be that sets up the rules or conditions for selecting material from 5_a. 5_a and 5_b cannot function independent of each other.

Carol Martin and Sally Harrison both examined figure 2.1 and suggested using the upper right quadrant, the future/subjunctive. They pointed out that a route $1 \to 5_a \to 5_c$ would describe the process of Grotowski's paratheater, some of Allan Kaprow's more recent happenings where there is no public, and the many workshops that use theatrical and dance techniques with no view toward public performance at all. Some of these workshops are therapeutic (dance therapy and psychodrama). But others fall into the category of aesthetics, or workshops run for "personal growth." This last is hard to pin down beyond saying that therapeutic techniques are used not to "cure" people but to extend their range of self-expression, to help them relate to each other, and simply as a source of pleasure. Thus some workshops use the performance process but not in the service of generating public performances. Sometimes not only are performances forbidden but workshoppers are told to keep what happened in workshops secret.

The model of the performative process shown in figures 2.1–2.4 is drawn from a Euro-American perspective. I will apply it to events that are not Euro-American. In doing so, I am not saying that the performances of many different cultures are equivalent. But I do think that performances in all cultures share the particular quality of twiceness that the model depicts, that performances everywhere are restored behavior. And I think restored behavior can best be understood processually by examining the rehearsal process: how the single behaved behaviors of ordinary living are made into the twice-behaved behaviors of art, ritual, and the other performative genres. I'm aware of the opinion of Goffman and others that "ordinary living" includes a lot of performing. Insofar as it does, the model applies. Maybe it is that art and ritual are more than "twice-behaved." Or maybe ordinary living is more artful than ordinarily supposed.

It is the work of rehearsals to prepare the strips of behavior so that when expressed by performers these strips seem spontaneous, authentic, unrehearsed. I don't mean unrehearsed only in the ways familiar to Western naturalism. Authenticity is a display of harmony/mastery of whatever style is being played, Chekhov or Chikamatsu. For the Brechtian actor to show that he is acting is no less difficult than for the Stanislavskian actor not to show he is acting. During rehearsals a past is assembled out of bits of actual experience, fantasies, historical research, past performances. Or a known score is recalled and replayed. Earlier rehearsals and/or performances quickly become the reference points, the building blocks of performances. Useful recollections are not of "how it was" but of "how we used to do it." The "it" is not the event but earlier rehearsals or performances. Soon reference back to the original—if there was an original—is irrelevant. How Christ offered his disciples wine and matzo at the Last Supper (a seder) is irrelevant to the performance of the Eucharist. The Roman Catholic church ceremony has its own performance history. The language of church ceremony has never been the language Christ spoke, Aramaic-Hebrew. Nor are the gestures or costumes of the priests modeled on Christ's. And if the church had chosen another of Christ's gestures as the keystone of the Mass—say, the laying on of hands to heal the sick—this would have developed its own traditional scripts. Indeed, in some Pentecostal churches the laying on of hands is the key representation of Christ, the demonstration of His presence. Or it may be speaking in tongues, dancing, or taking up serpents. Each of these scripts has developed its own way of being performed. What happens over years and centuries to the various church services happens much more quickly during rehearsals.

This is not just a thing of the West. John Emigh reports an example of $1 \rightarrow 5_a \rightarrow 5_b$ from the Sepik River area of Papua New Guinea. In the village of Magendo, sometime before the performance Emigh saw, an uninitiated boy named Wok wandered into the men's House Tamboran (forbidden to the uninitiated) and died. The story goes that a bird came to the boy's mother in a dream and told her what had happened and where to find Wok's body. The mother accused her brother of causing Wok's death. She said her brother had painted a dangerous spirit image in the House Tamboran. The brother accepted the blame, the house was torn down, a new one built, and the spirit of Wok resided in the new house. Wok is also credited by the villagers with teaching them how to build better canoes, how to catch fish, and how to plant crops. Emigh goes on:

Now there are several things about this story and its preparation for the event at hand that I find fascinating. First is the immediate and physical sense of relationship between past and present. The old House Tamboran stood *there* across the swamp. The reeds the child was found in were over *here*—people are very specific about the geography involved, and also about improvements in village life made possible by the intervention of Wok's spirit. Performing the dance at this time would be an act of renewal, of reconnection of past and present.[5]

But what's rehearsal at Magendo like? How does it use the material of Wok's story?

As the rehearsal proceeded an old man would stop the singing from time to time to make suggestions on style or phrasing, or, just as often, just as much a part of the event being rehearsed, he would comment on the meaning of the song words, on the details of the story. The rehearsal was at once remarkably informal and absolutely effective.

Questions of performing style are combined with interpretations of the story. The historical-legendary Wok is being transformed into his dance. A virtual or nonevent in the past—which, I grant, may have been itself based on something that happened, a dead child—is made into a concrete, actual present. But this is rehearsal: the present is something being made "for tomorrow," for the future when the dance will be danced.

As the rehearsal proceeded men and women would occasionally drift by. The assembled singers, drummers, and witnesses practiced the movements of the dance that accompanies the mother's lament. Lawrence, a school-teacher who spoke English, explained that this was an "imitative" dance, a dance in which both men and women imitated the movements of birds performing activities that loosely correlated to the events described in the mother's lament.

Wok is represented by his mother's lament—and the lament is represented by dancers, both men and women—and they are dancing as birds.

The dancers imitate birds because the clan the story is significant to is a bird clan, has a bird as its totem. The story is at once distanced—put at an artistic remove—by the translation of the woman's lament into gestures performed by both men and women acting as birds and made more immediate in its impact on all the people of the village by this artistic displacement.

"More immediate" because the bird clan exists now. A woman's lament for a murdered son is transformed into a dance of men and women imitating birds. A nonevent of the past, the killing of Wok (by a spirit?), is used as the jumping-off place for a theatrical event of the future: a bird dance commemorating a mother's lament. I say "nonevent" because the killing of Wok, however it happened, even if it happened, is not what makes him significant to Magendo. It's as if the role of hero/culture-bearer was there waiting for someone to play it, and Wok was selected. Wok's spirit taught the people how to fish, plant, build ceremonial houses. We don't know whether Wok's murder was the precipitating event or whether his role as culture bearer meant that he had to be killed (in myth, if not in fact). It doesn't much matter. It can't be found out. And the Wok who is the hero bears no necessary relationship to that other Wok who died or was murdered—except that by now they are both part of the same script, the same strip of behavior. The important event—the event that Magendo needs—is not Wok's death or his skills or his mother's lament but the performance of the dance that is none of these yet brings them all together.

The rehearsal Emigh saw works time as a single fabric of several strands, to be rewoven according to needs uncovered during rehearsals. The attention during rehearsal is focused as much on the technique of the dance as it is on what the dance signifies. The rehearsal looks backward to Wok and forward to a finished performance. Wok's dance, like rituals everywhere, disguises itself as a restoration of actual events when in fact it is a restoration of earlier performances. The ritual process is a shuttling back and forth between the nonevent and the restored event to be performed, between the significance of the event (as story, obligatory act, prayer, etc.) and the details of technique that make up the performance as performance. The rehearsals create the nonevent even as the nonevent is apparently creating the rehearsals. It is not because of Wok that the people of Magendo dance; it is because of their dance that Wok (still) lives. Their rehearsing, 1, re-collects what they "know" of Wok and his "work," 5_a, and this knowledge is combined with their ways of dancing to prepare the performance, 5_b.

Look again at figure 2.1. The fetch, or distance traveled, is more for $1 \rightarrow 5_a \rightarrow 5_b$ than for either $1 \rightarrow 2$ or $1 \rightarrow 3 \rightarrow 4$. This greater distance is in the scope of time as well as the scope of mood. $1 \rightarrow 5_a \rightarrow 5_b$ links rehearsal time, past, and performance time in both the subjunctive and indicative moods. I use "$5_a \rightarrow 5_b$" because the nonevent and the restored nonevent are versions of one another, not independent occurrences. Doing a known score is $1 \rightarrow 3 \rightarrow 4$, but even this known score has behind it a $1 \rightarrow 5_a \rightarrow 5_b$ and is best expressed as $1 \rightarrow 3 \rightarrow 5_a \rightarrow 5_b$, figure 2.4.

The model offers ways of comparing performances—and from comparisons the means of developing a theory that includes both aesthetic and ritual performances. The repetition of individual or social facts in the future indicative, $1 \rightarrow 2$, is ritual in the ethological sense. The repetition of a given or traditional performance score, $1 \rightarrow 3 \rightarrow 4$, is ritual in the social and religious sense. Aesthetic performances, such as Noh drama, whose proclaimed goal is to show audiences a 3 by presenting a 4 that has been tested against 3 is most often $1 \rightarrow 3 \rightarrow 5_a \rightarrow 5_b$. The invention of new performances or the substantial revision of traditional performances (either intentionally or unintentionally) is $1 \rightarrow 5_a \rightarrow 5_b$. Events that use the performance process but do not produce performances are $1 \rightarrow 5_a \rightarrow 5_c$. Performances that involves $5_a \rightarrow 5_b$ or $5_a \rightarrow 5_c$ draw together divergent times and moods; these kinds of performances are the most complex, multivocal, and symbolically rich.

These differentiations of performance types occur along a continuum. There is no need to specify a given performance as all this or that. A performance can be between modes: to be between $1 \rightarrow 3 \rightarrow 4$ and $1 \rightarrow 5_a \rightarrow 5_b$— as is Noh drama or Evanchuk's Shaker dancing—is to be $1 \rightarrow 3 \rightarrow 5_a \rightarrow 5_b$.

The model is meant to provide guideposts in a dynamic system. Performances of the type $1 \rightarrow 5_a \rightarrow 5_b$ may seem to be recollections of the past, but they are actually conjunctions whose center can be located not in any single time or mood but only in the whole bundle, the full and complex interrelations among times and moods. As performances, $1 \rightarrow 5_a \rightarrow 5_b$ are played in the indicative mood, but as performances of something they are in the subjunctive mood. "I am performing" is indicative; "I am performing Hamlet" is subjunctive. The difference between animal and human ritual is that animals are always performing what they are, while humans can choose to perform what/who they are not.

ℰ

A very clear example of a restoration of behavior of the $1 \rightarrow 5_a \rightarrow 5_b$ or $1 \rightarrow 3 \rightarrow 5_a \rightarrow 5_b$ type is the agnicayana that Frits Staal and Robert Gardner filmed in 1975 in Panjal, Kerala, India (plates 10, 11, and 12). Staal writes:

The Agnicayana, a 3000-year-old Vedic ritual, was performed in 1975 in southwest India by Nambudiri Brahmans. This event, which lasted twelve days, was filmed, photographed, recorded and extensively documented. From twenty hours of rough footage, Robert Gardner and I produced a 45-minute film, *Altar of Fire*. Two records are planned with selections from the eighty hours of recorded recitation and chant. Photographs of the ceremonies were taken by Adelaide de Menil. In collaboration with the chief Nambudiri ritualists and other scholars, I am preparing a definite [*sic*] account of the ceremonies, which will appear in two illustrated volumes entitled: "Agni—The Vedic Ritual of the Fire Altar." . . . Vedic ritual is not only the oldest surviving ritual of mankind; it also provides the best source material for a theory of ritual. . . . Hubert and Mauss . . . used the Vedic animal sacrifice as source material for a construction of a ritual paradigm. However, they did not know that these rituals are still performed, so that many data were inaccessible to them. [1978, 1–2]

10. Agnicayana: oblation with clarified butter from a long wooden ladle into the fire on the completed eagle-shaped altar. Photo by Adelaide de Menil.

By now (1983) Staal's ambitious program has been achieved. Note that he uses the 1975 agnicayana as the basis for his construction of a ritual paradigm. I am not concerned with that theory because of an irony: were it not being filmed, photographed, and tape recorded, the 1975 agnicayana would not have been performed. The impetus for the 1975 agnicayana was in America, not India: most of the money and much of the scholarly interest came from outside Kerala. Kerala was the 1975 agnicayana's location (as in ordinary films) but not its generative center. I doubt that American agencies would have responded with cash to an appeal from Nambudiri Brahmans to mount a ritual were it not to be filmed and studied. It was the threat of extinction—the sense that "this is the last chance to record this event"—that created the 1975 agnicayana. Actually, the 1975 agnicayana was either the one after the last of a series generated from within Kerala or the first of a new series generated by intercultural circumstances.

There are two related versions of the origins of the 1975 agnicayana. In the material accompanying the film, *Altar of Fire*, "a 16 mm color film on the world's oldest surviving ritual," a University of California publicist writes:

The background and problems of making *Altar of Fire* are perhaps as interesting as the ritual itself. The film's co-producer, Frits Staal, Professor of Philosophy and South Asian Languages at UC Berkeley, began studying Vedic recitation in southern India while a student in the 1950s. Later he discovered that the Nambudiri Brahmins not only transmitted the oral tradition through recitation but also continued to perform

11. Agnicayana: priests mark on a cloth the number of rounds of soma sequences they have chanted. Photo by Adelaide de Menil.

12. Agnicayana: the end of the ritual—and climax of the film—is the burning of the ritual enclosures. After the fire only the eagle-shaped altar remains. Photo by Adelaide de Menil.

some of the larger Vedic rituals, the largest of which, the Agnicayana, had never been witnessed by outsiders.

Western scholars had reconstructed this ritual from texts, but nobody had thought it possible that the ceremony survived. Yet it has. There are only a few Nambudiri families, however, whose members are entitled and able to carry out such a ceremony. It is expensive and requires years of training. Further, the tradition is rapidly dying because young people no longer believe in the efficacy of the ritual. As some Nambudiris became concerned about the disappearance of their tradition, Dr. Staal began to urge that the ceremony should be performed one last time so that it could be filmed and recorded.

After years of intermittent discussion, the Nambudiris agreed. They asked only that in exchange for being given the privilege of attending, filming, and recording the performance, the scholars help defray the cost of the ritual. . . . Finally, by the end of 1974, almost $90,000 was raised from grants and donations by institutions throughout the world. Robert Gardner, the noted ethnographic filmmaker *(Dead Birds, Rivers of Sand)* and professor at Harvard, was secured to direct the film. The Agnicayana was performed from April 12 to 24, 1975. [Extension Media Center, University of California]

The blurb goes on to describe the struggle involved in the filming itself. "There was a tendency to transform the sacrificial enclosure into a place of pilgrimage." Scuffles broke out between pilgrims and sightseers on the one hand and "scholars, Nambudiri youths, and six policemen" on the other. But despite all efforts,

At times, outsiders entered the sacrificial enclosure (a taboo place avoided scrupulously by the visiting scholars) and imperiled the filming—and indeed the ritual proceedings themselves. Some film footage was spoiled or its use made impossible by these fully dressed people who contrasted sadly with the Nambudiris in their white loincloths, themselves disfigured only by an occasional wristwatch.

The University of California brochure describes a drama not shown in *Altar of Fire.* An endangered species—in this case, a rare, ancient ritual—is saved by the timely intervention of dedicated conservationists from the outside who know both how to raise cash and how to behave on location. But the locals divide into two camps. The bad ones transform the event into something very postmodern: a combination media show and ad hoc pilgrimage center. These uncooperative locals dress according to their own mid-1970s codes—not as "natives"—and thereby "spoil" some footage. By contrast, and definitely in costume, the main actors—Nambudiri Brahmans—are "disfigured only by an occasional wristwatch." Scholarship plus media can turn the clock back three thousand years. Naturally enough, given the cinematic conventions of this kind of thing, the film itself shows very little of the struggle to make an "accurate" document of the agnicayana. The account of that struggle is reserved for the book, *Agni: The Vedic Ritual of the Fire Altar* (Staal 1983; two volumes, $250 for the set). Staal also gives the budgets for the project—a total of $127,207, of which $20,884 was spent in rupees on local expenses. That leaves more than $106,000 spent on the movie and all other non-Indian, nonlocal expenses. The agnicayana itself is probably out of financial reach for the Kerala Nambudiris. Certainly the filming is. The narrator of *Altar of Fire* makes no mention of the amount of money spent; credits at the film's end specify who, not how much. There is only the barest hint of the fierce local disagreements that surrounded the project. The UC press release makes a big thing out of these struggles because that underlines the heroic work of the film makers who were able to "overcome" all such difficulties.

But the UC brochure and the account in *Agni: The Vedic Ritual of the Fire Altar* are not the only "official" versions of what happened. Staal was attacked by Robert A. Paul (1978) for staging the agnicayana. In defending himself, Staal quotes the UC brochure. Then he adds:

The Adhvaryu, the main priest, and several of the other priests who officiated in 1975 had earlier officiated in 1955 or 1956, or both [the most recent Kerala-generated performances of agnicayana]. All our films and recordings had to be made from the outside. Under such circumstances, without two decades of experience and several years of careful planning, it would not have been possible to film and record this event, which was quite possibly the last performance of the world's oldest surviving ritual. All those who were present realized that this was not a humdrum affair, but a historical event. [1979, 346–47]

But what kind of historical event? Is a ritual "surviving" if the filmed version of it is also a document of its "last [that is, final] performance"? Before 1975, the agnicayana was previously performed in the 1950s. In *Agni* Staal lists 103 performances including 22 that occurred in Kerala over the past one hundred years. In a letter to me (15 June 1983) disputing whether the agnicayana of the *Altar of Fire* is an event of the $1 \rightarrow 5_a \rightarrow 5_b$ type, Staal states that "such performances took place for almost three thousand years, and are well documented for many periods." He says that a reader can compare the 1975 performance step by step with "the ritual as it was before 600 B.C."

What I am saying is that no matter what textual documentation exists we do not know what agnicayana was. The transmission of the ritual is a very complicated interaction among elements of the oral tradition and written texts and formulas. The transmission of the ritual itself—as a performance text (not a description, not a literary text, but as a thing done)—was largely oral, from man to boy, older Brahman priest to younger, employing a number of mnemonic devices used by Vedic reciters. Will *Altar of Fire, Agni,* and the eighty hours of sound tape, twenty hours of raw footage, and "thousands of color slides" now freeze the agnicayana texts? Freeze them in a way very different than the Sanskrit texts and memories of living persons charged with keeping and transmitting the oral tradition freeze things? In what way is the 1975 agnicayana a continuation of the oral tradition, and in what way is it a $1 \rightarrow 5_a \rightarrow 5_b$ or a $1 \rightarrow 3 \rightarrow 5_a \rightarrow 5_b$?

The agnicayana is very expensive by Kerala standards. That's why money had to be raised outside the community. Many priests are employed, a ritual enclosure built, an altar of firebrick constructed, food and shelter provided, and so on. The rite itself is archaic: long ago Vedic ritual gave way to later forms of Hinduism. Brahman priests reconstructed the 1975 agnicayana from a variety of sources: memory of previous performances, local opinion, Sanskrit texts. Also, and decisively for both the ritual itself and its filming, agnicayana requires animal sacrifice, a practice repugnant to many Kerala residents. Staal says, "Although discussion on the presence, dollars, and motives of foreign scholars and cameramen were relatively few, the outpouring of sentiment over the goats was practically unbounded" (1983, 2: 464). But it was the issue of the goats that was a magnet for discussions about dollars and foreign scholars. The controversy raged in the press, and because of Kerala's high literacy rate, 80 percent, almost everyone knew about the goats. In 1975 Kerala had a Marxist government, the Left is strong in the state, and animal sacrifice at the American-sponsored agnicayana became a prime political issue pitting old-fashioned entrenched interests, symbolized by the Nambudiri Brahman high-caste agnicayana, against more "proletarian" and "modern" interests. Finally, in Staal's words, "for the first time in the history of the Nambudiri tradition, the animals would be represented by rice flour folded in banana leaf" (1983, 2: 465). The heated politics of Kerala is absent from *Altar of Fire*.

The contextual situation of the 1975 agnicayana is extremely complex. The agnicayana is between an original event—the continuation of the oral tradition—and a social, political, and media event. In restoring agnicayana, considerations of how best to document the Vedic ritual—not the social or media event, certainly not the political controversy raging over the goats— were always first in the minds of Staal and Gardner. This intention to make a film of the agnicayana, as their texts and their Nambudiri Brahman priests said it was, rather than to make a film of what took place in 1975 is what makes *Altar of Fire* a $1 \rightarrow 5_a \rightarrow 5_b$. For *Altar of Fire* is what Staal and Gardner intended it to become—and to achieve their intention they had to shoot around the situation they found themselves in.

Their shooting script shows this—not that the passive recording of events is possible, even with the notebook and pencil. Like many rituals, agnicayana involves a great deal of simultaneous action over a wide range of spaces. But the camera and microphone are instruments of focus; and finished movies and sound cassettes are the outcomes of rigorous selective editing. As performed in 1975, the agnicayana took 120 hours, plus many more hours of preparations—not to count the hours negotiating the fate of the goats. Staal and Gardner could shoot only twenty hours, and their script says that for "numerous episodes filming depends on remaining quantity of raw stock."[6] The twenty hours of raw footage were edited into a forty-five-minute film. The shooting script breaks the twelve-day ceremony into numerous episodes convenient to the camera. The script is very specific about who the main performers are and what is of interest:

Adhvaryu 1 [chief priest]: as stage manager he performs most of the rites and commands the others. He is where the action is. . . .
    The final killing of the goat within the Camitra will not be filmed on this occasion [day 1] since this would upset many people; but hopefully on a later occasion. . . .
    [For day 2] No more than thirty minutes of filming for the entire day.

These procedures are only faintly reflected in *Altar of Fire*. On 11 April, the day before the agnicayana began, a statement was issued jointly in Malayalam and English by Muttathukkattil Mamunna Itti Ravi Nambudiri and Staal, explaining that a committee had been formed, government aid acquired, and a lot of money raised to "make it possible to film and record the [agnicayana] rituals so that a permanent record would be available to scholars all over the world." The statement ends by declaring that "inanimate substances" would be used instead of goats. "The organizers hereby assure the public that no animal sacrifice will take place. We request the cooperation of the public for the successful conduct of the Yagna [agnicayana]" (Staal 1983, 2: 467–68). The shooting script had to be revised.
    On camera, Edmund Carpenter, one of the visiting scholars invited to comment, says that there are three kinds of events going on simultaneously: the agnicayana, the social event surrounding the ritual, and the media event. He does not mention the political event. *Altar of Fire* focuses its attention on the agnicayana, all but forgetting social, media, and political events. But in India even noncontroversial ritual performances attract onlookers, merchants, beggars, entertainers, and crowds of curious. Media events are relatively rare, making the filming of the agnicayana a doubly powerful attraction for rural Panjal. On the last day, when the sacred enclosure was burned, a crowd of ten to fifteen thousand gathered. But *Altar of Fire* is carefully nonreflexive. The book, *Agni,* is more inclusive of these contextual events, but Staal still insists that the 1975 agnicayana is in no sense a reconstruction or restoration. The film he and Gardner made presents itself in such a way as to suggest that the film makers just happened to arrive and catch this ritual in time. But the film is actually at the convergence of two great

streams of events: one to raise the money and gather the people necessary to perform and film agnicayana; the other the controversy, media, and social events that accumulated around the doing and filming of the ritual.

We need no new educating to the idea that the instruments and means of observing and recording things deeply affect what's being observed. The substantial financial-logistical energies that made *Altar of Fire* possible also made the 1975 agnicayana possible and also brought into existence much of the turmoil surrounding the project. These bundles of events have to be considered in relation to each other; and they need to be understood as parts of one complicated meta-event. We are also used to questioning the authenticity of performances like the 1975 agnicayana. But it is not authenticity that needs to be questioned. Rather, we want ways of understanding the whole bundle of relations that joins Sanskrit scholars, film makers, Nambudiri priests, the press, Marxists, curious and agitated crowds, and performance theorists. If the discussion stops shy of considering this whole bundle, we miss the chance to recognize in the Staal-Gardner project another harbinger of an important shift toward the theatricalization of anthropology—and maybe not just anthropology. By replacing the notebook with the tape recorder, the still camera with the movie camera, the monograph with the film, a shift occurs whereby we understand social life as narrative, image, crisis and crisis resolution, drama, person-to-person interaction, display behavior, and so on. Theatrical techniques blur temporal and causal systems, creating in their stead bundles of relations that attain only relative clarity and independence from each other—and those only within contexts or frames that themselves need definition. For example, in film an effect may precede its cause. Something that happened later—in the shooting of a film, in the rehearsal of a performance—may be used earlier in the finished product. Only $1 \rightarrow 5_a \rightarrow 5_b$ shows this kind of performative circumstance.

If I fault Staal and Gardner at all it is because they did not make a second film, "On Filming *Altar of Fire*," that dealt fully with all the contextual events—dramas, arrangements, rehearsals, struggles, negotiations—that truly characterize late-twentieth-century social life, a social life that delights in on-location intensity and focus—as at Panjal—but that also extends around the globe and involves hundreds of persons who collectively decide whether or not an agnicayana gets performed without necessarily knowing what agnicayana is.

People may believe the 1975 agnicayana to be a $1 \rightarrow 3 \rightarrow 4$. But actually it is a $1 \rightarrow 5_a \rightarrow 5_b$. It was restored in order to be filmed. Its "future as a film," 5_b, created its "past as a ritual," 5_a. When events like the fight over the goats erupted at time 1, threatening the agnicayana's future as a film, these events were thought also to threaten its past as a ritual. To keep the ritual "accurate" and "genuine" the fight had to be excluded from *Altar of Fire*. The camera and narrator had to glide lightly over those packets of rice wrapped in leaves. An event of the $1 \to 5_a \to 5_b$ type can get away with not sacrificing goats while being proclaimed by Staal as an example of "animal sacrifice . . . still performed."

Altar of Fire ends with the narrator announcing that the viewer has seen what is probably the last performance of agnicayana. Not true. The viewer has seen the first of a new series of performances, a series where the event will never change because it is "on film." When people want to "see" the agnicayana they will not go to Kerala (where it may or may not be performed again), they will rent *Altar of Fire*. Funding agencies will not put up enough money to film agnicayana all over again; that would be redundant. Scholars using agnicayana will base their findings not on the series that ended in the 1950s—about which little is known—but on the material gathered by Staal and Gardner. And few, if any, scholars will examine all of the raw footage, listen to the full set of tapes, look at every one of the thousands of photographs. They will instead look at the movie, listen to the recordings, read the writings that came out of the Staal-Gardner project. Theories will be built on items extrapolated from strips of restored behavior.

Is this any different than building theories on writings? Writings are more easily recognized as interpretations than are restorations of behavior. Theories are presented in the same bundle as the data on which these theories rest. References are freely made to earlier interpretations and theories. Often writing is clearly reflexive. I don't prefer writings to restorations of behavior as a way of scholarship, but restorations are not yet understood as thoroughly as writing. Therefore, at present, restorations leave more mess than writing. People use restorations and consider them $1 \to 2$ or $1 \to 3 \to 4$ when actually they are $1 \to 5_a \to 5_b$ or $1 \to 3 \to 5_a \to 5_b$.

Figure 2.5 shows the full range of events flowing into and from the 1975 agnicayana. The movie becomes "now" for persons who in the future experience agnicayana through this medium. As Staal says, it is likely that most people will know agnicayana this way. Even if agnicayana is performed in Kerala again, it is possible that the Nambudiris will view the film and measure their ritual against it. The filming itself—as distinct from the finished film—is the core generative event. Before the filming comes planning, fund raising, consultations with ritual specialists, assembling people, material, and animals; and after the filming comes the work of archiving and editing raw goods and, ultimately, items of Euro-American culture such as movies, cassettes, books. There are also items shared among Indians and Euro-Americans: theories of ritual, data on the agnicayana "then," "now," and "later." Most of the events shown in figure 2.5 are "betwixt and between." They happen between original events and media events and between media events and scholarship. The original series of agnicayanas was liminal, an old-fashioned ritual; but from 1975 on the agnicayana has become liminoid, a voluntary performative event. Insofar as the agnicayana is liminoid it serves interests far beyond and different than those the old-fashioned agnicayana served when it belonged solely to Kerala. In terms of the "whole performance

	ORIGINAL EVENTS	MEDIA EVENTS		SCHOLARSHIP
Time "Then" 1	Agnicayana, 1950s and earlier: oral tradition			
"Now" 2		Agnicayana, 1975		
2		Deciding how to do the ritual: consultations with priests, scholars, locals, film makers, etc.; remembering and rehearsing		
2		Making a shooting script		
2			Rough footage Still photos Recorded sound	
2		People who came to see the ritual		
2			People who came to see the filming	
2		Fight over sacrificing the goats		
"Later" 3			Finished film Finished writings Finished recordings	
4				Theory of ritual

Figure 2.5

sequence" discussed in chapter 1, the emphasis of Staal's work on agnicayana is strongly, and increasingly as time passes, on the "aftermath."

Why not think of Staal and Gardner as film directors? Their work in India is more easily understood when seen in performative terms. An earlier event is "researched" and/or "remembered"—actions equivalent to rehearsals. A performance is arranged that presumably duplicates this earlier event, or selects from a series of earlier events what is most "essential," "typical," or "authentic." An event created in the future (the film, *Altar of Fire*, 5_b) is projected backward in time (the "original" agnicayana, 5_a) and restored "now" in order to be filmed (what happened in Kerala in 1975, 1). The items in this bundle cannot be separated; they must be considered as a unit. The so-called prior event (the "original" agnicayana is not strictly prior) certainly doesn't "cause" the 1975 performance. The 1975 performance is caused by the project of making a film. So in a sense the future is causing the present which, in turn, makes it necessary to research, remember—rehearse—restore the past. But this past—what is turned up by the rehearsal process—determines what is done in 1975, and those events are used to make the movie. The movie then replaces the "original" event. The movie is what we have of the past.

$\wp$

Restorations need not be exploitations. Sometimes they are arranged with such care that after a while the restored behavior heals into its presumptive past and its present cultural context like well-grafted skin. In these cases a "tradition" is rapidly established and judgments about authenticity are hard to make. Let me give examples from India, Bali, and Papua New Guinea.

Indian scholars trace Bharatanatyam (plate 13), the classical Indian dance, back not only to the ancient text on theater, *Natyasastra* (ca. second century B.C.–second century A.D.), which describes dance poses, but also to centuries-old temple sculptings that show these poses. The best known of these sculptings is the group at the fourteenth-century temple of Nataraja (Shiva, the king of dancers) at Cidambaram, south of Madras (plate 14). Most writings assume a continuous tradition connecting *Natyasastra*, temple sculptings, and today's dancing. According to Kapila Vatsyayan, India's leading dance theorist and historian,

Bharatanatyam is perhaps the oldest among the contemporary classical dance forms of India. . . . Whether the dancer was the devadasi of the temple or the court-dancer of the Maratha kings of Tanjore, her technique followed strictly the patterns which had been used for ages. [1974, 15–16]

Whenever the contemporary forms of Bharatanatyam and Manipuri and Odissi evolved, two things are clear: first, that they were broadly following the tradition of

13. Kumari Kamala in Bharatanatyam *Nrtta* (pure dance) posture. Photo courtesy Kumari Kamala.

14. Temple sculpting at Cidambaram, fourteenth-century India. Modern restorers of bharatanatyam studied this and other sculptings like it, as well as the *Natyasastra*. Photo courtesy Department of Archeology, Government of India.

the *Natyasastra* and were practicing similar principles of technique from their inception, and, second, that the stylization of movement began as far back as the 8th and 9th century. . . . Some contemporary styles preserve the characteristic features of this tradition more rigorously than others: Bharatanatyam uses the basic adhamandali [postures] most rigorously. [1968, 325, 365]

Vatsyayan's opinion is shared by virtually all Indian dance scholars. But in fact it's not known when the "classical" Bharatanatyam died out, or even if it ever existed. The old texts and sculptings surely show that there was some kind of dance, but nothing was remembered of this dance, not even its name, when moves were made in the first decades of the twentieth century to "preserve," "purify," and "revive" it.

There was a temple dance called *sadir nac* danced by women of families hereditarily attached to certain temples. According to Milton Singer,

The dancing girls, their teachers, and musicians performed not only on the occasion of temple festivals and ceremonies, but also for private parties, particularly weddings,

15. Purulia Chhau festival at Matha, 1976. Photo by Richard Schechner.

16. Purulia Chhau: training in a village, 1976. Photo by Richard Schechner.

and at palace parties. Special troupes of dancing girls and musicians were sometimes permanently attached to the courts. [1972, 172]

Many girls attached to temples were prostitutes. As dance scholar Mohan Khokar says,

the time-honoured tradition of the *devadasis,* or temple dancing girls, had fallen into such ignominy that the girls, considered sacred, continued to be considered sacred but in a different way—as prostitutes. And with this the dance that they professed—the avowedly divine Bharatanatyam—too promptly got lost to shame. [1983, 1]

From 1912 on a strong campaign was waged by Indian and British reformers to ban the devadasi system. But a countermovement led by E. Krishna Iyer wanted to "eradicate the vice but have the art." Opinions raged in the Madras press, especially during 1932 as Dr. Muthulakshmi Reddi, the first woman legislator in British India, led the attack on the devadasi system while Iyer and "lawyers, writers, artists, and even the *devadasis* themselves joined the fray."

The upshot of the brouhaha was that Krishna Iyer and his confreres emerged triumphant. The anti-nautch [devadasi] movement, which is how Dr. Reddi's crusade came to be called, was left in the lurch. The dance must survive, even if the *dasis* don't, boomed the slogan of the day. [Khokar 1983, 1]

That's exactly what happened—in a way. At the January 1933 Conference of the Music Academy of Madras, Iyer, for the second time (the first was in 1931, but this earlier show stirred scant interest), presented devadasi dancing not as a temple art or as an advertisement for or adjunct to prostitution but as secular art.

The *dasis* . . . took the fullest advantage of the sudden, buoyant interest in their art: a number of them—Balasaraswati, Swarnasaraswati, Gauri, Muthuratnambal, Bhanu-mathi, Varalkasmi, and Pattu, to name a few—readily quit the house of God for the footlights and in no time became public idols. [Khokar 1981, 1]

Scholar and critic V. Raghavan coined the word "Bharatanatyam" to replace terms associated with temple prostitution. "Bharatanatyam" connects the dance with both Bharata's *Natyasastra* and India: *natya* means dance, *bharat* means India.

Long before 1947 when Madras state finally outlawed the devadasi system, the dance moved out of the temples. People who were not from devadasi families, even men, danced. Rukmini Devi, "a singularly high placed Brahmin and wife of the International President of the Theosophical Society

. . . realized how great and lofty an art Bharatanatyam was and how pressing the need was to rescue it from corrupt influences" (Khokar 1983, 1). Not only did Devi dance, she and her associates codified Bharatanatyam. Their way to rescue the dance was to restore it in a $1 \rightarrow 5_a \rightarrow 5_b$ way. Devi and her colleagues wanted to use sadir nac but be rid of its bad reputation. They cleaned up the devadasi dance, brought in gestures based on the *Natyasastra* and temple art, developed standard teaching methods. They claimed that Bharatanatyam was very old. And, of course, a conformity to ancient texts and art could be demonstrated: every move in Bharatanatyam was measured against the sources it presumed to be a living vestige of. The differences between sadir nac and the old sources were attributed to degeneracy. The new dance, now legitimized by its heritage, not only absorbed sadir nac but attracted the daughters of the most respectable families to practice it. Today, many study Bharatanatyam as a kind of finishing school. It is danced all over India by both amateurs and professionals. It is a major export item.

The "history" and "tradition" of Bharatanatyam—its roots in the ancient texts and art—are actually a restoration of behavior, a construction based on the research of Raghavan, Devi, and others. They saw in sadir nac not a dance in its own right but a faded, distorted remnant of some ancient classical dance. That "ancient classical dance" is a projection backward in time: we know what it looks like because we have Bharatanatyam. Soon people believed that the ancient dance led to Bharatanatyam when, in fact, the Bharatanatyam led to the ancient dance. A dance is created in the past in order to be restored for the present and future. There is no single source for Bharatanatyam, only the whole bundle $1 \rightarrow 5_a \rightarrow 5_b$ or $1 \rightarrow 3$ (*Natyasastra*, temple sculptings) $\rightarrow 5_a$ (presumed ancient dance) $\rightarrow 5_b$ (today's Bharatanatyam).

Purulia Chhau, a masked dance of the arid region of West Bengal adjoining Bihar and Orissa, is an athletic dance-drama featuring many leaps, somersaults, struts, stamps, and ikonographic poses (plates 15 and 16). Stories usually are drawn from the Indian epics and Puranas and almost always depict duels and battles. Drummers of the Dom caste beat huge kettle-drums and long oblong drums, taunting the dancers into frenzied spinning jumps, screams, and confrontations. Rivalries among villages competing at the annual festival at a hill station, Matha, are fierce. According to Asutosh Bhattacharyya, professor of folklore and anthropology at Calcutta University, who has devoted himself entirely to Chhau since 1961, the Purulia region is inhabited by many aboriginal tribes whose

religious customs and social festivals show very little resemblance to those of Hinduism. . . . But, it is also a fact that the Mura of Purulia are very ardent participants in Chhau dance. With practically no education and social advancement the members of this community have been performing this art which is based on the episodes of the Ramayana and the Mahabharata and the Indian classical literature most faithfully, in some cases, for generations. . . . Sometimes an entire village, however poor, inhabited exclusively by the Mura, sacrifices its hard-earned resources for the cause of organizing Chhau dance parties. [1972, 14]

This presents a problem for Bhattacharyya.

The system which is followed in Chhau dance today could not have been developed by the aboriginal people who practice the dance. It is indeed a contribution of a higher culture keenly conscious of an aesthetic sense. [1972, 23]

He guesses that the drummers, the Dom, an outcaste group, originated Chhau, for the Dom were at one time a "highly sophisticated community, . . . brave soldiers in the infantry of the local feudal Chiefs" (1972, 24). Thrown out of work when the British pacified the region in the eighteenth century, failing to farm because of what Bhattacharyya calls the "vanity of their past tradition of warriors," they were reduced to their present untouchable status: workers of hides, drummers. But their war dance lives on as Chhau. Revealing biases sparkle from Bhattacharyya's account. Aboriginal peoples have no developed aesthetic sense; high-caste dancers are transformed into low-caste drummers after passing on their war dance because they are too proud to farm. (Why didn't they use their swords to steal land and become landlords?)

 The annual competition at Matha is not an ancient tradition but a festival initiated in 1969 by Bhattacharyya. It was discontinued in 1980 or 1981. Bhattacharyya recalls:

In April 1961 I visited an interior village in the Purulia District with a batch of students of the Calcutta University and for the first time observed a regular performance of the Chhau dance. . . . I found that there was a system of this dance and a definitely established method which was well-preserved. But it was on the decline due to lack of patronage from any source whatsoever. I wanted to draw the attention of the world outside to this novel form of dance. [1972, introd., n.p.]

And that he did. All-star parties of Chhau dancers toured Europe in 1972, Australia and North America in 1975, and Iran. They have danced in New Delhi, and as Bhattacharyya delights,

I attracted the notice of Sangeet Natak Akademi, New Delhi [the government agency established to encourage and preserve traditional performing arts] to this form of dance. It took immediate interest and invited me to give performances of the dance in New Delhi. In June 1969, I visited New Delhi with a batch of 40 village artists for the first time outside their native district. Performances were held there before very distinguished Indian and foreign invitees. . . .

Performances were also shown on TV in Delhi. Only three years later it was also shown on BBC television in London and five years later on NBC in New York, USA. [Program used in 1975 at the University of Michigan, p. 3]

Note how Bhattacharyya refers to the dances as his: "invited me to give performances of the dance." This is not bragging but an acknowledgment of the circumstances: without a patron the villagers would have gotten nowhere. And these days a patron needs more than money; he needs knowledge and a wish to devote himself to the form he's restoring. Government comes up with the cash.

Chhau 1961 and after is a creation of the mixture of what Bhattacharyya found and what he invented. But his invention is of the $1 \rightarrow 5_a \rightarrow 5_b$ type. As a folklorist-anthropologist he dug into the past and constructed a history of Chhau, and a technique, that he then proceeded faithfully to restore. His annual festival at Matha coincided with the Chaitra Parva celebrations common to the area and the occasion of the annual Chhau festivals of Seraikella and Mayurbhanj (related forms of the dance). These festivals—once paid for by maharajas—are now sponsored, less lavishly, by the government. In 1976 I went to Matha. The dances went on there all night for two nights. Villagers, arriving from towns as far away as two days' journey, set up camp. They roped together *charpois* (sleeping cots made of wood and twine) and jerry-built a theater. Women and children watched, and slept, sitting and reclining on the charpois elevated to a height of eight feet or more. Men and boys stood on the ground. A narrow passageway led from the area where performers put on costumes and masks to the roughly circular dancing ground. Parties enter down the passageway, stop, present themselves, then leap into their dancing. All dancing is done with bare feet on bare earth, swept clean of large rocks but still raw, pebbled, with turned-up clods and scrub grass. To me it felt like a rodeo in a backwater town. Torches and Petromax lanterns throw shadowy light, the drums bark and roar, the *shehanais* (clarinetlike) shriek, as party after party competes. Most parties consist of five to nine dancers. Some masks adorned with peacock feathers rise three feet over the dancers' heads. The mask of ten-headed Ravana is more than four feet long. Wearing these masks, dancers make full somersaults and twisting leaps. The dances are vigorous and it's very hot inside the papier-mâché masks, so each dance lasts less than ten minutes. Every village danced twice. There were no prizes, but there was competition, and everyone knew who danced well, who poorly.

Just in case there were doubts, each afternoon following the night's dancing, Bhattacharyya critiqued the performances. During the dancing he sat behind a desk, where two Petromax lanterns made him the best-lit figure of the event; next to him were his university assistants. All night he watched and wrote. One by one the villages appeared before him on the morrow. I listened to what he said. He warned one party not to use story elements not found in the Hindu classics. He chided another for not wearing the standard basic costume of short skirt over leggings decorated in rings of white, red, and black. Bhattacharyya selected this basic costume from one village and made it general. When I asked him about it he said that the costumes he chose were the most authentic, the least Westernized. In a word, Bhattacharyya oversaw every aspect of Purulia Chhau: training, dance themes, music, costuming, steps.

In January 1983 I attended a non-Bhattacharyya Chhau performance in a town near Calcutta. There I saw energetic dancing of stories from the *Mahabharata*. This same group of village dancers, while performing for performers and scholars assembled for a conference in Calcutta, sang at least one song that Bhattacharyya would have disapproved of. In English translation:

> We will not stay in India,
> We will go to England.
> We will not eat what is here
> But we will eat cookies and bread.
> We will not sleep on torn rags
> But on mattresses and pillows.
> And when we go to England
> We won't have to speak Bengali
> But we will all speak Hindi.

The villagers assumed that in England the "national language" was the same as it was in India: Hindi. The question: Is this village's Chhau, so full of contemporary longings, to be condemned for not being "classical"? Or is the syncretic mixing of *Mahabharata* and England to be accepted as the "natural development" of the dance?

Bhattacharyya selected individuals from different villages and composed them into all-star touring ensembles. He oversaw rehearsals and went with these "foreign parties" on tour. Dancers and musicians who toured returned to their villages with enhanced reputations. Touring, in fact, has had deep effects on Chhau. Three foreign parties have come into existence since the first tour in 1972: nineteen people went to Europe, sixteen to Iran, eleven to Australia and North America. Because foreigners won't sit through nine hours of dancing, Bhattacharyya made a program of two hours' duration. And because he didn't think that bare chests looked good on the male dancers he designed a jacket based on an old pattern. Both these changes became a standard back in Purulia. Many of the people who went abroad formed their own groups at home. Each of these groups are called "foreign parties"—and bill themselves as such; this gives them status, drawing power, and the ability to charge more. There is demand now for performances as performances, outside of the ritual calendar. A performance can be hired for about a thousand rupees, a lot cheaper than Jatra, the most popular entertainment in rural Bengal. But a thousand rupees is still a lot of money. In Bhattacharyya's opinion, as the financial opportunities have increased the subtlety of the art has declined. John Emigh spoke to Bhattacharyya in the summer of 1980. Reflecting on the tours, Bhattacharyya believes they saved a form otherwise doomed, but at the expense of stirring jealousies and rivalries and generating irreversible changes. Chhau is a masked dance, and one side effect of its popularity abroad has been the demand by tourists for masks. Many masks are shipped that have never been worn by a dancer.

These changes can be traced back to Bhattacharyya. He is the big Chhau man, and his authority is rarely questioned. He's a professor, a scholar from Calcutta. When he writes about Chhau he emphasizes its village base and ancient origins; he even suggests a possible link between Chhau and the dances of Bali. (Around the third century B.C. the Kalinga Empire of what is now Orissa and Bengal possibly traded across southeast Asia as far as Bali.) But he hardly mentions his own role in restoring the dance. Rather, he speaks of himself as "discovering" it.

This "discovery"—along with similar discoveries of the other forms of Chhau—will have lasting effects on the form, continuing the process of modernization. Since 1981 the festival at Matha has been discontinued. Some say that rivalries among villages heated up to such intensity that the festival became dangerous; others say that villagers rebelled against Bhattacharyya. In 1983, when Emigh returned to the Purulia district during the Chhau season (April–June), he saw children practicing steps, spins, and jumps: the dance is alive and well—and probably was even when Bhattacharyya came upon it. But it is also probably much different now because of Bhattacharyya's influence. Surely these days Chhau in each of its three variations is much more tightly knit into mainstream Indian and world culture than it was twenty years ago.

In February 1977 Suresh Awasthi, Shyamanand Jalan, and I thought of organizing a festival and workshop that would bring all three kinds of Chhau together. Awasthi is the former secretary (administrator) of the Sangeet Natak Akademi, the bureau of the central government in Delhi dedicated to studying and preserving traditional performing arts. Jalan is a Calcutta theater director and lawyer. His work has been in modern (Westernized) Indian theater. The 1977 Calcutta festival was the first time in many years that dancers from Purulia, Mayurbhanj, and Seraikella could see each others' dances. For three days dancers and scholars and directors explored the various ways that the three forms are related—and the possibilities for exchange between traditional and modern performing artists.

In January 1983, Jalan organized a much larger international gathering to look at the relationship, actual and potential, between several Indian classical forms and modern theater and dance. Not only Chhau but Bharatanatyam, Odissi, Kathak, Yakshagana, Manipuri, and Kathakali were presented both in their traditional ways and in uses being made of them by modern Indian and non-Indian theater people. Delegates from a dozen countries attended, including Eugenio Barba, Tadashi Suzuki, and Anna Halprin. The conference revealed the problems as well as the possibilities of "using" traditional forms in modern contexts. But, whatever the problems, such uses are growing—with deep effects both on modern theater and on the traditional genres (see Martin and Schechner 1983). It's neither possible nor (in my opinion) desirable to keep forms "pure." The question is how to manage, and whether to limit, the promiscuous mixing of genres.

Sometimes changes in traditional performances are made by insiders. One of the best-known films about non-Western performance is Margaret Mead's and Gregory Bateson's *Trance and Dance in Bali* (1938). At a showing of this movie shortly before her death, Mead said that the trance club of Pagutan decided that the visiting foreigners who were making the film would like to see young women go into trance and stab at their breasts with krises.[7] In Bali at that time women often went around with their breasts bare—naked breasts did not mean the same thing in Bali as they do in New York (where, ironically, in a semantic double twist, clubs where dancers are bare-breasted are called "topless"—perhaps a last-ditch puritanical revenge). But also—I suppose to please or at least not offend the foreign film makers—the Balinese women covered their breasts for the filming and young women replaced older ones as dancers. Without telling Mead or Bateson, the men of the trance club instructed the young women in proper techniques for entering trance and showed them how to handle the krises. Then the men of the club proudly announced to the film makers the changes made for the special filming. The film itself makes no mention of these changes. In *Trance and Dance* there is one old woman who, as the narrator says, announced beforehand that "she wouldn't go into trance" but who is nevertheless "unexpectedly" possessed. The camera follows her; she is bare-breasted, deep in trance, her kris powerfully turned against her own chest. Later, slowly, she is brought out of trance by an old priest who has her inhale smoke, sprinkles her with holy water, and sacrifices a small chicken on her behalf. There is a period of time when, seated, after the drama is over, her hands continue to go through the motions of dancing. It seems that members of the trance club were angry at this old woman because they felt that her trance disturbed the aesthetic refinements they had rehearsed for foreign eyes—and foreign lenses. As it turned out, the Mead-Bateson camera crew paid a lot of attention to this old lady: she appeared to be, and was, a very genuine trancer. But, speaking strictly from the Balinese point of view, which is "authentic," the young women prepared by the Balinese themselves or the solitary old woman doing the traditional thing? Is there not, in Bali, a tradition of modifying things for foreigners? And not only in Bali. Cases abound where, as in Patugan, local performances are adapted to suit foreign tastes. Hula dancers, for example, were traditionally heavy—that is, mature and powerful—middle-aged women. But tourist hula, now traditional in its own right, features slim-hipped young women. It's precisely when changes feed back into the traditional forms, actually becoming these forms, that a restoration of behavior occurs.

Sometimes, even, with tourist money in mind, performances are invented and presented as traditional when they are not. In 1972 I was in the Papua New Guinea highlands where I saw the tourist performance of the famous Mudmen of the Asaro River valley (plate 17). Their story is difficult to pin down but sad in any version. These white-clay-covered dancers—with their beautiful, grotesque masks made from hardened mud over an armature of banana tree bark—are, according to Margaret Mead, commemorating "a battle in which their ancestors, driven into the river by a marauding tribe, emerged covered with mud and frightened off the attackers, who thought they were evil spirits" (1970, 31). When photos of these dancers appeared in Western publications a demand was created for their dancing. Locally they danced at great regional shows such as the annual Mount Hagen festival, organized first by the Australian colonial administration and later continued when Papua New Guinea gained independence in 1975. The Mount Hagen festival was supposed to reduce intertribal hostilities while promoting international tourism. And in their own village of Makehuku the Mudmen put on daily displays for tourists minibussed in from nearby Goroka (a regional center). In Makehuku I saw the dancers dancing at midday instead of at dawn; they were nakedly visible in the center of the small village instead of only when necessary—that is, when threatened by enemies. And, of course, they were exploited: when I saw them they kept 10 percent of the tourists' dollars.

Edmund Carpenter challenges Margaret Mead's account of the origins of the Mudmen. In a letter to me, he said: "These were invented and designed by a TAA travel agent. They have no antiquity, no foundation in New Guinea aesthetics, no parallels elsewhere." I wanted to resolve the matter. I wrote to the National Library in Boroko, Papua New Guinea. The response did not

17. Mudmen of Asaro dancing for tourists, 1972. Photo by Joan MacIntosh.

18. Masked dancers of Kentasarobe, 1972. Squatting at the right making fire is Asuwe Yamuruhu. Photo by Joan MacIntosh.

help. The reference librarian checked holdings in Boroko and contacted both local anthropologists and theater people. No new data were turned up. Finally, the people in Papua New Guinea referred me to the American Museum of Natural History (where Mead was curator): so the circle closed. My point is: the Mudmen are by now dancing a $1 \rightarrow 5_a \rightarrow 5_b$. The origin of their dance is not locatable. It could be an authentic dance turned into a tourist attraction; it could be the invention of tourist agents, or the invention of the local dancers who themselves wanted to attract tourists. And what is "authentic" anyway? Even if "tourist art" is often shoddy and almost always syncretic, does that make it "inauthentic"?

Nor does the Mudmen story end here. In March 1972, while Joan MacIntosh and I were photographing not only the Mudmen but the tourists disembarking from their minibus at Makehuku, a man approached us and asked us in Pidgin to come with him to his village, Kenetasarobe. There Asuwe Yamuruhu, the headman, told us about his dancers for whom he wanted a tourist audience. The next day with two friends we paid $4 per person to photograph Yamuruhu's troupe's fire-making and dancing. Four dancers in magnificent grass, moss, and bamboo masks moved slowly in a crouch, raising their knees high, shouting phrases and expletives. Their show was equal to the Mudmen's. After about fifteen minutes of dancing, we spent an hour recording music, talking, and smoking. Yamuruhu wanted us to arrange for minibusses of tourists to come to Kenetasarobe. He gave me the pipe we had been smoking as a gift. I tried to explain to this choreographer that we could not help him market his dance, much as we enjoyed it.

In both Bharatanatyam and Purulia Chhau, a modern version of an old art is born through the intervention/invention of one or a few dedicated persons from outside the class and/or area of those they are leading. Maybe this is a version of the Moses myth or the Marxist fact: revolution comes to a group from the outside, typically brought in by a lost member of the tribe who in rediscovering his origins discovers also a responsibility to his now renewed connection. As Indians, Raghavan, Devi, and Bhattarcharyya are not outsiders as Staal and Gardner are. But Rhaghavan and Devi were not Devadasis, nor is Bhattacharyya a tribesman of the Purulia hills.

I see nothing amiss in restorations of behavior like Bharatanatyam and Purulia Chhau. Arts, and rituals too, are always developing, and restoration is one means of change. What happened in Bharatanatyam and Chhau is analogous to what the French dramatists of the seventeenth century did when they conformed to what they thought were ancient rules of Greek tragedy. The dramatists had at hand Aristotle, Horace, the Greek and Latin playtexts, architectural ruins, pottery, but they did not have the actual behaviors of the ancient Athenians. The restorers of Bharatanatyam and Chhau had living arts that they presumed were vestiges of older, more classical arts. They also had ancient texts, sculptings, and their own deep knowledge of Hindu traditions.

"Nativistic movements" want to bring back the "old ways." I'm talking about something else, something postmodern. Bharatanatyam and Chhau are close to what I mean, the Staal-Gardner agnicayana is even closer; and more restorations are on the way. Already the past fifty years are available on film, tape, and disc. Almost everything we do these days is not only done but kept on film, tape, and disc. We have strong ways of getting, keeping, transmitting, and recalling behavior. From the 1920s onward less and less behavior has been irretrievably lost. Waves of styles return regularly because of the relatively easy access to this behavior information. We live in a time when traditions can die in life, be preserved archivally as behaviors, and later be restored.

Sometimes these restorations take on their own life. Alan Lomax reports the experience of Adrian Gerbrands:

Gerbrands by chance screened a documentary on Eastern New Guinea mask-making for a native group in New Britain. The audience reacted powerfully during and after the screening. They, too, had once known how to make such masks and should, they felt, try their skill again, especially if their art too would be filmed. After Gerbrands had filmed the group's mask-making, a lone native approached him with the offer to perform a very important and defunct ceremony if he would film it. Naturally again Gerbrands used his camera. On his next trip to New Britain, the other men in the village insisted on seeing the film and were so distressed at the poor quality of the filmed ceremony that they vowed forthwith to reenact the whole ceremony, masks, costumes, ballet, feasting, and all, but at a length suitable for filming. This event and its resultant film were such successes locally that the ceremony is now being celebrated every year just as in former times. [1973, 480]

Celebrated, yes, but "just as in former times"? The intervention of the film as the stimulus for the restored behavior creates a complicated situation. In the Gerbrands case, the film showed the wrong way that made it necessary to do it the right way, "but at a length suitable for filming." It would take more research to disclose what is "right" and "wrong" and why.

Some proposed restorations pit outmoded behaviors against new behaviors; the lack of fit is revealing. The *Los Angeles Times* reported:

In an effort to boost tourism, tribesmen in New Guinea have offered to turn cannibal again. They told committee members of the Mt. Hagan show, the big territorial festival, that they were prepared to eat human flesh at the show in August [1975]. The tribesmen added, however, that they did not want to kill any of their enemies and would do instead with a body from the local hospital morgue. A government officer at the meeting politely but firmly declined the tribesmen's suggestions.

The rhetoric of this newspaper story is the key to the cultural contexts in conflict here. To American readers "tribesmen" = savages; "committee members" = Westernized savages; "government officer" = the New Civilized Order. The story is full of sly racist humor delectably alluding to a taboo appetite. That's why the item was run in a major American paper. But the local people have logic on their side. If old dances are being restored and the old warrior costumes and decorations worn, why not the cannibal feast that traditionally accompanied such displays? The locals know how far they can go: the body must come from a repository of corpses approved by the New Civilized Order. The Order has its role to play too: it must let it be known far and wide that, well, New Guinea is and isn't New Guinea anymore. So the story "gets out," and the sponsors of the Mount Hagen Show have their cake without having to eat it too.

⌒

Although restored behavior seems to be founded on past events—"Bharatanatyam is perhaps the oldest among the contemporary dance forms of India," "Verdic ritual is . . . the oldest surviving ritual of mankind"—it is in fact the synchronic bundle $1 \rightarrow 5_a \rightarrow 5_b$ or $1 \rightarrow 3 \rightarrow 5_a \rightarrow 5_b$. The past, 5_a, is recreated in terms not simply of a present, 1, but of a future, 5_b. This future is the performance being rehearsed, the "finished thing" to be made graceful through editing, repetition, and invention. Restored behavior is both teleological and eschatological. It joins first causes to what happens at the end of time. It is a model of destiny.

⌒

Restorations of behavior are not limited to New Guinea or India: the world of the non-Western other. All over America restorations of behavior are common, popular, and making money for their owners. Maurice J. Moran, Jr., has written an account of theme parks and restored villages (1978). Their diversity is undeniable: Renaissance Pleasure Faires in California and New York, restored villages in almost every state, Disneyland, Disney World and Epcot, safari and wildlife parks, amusement parks organized around single themes, Land of Oz in North Carolina, Storyland in New Hampshire, Frontierland, Ghost Town in the Sky, even Li'l Abner's Dogpatch. The Marriott Corporation, operators of parks and owners of hotels, describes a theme park as "a family entertainment complex oriented to a particular subject or historical area, combining a continuity of costuming and architecture with entertainment and merchandise to create a fantasy-provoking atmosphere" (Moran, 1978, 25). These places are large environmental theaters. They are related to get-togethers like the Papua New Guinea kaiko, the Amerindian powwow, and the Indian kumbhmela: pilgrimage centers where performances, goods, services, and ideologies are displayed and exchanged.

I'll concentrate here on only one kind of theme park, the restored village. As of 1978 there were over sixty of these in the United States and Canada and, it seems, more are coming. Millions of people visit them each year. Typically, they restore the colonial period or the nineteenth century; they reinforce the ideology of rugged individualism as represented by early settlers of the eastern states (Colonial Williamsburg, Plimoth Plantation), or the shoot-'em-up West (Buckskin Joe and Cripple Creek, Colorado; Cowtown, Kansas; Old Tucson, Arizona), or romanticized "heroic" industries like mining and whaling. Some like Amish Farms and Homes in Pennsylvania offer people actually living their lives; a few like Harper's Ferry in West Virginia commemorate historical confrontations. The scope of the architectural reconstructions and the behaviors of the persons who work in the villages make these restorations more than museums.

At Columbia Historic Park, California,

the tour of a still functioning gold mine is a major attraction—where would-be spelunkers are warned of the dangers of cave-ins and claim jumping. The miners are two retired men who can actually make a living from the little bit of gold left in the vein. [Moran, 1978, 31]

The twenty-five acres of historic Smithville in New Jersey contain a cluster of thirty-six buildings including a gristmill, schoolhouse, Quaker meetinghouse, cobbler's shop, and firehouse, "most of which are original structures from the Jersey shore area. 'Residents' of the town are dressed in period costume and work at the tasks of the 18th and 19th century citizens" (Moran 1978, 36).

Old Sturbridge Village in Massachusetts was started in 1946. By 1978 there were more than thirty-five buildings on the 200-acre tract. The crafts people are dressed in period costumes. On Sundays

a Quaker meeting is held. There is village dancing on Wednesday evenings. School is actually taught in the little faded schoolhouse two days a week, and there are presentations of plays from the period (*The Drunkard*, 1840, *Ever So Humble*, 1836). On July 4th the entire village celebrates as it may have been then. [Moran 1978, 40–41]

At Louisbourg, Nova Scotia, the employees of the village

assume the names of people who actually inhabited the village. The visitor is stopped at the gate and instructed to proceed only after an informal search, conducted in French. If you reply in English, a wary eye is kept on you as you proceed. [Moran 1978, 50]

Given the present temper of relations between English and French speakers in Canada, this entrance initiation reverberates across several centuries. Time is often merrily conflated:

One woman asked this writer if he had met her "husband." She was referring in the present tense to the man who had served as the chief engineer in the original Louisbourg. Her "maid" and "children" ("I had five, you know, but one died this past winter") cavort in the kitchen, smiling at the strangely clothed visitors with their major boxes [cameras]. [Moran 1978, 51]

The performance is carried further at Plimoth Plantation in Massachusetts (plates 19–24). According to materials sent to me by Judith Ingram, director of marketing at the Plantation, an attempt is made at a total re-creation, including the impersonation of actual residents of Plimoth in the seventeenth century.

Our efforts on this behalf began in the late 1960s. Since that time, visitors to our Pilgrim Village have been afforded the opportunity for total immersion in 17th century life. Staff members are trained in what might be termed "non-programmatic" interpretation which stresses the ability to converse with visitors naturally while putting in a hard day's work running the community in a holistic way. This approach assures that all the senses are brought to bear in the learning process. . . . No one who has entered the small, cluttered houses in our village in July and had to contend with the flies and dust, who has seen a fire on the hearth on a hot scorching day, or who has observed the difficulties just keeping the food edible, will come away with the traditional stereotype of the starched Pilgrim intact.
    In 1978 interepretation in the Pilgrim Village took another important step forward with the introduction of first person interpretation. Within the palisaded walls of the village no trace of the modern world can be found [except for special paths and access to several structures for the handicapped]. Now, we have recreated not only the houses and furnishings, but also the residents of 1627 Plymouth. Great care has been taken in replicating the attire, the personalities, and even regional English dialects of the Pilgrims.[8]

The Plimoth staff are careful to point out that the Plantation is not a "restoration" but a "re-creation." "We have no surviving original houses," said Ingram in a letter, "we do not know the exact design of the houses and must recreate structures typical of the period." These "re-creations" are built after much research. The same care goes into building roles—and these are modeled not on "typical" people of the period but on actual residents of the colony.
    According to Bob Marten, former cohead of the Plantation's Interpretation Department, ads are placed each January to fill about thirty roles representing the actual two hundred persons who lived in the colony in 1627. That is, thirty out of two hundred villagers are actually represented by what Marten calls "cultural informants."

19–20. Two views of the main street of the Plimoth Plantation. The picture above (19), issued by the Plimoth publicity office, shows the street as it "might have been" in the 1620s. The picture below (20), taken by Richard Schechner in 1982, is the same view of the same street. The tourists populating the street give the scene a very different feeling.

PERSONATION BIOGRAPH

Phineas Pratt
'FEHNYERZ PRUHT'

Dialect Specimen:
'Right there, through those there trees, I seein' the red Devils'
'ROIT THUR, DREW THUHZUHR DREEZ OI ZEEN THUR RID DUHFILZ'

Signature: Phineas Pratt.

Dialect Region: Southern Code 6

Current Wealth:

Friends, Associates:

Syllabus:

- Notes -

21. The "Personation Biograph" of Phineas Pratt. Biograph and photo courtesy Plimoth Plantation.

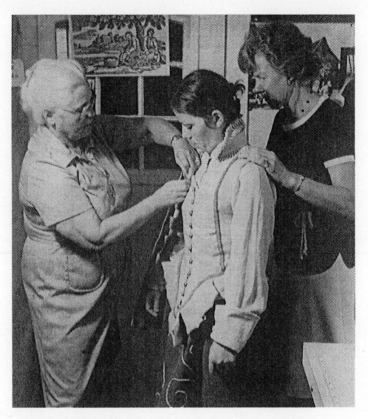

22. Putting on a costume at Plimoth. All costumes are custom fitted. They are designed and tailored as authentically as possible—but they are made by contemporary methods. Photo courtesy Plimoth Plantation.

Marten said the Plantation tries to find people who are similar to the characters they will play. "We're looking for the 20th-century counterparts of 17th-century people. If casting for the part of Elder (William) Brewster, we'll look for someone of approximately the same age with a gracious manner of expression and ready vocabulary. . . . John Billingston was a rogue, a con man. So we'll find someone who's capable of being in this role. He's usually played by a character actor who could sell a man his own shoes." [Miller 1981, n.p.]

As in movie acting, a lot of typecasting is done. "A truck driver makes a better yeoman than a teacher," says Marten.

Interestingly, there is little group rehearsal—for this is not a play the performers are preparing for but a more improvisatorial world of interaction not only among themselves but with the tourists who visit the Plantation daily. (The Plantation is open seven days a week, nine to five, from 1 April through 30 November.) Each performer is given a "Documentary Biograph" and a "Personation Biograph" (plate 21). The documentary biograph tells what is known about the character to be portrayed: age in 1627, place of origin, parents, social status, et cetera. Some of these data are noted as "current opinion" (rather than established fact) and some as "learned fabrication," a category that means invented but according to probability. The

23. Salting pork at Plimoth. Photo courtesy Plimoth Plantation.

24. Indian encampment at Wampanoag near Plimoth. Photo by Richard Schechner.

personation biograph includes dialect specimen, signature, names of the character's friends, some suggested readings, and, very important, a paragraph or two of "notes." For example, Phineas Pratt, we were told, is thirty-four, comes from Buckinghamshire, arrived in Plimoth aboard the *Sparrow* in 1622, and is a yeoman. The notes on Phineas's personation biograph tell the performer, in part:

P. Pratt is a man of Character; he cannot Lie, nor swear, nor suffer one heard— Quicker Master P. would unscabbard his temper a' his sword than tolerate a falsehood or an dissembilating man. Nor ought he, by his own Code of Good Word and Valient Deed. One doesn't find him continually Defending his or others verity, however, for the same disposition which causeth him to believe in his own Truth Telling, causeth him to trust the truth of Others—unless he find ample cause to Doubt. . . . He has lived as close to the red men—friends & foes—as anie English Man & accepted—nay, even *adopted* to his own ways, their customs & believs—but his animated telling of the sagacities & civilities of *The Beaver* causes some of the more canny & doubtful of the community to wince at "Finyuz's" acceptance of what they deem heathan apocrypha.

These notes are written in what I suppose is a seventeenth-century hand, in seventeenth-century grammar. The biograph also has a drawing of Phineas in his clothes—or costume, depending on whether you take his point of view or that of the performer playing him. Along with the biographs, a performer is given a cassette tape of talking in the proper dialect. Research is continuous. In 1983 revised documentary and personation biographs of Phineas Pratt (1593–1680) were issued. In the revision much is made of Phineas's experience with the Indians, especially his "exploits at Wassagusset" and his "deliverance from the Massachusetts who sought his demise." But the performer is advised that "The excitement of those times is past, however, and Phineas must now adapt to a quieter and less central role in the community." The writing style of the personation biograph seems less seventeenth-century than before.

Moran visited Plimoth:

In each building a member of the household that would have resided there greets you and asks "How be ye?" Within a few minutes you find yourself responding in a language that was foreign only moments ago. "I be well, thank ye." One little girl is asked, "Where be ye from?" "New Jersey," she answers. "I'm afraid I don't know that place." A parent intervenes. "You see, Susie, New Jersey isn't invented yet."
    . . . As the day proceeds, the villagers go about their work. Food is prepared in black kettles over hot coals, while they explain to their visitors the difference between pottage and ragout. . . . One young lad is helping building Mr. Allerton's house. With Irish brogue he explains, "I was in a shipwreck on my way to Virginia colony. When I washed ashore the Indians took me here. I was surprised to find anyone speaking English in these wilds." . . . One goat insisted on coming into the Standish household,

only to be shooed away by the maid. The houses are all hand-constructed, some with wooden floors, some with clay (damp in the spring thaw). The streets are uneven, rocky. . . . Many special events continue the theme of historic re-enactment. There is the opening of the Wampanoag Summer Settlement, staffed by native Americans in the style of the 17th century. There is a village barn-raising and a re-enactment of a typical wedding in the colony and also in the Indian camp. But the classical attraction, and one of the chief fundraisers for the village, is the Harvest Festival in October. . . . Here the villagers renew 17th century harvest customs with cooking and feasting, songs, dances, and a general show of high spirits. Native Americans from the summer settlement join in friendly challenges of skill and chance. [1978, 64–70]

The repartee between centuries is sometimes seasoned with ironies. A visitor to Plimoth apologized for interrupting a craftsperson with questions. "As many as you like, sir," the performer responded. "I have a few questions meself about your time period."[9]

When I visited Plimoth in the fall of 1982 I picked up some vibrations that signaled not $1 \rightarrow 3 \rightarrow 4$ but $1 \rightarrow 3 \rightarrow 5_a \rightarrow 5_b$. The place was very crowded, and although official photographs suggest a village full of persons of the seventeenth century, the actual experience is of anachronisms swimming in a sea of twentieth-century tourists (plates 19–20). Still, the reconstruction of the village is extraordinary. From the roof of an armory, looking down the main street to the sea, Plimoth reads perfectly. So much so that an article in *Natural History* magazine ("The Beautiful Yeoman," October 1982) concerning the daily life of the Pilgrim settlers is illustrated with photos taken at Plimoth. *Natural History* is published by the American Museum of Natural History and prides itself on its anthropological accuracy. The photographs give the impression of a backward time capsule. The only reference in the article to Plimoth is a very tiny photo credit. The name of the photographer, Cary Wolinsky, is writ large; the venue is barely visible. I can't help thinking that the editors wanted to make the readers feel that they were "actually there." The article is a detailed description of ordinary life in seventeenth-century New England, drawing extensively on documents of the time. The implication is that the illustrations are also "of the time." Of course, the editor can say that everyone knows there were no cameras back then. Still, a picture does speak a thousand words. And that tiny photo credit says: Forget where these pictures came from; think of what they are of.

Equally instructive, but in a different way, was my visit to the Wampanoag Summer Settlement "staffed by native Americans." The Settlement consisted of two small tepees inside which were some (maybe) Indians (plate 24). Although the brochure given to each visitor invites tourists to "meet the Native American people who have lived for centuries along the New England coast," I doubt that the Pilgrims and their descendants left a large stock of Native Americans alive. An avowed aim of the Plantation is to provide "the opportunity for members of the Native American community to learn about aspects of their own culture that are in danger of being lost" (Plimoth Plantation 1980, 3). The actors in the tepees are presented by Plantation officials as "Native Americans"—as if that made a difference. There is no attempt to present the Plimoth villagers as "white Anglo-Saxons." For all I know, some of them were Jews, Poles, or Hungarians. No blacks, though. It is not clear how far historical accuracy delimits theatrical contingency. When I asked to taste the ragout boiling in a stewpot, I was told by a seventeenth-century woman that twentieth-century Massachusetts state health law prohibits visitors from tasting food outside the established restaurant. Would state anti-discrimination laws be a basis for black actors to sue for roles as Pilgrims? Certainly in the Pilgrim village acting ability seems more prized than ethnic authenticity. A drama of the day I visited showed negotiations between the English Plimoth residents and visiting Dutch from New Amsterdam. A staff member bragged that a "Broadway actor" (not necessarily Dutch) had been hired for a key role. The point is that there is no way of avoiding anachronisms and the intrusion of today's values, political and aesthetic.

Whatever the underlying $1 \rightarrow 3 \rightarrow 5_a \rightarrow 5_b$ pattern of things, the "first-person interpretation" technique used at Plimoth is very effective theater. This technique is pushed hard by Plantation officials. According to the information sheet I got from Ingram,

First person interpretation not only encourages the personal involvement of visitors, it also facilitates the discussion of difficult concepts and ideas. Indeed, it has been our experience that since the implementation of this technique in the Pilgrim Village the frequency of questions dealing with matters that can collectively be termed the 17th century world view has risen. There has also been a corresponding decrease in the questions that fall into the "What is that?" category. By speaking in the first person, our staff can respond to questions in personal rather than abstract terms. [Plimoth Plantation 1980, 2]

In fact, the "first-person interpretation" technique has a kind of authenticity that the Plimoth architecture lacks. Nothing architectural survives from the original colony; the village has been totally re-created. But it is known who was there, and background information has been researched regarding individual inhabitants. Thus, while the buildings and furnishings are "typical" of the period, the people are "actually from" 1627—as much as good acting can make them so. Full "first-person interpretation" was not formalized at Plimoth until 1978. Before that, the interpretations were ad hoc. Performances took place for this or that occasion. After 1978 everyone in the Plantation played a role. Performers who've been at it a long time identify closely with their roles. Marten played Myles Standish from 1969 to 1981.

After living with Myles Standish for all these years, Marten said he's "more supportive and defensive" in his attitude toward the historical figure than a historian might be. Aside from appreciating Standish's virtues, Marten has gained an understanding of why the soldier committed some of his more controversial acts. "He killed a number of Indians—not in fair combat, but in ambush," Marten said. "If he had to knock off a few Indians for the good of the colony, he would do it without question. I don't think I'd have the stomach to do what he did, but in the context of that time, what Myles did made sense." [Miller 1981, n.p.]

What happened to Marten happens to all Euro-American actors: they build roles filling in from their own feelings what can't be located in any background study.

Occasionally the program of stepping back into the seventeenth century is undercut by a wink. The brochure tells visitors that Spanish and French persons, "if unarmed," are welcome to the Plantation even though England was at war with Spain and/or France for much of the seventeenth century. Actually the managers of the Plantation put great emphasis on separating the seventeenth from the twentieth century. "Unlike places like Sturbridge and Williamsburg," writes Ingram in her letter, "no items whatsoever are sold aboard the Mayflower or in the Pilgrim village. . . . Our program carefully separates modern element from period element, using the former to prepare the visitor for a suspension of doubt as he steps into the past." The only difficulty with this is that there are so many visitors stepping into the past that they are as likely to step on each other as into a Pilgrim environment. The concept Ingram celebrates would work if the number of visitors were limited so that they would be but a sprinkle amidst the Pilgrims and Indians. Try selling that to the Plantation's managers, who are trying to make ends meet. Economic requirements dictate that the visitors are a mass, and much of what I experienced at Plimoth was a crush of lots of people just like me: eager, camera-toting, question-asking explorers of earlier times. When I went into a less popular exhibit—like a simple home where two women were cleaning up from a lavish lunch—I felt some of what Ingram promised. I sat to the side and watched as they went about their chores. It was a nice piece of environmental theater. Or, when a duel drew most people to an open field, inside a house the negotiations between the Dutch from New Amsterdam and Governor Bradford went on—with neatly improvised dialogue. Still, somehow, I felt more that I was watching a period play than "actually being there" in the seventeenth century.

The attempt to separate out different elements so that distinct thematic areas of the environment are clearly defined is what places like the Disney parks do. Not only is there a sharp separation between the ordinary world—even the mechanics of running the park itself—and the park, but different parts of the park speak different thematic languages: in Disneyland, for example, there are big differences among Frontierland, Tomorrowland, and so on. At Florida's Disney World and Epcot the backstage is actually underground, and central control areas are several miles distant from where the visitors stroll. All Disney employees enter and leave the area underground and out of sight: they are seen in the Magic Kingdom only in costume and/ or character.

But despite—even because of—these attempts to separate realities, or spheres of experience in time/space, spectators enjoy what can best be described as a postmodern thrill at the mix or close coincidence of contradictory categories. At Plimoth hosts are twentieth-century persons trained in seventeenth-century English (more or less); the visitors are tourists who've paid to be treated as guests dropping in from another century. A brochure given to each visitor emphasizes the reality of the seventeenth-century world while encouraging the visitors to break that frame:

The people you will meet in the village portray—through dress, speech, manner and attitudes—known residents of the colony in 1627. Their lives follow the seasonal cycle of all farming communities—planting and harvesting crops, tending animals, preparing meals, preserving food—what you see will depend upon the time of your visit. Busy as they are, the villagers are always eager for conversation. Feel free to ask questions; and remember, the answers you receive will reflect each individual's 17th century identity.

The giveaway phrase is "Busy as they are." It's not true: they are paid to respond to the visitors. I doubt that a villager too busy to talk to the tourists would last long in the seventeenth century, for this preoccupied performer would have violated a rule laid down by his twentieth-century employers. The little one-page map and flyer are also full of the contradictions. The village is entered only after the tourist has gone through both reception and orientation centers. The reception center is where business is done: restaurant, gift shop, bookstore, tickets for the village itself; also telephones, toilets, a picnic area. The orientation center includes a multi-image slide show, which is, the flyer tells us, "an essential part of your visit." It gives historical background and lays out what's offered. The orientation to the seventeenth century "lasts about 15 minutes."

Inside the fence a seventeenth-century village atmosphere is kept up, as it is aboard the *Mayflower II* and in the Indian settlement. But a visit to the whole complex—reception center, orientation center, re-created environments alive with restored behavior—is a thoroughly postmodern experience, a theatrical experience. Spectators-participants generally go along with the seventeenth-century reality. John S. Boyd, who plays Stephen Hopkins, assistant to Gov. William Bradford and Plimoth's first tavern keeper, has had the following experiences:

"You are meeting people from all over the world," Boyd says. "I have met people from five different countries in one day." . . . Most visitors enter into the spirit of the Plantation, Boyd says, but a few are nonplussed when a plantation resident will claim never to have heard of Pennsylvania or ask visitors if they have a "good king." Most of them, though "really do accept us as from another century." [Reilly 1981, n.p.]

Plimoth Plantation is more than a theater or an educational facility; it's also a business. Attendance in 1979 was 590,000; costs were about $1.5 million. Everything is as authentic as possible, but the day ends for visitors at 5:00 P.M. and the actors go home. During the hard New England winter months—when the real Pilgrims endured their grimmest times—the Plantation is closed. By closed I mean that the performers no longer go about their daily chores. The Plantation is open for special programs; and as a show business the managers are gearing up for their spring opening. Maybe the village is closed during winter because the seventeenth-century ordeals of cold, hunger, and death can't be accurately portrayed in a way that would suit the tastes of twentieth-century tourists. Or maybe it's simply that outdoor entertainment in Massachusetts is a loser in winter. Probably it's both. The contradictions and anachronisms, framed and carefully kept separate, are what gives Plimoth and its sister restored villages their special kick. The contradictions are hidden, almost, to be revealed only at special times and places. Inside the village all is naturalism, but taken as a whole the Plantation is like the theater of Brecht or Foreman. The people who make Plimoth may not say it in these terms, but their creation is restored behavior mixing $1 \rightarrow 3 \rightarrow 4$ and $1 \rightarrow 5_a \rightarrow 5_b$: $1 \rightarrow 3 \rightarrow 5_a \rightarrow 5_b$.

But what of villages that specialize in restoring fantasies? These are pure $1 \rightarrow 5_a \rightarrow 5_b$. More than one Old West town features regular *High Noon* shootouts or an attack by "savage" Indians. These events are not taken from history; they are played back from the movies. They are reflexions not reflections of the American experience. Sometimes, curiously, they double back into movies. Buckskin Joe, Colorado, was created by Malcolm F. Brown, former art director at MGM. The town has been the setting for more than one movie, including *Cat Ballou*, a parody of Westerns. At Buckskin Joe a shoot-out takes place in front of the saloon, and the spectators—who are actual customers at the bar or other stores—duck for cover. At King's Island in Cincinnati a passenger train is held up, the conductor taken hostage, and passengers asked to intervene to save the day. Audience participation, on the decline in theater, is increasing in theme parks and restored villages.

Considered theoretically, restored villages, even those built on fantasies and/or movies, raise hard questions. How are they different than the Staal-Gardner agnicayana? Staal and Gardner based their Vedic ritual on a reconstruction of an "old India" as distorted, and as true, as the Old West of America where Amerindians attacked settlers and shoot-outs happened in front of saloons. The Brahman priests went to texts, their own memories, and what old people could recall of the agnicayana, just as architects, performers, and craftspeople of restored villages research their stuff. And as for things taken from pop mythology, as at Buckskin Joe, there are parallels in Chhau where the stories reenacted are from the *Ramayana* and *Mahabharata*, sacred in Sanskrit and very popular in numberless other versions, including movies and comic books. No, the difference between the American restored villages and the agnicayana and Chhau is that the performers and spectators in the restored villages know it's all make-believe.

In figure 2.6 there is a move from frame *A* into frame *B* resulting in a special consciousness, *AB*. *AB* is another way of stating the subjunctive mood of restored behavior: the overylaying of two frames that cannot coexist in the indicative: "being in" the seventeenth and twentieth centuries simultaneously, "doing" a Vedic ritual according to the old ways and before cameras, tape recorders, and media-curious crowds. What happens is that the smaller subjunctive frame temporarily and paradoxically expands, containing the indicative frame. Everything is "make-believe for the time being." Figure 2.7

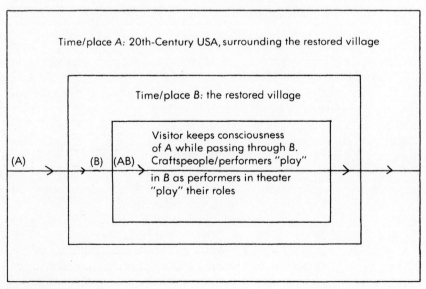

Figure 2.6

illustrates how the indicative world is temporarily isolated, surrounded, and both permeated and penetrated by the subjunctive: on the outside is the environment of the performance, on the inside is the special consciousness of performing and witnessing/participating in a performance. The famous "willing suspension of disbelief" is the agreement to let the smaller frame *AB* become the larger frame *AB'*.

At Plimoth, after a few hours in the village the visitors leave the seventeenth century. At the end of the day the "personators" take off their costumes and go home. In some restored villages a few people live "on location," but these people know very well about the twentieth century: their workday puts them in contact with hundreds of tourists each hour. But sometimes the choice to live anachronistically is radical. Sadhus in India often live without property, clothes, or contact with the ordinary world. I met people living without electricity and other modern conveniences in the mountains surrounding Santa Cruz, California. But the most studied examples of anachronistic living are performed for the media, like the Celtic encampment near London:

Five young couples and their children lived together in a house made of sticks, grass and mud, lighted only by fire and the daylight that came through two low doors. They grew vegetables, raised boars, cows, chickens and goats, and kept a polecat for catching rabbits. They shaped pottery, forged tools, built cartwheels, wove cloth, cured the skins of animals. They sound like the Celtic tribemen who lived not far from what is now London 2,200 years ago; they are actually 20th century Britons who have been living like Iron Age Celts for almost a year. Their experiment was conceived by John Percival, a BBC producer, to dramatize archeology for a series of 12 television documentaries. . . . Cameramen arrived at the Wiltshire village southwest of London every week to make films. Otherwise the "Celts" were well insulated from the modern world . . . Kate Rossetti, a Bristol teacher, had a long list of what she missed: "My

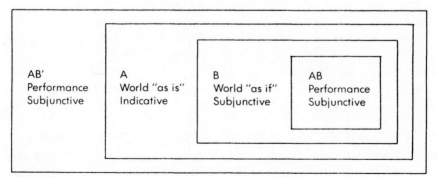

Figure 2.7

family and friends, chocolate, comfy shoes, Bach and Bob Dylan, being able to zoom up to Scotland." But she said she does not think she will ever live in a city again. [*New York Times*, 5 March 1978]

This kind of thing is no Arcadian return to nature. Contemporary Arcadians live in the Santa Cruz mountains. The BBC Celtic encampment is like a breeding zoo: a place where actions of bygone life can be bred and then recaptured (in this case on film)—a convergence of archaeology, anthropology, and media. It stands between the obvious fakery of a restored village and the not so obvious fakery of the 1975 agnicayana. By fake I mean something unable to live on its own, something that needs a media push or seems out of joint with contemporary life. Of course theater is fake, but it celebrates its fakery while restored villages slyly try to hide theirs. This sly faking is on the increase.

The BBC Celts are a little like the Brahman priests who restored the agnicayana for Staal and Gardner. For the 1975 agnicayana there were two audiences: an immediate one of locals, many of whom treated the ritual as a media event (this happens whenever a film is shot on location, even outside my window on Sullivan Street in Manhattan); and an audience outside Kerala who sees *Altar of Fire* mainly as a documentary of an actual ritual. But ritual with a difference: ritual for study, for entertainment—a "specimen." The inversion is ironic. The audience in Kerala sees the agnicayana as media; the audience for the Staal-Gardner film sees the media (version of agnicayana) as ritual. Both audiences are alienated from the "pure" agnicayana. But was there ever a pure agnicayana? Isn't every instance of it $1 \rightarrow 5_a \rightarrow 5_b$? When the narrator of *Altar of Fire* tells viewers they are seeing probably the last performance ever of agnicayana, more than a little dash of American P. T. Barnum showmanship has been added for flavor. And at Plimoth nothing (new) is going to happen; life there is finished. These restored behaviors are very much like theater in a theater: the script is fixed, the environment is known, the actors play set roles. But Bharatanatyam and Chhau are different. These restorations have healed seamlessly into their cultural surround; they are living arts. As such, these dances will change; their future isn't predictable, isn't a repetition of their past. Plimoth Plantation either continues as it is or it ceases to be; its very existence is knotted into its specific historicity. Each production of aesthetic theater is like Plimoth, but "the theater" as a genre is like Bharatanatyam and Chhau. The similarities and differences among various performance systems is summarized in figure 2.8.

One of the big differences among performance systems is the framing made by the physical environments—what contains what. In ordinary

	A	B
1	ARTS	RESTORED ARTS
	Theater, dance, etc.	Bharatanatyam, Purulia Chhau, etc.

Between these there is little or no phenomenological distinction, which makes it very hard to tell 1A from 1B without doing historical research—1B heals seamlessly into 1A. 1A and 1B each has a "life of its own." In both, performers know they're "in a show" and audiences know they're "watching a show."

	A	B	C	D
2	MEDIA FICTION	MEDIA SIMULATION	MEDIA "PUSH"	MEDIA "THERE"
	Regular Movies	Re-created especially for media, as were the BBC Celts	Without media there would be no event, as the 1975 agnicayana	Documentaries, news

A move to the right = decreasing dependence on media to make the event, though news items are edited, which creates a feedback between what "is" news and what media "makes into" news. Also, a move to the right = an increase in voice-overs explaining an independent event that needs an observer outside "objectively" explaining it. 2B, 2C, 2D merge into one another. Only in 2A is the performer sure he is "in a show" and the spectator sure he is "watching a show." A recent form, "docudrama," combines 2A and 2D (see below, n. 13).

	A	B	C
3	THEME PARKS	RESTORED VILLAGES	RESTORED VILLAGES
	Disneyland,	MADE FROM	MADE FROM HISTORY
	Land of Oz,	FANTASY AND HISTORY	Plimoth, Smithville,
	Dogpatch, etc.	Buckskin Joe, Frontierland,	Louisbourg, etc.
		Columbia Historic Park, etc.	

In 3A everyone knows they are "in a show" as spectator-participants or performers. In 3B and 3C even the performers begin to feel they are "in life." But, paradoxically, 3B and 3C are very close to 1A and 1B where the event begins to have a "life of its own." In 3A most of the machinery, mechanical and human, is hidden from the spectator, creating a fictive environment. In 3B and 3C there is an attempt, as at museums, to show as much as possible. But these days even museums are fictionalizing. For example, the Ice Age Art exhibit at the American Museum of Natural History (1978–79) was made mostly from simulated items.

Figure 2.8 *Performance systems: a comparative chart*

theater the domain of the spectator, the house, is larger than the domain of the performer, the stage, and distinctly separate from it. In environmental theater (see Schechner 1973b) there is a shift in that the spectator and performer often share the same space, sometimes they exchange spaces, and sometimes the domain of the performer is larger than that of the spectator, enclosing the spectator within the performance. This tendency is taken even further in restored villages and theme parks where the visitor enters an environment that swallows him. Every effort is spent on making the spectator participate. And while the visitor is aware of ordinary time and place, he simultaneously enjoys a temporary transformation of these. He is transported into another time and place. The 1975 agnicayana combines the qualities of film with those of a restored village. There are two frames working: that of the ritual and that of the film being made of the ritual. The Brahman priests are performers of the agnicayana, but they are also "visitors" absorbed into it (Vedic ritual being older and different than Brahmanic Hindu ritual); the local people watch both the ritual and the filming of it—neither of these events is familiar. If the priests had been totally absorbed into the agnicayana they would have insisted on sacrificing the goats, or they would have stopped the performance because in Vedic terms the goat sacrifice was necessary. But the priests, too, wanted the film to be made. The priests acted in regard to animal sacrifice not as Vedic priests but as modern Indians. More: they acted as performers in a film with a big stake in seeing that the shooting came off. Using their authority as priests, they devised the substitute effigies as a way of making the film, performing the agnicayana, and not offending the values of modern Kerala Indians. Thus the priests played three roles: Vedic ritualists, Brahman priests arbitrating a living tradition, film performers. In a way, the film performers convinced the Brahman priests that it was okay to tamper with the Vedic tradition. Or: as film performers Brahman priests were asked to play the role of Vedic ritualists. This double, or triple, life is typically that of theater actors; it is the theatrical brand of truth. And between the frame of the agnicayana and the frame of the film making stood the local audience, enjoying both spectacles.

But is it fair to say that the priests were playacting? In terms of Euro-American theatrical conventions, "acting" implies make-believe, even lying. The work of the great twentieth-century acting teachers from Stanislavski through Grotowski has been to make acting more "truthful." (A countermovement has been to acknowledge frankly that acting is artifice.) But even Goffman identifies the acting people do in ordinary life with con men and others who maintain a "front" different than their "true" selves. This understanding of acting derives from the Platonic idea of a hierarchy of realities in which what is most real is most distant from experience and the Aristotelian idea of art as an imitation and essentialization of life's experiences. But, from the perspective of Indian theatrical conventions, acting is both false and true because acting is playful illusion—as is the world itself. The boys who represent/are the gods in Ramlila are both "playing at" and "being" the gods.

I might think the priests officiating in front of rolling cameras at the agnicayana are acting, while Kerala villagers might think they are doing what priests always do, mediating between different orders of experience. Their training has prepared the priests to restore the behavior of the agnicayana; and birth has placed them in a caste enabled to do so. It is not accurate to call them actors, and it is not accurate to not call them actors. They are between "not actors" and "not not actors," a liminal realm of double negativity that precisely locates the process of theatrical characterization.

As for American restored villages, anyone with proper training (whatever his/her birth) can demonstrate colonial crafts and speak English in a seventeenth-century Yankee dialect. At the end of the workday, visitors assume the performers relinquish their roles even if the visitors don't see this divestiture with their own eyes. At Plimoth and elsewhere some of the conventions of orthodox American theater are dropped. The performers are not on a stage, not rewarded by applause, and they don't strictly follow a word-by-word script called a drama. In some restored villages and theme parks, actors interact with spectators, making the visitor enter into the world of the village and thereby further blurring the boundary between the performance and its nonacting surround. The performers at Plimoth are acting, but they try to seem like they are not acting. In America we say someone is "only acting" when we detect the seams between the performance and the nonacting surround. We also say someone is acting when they are performing on a stage. We say someone is not acting when they are doing what they ordinarily would do were there no audience. Documentary film imposes an acting frame around a nonacting circumstance. Documentaries like Curtis's *In the Land of the Head Hunters* or Flaherty's *Nanook of the North* combine people sometimes going about their ordinary tasks, sometimes restoring behaviors of a recent past, and sometimes acting for pay in fictive situations in an "on-location" set wearing costumes and saying lines written for the occasion.

Some performers at restored villages have become permanent residents, living off the income of their crafts and eating the food they have cooked that day in the presence of visitors. Their "lived lives" mesh with their "performed lives" in so strong a way that it feeds back into their performances. Their roles become their "ordinary life," supplying their restored behavior with a new source of authenticity. When this happens the residents of the restored villages can no more comfortably be subsumed under the category of "play-actors" than can the Kerala Brahman priests.

In T. McLuhan's 1974 film, *The Shadow Catcher*, a few of the original participants in Curtis's 1914 *Head Hunters* explain how Curtis's interest in the "old ways" rekindled their own interest—and led to restoring some ceremonies previously abandoned. Thus the values of the new dominant culture encouraged the enactment as fiction of what was previously performed in fact. Other actions—masked dancing, shamanic healing—were done "as usual," but before the rolling camera. Later, a new cultural whole developed, combining fiction and fact and including performances invented for tourists. Younger Kwakiutls said Curtis's movie helped them learn about the old life—because seeing something "really being done" is so much more powerful than just hearing about it. But what was "really being done" even the old-timers didn't do anymore by the time Curtis arrived. Who knows if they ever did it the way he filmed it? Curtis paid performers fifty cents an hour, five dollars when there was danger, like rowing the huge war canoes or hunting sea lions.

Increasingly, American theater of all kinds is like *Head Hunters* (whose title was changed to *In the Land of the War Canoes* because Curtis thought American audiences would find headhunting repulsive; the movie failed commercially anyway), combining documentary, fiction, history; in other words, restored behavior, $1 \rightarrow 5_a \rightarrow 5_b$. Today's experimental theater puts acting and nonacting side by side, as in the work of Spalding Gray, Leeny Sack, Robert Wilson and Christopher Knowles, and Squat Theatre. On the other side, such strongholds of "facts" as network news programs are anchored by people selected for their ability to perform, not to gather or edit news (see chapter 7 and Schechner 1982*b*).

Restored villages and Curtis's half-restoring, half-inventing for the sake of his feature film are performances in between that of Brahman priests restoring an archaic ritual for the benefit of the cameras and Olivier playing Lear on the Euro-American stage. Intermediate also are performances like those of Wilson and Knowles, Gray, and Squat. This kind of theater displays its ambivalence; it is explicitly reflexive. In restored villages as in environmental theater generally, the domain of the performance surrounds and includes the spectator. Looking at becomes harder; being in, easier. Where there is no house, spectators are thrown back on their own resources for whatever assurance they need to maintain who and where they are.

&

Restoration of behavior as a dynamic system is expressed in figures 2.1–2.4. The core of this system is $1 \rightarrow 5_a \rightarrow 5_b$. $1 \rightarrow 5_a \rightarrow 5_b$ is what happens during workshops and rehearsals. Workshops and rehearsals are two parts of a seven-phase performance process: training, workshop, rehearsal, warm-up, performance, cool-down, aftermath. Terminology varies from culture to culture, but the seven phases represent distinct functions that can be identified interculturally. The absence of one or more phases signals not "incompleteness" but an adjustment of the performance process to meet specific needs. For example, in Noh drama training is emphasized, but there is very little rehearsal; in Grotowski's paratheater there is a great deal of workshop but no performance.

Sense can be made of these differences by asking what it is that each phase in the performance sequence accomplishes. Training is where known skills are transmitted. Workshop is a deconstruction process, where the ready-mades of culture (accepted ways of using the body, accepted texts, accepted feelings) are broken down and prepared to be "inscribed" upon (to use Turner's word). Workshop is analogous to the liminal-transitional phase of rituals. Rehearsals are the opposite of workshops. In rehearsals longer and longer strips of restored behavior are arranged to make a new unified whole: the performance. This two-phase deconstruction-reconstruction process is exactly what Staal and Gardner did to the agnicayana; what the founders of Bharatanatyam did to sadir nac, the *Natyasastra*, and temple sculptings; what Bhattacharyya did to Purulia Chhau; and what the creators of Plimoth did to the data they researched regarding the Pilgrims.

Although the workshop-rehearsal process and the ritual process are analogous, the terms used to describe them don't fit together neatly. This is because scholars have often treated play, art, and religion separately. But the basic performance process is universal: theater is the art specializing in the concrete techniques of restoring behavior. Preparing to do theater includes memorizing a score of gestures, sounds, and movements and/or achieving a mood where apparently "external" gestures, sounds, and movements "take over" the performer, as in a trance. Behavior that is other is transformed into the performer's own; alienated or objectified parts of the performer's self—either his private self or his social self—are assimilated and publicly displayed. It is the assimilation of old and new material—and the transformations this material undergoes—that I have summarized as $1 \rightarrow 5_a \rightarrow 5_b$. The conclusion of the workshop-rehearsal process is the public performance; this is analogous to what Van Gennep calls "reincorporation" and what Turner calls "reintegration." Of course, the whole project can collapse, especially in modern and postmodern circumstances where performances are more likely to be voluntary, liminoid, than obligatory, liminal. When things go wrong and people scatter, a "schism" occurs.[10]

By examining the workshop-rehearsal process as it applies to individual performers, we will also be able to understand it in wider terms as it applies to performances like agnicayana, restored villages, and other large-scale productions.

How do workshops-rehearsals work? (See also chapters 5 and 6.) There are two basic methods. The first is by "direct acquisition," where a master uses bodily manipulation, imitation, and repetition to teach the neophyte actual items to be performed. The performance text is whole, and it is transmitted across generations. The second method of workshops-rehearsals is to teach a "basic grammar" that can be used to generate any number of performance texts. There is no one way, nor even any 250 ways, to perform *Hamlet*. There is continuity in how *Hamlet* has been performed from the time Shakespeare wrote it in 1604 to now. Training performers to play *Hamlet* means teaching them how to invent a performance text.

The separation of dramatic texts from performance texts that characterizes modern Euro-American theater leads to the separation of training from workshop and rehearsal. In many Asian forms training, workshop, and rehearsals are one; in Euro-America training is generalized in the sense that techniques are taught as "tools" that can be used to make any number of different kinds of performances. An actor pants not so that she may pant in performance but in order to strengthen her diaphragm, get in touch with the different ways her voice can resonate, control her breathing so that demanding physical work can be done without losing breath. Or, scenes from plays are practiced not because they will be played this way when the student enters the professional theater but so that the neophyte can learn how to prepare a role, evoke genuine emotions (or feign them), and in other ways acquire the necessary skills to "become an actor." These skills are eclectic. But how absurd it would be for a traditionally trained Noh shite to claim—or even desire—a similar eclecticism.

Just as there are intermediate or liminal performance styles, so there are some training methods that occupy a position in between these extremes, combining elements of both. Guru Kedar Nath Sahoo, dancer of Seraikella Chhau, teaches first a set of sword and shield exercises that will later be transformed into moves used within the dance drama. These exercises also strengthen the body and familiarize the performers with Chhau's martial roots. In Kathakali, the massages administered by the guru's feet literally reshape the student's body, making possible the wide turnout and arched lower spine used in Kathakali. The massages coincide with rigorous exercises that are later used with only a few variations in the dancing. Neither in Chhau nor in Kathakali are the exercises the basis for invention. The exercises are part of both the "breaking down" and the "building up" process. In themselves, the exercises don't help performers understand the dances theoretically. Such knowledge comes only after years of dancing as performers decipher for themselves what they have been doing. Many fine performers never acquire theoretical knowledge. Some do, and these are the ones most likely to introduce changes.

In situations where a performance text is invented, or a "lost" or "decayed" performance is restored, workshops are where items are discovered and "kept" for use later. The director says, "Keep that." What the director means is not to do it again right now but to throw it ahead in time—to store it in the "future subjunctive," 5_c. This is the place where material "thrown forward" and "kept" for later use in the performance-to-be is stored. Imaginary or nonevent material, 5_a, is combined with material from the personal or historical past, 3, and thrown forward into 5_c. As workshops become rehearsals the performance-to-be "takes shape" as 5_b. 5_c is emptied as more and more material either finds a place in the performance text or is discarded. The bits kept in 5_c provide clues about what the finished performance text might be. In making a film, or restoring a Pilgrim village, 5_c is full of images "in the can" and/or items gleaned from research. This process of the development from $1 \rightarrow (3-5_a) \rightarrow 5_c$ to $1 \rightarrow 5_a \rightarrow 5_b$ is depicted in figure 2.9.

The workshop-rehearsal process is liminoid. It is "betwixt and between" the fixed world from which material is extracted and the fixed score of the performance text.

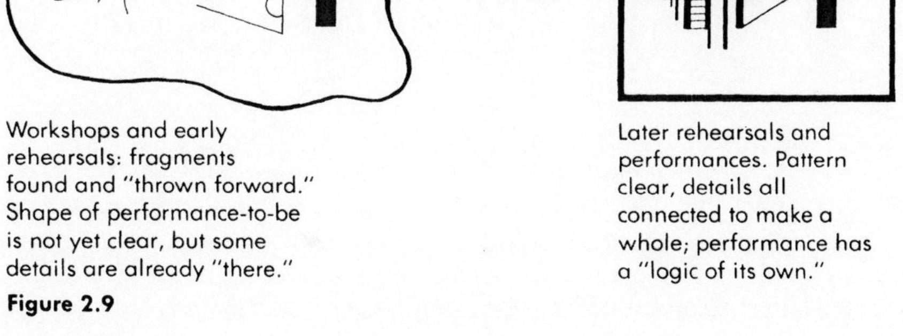

$1 \rightarrow (3-5_a) \rightarrow 5_c$ $1 \rightarrow 5_a \rightarrow 5_b$

Workshops to rehearsals:

a liminoid world

Workshops and early rehearsals: fragments found and "thrown forward." Shape of performance-to-be is not yet clear, but some details are already "there."

Later rehearsals and performances. Pattern clear, details all connected to make a whole; performance has a "logic of its own."

Figure 2.9

During the past fifty years, since Artaud at least, the two kinds of performance processes—transmission of whole items by direct acquisition and transmission by means of learning a generative grammar—have been linked. This
linkage is, in fact, one of the great achievements of experimental theater in
this century. Richard Foreman, for example, transmits to relatively passive
performers a complete performance text in a method parallel to that used by
the Ramlila vyases (see chapter 4). Foreman writes his plays, makes a sche-
matic of how they are to be staged, designs the setting, and often is present
as chief technician at each performance. And the "grammatical" methods of
guru Sahoo and the teachers at the Kathakali Kalamandalam may be due to
extensive contact with European methods. Also, techniques such as yoga,
martial arts, mantra chanting, and so on, transmitted as whole texts in their
cultures of origin, are now used in the West as items of training of the
generative grammar kind. In 1978, at a meeting outside of Warsaw convened
by Grotowski, I saw Kanze Hideo put on a Noh mask, crawl on the floor,
and improvise actions having nothing to do with classical Noh. And his
friend, director Tadashi Suzuki, in a production of Euripides' *Trojan Women*,
combined Noh, Kabuki, martial arts, modern Western experimental theater,
and ancient Greek tragedy. The play was as much about post-atomic-bomb
Japan as about defeated Troy. Examples multiply, bearing witness to
exchanges between, especially, Asian and African and Euro-American
theater. Three kinds of workshop-rehearsal are now occurring: (1) those used
to transmit whole performance texts; (2) those based on grammars that
generate new performance texts; (3) those combining 1 and 2. This last, far
from being a sterile hybrid, is a most fertile response to postmodern circumstances.

There is another way of looking at the workshop-rehearsal process, one
that connects Turner's ideas of subjunctivity/liminality to Stanislavski's
"magic if." In *An Actor Prepares* Stanislavski says:

You know now that our work on a play begins with the use of *if* as a lever to lift
us out of everyday life onto the plane of imagination. . . . There is no such thing
as actuality on the stage. Art is a product of the imagination. . . . The aim of the
actor should be to use his technique to turn the play into a theatrical reality. [(1936)
1946, 51]

The use of "if" encourages the actor to be in the "given circumstances" of
the character. "What would I do *if* certain circumstances were true?" (Stanislavski, 1961, 33). It is during workshops-rehearsals that the "if" is used as
a way of researching the physical environment, the affects, the relationships—everything that will sooner or later be fixed in the performance text.

Figure 2.10 shows how the deep structure of workshop-rehearsal inverts the deep structure of performance.[11] In workshop-rehearsal real work is being done, work that is serious and problematical: indicative, "is." But the daily experience of workshop-rehearsal—what a casual observer might feel—is an "as if," something tentative, subjunctive: "Let's try that," "This could work," "What would happen if?" Workshop especially is playful. There the techniques of "as if" flourish: games, role exchanges, improvisations—participants bring in stuff from all over. Workshops find, reveal, and express material; rehearsals give this stuff performative shape. Despite the fact that deep things are "brought up" during workshop, the feeling of openness, of experimentation, of transition, is maintained. Workshops are liminoid, creating an "as if" scalpel used to cut into the actual lives of those making the performance.

The finished performance text is the inverse of the workshop-rehearsal. The performance text displayed before an audience, or requiring their participation, is "indicative": 2, 4, or 5_a. In Euro-American theater secular rituals such as reviewing by critics, attendance by a paying audience of strangers,

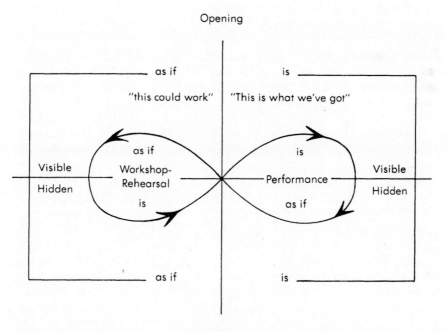

Figure 2.10

and an opening-night party mark the transition from rehearsal to performance. The performance text is an "is," the more or less invariable presentation
of what's been found, kept, and organized. But the deep structure under this
"is" is a subjunctive "as if." The tears Ophelia sheds for Hamlet are actual,
hot, and salty, but her grief is subjunctive. The cause of that grief may be
something wholly unrelated to *Hamlet* or the actor playing Hamlet. The cause
is possibly some intimate association the actress found during workshops or
rehearsals. The Balinese dancer in trance may violently thrust a kris against
his chest, but the cause of this action is not self-hatred but a manifestation of
trance possession by the demon Rangda. The two processes—the American
actress who uses her personal life, and the Balinese trance dancer who aban-
dons his—may appear to be opposite, but they are actually identical. In each
case the "given circumstances," the "as if" of the preparatory phases of
performance, sink out of sight but underlie and cause the "is" of the performance text.

Of course, there are variations of this process: to experiment means to
"play around" and in so doing to create new situations. Brecht asked his
actors to be in character ("is") most of the time but sometimes to stand beside
their characters ("as if"), questioning the very actions they were performing. Thus Brecht introduced into the public performance a quality of the
workshop-rehearsal process.

This breaking of frames occurs not only in serious drama but in the circus,
nightclub acts, and Broadway musicals, too. There was a scene in *Sugar Babies*
where the star, Mickey Rooney, loses his wig. He laughs, his face turns red,
he runs to the edge of the stage and shares a wisecrack with the audience.
Then he puts his wig back on and resumes his role. This break is Rooney's
acknowledgment that underneath all the roles he plays there is the person,
the star, the "real" Mickey Rooney. Losing the wig looks accidental, but
actually it was a set piece of business. Probably Rooney lost his wig "for real"
during a rehearsal, and the bit was kept. It helps the audience feel good about
paying so much money; for a brief moment each spectator thinks she's been
treated to a special glimpse of the star unmasked. Of course, the unmasking
is a trick, not an unmasking at all.

I do not criticize the rehearsedness of such scenes.[12] When I direct I hold
"open rehearsals" where the public actually sees a work in process; or, during
finished performances, I try to include "raw elements" like having the green
room visible during *Mother Courage*. But almost always the genuine processual nature of workshop-rehearsal is lost.[13] The "as if" wants to submerge
itself when the public is present. Only while working with those they can
really trust, usually a few comrades who have shared a lot of experiences
together, can performers play "as if" with "is" material. When working

under the eye of a critical public, performers want to show only the "is" of their "as if."

The last part of rehearsal is practice. Longer and more complicated strips of restored behavior are organized into the actual performance. Music, costumes, lighting, makeup, et cetera, accumulate. Each of these is blended in with the intention of making an integrated whole. During this final push, gestures are edited so that they send the clearest signals and practiced until they become second nature. Pacing—the relation of the rhythm/tempo of each part to that of the whole—becomes very important. This last phase of rehearsal is comparable to the phase of reintegration in a ritual. Strangers to the theater often think only of this last phase when they hear the word "rehearsal." But as I have tried to show, reintegration is only the final part of a long process.

Immediately before going on stage, most performers engage in some ritual. The Noh actor contemplates his mask; Jatra performers in Bengal worship the gods of the performance who manifest themselves in the props and images of gods set up on the trunks backstage; Stanislavski advised thirty seconds of silent concentration. Sometimes preparatory "moments" are very long. Tribesmen in Papua New Guinea spend many hours putting on makeup and costumes. I always met The Performance Group at least two hours before a performance to clean up the theater, give notes, and do warm-ups. The main function of these preparations is not to make the performer "look" the role (though this task is accomplished) but to recapitulate and reactivate the training, workshop, and rehearsal process. The audience, too, usually is quieted down and transported across the threshold separating preperformance hubbub from the event itself. The houselights slowly dim; in France a staff is rapped clearly on the stage floor; at sports matches the national anthem is sung; sometimes a prayer is recited or a moment of silence observed.

Seeing what of the ritual process is missing from a performance can be a useful way of understanding what's going on. Grotowski's paratheatrical work took participants from cities and brought them to remote areas to perform actions with and under the supervision of Grotowski's people.[14] These actions varied according to who the participants were and what were the current interests of the Polish Laboratory Theatre. But the actions always involved discovering and revealing hidden personal themes, finding new ways of behaving (alone or with others), and sharing I-Thou relationships. Many of the physical actions—running through the forest at night, sudden immersion in water, dances around fire and the passing of fire from person to person, group chanting, singing, storytelling—are very like those in initiation rites. Maybe initiation rites were a model for Grotowski. When participants returned home after a few days or weeks they often said that they couldn't talk about what happened. This silence wasn't due to a vow of secrecy; it was due to the conviction that words couldn't do justice to the experience. "It changed my life" was a frequent laconic summary. As performative action Grotowski's paratheater resembled an initiation rite in which a transformation of self, a change of status, was effected. But ex-Grotowskiites have been surprisingly unsuccessful in starting their own theaters or feeding what they've done with Grotowski into their own theater work. Paratheater seemed to disable rather than invigorate them. Grotowski did not work out, nor were his clients able to supply, phase 3 of the workshop-rehearsal/ritual process: reintegration. There was no way that the participants in Grotowski's paratheater could bring it home or do it publicly. Participants were left hanging: they were separated, stripped down, made into tabulae rasae; they had deep experiences, were "written upon," made new; but these "new selves" were not reintegrated into the ordinary world. Not only did Grotowski's theater no longer perform publicly, he denied any religious aspect to his paratheatrical work. He intentionally prevented it from knitting in with any social, aesthetic, or religious system.

The absence of reintegration in Grotowski's paratheater reveals his intentions while he was conducting his paratheatrical experiments (ca. 1969–76). Theater has but two stances in relationship to society at large: either to be tightly woven into broader social patterns, as rituals are, or to serve as an analytical and dialectical instrument for a critique of society, as Brecht's theater tried to be. Most theater people are not conscious of these stances, their work drifts. But Grotowski is a most conscious individual. He intentionally avoided taking either of these stances while making paratheater. More recently, in his Theatre of Sources, Grotowski gathered masters of performance from different non-Western cultures. In a "transcultural village" (a kind of performative theme park) masters and visitors exchanged techniques. Grotowski has also spent many months in the field, particularly in India and Haiti. Barba has adapted aspects of Theatre of Sources for his "theater anthropology" project.[15] And very recently Grotowski began work on "objective drama"—trying to locate efficacious performance processes regardless of their religious or other ideological bases/contexts. This work may synthesize Grotowski's multifaceted career—poor theater, paratheater, theater of sources—into something that includes a reintegrative phase. (For more on Grotowski's paratheater and related work, see chapter 5.)

℘

Far-fetched as such projects may seem, they signal a very deep attempt to integrate the performative knowledge of several Asian, African, Caribbean, and Native American cultures with the social, political, and aesthetic life of Euro-America. Such an attempt may have enormous consequences for the development of an intercultural theater. And just as theater workers are increasingly interested in anthropological thought and the techniques of fieldwork, so anthropologists find themselves more and more like theater directors.

Staal and Gardner are not alone in entering the field as theatrical producers-directors in the guise of anthropological fieldworkers. Not finding a ritual worthy of being filmed, they arranged for one to be performed. They made sure there was enough lead time to get money to make the movie and to import a planeload of important scholars. Their lie, if there is one, comes with the marketing of *Altar of Fire* as a document of a "living ritual" they just happened on in the nick of time. The film's audience may construe agni-cayana as a "living ritual" when in fact it is a complicated kind of playacting. But I think I've shown how playacting is a kind of living ritual—though one made reflexive through the use of training, workshop, and/or rehearsal. *Altar of Fire* is more than a film of Vedic ritual. The filming itself ritualizes the action of restoring the agnicayana. But that work of ritualization took place in the out-of-sequence shooting, in the disputes surrounding the sacrifice (or non-sacrifice) of the goats, and in the editing room.

Maybe even today most anthropologists would agree with Turner, who in 1969 said of his stay with the Ndembu, "We never asked for a ritual to be performed solely for our own anthropological benefit; we held no brief for such artificial play-acting" (1969, 10). But the presence of the fieldworker is an invitation to playacting. And what should be done regarding traditions that are near extinction? Old-style patronage is finished. Yesterday patrons wanted performances either as entertainment, as celebration, or for ritual benefit. Today patrons want performances for the archives or as data from which to develop theories. Patrons such as the National Endowment for the Arts sponsor performances to "enrich cultural life"—which means a whole spectrum of things from paying off the upper middle class to keeping unruly youth in tow.

But what ought our response be to genres doomed by modernization and postmodernization? In Karnataka, South India, not too many miles from where Staal and Gardner filmed, Martha Ashton was "not only the first foreigner to study Yakshagana in detail, but . . . also the first and only female to perform it."[16] Ashton joined with her teacher Hiriyadka Gopala Rao in reconstructing old-style Yakshagana. They assembled a company, helped recollect old stories, steps, and songs. Not only did Ashton film the results of this reconstruction, she also wrote a book on Yakshagana (Ashton and Christie 1977) and organized a tour of the Rao-Ashton company to America in 1976–77. Was she wrong in doing all this? When I visited Karnataka in 1976 I saw three kinds of Yakshagana: the popular version; a style for modern audiences developed by K. S. Karanth, a well-known writer; and "classical Yakshagana" restored largely through the efforts of Rao and Ashton. Which style is most or least Indian?

The position of purists who refuse to stage the rituals or performances they are studying and recording (on film, on tape, and in books) is not pure but ambivalent. Their position is analogous to that of experimental theater auteur Richard Foreman who, in many of his productions, sat between his players and the audience, often running a tape recorder broadcasting his own voice interpreting and asking questions and giving instructions. To the society the fieldworker temporarily inhabits, he represents his home culture in one of its most inexplicable aspects: Why send somebody around the world to observe and record how another group lives? And to those of us who see or read the reports of the fieldworker, he is our main link with both fresh aspects of human behavior (fresh to us, that is) and our often asserted, sometimes tested, but never proven assertion that humans are one species culturally, "humanly," as well as biologically.

The situation precipitated by the fieldworker's presence is a theatrical one: he is there to see, and he is seen. But what role does the fieldworker play? He is not a performer and not not a performer, not a spectator and not not a spectator. He is in between two roles just as he is in between two cultures. In the field he represents—whether he wants to or not—his culture of origin; and back home he represents the culture he has studied. The fieldworker is always in a "not . . . not not" situation. And like a performer going through workshops-rehearsals the fieldworker goes through the three-phase perform- ance process isomorphic with the ritual process:

1. The stripping away of his own ethnocentrism. This is often a brutal separation, which in itself is the deepest struggle of fieldwork, and is never complete. What should he eat, how? And his toilet habits, his problems of hygiene. And the dozens of other things that remind the worker of the distance between his own culture and the one he wants to get inside of. But if his work is to succeed, he has to undergo some kind of transformation.

2. The revelation, often coming suddenly like inspiration, of what is "new" in the culture he temporarily inhabits. This discovery is his initiation, his transition, the taking on of a new role in his adoptive society, a role that often includes a new identity, position, or status. The worker "goes native," even inside himself.

3. The difficult task of using his field notes (or raw footage and sound tapes) to make an acceptable "product"—monograph, film, lectures, whatever: the way he edits and translates what he found into items understood by the world he returns to. In brief, he must make an acceptable performance out of all workshop-rehearsal material. His promotion to full professor ratifies his reintegration into his own society.

As fieldwork converges on theatrical directing, the third phase of the process includes making films—or, as Victor and Edith Turner did with their students, "performing ethnography" (see chap. 1 and Turner and Turner 1982). It is this third phase of the process that is most problematical. Clearly, monographs are written in the style of the "home culture." Only recently, with an increase in "life histories," has there been some effort to make writing speak in the voice of the "away culture." But even life histories are translations. Films use images drawn directly from the away culture. These images make it seem as if the away culture were speaking for itself. But of course camera angles, methods of shooting, focus, and editing all reflect the world of the film maker. If the film maker is from the away culture, the point of view may be more from the inside—but maybe not: technology enforces its own logic. Or the resultant film may not be "ethnographic" in the classic sense. Ethnography demands a double vision, inside and outside simultaneously or alternately. If the fieldworker is able to show all this (maybe using local camerapersons and editors), the third phase of the fieldworker's progression folds back into phase 1. He tries to show his own people what the away culture is like in its own terms. It may be too much to ask—or the wrong thing.

In the past anthropologists have fancied themselves siblings of "hard scientists." But hard science works from models strictly fenced off from ordinary life; and it depends on predictive theory. The soft sciences are actually extensions of the arts and humanities. Ordinary life and performative life are related in the looped way I showed in figure 2.10. Theory in the social sciences is little more than what Geertz calls "thick description" (1973, 3–32). Presently the theater director is leaving the shadowy, out-of-sight offstage and entering the stage not just as another performer but as a unique figure: the embodiment of the workshop-rehearsal process. Fieldworkers now not only watch but learn, participate, and initiate actions. Directors have been, and fieldworkers are becoming, specialists in restored behavior. In this epoch of information and reflexive hyperconsciousness we not only want to know, we also want to know how we know what we know.

❧

D. W. Winnicott's ideas add an ontogenic level and a new set of categories to my description of what the performer does. Winnicott, a British psychoanalyst, studied the mother-baby relationship, especially how the baby learns to distinguish between "me" and "not me." Winnicott called certain objects "transitional"—in between the mother and the baby, belonging to neither the mother nor the baby (the mother's breasts, a security blanket, certain special toys). And the circumstances in which these transitional objects were used constituted "transitional phenomena."

I am here staking a claim for an intermediate state between a baby's inability and his growing ability to recognize and accept reality. I am therefore studying the substance of *illusion*, that which is allowed to the infant, and which in adult life is inherent in art and religion. . . .

I think there is a use for a term for the root of symbolism in time, a term that describes the infant's journey from the purely subjective to objectivity; and it seems that the transitional object (piece of blanket, etc.) is what we see of this journey of progress toward experiencing. . . .

The transitional object and transitional phenomena start each individual off with what will always be important to them, i.e., a neutral sense of experience which will not be challenged. . . .

The important part of this concept is that whereas inner psychic reality has a kind of location in the mind or in the belly or in the head or somewhere within the bounds of the individual's personality, and whereas what is called external reality is located outside these bounds, playing and cultural experience can be given a location if one uses the concepts of the potential space between the mother and the baby. [1971, 3, 5, 12, 53]

This potential space is workshop-rehearsal, the liminal/liminoid space, the $1 \rightarrow 5_a \rightarrow 5_b$ bundle.

Winnicott's ideas mesh nicely with Van Gennep's, Turner's, and Bateson's, in whose "play frame" ([1955] 1972, 177–93) "transitional phenomena" take place. The most dynamic formulation of what Winnicott is describing is that the baby—and later the child at play and the adult at art (and religion)—recognizes some things and situations as "not me . . . not not me." During workshops-rehearsals performers play with words, things, and actions, some of which are "me" and some "not me." By the end of the process the "dance goes into the body." So Olivier is not Hamlet, but he is also not not Hamlet. The reverse is also true: in this production of the play, Hamlet is not Olivier, but he is also not not Olivier. Within this field or frame of double negativity choice and virtuality remain activated.

In children the movement from "not me" to "not not me" is seen in their relationship to security blankets, favorite toys that cannot be replaced no matter how old, dirty, or broken. Play itself deconstructs actuality in a "not me . . . not not me" way. The hierarchies that usually set off actuality as "real" and fantasy as "not real" are dissolved for the "time being," the play time. These same operations of dissolving ordinary hierarchies, of treasuring things beyond their ordinary worth, of setting aside certain times and places for the manipulation of special things in a world defined nonordinarily: this is also a definition of the workshop-rehearsal process, the ritual process, the performative process.

When such performance actualities are played out before audiences, the spectators have a role to play. Winnicott puts into his own terms an audience's "willing suspension of disbelief."

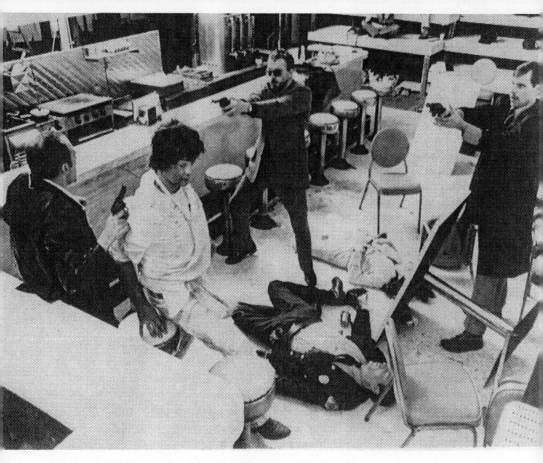

25. The Performance Group's production of Terry Curtis Fox's *Cops* staged in a hypernaturalistic style. Photo by David Behl.

The essential feature in the concept of transitional objects and phenomena . . . is the paradox, and the acceptance of the paradox: the baby [performer] creates the object but the object was there waiting to be created [performance text]. . . . We will never challenge the baby [performer] to elicit an answer to the question: did you create that or did you find it? [1971, 89]

Olivier will not be interrupted in the middle of "To be or not to be" and asked, "Whose words are those?" And if he were interrupted, what could his reply be? The words belong, or don't belong, equally to Shakespeare, Hamlet, Olivier. If such an interruption did take place the audience would assume Pirandello or Brecht was at work, building into the performance text its own reflexive double. But to whom would such an interruption belong? You see, in the theater there is no place that is not make-believe. Even the shot that killed Lincoln, for a split second, must have seemed part of the show.

Restored behaviors of all kinds—rituals, theatrical performances (plate 25), restored villages, agnicayana—are "transitional." Elements that are "not me" become "me" without losing their "not me-ness." This is the peculiar but necessary double negativity that characterizes symbolic actions. While performing, a performer experiences his own self not directly but through the medium of experiencing the others. While performing, he no longer has a "me" but has a "not not me," and this double negative relationship also shows how restored behavior is simultaneously private and social. A person performing recovers his own self only by going out of himself and meeting the others—by entering a social field. The way in which "me" and "not me," the performer and the thing to be performed, are transformed into "not me . . . not not me" is through the workshop-rehearsal/ritual process. This process takes place in a liminal time/space and in the subjunctive mood. The subjunctive character of the liminal time/space is reflected in the negative, antistructural frame around the whole process. This antistructure could be expressed algebraically: "not (me . . . not me)."

Figure 2.11 portrays this system. Figure 2.11 is a version of $1 \rightarrow 5_a \rightarrow 5_b$. Actions move in time, from the past thrown into the future, from "me" to "not me" and from "not me" to "me." As they travel they are absorbed into the liminal, subjunctive time/space of "not me . . . not not me." This time/space includes both workshops-rehearsals and performances. Things thrown into the future ("Keep that") are recalled and used later in rehearsals and performances. During performance, if everything goes right, the experience is

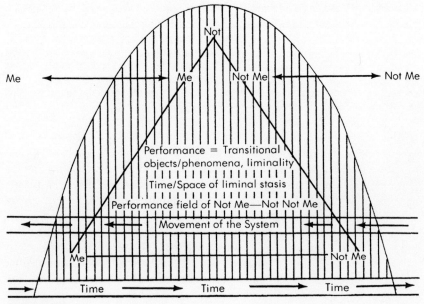

Figure 2.11

of synchronicity as the flow of ordinary time and the flow of performance time meet and eclipse each other. This eclipse is the "present moment," the synchronic ecstasy, the autotelic flow, of liminal stasis. Those who are masters at attaining and prolonging this balance are artists, shamans, conmen, acrobats. No one can keep it long.

By integrating the thought of Winnicott, Turner, and Bateson with my own work as a theater director, I propose a theory that includes the ontogenesis of individuals, the social action of ritual, and the symbolic, even fictive, action of art. Clearly these overlap: their underlying process is identical. A performance "takes place" in the "not me . . . not not me" between performers; between performers and texts; between performers, texts, and environment; between performers, texts, environment, and audience. The larger the field of "between," the stronger the performance. The antistructure that is performance swells until it threatens to burst. The trick is to extend it to the bursting point but no further. It is the ambition of all performances to expand this field until it includes all beings, things, and relations. This can't happen. The field is precarious because it is subjunctive, liminal, transitional: it rests not on how things are but on how things are not; its existence depends on agreements kept among all participants, including the audience. The field is the embodiment of potential, of the virtual, the imaginative, the fictive, the negative, the not not. The larger it gets, the more it thrills, but the more doubt and anxiety it evokes, too. Catharsis comes when something happens to the performers and/or characters but not to the performance itself. But when doubt overcomes confidence, the field collapses like popped bubble gum. The result is a mess: stage fright, aloneness, emptiness, and a feeling of terrible inadequacy when facing the bottomless unappeasable appetite of the audience. When confidence—and the skills necessary to achieve what's promised—prevails, there is nothing performers can't do. A special empathy/sympathy vibrates between performers and spectators. The spectators do not "willingly suspend disbelief." They believe and disbelieve at the same time. This is theater's chief delight. The show is real and not real at the same time. This is true for performers as well as spectators and accounts for that special absorption the stage engenders in those who step onto it or gather around it. Sacred a stage may or may not be, special it always is.

e

The workshop-rehearsal process is the basic machine for the restoration of behavior. It is no accident that this process is the same in theater as it is in ritual. For the basic function of both theater and ritual is to restore behavior—to make performances of the $1 \rightarrow 5_a \rightarrow 5_b$ type. The meaning of individual rituals is secondary to this primary function, which is a kind of collective memory-in/of-action. The first phase breaks down the performer's resistance, makes him a tabula rasa. To do this most effectively the performer has to be removed from familiar surroundings. Thus the need for separation, for "sacred" or special space, and for a use of time different than that prevailing in the ordinary. The second phase is of initiation or transition: developing new or restoring old behavior. But so-called new behavior is really the rearrangement of old behavior or the enactment of old behavior in new settings. In the third phase, reintegration, the restored behavior is practiced until it is second nature. The final part of the third phase is public performance. Public performances in Euro-America are repeated until there are no more customers. In most cultures performances occur according to schedules that ration their availability. What we call new behavior, as I said, is only short strips of behavior rearticulated in novel patterns. Experimental performance thrives on these rearticulations masquerading as novelties. But the ethological repertory of behaviors, even human behaviors, is limited. In rituals, relatively long strips of behavior are restored, giving the impression of continuity, stasis: tradition. In creative arts, relatively short strips of behavior are rearranged and the whole thing looks new. Thus the sense of change we get from experimental arts may be real at the level of recombination but illusory at the basic structural/processual level. Real change is a very slow evolutionary process.

Many people these days fear a disruption of historical cultural variety brought about by world monoculture. Just as physical well-being depends on a varied gene pool, so social well-being depends on a varied "culture pool." Restored behavior is one way of preserving a varied culture pool. It is a strategy that fits into, and yet opposes, world monoculture. It is an artificial means of preserving the wild. Usually it is not local people who practice restored behavior in this conscious way. The devadasis were content to dance their sadir nac, even if it was doomed. The Mura and Dom danced and drummed their Chhau before Bhattacharyya arrived in 1961, even if it was "in decay." The agnicayana would or would not have been enacted again in Kerala without Staal and Gardner. As for Plimoth, the Pilgrims are long since gone. Modern sensibility wants to bring into the postmodern world "authentic cultural items." Maybe this is just a kind of postimperialist souvenir hunt. Or maybe it is something more and better. Within the frame of postmodern information theory all knowledge is reducible/transformable into bits of information. As such, these bits can be reconstructed in new ways to create new orders of facticity. An illusion of diversity is created backward in time to 5_a and forward to 5_b. This illusion is artful because it is art itself, pure theater. This illusion may have the status of "reality" as actual as any other order of reality. The underlying idea that information, not things, is the matrix of cultures, and maybe of "nature" itself, is at the root of such recent exploration as recombinant DNA, gene splicing, and cloning. What these experiments "create" is a liminal existence between nature and culture. The experiments suggest what the performing arts have long asserted, that "nature" and "culture" may be a false dichotomy, that actually these are not opposing realms but different treatments of identical information bits.

NOTES TO CHAPTER 2

[1]In *Frame Analysis* Goffman used the term "strip of activity": "The term 'strip' will be used to refer to any arbitrary slice or cut from the stream of ongoing activity, including here sequences of happenings, real or fictive, as seen from the perspective of those subjectively involved in sustaining an interest in them. A strip is not meant to reflect a natural division made by the subjects of inquiry or an analytical division made by students who inquire; it will be used only to refer to any raw batch of occurrences (of whatever status in reality) that one wants to draw attention to as a starting point for analysis" (1974, 10). My "strip of behavior" is related to Goffman's term, but it is also, as will be seen, significantly different.

[2]Labanotation, roughly analogous to musical notation, was developed by Rudolf von Laban in 1928. According to an article in the *New York Times* (6 May 1979, "Arts and Leisure" section, p. 19) by Jack Anderson: "The system records dance movement by means of symbols on a page that is read from the bottom up. Three basic vertical lines represent the body's center, right, and left sides. Where the symbols are placed on the lines indicates what parts of the body are moving. The shape of the symbols indicates the direction of the movement, and their length indicates the movement's duration." This, plus other kinds of notation such as "effort-shape," makes it possible to more or less "keep" a dance or other bodily mise-en-scène long after it has stopped being performed. Such systems are now widely used in dance, less so in theater.

[3]Andrews has done more research than anyone on the Shakers' rituals. See References.

[4]"Actual" is a term I adapted in 1970 from Eliade's "reactualization" (1965). In 1970 I wrote: "A try at explaining actuals involves a survey of anthropological, sociological, psychological and historical material. But these are not organized to promote the search. . . . [In the literature] I find an incipient theory for a special kind of behaving, thinking, relating, and doing. This special way of handling experience and jumping the gaps between past and present, individual and group, inner and outer, I call 'actualizing' (perhaps no better than Eliade's 'reactualizing,' but at least shorter). . . . An actual has five basic qualities, and each is found both in our own actuals and those of primitive [*sic*, and excuse me] peoples: 1) *process*, something happens *here and now;* 2) *consequential, irremediable,* and *irrevocable* acts, exchanges, or situations; 3) *contest*, something is *at stake* for the performers and often for the spectators; 4) *initiation, a change in status* for participants; 5) space is used *concretely* and *organically*" (1977, 8, 18).

[5]All Emigh citations are from a letter he distributed to a few persons concerning his 1975 work in West Irian. He has since returned to Asia to continue his researches. Emigh was trying to establish connections relating Balinese performance to performances and ritual practices in West Irian, specifically forms of ancestor worship. Emigh saw a pan-Micronesian aspect to Balinese and West Irian performances. Most of Emigh's stuff has not yet been published, but I think he is onto relating a stratum of performance including masks, dance styles, and relationships to sacred geography that was/is present across vast areas of the Pacific—at least from Japan to aboriginal Australia, from Papua New Guinea to India, and including many of thousands of islands within this big area. W. H. Rassers (1959) has shown a definite link between Balinese shadow puppetry and Sepik River ceremonies. These connections can still be seen because in styles and techniques of performance people tend to be conservative, maintaining very old practices, some of which are expressed in a Euro-American way in Grotowski's *Towards a Poor Theatre*. This keeping of old ways, almost in decipherable archaeological-behavior layers, makes the study of contemporary performance also the study of old performance. The old ways are constantly being worn away and then restored: never the same, never essentially different.

[6]The *Altar of Fire* shooting script (Gardner(?) 1975) was given to me by someone who worked on the film—a local person. I obtained the script, in 1976. The script also gives detailed instructions to camerapeople, technicians, etc. It also provides drawings of the site, altars, etc. It includes lots of background material on agnicayana, as well as descriptions of what will happen.

[7]Until John Emigh—who heard Mead talk on the subject at the American Museum of Natural History—told me what she said, I thought *Trance and Dance* wholly "authentic." My experience proves how easily people can fall into the trap. To many American scholars and students, *Trance and Dance*—because of its age, and because of the authority of Mead and Bateson—is the most powerful example of what Balinese trance "really is."

[8]From a three-page mimeographed information paper dated "2/80" sent to me by Ingram. (Plimoth Plantation 1980, 1–2).

[9]For more on restored villages, theme parks, and related entertainment-performance environments, see Haas 1974, Kriazi 1976, Mackay 1977, McNamara 1974, 1977, Bierman 1979, Moore 1980, and Wilmeth 1982. Moore treats Disney World as a "bounded ritual space."

[10]I'm taking a term Turner applies to "social dramas" and applying it to the performance process. But his conception of social drama is performative, and closely related to his understanding of the ritual process. Turner uses key terms like "liminality," "communitas," and "process" in laying out his theories of both ritual and social drama. See, especially, Turner 1969, 1974, 1982*a*.

[11]I first used this figure in 1977 when I was relating "social drama" to "aesthetic drama" (1977, 144). Turner used the model a few times (see Turner 1982, 73). In my 1977 use I hypothesized that theatrical techniques are the hidden, implicit underground of social and political action, the dramatic ordering of events; and, conversely, that social and political action underly theatrical works. Thus I was denying the one-way action of Aristotelian mimesis and at the same time denying the proposition that "all the world's a stage." I accept both statements as dialectically true: each making the existence of the other necessary. Artistic action creates the rhetorical and/or symbolic possibilities for social drama to "find itself," and the events of ordinary life provide the raw stuff and conflicts reconstructed in art works. The visual pun on the figure for infinity was not intended—but when I saw it I was pleased.

[12]Bouissac (1982) deals with this problem of planned accidents. He asks, provocatively, whether such acts should be analyzed from the point of view of the naive spectator who thinks the accident is "for real" or of the observer who knows what's "really happening." In my own theater work I've tried to make my intentions as clear as possible—on the principle that whatever is made conscious uncovers a further horizon of unknown potentially emergent stuff and that the work of the artist these days is to demystify.

[13]A particular kind of performance has surfaced over the past ten years or so: performances of "the real as real." Sometimes these are documentary films. But such movies always have the taint of editing (falsification). More impressive is some of the work of Spalding Gray, Robert Wilson, and various Performance Artists who include unedited slices of their lives as lived. See "The Natural/Artificial Controversy Renewed" in *The End of Humanism* (Schechner 1982*b*). For a good survey of this kind of work in California—one of the places it is most popular—see Loeffler, ed., 1980.

[14]Grotowski's paratheatrical work has been written up in a number of places. See Grotowski 1973; Mennen 1975; Kolankiewicz, ed., 1978; Burzynski and Osinski 1979; and Grimes 1982.

[15]For information about the Theatre of Sources, see *International Theatre Information*, winter 1978, and Grimes 1981. For Barba's "theatre anthrolopolgy," see Barba 1982*a*.

[16]From a publicity release announcing the Rao-Ashton company's tour to America.

3

PERFORMERS AND SPECTATORS
TRANSPORTED AND TRANSFORMED

By using masks, costumes, and physical actions arranged in a set way or improvised according to known rules; by performing following a script, scenario, or set of rules; by performing in special places or places made special by performing in them; by performing on holidays or at times set aside "after work" or at crisis in the life cycle such as initiations, weddings, and funerals: by all these means, and more, theatrical reality is marked "nonordinary—for special use only." Furthermore, what is performed is encoded—I want to say nested, trapped, contained, distilled, held, restrained, metaphorized—in one, or more, special kinds of communication: either as a mixture of narrative and Hindu temple service as in Ramlila; or as fixed narrative and individual creativity as in any of the productions of, say, Chekhov's *Cherry Orchard;* or as a well-known sequence of events better known to connoisseurs than to common spectators as in the kuse mai of the Noh drama *Yorimasa* as performed by the Kanze school; or as closely guarded secrets revealed to initiates during the performance itself as in the vomiting and bleeding that is part of the initiation of Gahuku boys in Papua New Guinea; or as a script imposed by a single writer-director-scenographer such as Richard Foreman's *Pain(t);* or as words and actions devised collectively as the *Mysteries and Smaller Pieces* of the Living Theater; or as a scenario sent to hundreds of people, some of them friends, some strangers, to be acted (or discarded) separately, and in many different settings and styles, by recipients of one of Allan Kaprow's happenings. This Homeric list may exhaust you, reader, but not the field. They are mere smatterings of evidence of the incredible diversity of performance events. And I have pointedly omitted events like the Mass, professional football, psychodrama, whirling dervishes in devotion, Sumo wrestling: a wide variety of performative rituals, games, sports, and hard-to-define activities that lie between or outside established genres. After all, "established genre" indicates a record of what has found its place, while performance activities are fundamentally processual: there will always be a certain proportion of them in the process of transformation, categorically undefinable. But all performances—defined and undefined—share at least one underlying quality. Performance behavior isn't free and easy. Perform-ance behavior is known and/or practiced behavior—or "twice-behaved behavior," "restored behavior"[1]—either rehearsed, previously known, learned by osmosis since early childhood, revealed during the performance by masters, guides, gurus, or elders, or generated by rules that govern the outcomes, as in improvisatory theater or sports.

Because performance behavior isn't free and easy it never wholly "belongs to" the performer. In Euro-American theater (Stanislavski and after) much of the work of training and rehearsal makes performance behavior seem "as if" it belongs to the performer,

Because the very best that can happen is to have the actor completely carried away by the play. Then regardless of his own will he lives the part, not noticing *how* he feels, not thinking about *what* he does, and it all moves of its own accord, subcon-sciously and intuitively. [Stanislavski 1949, 13][2]

Stanislavski also felt the opposite (see chapter 1): that intuitive flow needed to be consciously controlled. He wanted a trained intuition. He wanted the actor to be carried away not into chaos but into the precise score of what had been prepared through rigorous training, workshop, and long rehearsals of often a year or more. Thus the "Stanislavski system" is largely devoted to training the actor so that flow can be generated through a conscious process. But such a seamless knitting of the "life" of the character and that of the actor is not the goal of all theater everywhere. In the West, Brecht distrusted it, but Brecht himself modeled his ideal actor—one who alternated between flow and reflexivity, between "being the character" and speaking about the char-acter—after what he had learned of Asian theater, especially Chinese theater.

26. Vyases holding the books that contain the samvads (dialogues) and stage directions of the Ramnagar Ramlila. One vyas trains the swarups; the other is responsible for the remaining roles. Both make sure that during the actual performances everything goes as it should. Photo by Carolyn and Martin Karcher.

And in the Ramlila of Ramnagar, India's best-known Ramlila, the directors of the spectacle, the vyases, stand behind the performers, open promptbooks in hand, speaking the words and actions (plate 26): making certain that everything happens according to the book. Interestingly, the crowds at Ramlila are not troubled into supposing that the actions of Rama or Hanuman are any less "real" due to the presence of the vyases or even to their intervention. Clearly the "lives" of Rama and Hanuman intersect but are not identical to the "lives" of the actors. Like the presence of director-author Tadeusz Kantor during the performances of *The Dead Class*—where Kantor makes slight adjustments in the performance by lowering a performer's hand or whispering to another to speed up the delivery of some lines—the corrections of the performance become part of the performance. The stage—and I mean not only the physical place but the time/space/spectator/performer aggregate—generates a centripetal field that gobbles up whatever happens on it or near it. This absorption into the center is the chief parallel between performance process and ritual process; it's what Kafka meant when he wrote the miniparable: "Leopards break into the temple and drink to the dregs what is in the sacrificial pitchers; this is repeated over and over again, finally it can be calculated in advance, and it becomes part of the ceremony" (1954, 40). After some performances Kantor's corrections became predictable; people who saw *The Dead Class* many times say that Kantor's gestures are no longer free but part of the performance score. But even the intervening-when-needed, and therefore unpredictable, actions of the vyases at Ramlila are part of the performance score—just as the officials moving in and out of a football game intervene only when there is an infraction but still play decisive and well-defined roles in the game.

As Kafka says, accidents become part of the ceremony, even adding a special thrill. During the 1980 Ringling Brothers Circus at Madison Square Garden, a trapeze artist attempts to rise from a position where she is hanging by her ankles. She starts, hesitates, reaches, almost falls. The music stops, the crowd gasps—if she cannot reach the bar she will drop forty feet. Finally, inching her way up, grabbing her left forearm with her right hand, she reaches the bar. The music crescendoes, the crowd sighs relief and then cheers. The whole bit is repeated each show. It doesn't matter whether this bit actually happened once and then was kept as business or whether it was invented wholesale. It is now "calculated in advance": part of the show. And each show—of theater, sports, ritual—is a palimpsest collecting, or stacking, and displaying whatever is, as Brecht says, "the least rejected of all the things tried." The performance process is a continuous rejecting and replacing. Long-running shows—and certainly rituals are these—are not dead repetitions but continuous erasings and superimposings. The overall shape of the show stays the same, but pieces of business are always coming and going. This process of collecting and discarding, of selecting, organizing, and showing, is what rehearsals are all about. And it's not such a rational, logical-linear process as writing about it makes it seem. It's not so much a thought-out system of trial and error as it is a playing around with themes, actions, gestures, fantasies, words: whatever's being worked on. From all the doing, some things are done again and again; they are perceived in retrospect as "working," and they are "kept." They are, as it were, thrown forward in time to be used in the "finished performance." The performance "takes shape" little bit by little bit, building from the fragments of "kept business," so that often the final scene of a show will be clear before its first scene—or specific bits will be perfected before a sense of the overall production is known. That is why the text of a play will tell you so little about how a production might look. The production doesn't "come out" of the text; it is generated in rehearsal in an effort to "meet" the text. And when you see a play and recognize it as familiar you are referring back to earlier productions, not to the playscript. An unproduced play is not a homunculus but a shard of an as yet unassembled whole.

During the run of a play—or over the calendrically fixed course of the performances of a ritual—even in the most traditional genres (I've seen performers in Noh, Ramlila, Kathakali, and Balinese dance-drama do this), new business is accumulated and stale business eliminated. A person going to a particular performance only once, as is the habit in our culture, can't notice the process of continuous change. Sometimes, where a performance is frozen tight, it takes great effort, and ceremony, to update the show, as when a pope summons a council to revise the Mass. But on the local level, the Mass is always being adjusted to suit the living relationship between priest and parishioners. This relationship is as much one between performer and participating spectators as between religious leader and faithful. Individual performative variation will be appreciated even more when one realizes that a performance of the Mass far transcends the recitation of a set text: it involves the particular and peculiar styles of the performers. And as with the Mass, so with all ceremonies/rituals everywhere.

I wrote earlier that performing isn't free and easy: it is behavior that is "put on." This is what gives theater its bad name. Theater is that art where the master teacher says, "Truth is what acting is all about; once you can fake truth you've got it made." This is not a wholly cynical statement, as can be seen in the story Levi-Strauss tells of Quesalid, a Kwakiutl who wanted to expose the quackery of the shamans (1963, 167–85). "Driven by curiosity about their tricks and by the desire to expose them, he began to associate with the shamans until one of them offered to make him a member of their group. Quesalid did not wait to be asked twice." He was thoroughly trained in acting, magic, singing; he learned how to fake fainting and fits, how to induce vomiting, and how to employ spies who would tell him about the lives of his patients. He learned how to hide a wad of down in the corner of his mouth and then, biting his tongue or making his gums bleed, to produce this bloody evidence before patient and spectators as "the pathological foreign body extracted as a result of his sucking and manipulations." Quesalid mastered the art so well that he not only exposed the other shamans as quacks but built a powerful reputation for himself as a true shaman. Over the years he began to believe in his cures, even though he always knew that they were based on tricks. He reasoned that the ill got better because they believed in him, and they believed in him because he knew his art so well and performed it so stunningly. Finally he thought of the bloody down and all his other tricks as manifestations of his own authentic powers. As Levi-Strauss says, "Quesalid did not become a great shaman because he cured his patients; he cured his patients because he had become a great shaman." Quesalid, like the leopards in Kafka's parable, was absorbed into the field of his own performing. He was transformed into what he had set out to expose.[3]

At the Ramlila of Ramnagar, India, one of the best actors is the man who plays the semidivine sage, Narad-muni (plate 27). When Narad-muni speaks or sings, the audience—sometimes of more than twenty-five thousand—listens with special care; many believe the performer playing Narad-muni has powers linking him to the sage/character he plays. This man is no longer

27. Narad-muni in the Ramnagar Ramlila. Photo by Richard Schechner.

28. Mahant Baba
Omkar Das, who
performs the role of
Narad-muni. Photo by
Richard Schechner.

called by his birth name (Omkar Das, plate 28), not even by himself. Over the thirty-five years he has performed Narad-muni he has increasingly been identified with the legendary figure. Because he is a Brahman, and any Brahman can perform priestly ceremonies, Narad began some years ago to practice priestcraft. Now he is the *mahant* (owner and chief priest) of two temples in Mirzapur, a city about forty miles from Ramnagar. He is rich. People come from far away to his temples because they believe Narad-muni speaks through Narad-priest. Narad never claims to be an incarnation of Narad-muni, but each year at Ramlila his connection to Narad-muni is renewed, displayed, deepened, and ritualized before an audience of thousands. This man is not Narad-muni, but also he is not not Narad-muni: he performs in the field between a negative and a double negative, a field of limitless potential, free as it is from both the person (not) and the person impersonated (not not). All effective performances share this "not–not not" quality: Olivier is not Hamlet, but also he is not not Hamlet: his performance is between a denial of being another (= I am me) and a denial of not being another (= I am Hamlet). Performer training focuses its techniques not on making one person into another but on permitting the performer to act in between identities; in this sense performing is a paradigm of liminality.

Indian culture with its tradition of reincarnation encourages this kind of multiplication of (im)personations. When the beautiful black god Krishna was desired by all of the gopis, he multiplied himself so that each woman had Krishna with her: this theme is a favorite of Indian artists, both visual and performative, and forms the praxis-core of many kinds of Krishna worship.[4] And who is the "genuine" Hamlet? Olivier? Burton? Bernhardt? Or Burbage, who played it first in 1603? Or a nameless English actor who toured France even earlier in a lost play now known only as the ur-*Hamlet*? This question of multiple realities, each the negative of all the others, does not merely point to a peculiarity of the stage but rather locates the essence of performance: at once the most concrete and evanescent of the arts. And insofar as performance is a main model for human behavior in general, this liminal, processual, multireal quality reveals both the glory and the abyss of human freedom.

Few are the performers who have experienced Narad's transformation. Even at Ramlila most performers don't get absorbed into their roles. This is not to say that the roles don't deeply affect the performers' lives. Approaching the village where the family who has played the demon-king Ravana lives, I was told that "Ravan-raj [King Ravana] lives over there." Everyone knows Ravana: he is royalty among peasants. The family has grown rich since the 1860s when a forefather was auditioned by the Maharaja of Benares to play Ravana, a role roughly like that of Satan in *Paradise Lost*. Over the years the situation of Ravana's family has become more and more a structural anti-thesis to that of the boys who play Rama, Sita, and Rama's brothers, the protagonists of the Ramlila and archenemies of Ravana. The boys are picked by audition yearly. Sometimes boys will remain in the Ramlila for several years, playing Shatrughna one year and Lakshman or Rama the next. Once a boy's voice changes or he grows facial hair, he is no longer suitable to play a swarup.

The boys who play the swarups come mostly from city families and attend school; after their stint in Ramlila many enter professions ranging from the priesthood to journalism to acting. During the thirty-one days of the cycle play, the boys playing Rama, Sita, and Rama's brothers live in seclusion in three different dharamsalas in Ramnagar—moving along with the play itself to different locations. Ravana returns each night the several miles to his native place: his village, like the mythic Lanka, is away from the places where Rama, Hanuman, Sugriva, or any of their party resides. But at the climax of the cycle, when Ravana is killed in battle by Rama, the man playing Ravana signifies this moment by taking off his ten-headed mask and prostrating himself before Rama, kissing his feet. But again, I ask, who is doing the kissing? The actor without his mask is doing devotion to the boy who, with his sacred crown, is Rama incarnate. Both man and boy are "between personae," in that liminal, double-negative field where they are neither them-selves nor their roles. And if few performers have experienced Narad's trans-formation, most have felt Ravan-raj's and Rama's doubling: the sense of being taken over by a role, of being possessed by it—in its "flow" or in the flow of the audience's appetite for illusion, ludus, lila: play.

This surrender to the flow of action is the ritual process. Here it is that the two root meanings of *ri* converge: the action is orderly, even numerical—"Play it by the numbers"—but the sense of being in it is, as Csikszentmihalyi says, "the merging of action and awareness. A person in flow has no dualistic perspective: he is aware of his actions but not the awareness itself. . . . The steps for experiencing flow . . . involve the . . . process of delimiting reality, controlling some aspect of it, and responding to the feedback with a concen-tration that excludes anything else as irrelevant" (1975, 38, 53–54). Or, as Ryszard Cieslak, the great actor who performed in many of Grotowski's works, told me:

The score is like a glass inside which a candle is burning. The glass is solid; it is there, you can depend on it. It contains and guides the flame. But it is not the flame. The flame is my inner process each night. The flame is what illuminates the score, what the spectators see through the score. The flame is alive. Just as the flame in the glass moves, flutters, rises, falls, almost goes out, suddenly glows brightly, responds to each breath of wind—so my inner life varies from night to night, from moment to moment. . . . I begin each night without anticipations. This is the hardest thing to learn. I do not prepare myself to feel anything. I do not say, "Last night, this scene was extraordinary, I will try to do that again." I want only to be receptive to what will happen. And I am ready to take what happens if I am secure in my score, knowing that, even if I feel a minimum, the glass will not break, the objective structure worked out over the months will help me through. But when a night comes that I can glow, shine, live, reveal—I am ready for it by not anticipating it. The score remains the same, but everything is different because I am different. [Schechner 1973*b*, 295]

Cieslak is the Zen master for whom the moment of action is when all the preparation falls away: what remains is readiness. As Shakespeare says, "ripeness is all."

When the performance is over, Cieslak "cools down." Often he drinks vodka, talks, smokes a lot of cigarettes. Getting out of the role is sometimes harder than getting into it. Little work has been done on the cool-down, at least in the Euro-American tradition. In Euro-America the emphasis is on training, workshop, rehearsal, and warm-up. In Bali, by contrast, there are rituals for cooling down: sprinkling with holy water, inhaling incense, massage, and even sacrifice of animals and blood sprinkling. What the cool-down does is return the performer to an ordinary sphere of existence: it transports him back to where he began. Acting, in most cases, is the art of temporary transformation—not only the journey out but also the return. Quesalid and Narad both, over the long run, gave in to their roles; Cieslak knows how to prepare and be ready to flow with his role. But he has hardly an inkling of what to do afterward. And some roles effect a swift and permanent transformation, as in initiation rites and other "rites of passage." I am interested in these different kinds of changes that occur within performers—and the concomitant changes that happen in an audience—not from a psychological point of view but as a baseline from which to project several stops along a continuum of performance types. This continuum will tell something about performance in a number of cultures, and also interculturally. The continuum runs from those performances where the performer is changed through the "work" of the performance to those in which he is transported and returned to his starting place. Vertical axes on this continuum would show whether transformation occurs gradually, as with Quesalid and Narad, or suddenly, as when a Gahuku boy is changed into a man through the work of a single set of initiatory performances. Also, I will show how these two kinds of performances—transportative and transformative—occur together, working together.

I call performances where performers are changed "transformations" and those where performers are returned to their starting places "transportations"—"transportation," because during the performance the performers are "taken somewhere" but at the end, often assisted by others, they are "cooled down" and reenter ordinary life just about where they went in (figure 3.1). The performer goes from the "ordinary world" to the "performative world," from one time/space reference to another, from one personality to one or more others. He plays a character, battles demons, goes into trance, travels to the sky or under the sea or earth: he is transformed, enabled to do things "in performance" he cannot do ordinarily. But when the performance is over, or even as a final phase of the performance, he returns to where he started. Actually, the ways in through preparations and warm-ups and the ways out through cooling down are liminal, between the ordinary and the performative realms, serving as transitions from one to the other. If the cool-down is incomplete, as it so often is especially in Euro-American performance, the performer is left hanging—as some movie actors, not all happily, have found out. If John Wayne was satisfied in becoming (like Narad) what he portrayed—Big John, The Duke—Bela Lugosi was not. I want to point out that if a change occurs within the performer, or in his status, it happens only over a long series of performances, each of which moves the performer slightly (figure 3.2). This is what happened to Narad and John Wayne. Thus each separate performance is a transportation, ending about where it began, while a series of transportation performances can achieve a transformation. It's not my task here to describe the ways the ordinary world is different from the performative world. In some kinds of performances—trance dancing, for example—extreme care is exercised in bringing the performer out of trance. This is so because trance exhibits qualities of both personality change and involuntariness: the trancer clearly needs help "coming back," while the

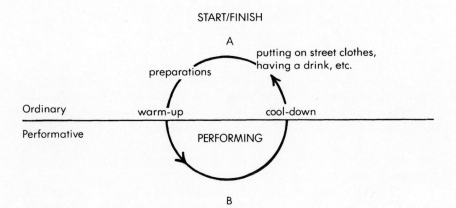

Figure 3.1

character actor appears to be in control of himself. We might even say that there are two kinds of transportations, the voluntary and the involuntary, and that character acting belongs to the first category and trance to the second. However, having watched trance—and having seen many films depicting it—I suspect that the differences between these kinds of transportations have been overemphasized. The character actor is self-starting (at least if he has orthodox Euro-American training), but once warmed up and in the flow of things he is deeply involved in what Keats called the "negative capability" and what I've schemed out as the "not me–not not me." The character actor in flow is not himself, but he is not not himself at the same time. Also, trance performers are frequently conscious of their actions even while performing them; and they too prepare themselves by training and warm-up. The difference between these kinds of performance may be more in labeling, framing, and cultural expectations than in their performance processes.

Transformation performances are clearly evidenced in initiation rites, whose very purpose it is to transform people from one status or social identity to another. An initiation not only marks a change but is itself the means by which persons achieve their new selves: no performance, no change. In *The High Valley* Kenneth E. Read tells how a Papua New Guinea boy, Asemo, was taken from his mother's home, secluded in the bush for several weeks, put through initiatory ordeals and training with his age-mates, and finally brought back to his village (along with his age-mates) transformed into a man. Read lets us know that the underlying action of the initiation is performative. To give but two examples, after two weeks of seclusion the boys are brought back to Susuroka, their village:

The noise and movement were overwhelming. Behind us, the shrill voices of women rose in keening, ritual, stylized cries informed by genuine emotion that were like a sharp instrument stabbing into the din around me. The ululating notes of male voices locked with thumping shouts, deep drumbeats expelled from distended chests counterpointed the crash of bare feet on the ground, and, rising above it all, came the cries of the flutes. [1965, 159]

Asemo and his age-mates were somewhere in the middle of the throng, almost certainly blinded by the dust, carried along by the press of stronger bodies. . . . Other

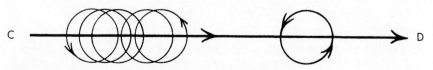

Figure 3.2 *A series of transportations results in a transformation*

youths had told me, laughing, of their panic during these opening minutes of their day-long ordeal. [1965, 160]

This ordeal included forced vomiting and nosebleeding. Read describes how Asemo and the other boys were "sadly bedraggled" and "dejected" and "limp." Literally exhausted, the boys were carried, dragged, and pushed into running a gauntlet where Gahuku women attacked the men and boys with "stones and lethal pieces of wood, an occasional axe, and even a few bows and arrows." The men picked the boys up and put them on their shoulders and together they ran through no-man's land.

The men had bunched together as they ran, so closely packed that they struck each other with their legs and arms. In the center of the throng the initiates, riding the shoulders of their escorts, swayed precariously from side to side, their fingers clutching the feathered hair of the head between their legs. (1965, 172)

Read says that "there was no mistaking the venom in the assault" of the women; and the men didn't think of the attack as a "ceremonial charade" but recognized that it "teetered on the edge of virtual disaster." On the edge, but not over: the attack was contained within its performative boundaries much the way a bloody hockey game barely but reliably remains a game. The ordeal, the gauntlet, the attack: these are all "twice-behaved behaviors"—scored, expected, performed.

Six weeks later the "final act was played out in the . . . village." Asemo spent those weeks absorbing training. The day of his coming out—a day of feasting and dancing—culminated in the presentation of the initiates to the whole village (plate 29). This time the women didn't assault the men but greeted them with a "rising chorus of welcoming calls." Then the initiates danced as a group, without the assistance or protection of the older men.

They moved unsteadily under the ungainly decorations, and I failed to see the splendid stirring change that had been apparent to their elders' eyes. But dignity touched them when they began to dance, a slow measure based on the assertive stepping of the men but held to a restrained, promenading pace by the weight [of their headdresses]. . . . For a moment I was one with the crowd of admirers. . . . Asemo was in the front rank of the dancers, his legs moving in unison with his age mates, his face, like theirs, expressionless, his eyes fixed on some distant point only he could see. [1965, 177]

Asemo and his age-mates had become men in the Gahuku scheme of things. During and after his day of dancing Asemo was a male Gahuku with the responsibilities and privileges of that status. Abolition of the initiation rites— and Read thought when he wrote *The High Valley* in 1965 that they would not be performed again—signals a shift in the whole basis of Gahuku society.

That is because the initiation doesn't merely mark a change that has occurred elsewhere in the social scheme—as bar mitzvah, graduation, or entrance into a professional association usually does in the Euro-American context—but is in its whole duration the machine that works the changes transforming boys into men. Without this machine, Gahuku boys will be different kinds of men. To be taken from Susuroka, to undergo the ordeals, to be trained in lore and dancing, to return and dance: that process equals becoming a Gahuku man. This status—whatever its personal meanings and effects, whatever private style it accommodates—is fundamentally social, public, and objective. It does not determine what kind of Gahuku man Asemo will be, or even how he feels about it, any more than a wedding ceremony determines what kind of husband the groom will be. But definite acts have been performed. These acts accomplish a transformation.

29. Men dancing on the final day of Asemo's initiation. Photo by Kenneth E. Read.

People are accustomed to calling transportation performances "theater" and transformation performances "ritual." But this neat separation doesn't hold up. Mostly the two kinds of performances coexist in the same event. Just as Asemo and his age-mates were being transformed, the Gahuku men who vomited and bled with them, who carried them on their shoulders through the attack by the women, who trained them to dance, were transported, not transformed. They were trainers, guides, and coperformers. Those who no longer change—or who do not change "this time," through the work of this performance—effect the changes wrought in the transformation. This relationship is shown in figure 3.3. The experienced performers enter the performance and share in its actions of bleeding, vomiting, gauntlet running. But when the performance is over, the already initiated Gahuku men reenter ordinary life approximately where they left it. If any change among them occurs, it is subtle: the way persons achieve more respect, or lose it, through doing what their social lives require. When the performance is over the transported have been returned to their place of entry and the transformed have been changed. The system is analogous to a printing press, where information is imprinted upon a piece of paper as it is fed through. The performance—and the training leading up to it—is a point of contact between the "press" (transported) and the "paper" (transformed). Point B— the performance witnessed by spectators who are far from casual seekers of entertainment—takes place at this decisive point of contact between transported and transformed. What the transported imprint upon the transformed at that point of contact is there to stay: circumcision, scarring, tattooing, and so on; or the giving of special clothes, ornaments, and artifacts, such as wedding bands, the sacred four-strand thread of Hindu initiation, the tefillin to be bound and unbound daily by Jewish males, and so on. Or something is taken from the transformed: the bloody down Quesalid displays, the foreskin taken from the circumcised, a ceremonial haircut, or, as in the Gahuku case,

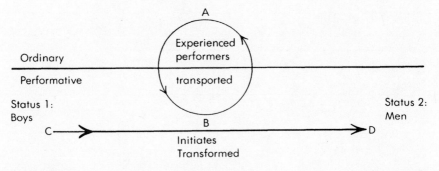

Figure 3.3

blood and vomit. These markings, additions, and subtractions are not mere arrows pointing to deeper significance. They are themselves loaded with power: they bind a person to his community, anchor him to a social identity; they are at once intimate and public. Theater people especially ought to be sensitive to the force of the surface. The surface of the social being is like the surface of the sun: always seething, throwing up from the depths material heretofore hidden, and sucking down into the depths what just now was surface.

For the system to work, the transported must be as unchanged as the transformed is permanently changed. The work of the transported is to enter the performance, play his role, wear his mask—usually acting as the agent for larger forces, or possessed directly by them—and leave. In this process the transported is identical to the actor. Or, to put it another way, the actor in Euro-American theater is an example of a transported performer. For reasons that will be made clear later, the Euro-American theater is one of transportation without transformation. Many performance workers, especially since 1960, have sought to introduce into the Euro-American performing arts the process of transformation.

And the audience? Spectators at transformation performances usually have a stake in seeing that the performance succeeds. Often they are relatives of the performers or part of the same community. Thus, in transformation performances the attention of the transported and that of the spectators converge on the transformed (figure 3.4). This convergence of attention—

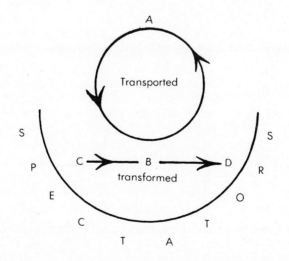

Figure 3.4

and the direct stake spectators have in the performance—is why so many transformation performances use audience participation. All of Susuroka gathered for the final day of dancing as Asemo and his age-mates made their debut as men. At first only the boys-now-men dance, but then everyone joins in a general celebration. So it is also with bar mitzvahs, weddings, and even funerals.

In a transformation performance the stars of the show may not be the best performers, technically speaking. Asemo and his age-mates can't dance as well as the older men, any more than a bar mitzvah boy sings his part from the Torah as well as the chazan. Throughout the initiation process the older men have concentrated on getting the boys through—doing what must be done for the initiation to be completed, for it to work. And on that last day the concentration of the village is on what has been made: new men, the work done. Interestingly, the word "drama" derives from the Greek root *dra:* to do, to make. Similarly, at a wedding the attention is on the marrying couple, at a bar mitzvah it's on the bar mitzvah boy, and so on. But whatever the abilities of the transformed, the transported need to be skilled performers. Everywhere the pleasure an audience gets from a transformation performance depends greatly on the skills of the elders and/or professionals who train, guide, officiate, and often perform with the transformed. The bar mitzvah boy is praised for his singing, but the chazan better sing better; ditto for the dancing of Asemo's father and uncles.

It would be easy if it ended here. But the status of the transported can be more important than their skills as performers—even if, as in Quesalid's case, this status derived from performative skill. Think what an event it would be if the pope played Christ at Oberammergau. As it is, Pope John Paul II cooing to an audience/congregation of seventeen thousand teenagers bussed into Madison Square Garden is flashed on national TV. John Paul's performance is "out of character" for a pope but good footage evidencing his "human-ness." John Paul's "human image" often makes people forget his conserva-tive theology. And Polish John Paul is an unusual bit of casting in a role usually reserved for an Italian. But what would happen to a common parish priest if, on national TV, he cooed to a big bunch of teenagers brought before him? An absurd question, because why would the networks broadcast the doings of an ordinary priest? And yet this same parish priest celebrating Mass is more powerful, in the church's view, than an actor playing the pope in *The Deputy.* And how about the unlikely possibility of a priest (or the pope himself) playing the role of pope in a play? However unlikely these combi-nations are, they point to the four variables operating in every performance: (1) whether the performance is efficacious, directly making changes in ordi-nary life (initiations, weddings, and so on), or whether it is fictive, even about "real events" (*The Deputy*, ordinary plays, documentaries); (2) the status of the roles within a performance; (3) the status of the persons playing the roles—whether they are playing themselves (as in initiations), are possessed by others, or have, in the Stanislavskian sense, "built a role" (remember that Quesalid started by playing the role of unmasker/investigator and ended behind the mask he wanted to rip off others, and that Carnival and other celebrations pivot upon the inversion of roles where fools play the king and the king is required to act foolishly); and finally (4) the quality of the performance measured by the mastery performers have over whatever skills are demanded (and these vary from society to society, occasion to occasion)— even, sometimes, the skill to feign a lack of skill, as in many con games. None of these four variables is absent from any performance, transformative or transportational.

My model of transportation/transformation performance is open. It can be applied across cultures and genres. I have already applied it to the initiation rites of Gahuku boys in Papua New Guinea. And presently I will apply it to a few more kinds of performances, selected not only to be representative but also because I have had some personal experience with most of them. In the Greek case, obviously I wasn't around in the fifth century B.C., but I have directed versions of Euripides' *Bacchae*, Sophocles' *Philoctetes*, and Sophocles'/ Seneca's *Oedipus*. I will also look at theater according to the Indian treatise *Natyasastra* (second century B.C.–second century A.D.), the Noh drama according to the writings of Zeami (fourteenth-fifteenth centuries), and as practiced today in Japan; *The Elephant Man* on Broadway; and my own production of *Dionysus in 69* as an example of environmental theater using audience participation.

First, let me show how the model looks when applied to that period of Athenian theater when writers alone received prizes (figure 3.5). This is the opposite of what happened in the village of Susuroka. There people of different status were transformed by the initiation performance into people of the same status: boys + men became men. Here people of the same status, competing poets, are transformed by the performance into unequals: a winner + losers. This competitive differentiation is of course that of the agon: the core action of each Greek tragedy is identical to that of the City Dionysia as a whole. The revelation through direct competition among agonists (prot- and ant-) of who wins and who loses is deep not only in Greek tragedy but, by derivation, in Euro-American theater, whose narratives until very recently always involved conflict and resolution into winners and losers.

The Greeks so loved competition that they preferred it over aesthetics. At first, prizes were given only to the writers, and each formed an ensemble of those he thought could best present his play. Aeschylus was noted for training his own chorus. But commencing in 449 B.C., prizes were also given for the best actor. From then on writers were not allowed to select their own protagonists—these were assigned by lot and paid by the archon out of public funds. This lessened the possibility that writers and actors would form teams, but it was certainly a strange regulation from the modern viewpoint because it foreclosed one of the ambitions of twentieth-century theater: to form an aesthetically balanced company. But the Greeks wanted to reduce the possibility that the two competitions—one in writing, the other in acting—although they occurred at the same time and used the same medium and clearly affected one another, would in practice become one. What happened was that writers were transporters for actors and actors for writers: each was the means the other used to achieve victory. The model thus could be drawn twice: once with the writers as the "straight line" and once with the actors.

In Susuroka the men compete with each other. But even as they do they collaborate to help the boys through. The object of the performance is to eliminate winners and losers—the boys helped the most are those least able to do what's needed. Ultimately, all the boys are initiated, all win, all dance together on the village ground. This isn't saying that among the Gahuku there aren't better or worse dancers; but these differences, during the initiation, are effaced as much as possible, or at least not made a formal part of the ceremonies. With the Greeks the differences are displayed as much as possible, though even the Greeks made mistakes: Sophocles lost the year he entered with *Oedipus.*

I said that among the Greeks competition was preferred over aesthetics.

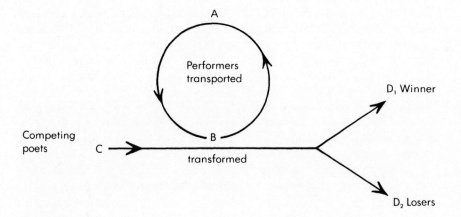

Figure 3.5

And Euro-American aesthetics, thanks to the Greeks, is a function of competition. If aesthetics is a concern for how well (= how beautifully) a thing is done, this concern developed among the Greeks when they ceased looking at a group in the process of being transported—as in the dithyrambic dances—and began selecting from the group individuals who "do better" than others (see figure 3.6).

Only by observing the details of performance—the what and how—could the Greeks, and any who follow the Greek model, discern winning poets and actors from losers. This process of differentiation is even more demanding when it's possible for a winning actor to perform in a losing play and a losing actor in a winning one. Spectators and judges—who actively claim to represent the "whole city," just as the judges who award Obies and Tonys claim to represent the "theatrical community"—confront the artists directly; they are neither absorbed into the performance as participants nor simply "enjoying" it. Critics must, and spectators often do, rank performances in relation to other performances, even separating out within a given performance the "good" from the "bad." And writers and players—knowing they are being judged, that something important is at stake—react by playing up to the audience or intentionally scorning it. Rare is the performance, especially on opening night when the critics are there, in which performers feel the audience working with them, mutually absorbed in the task of making the show go. Instead, the experience is of confrontation: the radical separation of audience and judges/critics on one side and performers, playwrights, and other theater people on the other. This basic confrontation leads to the accumulation of "values" by which artists are transformed into winners and losers. Again, much of the experimental work during the last twenty years has been directed—through devices of audience participation, environmental staging, and collective creativity—at abolishing this agony.

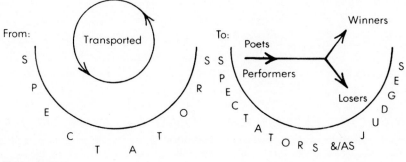

Figure 3.6

Aesthetics need not be built from competition, as is clear when you look at theater according to the *Natyasastra*. This book, called the "Fifth Veda," was compiled between the second century B.C. and the second century A.D. It is almost certainly not the work of a single person. The details it contains describing theater architecture, staging, exact gestures of the body, limbs, face; the discussion of emotions, of acting styles, of the different types of plays; the book's mythical narrative frame of a theatrical performance decreed by the gods and later brought down to earth for people to enjoy—all point to a flourishing theater-dance tradition long before extant Sanskrit dramas. Unlike Aristotle, who wrote after the heyday of Attic tragedy, and whose *Poetics* is so laconic as to be possibly no more than notes toward a text, the *Natyasastra* is so full of details, of exact descriptions and specifications, that it can be nothing other than a how-to-do-it manual, collectively authored (compiled) over four or five centuries. Out of all this I will look only at the relationship between the means of theatrical production—gestures, dance steps, modes of dialogue delivery, costumes, makeup, masks, theater architecture and stage design, and so on—and the particular kind of "entertainment" enjoyed by the spectators.

This relationship is epitomized in the Sanskrit notion of *rasa*. Rasa literally means "flavor" or "taste," and Indian theater—like the Indian painting and sculpting of roughly the same period, especially the caves at Ajanta and the sculptural group at Mahabalipuram—is, in Richard Lannoy's McLuhanesque term, "synaesthesic." As Lannoy says,

The Ajanta style approaches as near as it is likely for an artist to get to a felicitous rendering of tactile sensations normally experienced subconsciously. These are felt rather than seen when the eye is subordinate to a total receptivity of all the senses. . . . The seated queen with the floating hand is drawn so that we obtain information which cannot be had by looking at her from a single, fixed viewpoint. . . . The logic of this style demands that movements and gestures can only be described in terms of the area or space in which they occur; we cannot identify a figure except by comparing its position with others around it. . . . It could be said that the Ajanta artist is concerned with the order of sensuousness, as distinct from the order of reason. [1971, 48–49]

Lannoy shows how the Sanskrit drama, based on the *Natyasastra* (or probably vice versa), is analogous—especially in its synaesthesic technique—to the cave art and even to the caves themselves. "The structure and ornamentation of the caves were deliberately designed to induce total participation during ritual circumambulation. The acoustics of one Ajanta vihara, or assembly hall (Cave VI), are such that any sound long continues to echo round the walls. This whole structure seems to have been tuned like a drum" (1971, 43). This tuning was not fortuitous—these caves are human-made, excavated and carved out of a solid mountain wall.

In both cases [the caves, the theater] total participation of the viewer was ensured by a skillful combination of sensory experience. The "wrap-around" effect [of] the caves was conveyed on the stage by adapting the technically brilliant virtuosity of Vedic incantation and phonetic science to the needs of the world's most richly textured style of poetic drama. [1971, 54]

What the *Natyasastra* supplies are the concrete details of that style which is at its core not literary but theatrical. Even today, in such popular forms as Ramlila, Raslila, and the Krishna bhajans, there is circumambulation, trance dancing, sharing of food, open or cyclical rather than confrontational narrative, wrap-around environmental-theater-type staging, processions; phases of the performance where the spectators watch and phases where they participate: a total blending of theater, dance, music, food sharing, religious ceremony, and a resulting sensuous overload that convinces me that the *Natyasastra* informs not only the classical Sanskrit drama, extinct for twelve hundred years, but also dozens of living forms beloved by the Indian people.

I said that rasa is the essence of the performance theory of the *Natyasastra*, and rasa means taste or flavor: a sensuous essence that enters through the snout—nose, mouth, tongue—and engages the eyes and ears the way a sumptuous meal does, ultimately satisfying the belly which, to minds conditioned by yoga, is the seat of breath. Thus rasa is neither gross nor leaden but highly sophisticated and subtle. Food-sharing symbolism is a paradigm of more than Indian theater. Food, along with ghee (clarified butter), water, flowers, bells, fire: these are the integers linking Indian theater and puja, the basic Hindu ceremony whose roots reach down to pre-Aryan Harappa. At the core of puja is the offering of *prasad* (food) to the gods. This food is sanctified by the gods and returned to the people. The food makes a circular journey but is transformed in the process from human offering to divine gift. Different foods—different flavors, aromas, and textures, different references and associations—have different functions and meanings. Fruits, sweets, rice, and so on, prepared in various ways, constitute a language of food. Indian theater, derived from the entertainments among the gods (according to the *Natyasastra*), also is an offering to the gods: a food for the gods, which the gods return to people for their enjoyment. Natya is theater is prasad. And the gods are frequent characters in the plays, as well as spectators of the human and divine show. In Ramlila of Ramnagar long poles topped by effigies represent the gods on high looking down at the performance. This appearance of the gods as performers and spectators is natural and easy among a people who believe in reincarnation and whose basic religious texts, the Vedas, depict gods modeled on "primal man" and not the other way round. Also, the occasion for theater in India is not, nor was it ever, a competition among poets and actors. Performances occur for any number of reasons, ranging from the celebrations of fixed annual events like Ramlila, Raslila, and Chhou to pure enjoyment of commercial theater like Jatra and Tamasha to the marking of auspicious events like marriages, the visit of a dignitary, or recovery from an illness. The performance is sometimes thought of as an offering. Need I add that these occasions and functions overlap? At the Ramlila of Ramnagar the outskirts of the performing area are occupied by sellers of food, trinkets, and clothes and the operators of games of skill and chance. Everyone attends the Ramlila, from the nursing infant to the highest god. On one night, from a tower later to be occupied by the maharaja of Benares's family, performers representing Vishnu and Lakshmi watch as Rama and Sita are displayed; these two couples are manifestations of the same deities, doubled in time and space like flower petals or tossed rice and saying the same thing: This is an auspicious, prolific event.

Rasa is the flavor of the performance—how it tastes, how it appeals to the tastes of people from different *jati* (castes) and experience; and Indians use the word "taste" with a great deal more subtlety and range of socioaesthetic signification than we do. If some theater needs an audience to hear it, and some need spectators to see it, Indian theater needs partakers to savor it. I don't have the space here to discuss exactly how rasa is used. What I do want to point out is that according to the *Natyasastra*—and in many Indian performances of today—the enjoyment of the performance is shared between the performers and the spectators or, as I shall say from this point, between the preparers and the partakers. Rasa happens where the experience of the preparers and partakers meets. Each, using skills that have to be learned and that are not easy, moves toward the other. The experience of the performance is like that of a banquet where the cooks and servers must know how to prepare and serve, but the diners must know how to eat. And, as in Asian banquets in general, there is more food than can possibly be consumed: a great part of the skill is in knowing how and what to select for any given occasion. This relationship can be depicted as in figure 3.7. A successful performance is one where the levels of both skill (preparers) and understanding (partakers) are high and equal. If the partaker expects more than the preparer can deliver, the performance is inadequate; if the preparer does more than the partaker can savor, the performance is wasted. Low skill matched by low understanding is preferable to imbalance. Perfect rasa is a meeting at a very high level of preparer and partaker. Noh drama in Japan works in a similar way, except that the root metaphor is gardening and what is shared is *hana* (flower). More on that later.

This Indian system of participant enjoyment—a system exported to Southeast Asia, China, and Japan—is one of the main things that attracted Brecht to Asian theater. This system actively involves the audience while at the same time enhancing its enjoyment. The system is a set of relations among four variables:

```
 1            2                                            4          3
performer/performed  ——————————→ RASA ←——————————  savored/spectator
preparer                                                partaker
```

Rasa is the interface of 1/2 : : 4/3. Rasa doesn't exist except as a function of the interface. Each term of the system can be varied independently of the others. That is, some spectators can savor one part of a performance, others another; a performer can be absorbed into his role at one moment and detached from it at another. Brecht took from Asian theatre this technique of independently variable elements and developed from it his theory/practice of *verfremdung* (alienation or distance). Let me emphasize again how close this system is to the way fine food is eaten. At a banquet, feast, or fine restaurant—and this is even more striking at ceremonial occasions and ritual observances—it is presumed that all food is superb or sanctified, but only some of it is eaten: one of the meanings of "taste" is "to partake of only a little bit in order to savor its essence."

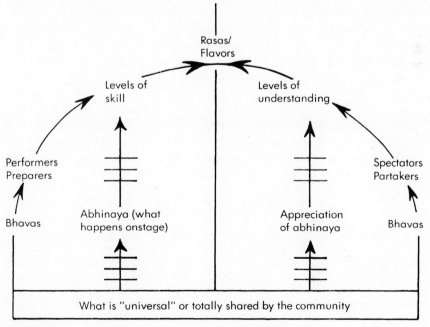

Figure 3.7

Thus, according to the *Natyasastra*, both performers and partakers are transported, and no one is transformed (figure 3.8). Rasa is the mutuality, the sharing, the cocreation of preparers and partakers. Every detail of the presentation is worked out but variable: theater architecture, mise-en-scène, gestures, music, types of plays, spectator comportment, the proper occasions for theater, et cetera, et cetera, et cetera. But while the details are worked out to a degree unknown in the West, there is much liberty within the scheme because the parts are variable.

For example, how much should be presented at one time? There is a "start" and a "finish" to each night's performance—and many plays in the Sanskrit and folk traditions extend over a number of days and/or nights—but there isn't any definite "beginning" or "end" as there is in Greek drama. Where to stop in a given series again depends on circumstances. At Ramlila the size of the crowds, the weather, the energy of the performers, and the wishes of the maharaja all can determine how much is done on a given day. Like postmodern performance in Europe and America, the Indian system is a braid of several strands of activities; these require that performer and partaker attend together to the here and now of the ever-changing relations among the strands. The two systems, Greek and Indian, can be diagramed as in figures 3.9 and 3.10. This difference affects not only the performance but training, rehearsals, and the means of transmitting performance knowledge. Paradoxically, the Greek system—as it has been worked out historically in Western theater—is freer than the Indian in training and rehearsal but more fixed in perfomance. Through training and rehearsal, the "idea" or "action" of the performance is "discovered," and this takes searching; in performance this idea is "shown," and this needs a fixed score. In the Indian system training and rehearsal are fixed because what is being transmitted is not a means of discovery but the performance elements themselves broken into learnable segments. The performance, however, is truly contingent. The more experienced and respected the performer, the more he is permitted to vary

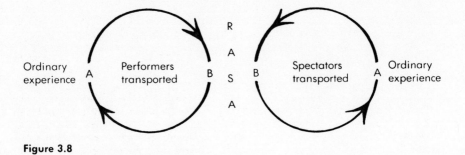

Figure 3.8

elements of the show during performance. The performance is truly contingent, an ever-changing lila (play, sport, illusion) created between preparer and partaker. But these days, as even classical folk arts are restored according to Westernized training methods, Indian theater is losing some of its quality of contingency.

This view of the difference between causal chains and braided relations also helps explain why Western theater develops from crises that are then the business of the performance to resolve, while Sanskrit drama, and much contemporary Indian theater, "doesn't go anywhere." It's not supposed to go anywhere; it's not a "development-resolution" kind of drama but an expository, synaesthesic, and playful set of variations much more akin to the Indian raga system of music than to anything Aristotelian.

This "playing around with"—performances that mutually transport preparers and partakers—describes not only Indian theater but the experiments Grotowski made in "paratheater" and the "rituals" Anna Halprin has been devising in California for nearly thirty years. The weakness of both Grotowski and Halprin is that they rely on the I-thou immediacy, what Turner labels "spontaneous communities," to generate the rules of the game, and they depend on "group creativity" to come up with the elements to be bunched and braided. Without the benefit of a worked-out, culturally elaborate theatrical system (which the *Natyasastra* both describes and provides and which is ever-present in the Indian oral tradition), the participants are thrown

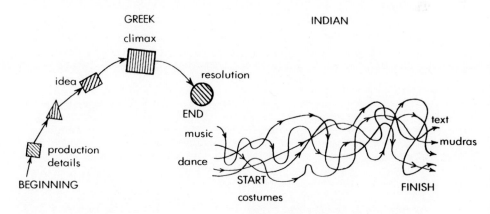

Figure 3.9. CHAIN: All theatrical "effects" or "elements" serve the driving idea, the causal chain.

Figure 3.10. BRAID: There may be many or few strands operating at any moment; the performance bunches and relaxes. No strand is necessarily more important than any other, or causes them.

back on their own "sincerity," their own "personal truth." This truth is but a version of that radical individualism so rampant in twilight capitalist culture: all too often a combination of clichés of intimacy, unexamined cultural fact, and romantic distortions of preindustrial religious experience. The results— as I've witnessed them and heard them described—are actions like staring deeply into your partner's eyes, swaying or moving in circles in "ritualistic" dances, passing fire, telling personal stories during long hours spent quietly in candlelight, running through the woods at night, and so on. Yet the underlying tendency of this kind of experiment is, I think, valid: to restore to performance, or invent anew, that quality of mutuality so powerfully present in rasa.

Nothing could be further from the narcissistic experiments of today's theater than Japanese Noh, a form that is describable by the figures I devised for the *Natyasastra*. In Noh there is a close relationship between highly skilled performers—many of them apprenticed in the art from early childhood by their fathers, uncles, and grandfathers—and an audience of connoisseurs. Zeami and his father, Kanami, gave Noh its definitive shape in the fourteenth and fifteenth centuries. Zeami, in a series of monographs, is very specific about how Noh performers are to be trained, how Noh is to be performed, and what the underlying theory of the art is. I can only touch on this rich literature, one of the most detailed theatrical accounts ever written by an individual. And Zeami was not only a director and actor of great force but the author of the largest number of Noh plays still in the repertory. His output and range are roughly that of Brecht and Stanislavski combined.

Zeami is specific about how a performance of Noh is to be adjusted according to a number of circumstances outside the mise-en-scène: the season, weather, quality and comportment of the audience. For example:

When Noh is performed in a shrine or in the presence of a noble, there are many people assembled, and it is very noisy with the buzz and murmur of their voices. In that case, the performer better wait until they become calm and quiet and all their eyes are concentrated on the entrance. . . . If he begins to sing *issei* [entrance music] immediately, the atmosphere of the theatre will take on the tone of the performance, the attention of the audience will be concentrated on the movements of the shite [main actor] and the noisy voices will become quiet. . . . But as one of the principles of Noh is that it should be performed in front of nobles, if the noble arrives at his box earlier than usual, the shite must begin the play as soon as possible. In this case, the audience has not yet become quiet, or latecomers are entering the boxes, and everyone's mind is not yet prepared to the Noh, some standing, others sitting in their boxes. In this case, one will not have a sufficiently calm atmosphere in which to perform. At such a time . . . the player had better be clad in more ornamental dress than usual, sing more strongly, step more loudly on the floor, and his carriage should be much more vivid and attractive. This will calm down the atmosphere of the theatre. . . . So to judge whether the audience is ready for the play to begin, or whether their minds are not yet concentrated on it, is very difficult. Only the experienced shite can do it. . . .

The audience whose eyes are not sharply appreciative will not praise the talented shite, and, on the other hand, the audience who can really appreciate Noh cannot endure to see an immature shite performing. It is natural that the unskilled shite is never admired by a cultivated audience; but that the real master sometimes cannot hold the attention of an unappreciative audience is partly because these people do not have enough taste to recognize the master's talent. . . .

The purpose of this art is to pacify and give pleasure to the minds of the audience and to move them, both nobles and the common people, and this will also assure prosperity and long life [for the actor]. [Zeami 1968, 36–39, 63–65]

So close and immediate is the relationship between performers and spectators that if the audience is noisy the costumes are changed at the last minute; a kind of homeopathy is tried where brighter costuming is used to calm a too flashy audience. Noh's apparent solemnity and fixity are deceptive. At its core is a set of contingencies unmatched elsewhere in world theater. The shite rehearses only with the chorus. The waki (second character), kyogen (comic actor), flutist, and drummers are all from different families and rehearse separately from each other. The whole group of actors, chorus, and musicians meets only once or twice before a public performance. The shite outlines his plans. Rehearsals as such are rarely held. The performance itself is the meeting place of the strands—singing, chanting, dancing, reciting, music making— that are braided into the public Noh. And the performance is variable not only in the ways Zeami describes but also because the shite can signal the musicians to indicate that a dance will be repeated or shortened. Again, like Indian raga music, Noh takes advantage of the immediacy of the encounter among artists and between the ensemble and the audience. An audience of connoisseurs is aware of, and delights in, these contingencies. Noh—the very word means "skill"—is like a sport, and the spectator's enjoyment is increased if, like the baseball fan who can read the third-base coach's signs to batter and runners, he knows the details of the interplay on stage. Many spectators of Noh also study its chanting or dancing and are attached to one school or another. For their part, Noh performers complain of boredom when, for tours, a company is assembled to repeat a fixed repertory. The onceness of Zen—a meditation and a martial art—is the heart of Noh.

Not rasa (flavor) but hana (flower) is the root metaphor of Noh. To understand hana you must see many sumi-i paintings, where each stroke of the brush is allowed just once, there are no corrections, so that a great work, when it occurs, is what happens when all training drops away in an unrevised meeting of artist and medium. Zeami speaks of hana often but at no time more cogently than here:

My father Kanami died on the nineteenth of May [1384] at the age of fifty-two. On the fourth day of the same month he gave a dedicatory performance in front of Segen Shrine in the province of Suruga. His own performance on this program was especially brilliant, and the audience, both high and low, all applauded. He had ceded many showy plays to uninitiated shite, and he himself performed easy ones, in a subdued way; but, with this additional color to it, his flower looked better than ever. As his was *shin-no-hana* [hana acquired through training; literally, "true flower"] it survived until he became old without leaving him, like an old leafless tree which still blossoms. [1968, 23–24]

Pure Beckett: an art of distilled discipline. Not only sumi-i but Zen rock gardens and bonsai trees are analogues to Noh. Hana exists between performers and spectators; when it is there both performers and spectators are transported (see figure 3.11). But unless the spectators know what's going on through specific instruction in Noh, the hana is missing. As in the Tea Ceremony, the ability to appreciate the service and the objects shown is directly proportional to what the guests know. This is different from the Indian situation where mutuality but not special knowledge is required. Living in a North Indian village will give a person by the age of five all that he needs to participate in Ramlila; from then on the experience will deepen year by year. But the Noh spectator must become a connoisseur or he will fail the performance. And that is why so many newcomers to Noh find it impenetrable.

It doesn't take special training to like Broadway theater or to dislike it. In this trait Broadway is like experimental theater. Almost all Euro-American theater prides itself on its popularity. What it asks of its audience is not special knowledge but responsivity. The historic sources of this theater are not so much religious ritual or initiatory ordeals but popular entertainments. I saw

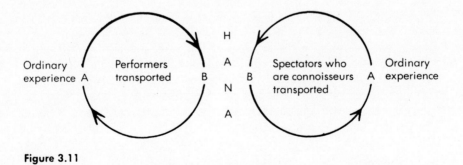

Figure 3.11

The Elephant Man on Broadway in 1979. Philip Anglim's portrayal of the title role was a model of professionalism as understood in the American theater: physical, restrained, precise, and according to the conventions of a stylized naturalism. By holding his right arm extended and twisted from the shoulder and again at the wrist, by dropping his right shoulder and turning his neck to the left, by rotating his left wrist and clenching his fist—and then keeping this excruciating position for more than two hours (except when offstage)— Anglim gave the impression of deformity without help from the costumer or makeup artist. This is in contrast, say, to Lon Chaney's *Hunchback of Notre Dame* in the movies—or to dozens of other films—where the actor is an armature for a construction. But Anglim's work on himself serves another purpose too. It allows individual spectators to sympathize with the character Anglim is playing and not be repulsed. In admiring Anglim's skill, and in recognizing his discomfort, a spectator is relieved from confronting directly the Elephant Man's look and stink. A spectator can congratulate herself: ''I saw Anglim/Elephant Man, and I was not disgusted. I saw that he was a human being, just like me.'' This kind of sentimental empathy, earned by acting skill, is what got the production its critical and commercial great success. The performer is transported while individual spectators experience their own reactions at the level of private responses. Some, like me, may simply respond to Anglim's skill. There is no collective work set out for the audience to do or participate in (see figure 3.12).

The difference (can I say emptiness?) betwen this experience, these sets of individual experiences—parallel but not collective—and Asemo's initiation, Greek theater, *Natyasastra,* and Noh is clear. In each of the others the

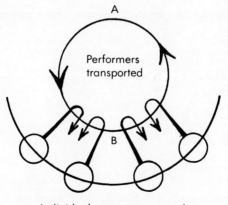

Individual spectators respond

Figure 3.12

30. The Performance Group's production of Bertolt Brecht's *Mother Courage and Her Children* in New York, 1975. Kattrin (Leeny Sack) is in Wooster Street; Mother Courage (Joan MacIntosh) and the Cook (James Griffiths) stand by the open Garage door and sing as the audience watches from inside. Photo by Clem Fiori.

31. Kattrin is buried in *Mother Courage*, New York, 1975. Photo by Clem Fiori.

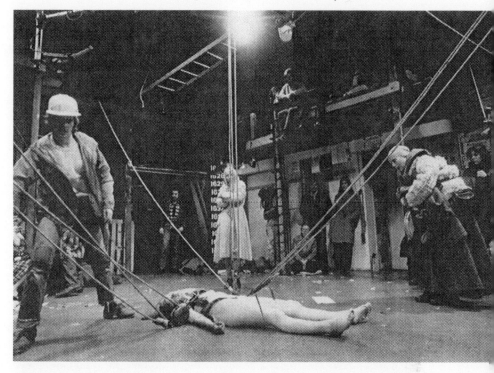

32. The environment for The Performance Group's production of Seneca's *Oedipus*, New York, 1977. The *Oedipus* environment was built in the same space that previously housed the *Mother Courage* environment. *Oedipus* was designed by Jim Clayburgh. Photo by Jim Clayburgh.

audience has a definite collective role to play. The tie-ins do not stop with responsivity but go on to include consciously articulated and practiced inter-actions. Asemo and his age-mates as initiates exist between the men and the rest of Susuroka, somewhat the way rasa and hana are cocreated by audience and performers in Indian and Japanese theater. And in the Greek theater, the response of the judges to a particular performance determined who won the prizes. The only thing close to this kind of celebratory play/work in our culture is what fans do at football, baseball, boxing, or other sports events.

Brecht knew this and wanted people to attend theater with the same critical/supportive mind they take to sports. It was this lack of mutuality, a symptom of the audience's lack of power, and the performances' lack of transformative potential that led to the experiments of the sixties and seven-ties. These involved audience participation, creation of new kinds of spaces for theater, a widespread interest in shamanism: performances that heal, transport, transform. And conscious links were forged between theater and religion. I do not have space to investigate these experiments here; I have written extensively about them elsewhere.[5] But I do want to say that in my own work— *Dionysus in 69, Commune, Mother Courage,* and *Oedipus* (plates 30–32) especially—I positioned my company, The Performance Group, somewhere between the individualist practice of Broadway and the collective social process of Susuroka. Also, I had the ambition to develop a performing style as precise as that described in the *Natyasastra.* I even sought to train the audience by holding many discussions after performances, giving public workshops, holding open rehearsals, and lecturing/writing a lot about the work. I didn't know it at the time, but I used workshops with The Perfor-mance Group as a way of transforming individuals into a group and then used The Group as transporters in an attempt to make a collective out of the individuals who constitute an audience, a temporary collective—a commu-nity for the time being (see figure 3.13).

I treated the members of the audience as if they were joining a workshop, and I tried to condense the workshop into a single performance. Grotowski, recognizing as early as 1967 that this couldn't be done, did away with the audience altogether. In his paratheatrical work he broke his acting company into subgroups who led people in attempts to generate "spontaneous communitas." In 1980 Eugenio Barba started the International School of Theatre Anthropology to bring together master teachers from Asia and performers from Europe and America. Barba doesn't want to teach Oriental techniques; he wants to get at "certain laws that determine organic tensions in the actor's organism. . . . The study and understanding of these laws, going beyond the styles and conventions of their theatrical forms, can, for the European actor, facilitate an awareness of his own energy process."[6] Barba says that "theatre anthropology is the study of the biological and cultural behavior of man in a theatrical situation, that is to say, of man presenting and using his physical and mental presence in accordance with laws differing from those of daily life." My own attention has turned, temporarily I think, from actually making performances to the writing of "performance theory."

Today there is a quiet in the American theater. But the surface calm lies. Tectonically, there is movement toward a collision of cultures. And where traditions collide—or separate radically—up bursts creative magma. If this is not happening right now on the "art front," it is happening in the social sciences—disciplines undergoing transformation. In the spring 1980 issue of the *American Scholar*, Clifford Geertz wrote about "blurred genres"—his attempt to summarize, and criticize, movements in social thought dealing with cultures in terms of games, dramas, and texts. Geertz, a pioneer of these processes (they are not yet frozen into "methods"), recognizes them as ways of handling the new world that has given birth to itself since World War II: a world of colliding cultures no longer dominated by Europeans and Americans, and no longer capable of being dominated by anyone. Dominance, of course, can be political, economic, cultural, scientific, philosophical, artistic. In none of these spheres is there hegemony. Soon enough, as the changed relations among peoples are more clearly manifested, the term "international" will be replaced by "intercultural." The intercultural phase of human history will not bring the "retribalization" of industrial societies, but it will promote the coexistence of metaphoric and linear knowledge. Metaphoric knowledge—the kind of knowledge released by the arts—is gaining an equal

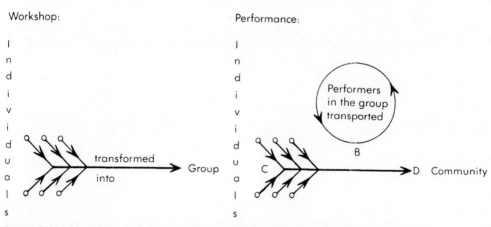

Figure 3.13. *An attempt, in American society, to duplicate the initiatory/transformative process*

footing: it is not inferior to "realer" facticities but is a primary reality, one of several that braid into the human helix. And theatrical metaphor—restored and reactualized behavior—is a root metaphor. It is a root because theater = action = transportation/transformation. Chased from Plato's republic as nonrational and subversive but existing always, sometimes marginally, theater is now showing itself everywhere: in social dramas, personal experience, public displays, political and economic interaction, art.

NOTES TO CHAPTER 3

[1] I discuss the idea of "twice-behaved behavior" extensively in chapter 2. I see in the rehearsal process itself the paradigm of ritual, and in "restored behavior" the operation linking such diverse activities as ritual, theater, psychotherapy, shamanism, and reflexivity.

[2] This sense of being "carried away" is what Mihaly Csikszentmihalyi calls "flow," and it characterizes a number of activities, such as sports, mountain climbing, chess, surgery (for the surgeon), theater, dance. It is the opposite of reflexivity. Probably many human activities are dialectical, depending on a wavelike alternation of flow and reflexivity. It may also be that some activities—theater being among them—have a reflexive rehearsal phase followed by a flowing performance. For more on flow, see Csikszentmihalyi 1975.

[3] This is another example of the peculiar power of performance to invert causal progressions so that effects precede causes. That is, the "power" of a performer is both cause and effect of his performance. Performance—and its effect on the audience—and feedback compose a synchronic bundle that, paradoxically, unfolds during the performance diachronically.

[4] The best discussions I know of are in Singer 1972 (199–244), Hein 1972, and Hawley 1981.

[5] See especially Schechner 1973a and 1977.

[6] From a three-page announcement of the first session of the International School of Theatre Anthropology, held in Bonn, West Germany; Holstebro, Denmark; and Stockholm, Sweden, from 1 October through 30 November 1980. Barba's school is only the most recent of a very extensive set of exchanges among the world's theaters, both ritual and aesthetic. Peter Brook has run his International Centre for Theatre Research in Paris for more than ten years, using performers from Africa, Asia, Europe, and America and experimenting with forms as diverse as Shinto worship and African storytelling, and texts ranging from the *Mahabharata* to *The Ik*, adapted from Colin Turnbull, *The Mountain People*. Ellen Stewart at La Mama ETC in New York sponsors the Third World Institute of Theatre Arts Studies which, for example, in October 1980 ran performances and workshops of traditional theater and rituals from Nigeria, Japan, the Dominican Republic, the Philippines, Korea, Indonesia, India, and Haiti. This work, and much more like it, is laying the foundation for an extensive reconstruction of theatrically—what it means, how it works—on a worldwide basis. The exchange is not one-way: a Nigerian explained how TV is used to reawaken among children interest in traditional games and ceremonies. The Performance Group's tour of India in 1976 had an effect on directors, actors, and writers in India.

4
RAMLILA OF RAMNAGAR

Texts, Oppositions, and the Ganga River

The subject of Ramlila (plates 33–48), especially the month-long Ramnagar Ramlila,[1] is like the story of Krishna's mouth. I have seen the great Bharatanatyam dancer Balasaraswati perform this story. Krishna's mother fears that the little Krishna has put some dirt, or something dangerous, in his mouth. She asks him to open his mouth. He refuses. She asks again and again. Finally he opens his mouth and she looks in. There, in amazement, bewilderment, even terror, she sees all the worlds. Contained in her baby's tiny mouth is the unspeakable Absolute. Revealed, Krishna closes his mouth, and with it his mother's memory of what she has seen therein. The dance ends with mother and baby playing once more simply as mother and baby. So it is with Ramlila. I look into its mouth and see all there is to be seen. I am not so certain, even though I am an American, a rationalist Jew (but Talmudic: given to inquiries and commentaries of all kinds), that I should remember what I have seen. And, doubtless, to those who have experienced Ramlila many times more often than I, this writing will be evidence of my forgetting.

Ramlila incorporates several texts, both literary and performative. The

Ramayana of Valmiki, never uttered but present all the same, is in the very fiber of Rama's story. The text chanted by twelve Ramayanis is Tulsidas's Hindi *Ramcharitmanas*, composed in the sixteenth century. The *Ramcharitmanas* is as familiar to the people of North India as the King James version of the Bible is to English-speaking people. The Ramayanis spend ten days before the first lila up on the sheltered roof of the small tiring-house green room next to the square where on the twenty-ninth day of the performance the Bharat Milap—the reunion of Rama, Sita, and Lakshman with Bharat and Shatrughna—will take place. There, under a veranda on that hot roof, the Ramayanis chant the *Ramcharitmanas* from its first word till the birth of Ravana. With Ravana's birth, the theatrical portion of Ramlila begins—after ten days of chanting on the roof. On the first day of chanting a special Ganesh puja is celebrated—a traditional beginning of auspicious events. Gathered on the roof with the Ramayanis are the five boys who perform the swarups—the divine incarnations of Rama, Sita, and Rama's brothers; performers of other leading roles; technicians and craftspeople; and the Adhyaksha, the administrative head of Ramlila, a man who works directly under the maharaja and is responsible for seeing to it that everything goes right. But after Ganesh puja attendance on the roof is sparse.

None of Tulsidas's text prior to "Listen, sage; in due time this king and all his household were born as demons of the night. He had ten heads and twenty arms; his name was Ravana, a formidable and valiant warrior" (Tulasi Das 1952, 81) is heard by the maharaja of Benares, patron of Ramlila, or by the faithful daily audience called nemis, or by the hundreds of sadhus (holy men) who stream into Ramnagar for Ramlila, summoned by Rama and sustained by the maharaja's generosity in providing dharamsalas (pilgrim dormitories) for rest and rations for the belly. These "sadhu rations" are by far the largest single specifically Ramlila expense in the Ramnagar Ramlila budget—eighteen thousand rupees in 1976. Only the Ramayanis and a few others hear the start of the *Ramcharitmanas*—a title that means "The Holy Lake of the Acts of Rama"—for it is with Ravana's birth that the theatrical Ramlila, the core dramatic conflict, begins. Ravana, by performing all kinds of austerities, earns a boon from Brahma. Ravana asks: "Hear me, Lord of the world. I would die at the hand of none save man or monkey" (Tulasi Das 1952, 82). Such will be Ravana's fate, for he, like Macbeth ("For none of woman born shall harm Macbeth") or Milton's Satan, is too proud.

As scholars researching Ramlila, Linda Hess and I felt it was our duty to see and hear everything. But this, we soon discovered, is impossible. Too many things happen simultaneously, scattered across Ramnagar. While Rama is in Chitrakut, Bharat sits in Nandigram; while the army of monkeys and bears moves toward Rameshwaram in pursuit of Ravana, Sita with a band of devoted spectators is already awaiting them in the Ashoka Garden of Lanka where Ravana holds her prisoner; when Lakshman is wounded by Meghnad's shakti and Rama pitifully mourns his fallen brother, Hanuman is more than a mile away chasing after the herb that will revive Lakshman. And even when the story is all but over, Rama already crowned, his lesson preached in the marble gazebo of Rambagh, he and his family received as royalty by the maharaja and his family in a special Ramnagar ceremony known as Kot Vidai (Farewell), the chief Ramayani continues to quietly chant the *Ramcharitmanas* until every last syllable of Tulsidas's text is sounded. It is not until the *Ramcharitmanas* is completed that the final arati (temple service to the swarups) can be performed, and the five boys who have performed/been gods be returned to ordinary life, and the masks—some papier-maché, some fashioned from copper and brass—put away.

But there is more to the Ramlila texts than the *Ramcharitmanas*. Tulsi's masterpiece is the generating kernel of the performance, but it is like a tree springing from a great taproot, branches spreading far and wide. There are the *samvads,* dialogues actually spoken during the thirty or thirty-one nights (depending on the lunar calendar) of the performance. These samvads were assembled and written during the nineteenth century.[2] They are intended to translate the feelings—the bhavas and rasas, if you will—of the *Ramcharit-manas* into a spoken language that ordinary people can understand. Thus Rama's story is twice told, at least. For each segment of narrative, the chant of the Ramayanis alternates with the dialogues of the characters speaking samvads. And if the maharaja is the principal audience of the *Ramcharit-manas*—the twelve Ramayanis always sit close to him—the sadhus and others especially devoted to Rama crowd up near the swarups (who speak most of the samvads) singing bhajans: devotional songs. In between are vast numbers of spectators—literally, people who see more than hear, as the story is acted out. Thus there are four main texts: *Ramcharitmanas,* samvads, bhajans, spectacle.

Consider: The Ramayanis sit in a tightly closed circle, their leader concentrating on the manuscript on which Tulsi's text is written. This text is illuminated at night by burning torches. Far away from the Ramayanis, lit by Petromax lanterns and sometimes by blazing flares, are the characters of the Ramlila who utter the samvads. There are many such characters: Rama, Ravana, Lakshman, Sita, Hanuman, Angad, Guha, Narad, Bharat, Dasharatha, Kaikeyi, Sugriva, Shiva, Brahma, Indra, Manthara, Parashuram, Vasishtha, Sumantra, Janak, Vibhishan. I list them this way, and not strictly according to their ritual importance, because in Ramlila these gods-characters-beings present themselves to me simultaneously as actors, as performers of a story, as physical theatrical presences. I am not alone in considering them thus. I spoke with a man in the crowd of spectators, who told me:

Everything there [at Ramnagar Ramlila] is a naturality. If they say "ashoka tree" they have an ashoka tree, if they say "jungle" they go to a jungle, if they say "Ayodhya" they show Ayodhya. Other Ramlilas, it is more drama. There are fancy clothes and loudspeakers and electric lights. Here the maharaja preserves the spiritual side. He makes certain everything is done right.

So, in addition to the literary texts, there is the performance text: the actual mise-en-scène, supervised by the maharaja (plate 34), who is the overseer of everything: the director of the vyases who do the day-to-day directing and who can always be seen standing onstage, promptbooks in hand, whispering the dialogue into the ears of the role players, making certain that each samvad is correctly spoken, giving signals to the leader of the Ramayanis so that the alternation between samvads and *Ramcharitmanas* is correct. Behind all this intricate staging is the maharaja. The performance text he preserves is a nineteenth-century one.

Actually, the mise-en-scène and the Ramlila environments—the settings for Ayodhya, Janakpur, Chitrakut, Panchavati, Lanka, and Rambagh—were mostly constructed in the nineteenth century, when Ramnagar Ramlila probably took its present form. Some parts of the environment preexist the Ramlila: the pathways through the back parts of Ramnagar, the countryside setting of Nishad's ashram, the two-hundred-year-old Sumeru temple of Durga and Kali with its large Pokra pool (called "tank") that serves as the *kshir sagar* ("ocean of milk") on which Vishnu sleeps prior to his incarnation as Rama and the other swarups. The temple and tank are next to Rambagh, once a maharaja's pleasure garden. And then there is the Fort, the maharaja's palace, residence, office, museum, and nerve center of Ramlila. The Fort is the setting of one of Ramlila's most spectacular scenes, one unique to Ramnagar. Furthermore, the Fort extends into the Ganga, linking the maharaja and Ramlila to the holy river. Whatever their histories, these environments belong partly or wholly to Ramlila, drawing significance from the performance and giving significance to it. Rambagh is a good example. It is no longer in use, except as a setting for Rama's teachings at the close of Ramlila, as temporary quarters for the boys who play Rama, Sita, Lakshman, Bharat, and Shatrughna, and as the scene-and-technical shop where Atmaram, a man in the maharaja's employ for decades, working with a pitifully small crew, supervises all technical aspects of the Ramlila. Almost single-handedly, Atmaram—whose name literally means "soul of Rama"— makes the props, maintains many of the large environments, and sees that, despite declining budgets, wind and rain, and the unpredictable obstacles that always occur, the show goes on. Some technical aspects of this Hindu epic are handled by Muslims: the construction of the large effigies (mostly of demons); the fireworks-flares illuminating the swarups at arati and at other times, bathing important scenes in brilliant red and then white light; and the painting, handling, and driving of the elephants. Some environments, like the Pokra tank and Sumeru temple, sacred to Durga and Kali, keep their own very powerful existence throughout the year, lending themselves to Ramlila annually—in much the same way as Shiva comes to worship Rama during this season as part of the Ramlila. Other environments need almost total reconstruction each year.

Benares is a Shaivite city, and the maharaja is identified with Shiva. As he passes, the crowd roars great, approving chants of "Hara, Hara, Mahadev!" ("Shiva, Shiva, the Great God!"). But, like the Ramlila itself, Benares is a multitexted place. It is ancient, holy Kashi and British Benares and Indian Varanasi (the city between the small rivers Varuna to the north and Asi to the south). The city is also sometimes called Ananda Kanana ("the Garden of Bliss") and Avimukta ("a place where Shiva always is"). Indeed, Varanasi is—as I was told on many occasions—an island of Shiva in the great North Indian sea of Rama. Nowhere, and at no time, is this clearer than during Ramlila. Perhaps the most ecstatic crowds, if not the largest, are those who assemble twice during the month-long performance when Rama himself performs the puja (worship) to the Shiva lingam: once after crossing the make-believe Ganga during his first day of exile; and once at make-believe Rameshwaram when the bridge to Lanka is built.

I am still talking about the layering of texts: literary and performance texts. Each of these texts may be "read" independently of the others. They each yield a part of what is in Krishna's mouth.

There is, too, the text of movement. For Ramlila is a performance made of movements: pilgrimage, exile, circumambulation, pursuit, kidnapping and running away, processions. All this movement—movement in the story, actual movement through the environments of Ramlila, movement to get to Ramnagar from Varanasi and back by crossing the Ganga—is balanced by the stasis of arati closing each day's performance. During arati the swarups (literally, "the gods incarnate") freeze and become pure murtis: images as in a temple of what they are, action suspended in/out of time (plate 35). Thus, in Ramlila dialectical oppositions are not so much resolved as suspended. The Ramlila then is composed of many texts of complementary oppositions.

Let me name a few as they operate both conceptually and spatially in both the narrative and the environments of Ramlila. These oppositions are more comprehensible if I summarize them as follows:

33. A scene from one of the first days of the 1978 Ramlila. The action takes place in Ayodhya, an environment built close to the maharaja's residence, the Fort. Note the maharaja on his large elephant, *upper left*. Photo by Richard Schechner.

34. Maharaja Vibhuti Narain Singh, on the throne since 1935, greets the crowd as he rides in his carriage to the day's lila site, 1978. Photo by Richard Schechner.

Maharaja and Ramayanis: Shiva	vs	Rama, Sita, and the other swarups and sadhus: Vishnu
Tulsidas, Valmiki, and the Great Tradition[3]	vs	Samvads, bhajans, and the Little Traditions
West bank of Ganga, the Varanasi side	vs	East bank of Ganga, the Ramnagar side
Stillness: murtis, arati, "stations"[4]	vs	Movement: processions, pilgrimage, exile, flow
Town space	vs	Theater space
Present historical time	vs	Time of the Ramlila story
Mela (fairground and marketplace)	vs	Lila (theater and dance)

These oppositions—and there are more—are not mutually exclusive or hostile to one another. They complement each other, constructing among themselves a vision of the world that is whole. For example, the maharaja exists in the field of energy created by Rama; and Rama exists as arranged for by the maharaja—not any Rama but the Rama of Ramnagar Ramlila, a Rama who has auditioned for the maharaja, who is paid more than a token, less than a wage after the month of performing is over. For his part, the maharaja is in a way a fictional character. There is no kingdom in secular modern India

35. Lakshman, Rama, and Sita in 1978 during the arati ceremony that closes each day's lila. Photo by Richard Schechner.

over which Vibhuti Narain Singh actually rules (as his predecessors and he himself, until Independence, actually ruled). His existence as maharaja is confirmed by his function as sponsor-producer of Ramlila. For the month of Ramlila is when the maharaja of Benares is most visibly and demonstrably a king. It is during this month, more than at any other time, that he rides on his elephant, or in his 1928 Cadillac; that he is accompanied by troops and a military marching band; that he shows himself again and again as a king to assembled thousands who chant an homage to the king of the city of Shiva that corresponds neatly to the homage this Shaivite king gives to Rama, Vishnu incarnate. Thus it is that a mediation occurs between Shiva and Vishnu, between the west bank of the scared Ganga River where Varanasi is and the east bank where Ramnagar is.

Nowhere is this mediating dynamic more clearly operating than in crossing the Ganga. The Ganga is no ordinary river—she is a goddess and her waters are holy. And for thousands who cross this holy river daily to attend Ramlila some special dharma accrues. That the maharaja's Fort is across the river from Varanasi is a result of the strategy of Maharaja Balwant Singh, who ruled from 1740 to 1770. He built the Fort as a barrier between the Nawabs (Muslim rulers) of Avadh and Benares. Thus the Fort predates Ramnagar Ramlila. Maharaja Balwant Singh's military and political strategy has had more than military consequences. I do not doubt that Ramnagar Ramlila has gained in importance because it is just near enough to Varanasi to gather audiences from there and far enough to require crossing the Ganga. A very special balance and tension are thus obtained. So, too, the sharp bend in the Ganga's flow, making it stream from south to north as it passes Varanasi, putting the city on the west (rather than south) bank, has more than geographical consequences. At dawn one can bathe in the Ganga and witness the sun rising over her vast waters (during flood season). Sometimes, even, the water's surface is broken by the surging backs of the population of dolphin who inhabit the river.

To get to Ramnagar Ramlila from Varanasi one must cross the Ganga—travel in the afternoon away from the westward declining sun and toward the brightly illuminated face of the Fort. Each day many thousands cross the river to attend Ramlila. There are several ways of crossing. A large steel bridge spans the river a few miles downstream from the Fort; a motor ferry leaves from the ghat near Benares Hindu University and docks close to the Fort; many private small rowboats ply the river. It was my impression that most people who attended Ramlila from Varanasi went by boat. Because the ferry operated only during daylight hours a great fleet of rowboats, each seating around thirty persons, assembled at night to take riders back to Varanasi. As a spectator said: "Each goes to Ramlila as an individual but returns from it as part of a group."

What a trip. Leaving amidst the tumult of the after-show surge of people looking for their friends, their prearranged boats, the fleet separated on the river as each boat went its own way. On many boats persons sang bhajans. By midriver it was as if the boat I was on, appropriately skippered by an old man, gaunt and beautiful, named Ramdas (meaning "servant of Rama"), was alone on the river. Another opposition: the seething surging crowds of Ramlila versus the ascetic, quiet aloneness of the river. The Ganga is wide and rough enough during flood season that it was almost as if we were rowing across the sea. Some nights blue lightning flashes, and the wind is fresh: we hasten to avoid storms, storms that capsize more than one small boat. Toward the end of Ramlila, as the rainy season gives way to the glorious clear autumn weather and the moon swells to full, the river sparkles. I experienced the vastness of Ganga, and her intimacy. After about one-half hour of rowing and being carried by the swift current, the west bank is reached: Different passengers alight at different ghats. I stepped off at Asi. Others went down toward Dashashvamedh.

At least seventy-five boats work the river. I realize that this accounts for only 2,250 persons and sometimes crowds at Ramlila exceeded 50,000. There is disagreement about how many attend the popular lilas: the day Rama breaks Shiva's bow and wins Sita's hand; Dashahara, when Ravana is killed; the Bharat Milap; and Coronation Day. Estimates go as high as 100,000. Shrinath Mishra, senior superintendent of police for Benares estimates 40,000–50,000. On an average day around 20,000 people attend and on the least popular days, or during heavy rains, there are as few as 1,500.

Be that as it may, crossing to and from Ramnagar constitutes a big part of the experience of Ramlila. Crossing the Ganga means literally to be in touch with India's great life stream. Songs sung on the boats crossing back from Ramnagar include hymns that are identified with both Rama and Gandhi. On our boat, as on many others, the same people traveled together with the same boatman, night after night, year after year. This boatman, Ram Das, led the singing (in Hindi):

King Rama, leader of the Raghu dynasty,
Born from Shankara's [Shiva's] drum,
Born from the waves of the Ganga,
Husband of pure Sita

Born from the mouth of the wise.
Hail to Sita's Rama,
And to Hanuman, who relieves us of our burdens
And grants us favors.

Hail to Mother Ganga.

This is very close to Gandhi's song (sung to the same tune):

> King Rama, leader of the Raghu dynasty,
> Husband of pure Sita:
> May we worship this Sita-Rama.
>
> He is known as Ishwara or Allah.
> May this God bestow good sense on everyone.

But the crossing of the river is not always peaceful. Sometimes boats overturn and people drown. Always, in the afternoon on the ferry, there is a great rush and crush.

On 23 September 1978, for example, I noted what it was like to cross the Ganga by ferry:

Boatrush. Pushing down the muddy flood-slicked slope of Samneghat toward the ferry. People rush furiously to get on the old boat. There used to be two of them, but one is laid up about a half-mile upstream. Who knows why, or when it will return to service? The ferry is free. The private boats can cost a rupee or more. On the ferry people pile up, bikes and all. From the shore to the boat is a narrow gangplank not more than three feet wide. So soon a wild, shoving, shouting bottleneck develops. There is screaming and jostling. Bikes are handed over the tops of peoples' heads to friends already aboard. People squirm into the crowd or cling to the handrope and edge along the side of the gangplank. But often everything just stops: things get jammed up. There is a raging crowd on shore, an empty gangplank, a half-empty boat blowing its whistle signaling departure.

Three days ago as we arrived very early for the three o'clock boat three women with head bundles of sticks squatted by the shore. They were the epitome of patience and labor. Their bodies were dark and as thin as the sticks they carried. (Someone told us that these sticks would be made into toothpicks.) It was hot, in the nineties, and humid. After thirty minutes the boat arrived and the ordinary riot occurred. Finally the bikes were loaded; most of the men who wanted to go were on board. Only a few women. Occasionally they approached the gangplank, and then they slid back as aggressive men shoved on by. The boat whistled; there was a last-minute rush and surge of bikers. Always, here, there's more demand than supply. Over the little mudhill at the shore, more passengers and bikers rushing to the boat. The boat's motor began. More men leaping from shore to ship. A single black bike passed over the heads of some men and women on board on top of the other bikes. Shouting. The boat pulls away.

And the three women were as they had been, standing helpless, and then squatting, to wait out the hour till the next boat.

I quote this because there is a tendency, in writing about Ramlila, to be swept up in devotion and admiration and to forget the ordinary grind and helplessness of lots of people who may never themselves attend Ramlila in Ramnagar but who still, for me at least, comprise part of the Ramlila experience, even (paradoxically) in being excluded.

So one of the deepest oppositions is between the extraordinary time-space-narrative adventure of Ramlila and the ordinary grind of daily living in North India. In a real way, Ramlila provides for a number of people a temporary relief from this grind; a festive season, a time-out. For others, those who sell food or row boats, for example, Ramlila is a busy work time.

Narrative Structure

The narrative structure of Ramlila is very important: it is through the story that much information concerning values, history (both mythic and conceptual), hierarchy, and geography are transmitted. People begin attending Ramlila as children, even as babies; much is learned through osmosis. Naturally, the basic story of Ramlila is that of the *Ramayana* and the *Ramcharitmanas:* the birth of Rama, his childhood adventures culminating in his breaking of Shiva's bow and winning Sita in marriage. Then, just before Rama is to be crowned king in Ayodhya, Kaikeyi—one of old king Dasharatha's wives—insists that Dasharatha make good two promises he made earlier. "What do you want?" Dasharatha asks. "That my son Bharat be made king and that Rama be sent into the forest in exile for fourteen years." Dasharatha dies of grief, but Rama, knowing he is an incarnation of Vishnu and that all these troubles are merely parts of Vishnu's great lila (sport, play, game, illusion, theater: the way the world operates on the human scale), willingly goes. Along with him go his brother Lakshman and his bride Sita. In the jungle live both *rishis* (sages) and *rakshasas* (demons). Rama and his party have many adventures with both.

Rama establishes a kind of royal house in exile at Chitrakut. His brother Bharat visits him there and begs him to return to Ayodhya. Rama refuses and moves farther into the jungle—farther south in India, to Panchavati. Then Shurpanakha, sister of the ten-headed demon king of Lanka, Ravana, sees Rama and Lakshman, is struck by their beauty, and tries to seduce first Rama and then his brother. Lakshman cuts off her nose and ears (a bloody but comic scene in Ramnagar Ramlila). In rage and humiliation Shurpanakha flees across the sea to her brother Ravana's kingdom. Ravana dispatches an army to avenge her—and the army is slaughtered. Then, using a golden deer as a decoy, Ravana lures Rama and Lakshman from Sita, kidnaps her, and carries her to Lanka. On the way he fights a battle with Jatayu, the old vulture king who tries to stop Ravana. The demon king cuts off the bird's wings and leaves him dying. Before he dies Jatayu tells Rama that Sita has been kidnapped by Ravana. Rama and Lakshman gather an army of monkeys and bears (including the great monkey hero, Hanuman) and pursue Ravana the length of India and across the narrow sea separating the mainland from Lanka (plate 36), these days, Sri Lanka. Meanwhile, Sita has refused Ravana's proposals. He imprisons her in a garden of ashoka trees and awaits the time when she will submit to him and become his wife. After many preparations and adventures—including Hanuman's entry into Lanka where he meets with Sita, is captured, and, when Ravana sets fire to his tail, grows to gigantic size and burns down the capital city—Rama's army crosses the sea at Rameshwaram and a great war is fought in Lanka. Systematically, Ravana's armies and heroes are destroyed, his family annihilated. Finally, Ravana meets Rama in single combat and is killed. Sita is rescued, her chastity tested and proved in a fire ordeal, and Rama's whole party begins a slow progression (in the Elizabethan sense) back to Ayodhya. Wherever they go—traveling in Ravana's magic chariot, the *pushpaka,* roughly retracing on the homeward journey their outgoing path—great, joyous crowds greet them. The fourteen years of exile are coming to an end. As they approach Ayodhya, Bharat comes out with Shatrughna, and the four brothers are reunited in the famous Bharat Milap. Rama is crowned and the kingdom turned over to him. The golden age of his rule, Ramraj, begins.

Every Indian knows this story: many believe it to be historical fact. In North India, especially, Rama is king of kings. The details of Rama's story combine themes found also in both the *Iliad* (the war fought over an abducted woman) and the *Odyssey* (the wanderings of the warrior). There is something deeply Indo-European about the *Ramayana*: movement over great distances; wars that mix lust and politics; admiration for and collaboration with animals; gods of high heaven and demons of the underworld using the middle earth, this earth, as a focus of combat between these two forces—a combat that involves human beings and depends on them. For Indians specifically, the *Ramayana* more than the *Mahabharata* defines the whole subcontinent. From Mount Kailasha in the north to Ayodhya and Mithali (Janakpur) on the Gangetic plain, to the hot and once dangerous forest of Dandaka, across the great rivers Ganga, Jamuna, and Godavari, to the southern hills leading down to Rameshwaram, and on to Lanka (see figure 4.1): today's terrain is also Rama's mythic nation. A small book by H. D. Sankalia, *Ramayana: Myth or Reality?* (1973), deals effectively, in my opinion, with questions concerning not only the *Ramayana*'s historicity but also the more interesting problem of its continued historical presence within the Indian popular consciousness. This presence is renewed, enhanced, each year by thousands of Ramlilas performed all across North India; and each of these Ramlilas sets up as theater a model of the Indian subcontinent. Nowhere is

Figure 4.1. *Map of India with ''historical Ramayana'' and ''mythic Ramayana'' indicated. The ''historical Ramayana'' is drawn after the opinion of Sankalia (1973).*

36. Hanuman leads Rama and his army across the sea at Rameshwaram and into Lanka, 1978. The sea is a small pool only several feet wide. This photo was probably taken in the 1960s. Photo courtesy Sangeet Natak Akademi, New Delhi.

this historical-mythical consciousness more effectively actualized than at Ramnagar.

At Ramnagar the whole *Ramayana* story is told, but with a few emphases and an addition that distinguishes it from what is related in Valmiki or the *Ramcharitmanas*. The classic Rama story has three main parts: (1) initiations, culminating in the breaking of Shiva's bow and the marriage of Rama to Sita; (2) exile and growth to maturity through battle and ordeal—a maturity that is as much spiritual, ethical, and political as it is physical in terms of effective war making—culminating in the war against Ravana; (3) Ramraj, which barely begins as the narrative ends, though it is actually in existence before the story starts since one of the "nests," or frames, of the entire epic is that the story of Rama the hero is sung to Rama the king. The various frames— very interesting from a literary and philosophical point of view (see O'Flah- erty 1982)—are not so relevant theatrically where the story of Rama is acted out, not told.

The three big movements of the epic are divided into five main parts at Ramnagar: (1) a prelude where Brahma implores Vishnu to take human form and rescue the world, which is being terrorized by Ravana and his demon cohorts; (2) the initiations of Rama, his growth to maturity through training, contesting for Sita's hand, and finally being named by Dasharatha to become king of Ayodhya; (3) his fourteen years in exile, divided into the thirteen years before Sita's kidnapping and the year after, during which the war with Ravana is fought; (4) the resumption of Ramraj, from the Bharat Milap—the moment when the exile ends and the four brothers are reunited—to Rama's coronation and teachings; and (5) the postlude, performed only at Ramnagar, where the maharaja and his family welcome the swarups to the Fort, feed them in a ceremony witnessed by a huge assembled audience, and honor them publicly. The next day, in private, the maharaja pays the performers for their services. These two actions—honoring Rama and his party publicly, paying the actors—bring the story of Rama into a field controlled by the maharaja: it frames the mythos within the political- economic realities of contemporary India. But not quite, as I shall show. Still, first as guests, then as employees; first as mythic heroes, then as subjects, the personae of Ramlila conform to the double actuality—the multiple realities— of Benares and its maharaja. The five-part narrative scheme can be presented in linear form as in figure 4.2. In terms of theatrical time, the whole cycle consists of a one-day prelude, seven days of initiations, twenty days of exile, two days of Ramraj, and two days of postlude.

This theatrical structure can be represented in another, more revealing, configuration (figure 4.3). Without the interruption of Rama's coronation brought about by Kaikeyi's insistence that Dasharatha keep his promise to her, there would be no drama, just a straight line from Rama's birth to his Ramraj. The heart of the drama is Rama's exile, the kidnapping of Sita, the war against Ravana—in a word, the drama makes plausible and exciting Vishnu's incarnation as Rama and his earthly acts as a student, son, kshatriya (warrior), king, husband, householder, protector of Brahmans, sadhu (wandering ascetic), and teacher: all of the roles possible for a devout Hindu male. The loop from day 9 through day 28 is where most of the adventure takes place. It is, literally and theatrically, Rama's journey in time and space

	1			2	
	PRELUDE			INITIATIONS	
Event	Gods beg Vishnu to incarnate himself as Rama	Rama's boyhood adventures killing demons		Contest for Shiva's bow; courtship of Sita; Marriage	Coronation stopped
Day	1	2–5		6–8	

		3A		
	MATURITY	EXILE	CRISIS	
Event	Exile begins	Journey through the forest to Chitrakut and Panchavati	Shurpanakha appears. Sita kidnapped	
Day	9	10–15	16	

		3B		4	5
		WAR	RETURN	RAMRAJ	POSTLUDE
Event	Rama pursues Ravana	War in Lanka	Return to Ayodhya Bharat Milap	Coronation and teaching	Ceremony Pay at Fort
Day	17–19	20–26	27–28	29–30	31–32

Figure 4.2

from the safety of Ayodhya to the adventures that lie in store for him at Chitrakut, Panchavati, and Lanka.

Victor Turner outlined a four-part sequence of what he calls "social dramas." These social dramas occur in trials, combats, rivalries, wars. Turner's idea applies very well to the Ramlila of Ramnagar, where a great myth has been translated into a religious-aesthetic drama with many overtones of social drama.

I define social dramas as units of aharmonic or disharmonic social process, arising in conflict situations. Typically, they have four main phases of public action. These are: (1) *breach* of regular norm-governed social relations; (2) *crisis* during which there is a tendency for the breach to widen . . . ; (3) *redressive action* ranging from personal

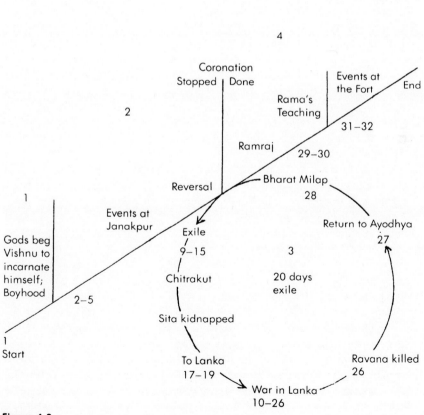

Figure 4.3

advice to informal mediation or arbitration to formal juridical and legal machinery, and, to resolve certain kinds of crisis or legitimate other modes of resolution, to the performance of public ritual . . . ; (4) the final phase consists either of the *reintegration* of the disturbed social group, or of the social recognition and legitimation of *irreparable schism* between the contesting parties. [Turner 1979*a*, 63–64]

It is no surprise that Turner's scheme fits Ramlila exactly: Turner constructed his concept of social drama from what he knew of aesthetic drama. What is interesting is how well this model works cross-culturally—in India as well as Africa, where Turner developed it to account for conflicts among the Ndembu, and Euro-America, where Shakespeare's plays and the works of other dramatists can be analyzed according to Turner's model.

For Ramlila the phases of the social drama are: (1) breach—when Kaikeyi makes her claim on Dasharatha; (2) crisis—Rama's exile, complicated by the kidnapping of Sita; (3) redressive action—the war against Ravana; (4) reintegration—the reuniting of Rama and Sita, the Bharat Milap reuniting the four brothers, the coronation of Rama, and Ramraj. At all levels a reintegration takes place: at the level of lovers, family, state, and cosmos. One could also look at Ramlila in a broader perspective and identify the breach as when Ravana obtains his boon and destroys the altars of the Brahmans, terrifying the earth. Redressive action begins immediately with the incarnation of Vishnu as Rama. But then Vishnu's lila makes necessary the performance of the Ramlila story as a narrative within a cosmic reality in order to restore the earth to harmony. In this scheme, Ravana's surrender to Rama is the decisive moment of reintegration, for it ends his rebellion.

At Ramlila itself, on Dashahara day, this surrender of Ravana is performed with particular simplicity and beauty. On preceding days there have been great battles, involving Lakshman, Hanuman, Kumbhakarna, Meghnad, Ravana, and Rama (plates 37–40). The victory in these battles goes to Rama's side but not decisively enough to end the war. On Dashahara day the narration of Ramlila itself is interrupted so that the maharaja can play out his own story, a story that he shares with other Indian kings. On Dashahara there is a special "weapons puja" where the maharaja displays in the courtyard of the Fort a panoply of swords, daggers, guns, and other implements of war (mostly from the nineteenth century, when maharajas were really kings, almost). We were not allowed to photograph this display. This prohibition signaled that it was a very special manifestation. The only parts of Ramlila off-limits to us were scenes centering around the maharaja himself: his daily puja celebrated between the afternoon and evening portions of the lila; the ceremony the day after Ramlila when the maharaja meets with, thanks, and pays the performers. We, and all of Benares, could see the weapons display, but photographs were forbidden.

After the "weapons puja" display, in an extraordinary and magnificent theatrical procession of elephants, the maharaja makes his way amidst immense crowds from the Fort, down the main street of Ramnagar, and out to Lanka more than three miles to the southeast. I noted in 1978:

Maharaja enters Lanka on his elephant, followed by the others. They ride straight through the crowd, past the battleground, turn and ride up and over the battleground. They leave Lanka the way they came—having stayed less than ten minutes, never stopping, just passing through and over. What is the meaning of this strange procession that violates the performing space? It is the only time in the Ramlila that the maharaja literally invades the performing space. Otherwise he remains firmly anchored at the back of the spectators, defining where the audience is. The "weapons puja" is what's left of a very warlike traditional display of kingly might that used to occupy maharajas on Dashahara. They would march their armies to the borders of their domain, proclaim the territory as theirs, and go home. Thus they showed their ability to make war; and they identified themselves, however vaguely, with the ancient horse-sacrifice, which Dasharatha himself performs in the *Ramayana*. Thus the maharaja here in Ramlila is staking out his territory, saying in effect that the Ramlila is his. He boldly penetrates the performing space and cuts across the battleground, showing who's boss, who's king, and over what territory. He rides to the very edge of the Ramlila ground, the end of the Ramlila world—and he goes a few hundred feet beyond, then turns his elephants, and returns. This is the farthest out anyone playing a role in Ramnagar Ramlila goes. Then the maharaja leaves Lanka; he does not see Ravana defeated. "It is not right," he told me, "for one king to watch the death of another."

In the *Ramcharitmanas* Ravana dies when one arrow "dried up the depths of Ravana's navel, others furiously smote his heads and arms and carried them away with them." The headless, armless trunk "danced upon the ground," and then Rama strikes it with an arrow, cutting it in two. But "even as he died, he roared aloud with a great and terrible yell, 'Where is Rama that I may challenge him and slay him in combat?' Earth shook as the Ten-headed fell; the sea, the rivers, the mountains and the elephants . . . were troubled. Spreading abroad the two halves of his body, he fell to the ground, crushing beneath him crowds of bears and monkeys. . . . His spirit entered the Lord's [Rama's, Vishnu's] mouth" (Tulasi Das 1952, 418–419). This furious scene is not played out in the Ramlila the way it is described by Tulsidas in the *Ramcharitmanas*. I find the differences very important. First, let it be noted that the vyases, Atmaram, and the effigy makers are perfectly capable of staging the battle as written. Kumbhakarna is beheaded and cut in two; Jatayu loses his wings. What actually happens on Dashahara is this. Late in the afternoon, after the maharaja has come and gone, Ravana sits in his chariot across the raised battlefield from Rama. About 150 feet separate them. Then Rama begins shooting arrows at Ravana. After an arrow has been

37. Hanuman and Ravana fighting, 1978. Photo by Richard Schechner.

38. Effigy of Kumbhakarna from around 1920. Photo courtesy of the Maharaja of Benares.

39. Effigy of Kumbhakarna in his Fort at Lanka, 1976. Photo by Richard Schechner.

40. Dashahara day, ca. 1825. As described by James Princep in his *Benares Illustrated* (1830), "To the right and left are observed the camps of the adverse chiefs, the fort of Lunka [*sic*] is farther behind, with giants guarding the gates. . . . The last battle, in which Rawun [*sic*] is killed, occurs on the usera [*sic*] or tenth day. This is, at Ramnugur [*sic*], the principal day of the spectacle, and is represented in the accompanying plate."

shot for each of Ravana's arms (twenty) and each head (ten), Rama shoots two more arrows—one to sever Ravana's body, one to dry up his navel. To signal that this has happened, the performer playing Ravana removes his mask of ten heads and body piece of twenty arms. Then the demon king walks the length of the battlefield and touches his head to the feet of Rama. The crowd surges to see this death, this surrender, this acceptance of Ravana by Rama. The crowd, like Brahma and Shiva in the *Ramcharitmanas*, is glad. "The universe was filled with cries of triumph." Ramnagar cops wave great staves, threatening the roaring, surging, seething crowd. What has been staged is not the final battle with its gory dismemberments—these were seen earlier with the death of Kumbhakarna. What is staged is Ravana's surrender. What is seen is Rama's lila, his "sport": the absolute ease with which he defeats the demon. What Ravana's surrender and Rama's lila signify is the reintegration of the world. The climactic military encounter is theatrically transformed into a scene of religious and cosmic harmony. The crowd is ecstatic.

Then, after giving up his spirit to Rama, the performer who was Ravana

41. Sadhus dancing and singing on Dashahara night, 1978. Photo by Richard Schechner.

42. Ravana's effigy being cremated, 1978. Photo by Richard Schechner.

turns and walks off into the crowd. His son carries the mask and body piece. The two of them are swallowed by the masses. Someone told me, though others deny it, that later in the afternoon, when his role in Ramlila is over, Ravana goes to the owners of food and tea stalls set up in Lanka to collect "Ravana's rent." In this way he gets paid something extra for his perform- ance. Those who operate businesses as part of the mela pay Ravana for occupying space in Lanka, Ravana's kingdom. Ravana does not stick around for the end of Ramlila but returns to his village some ten miles away. "I never see the end," he told me.

What remains in Lanka is the fifty-foot-high effigy of Ravana's upper torso and head(s). This giant effigy will be cremated on Dashahara night after a wild evening of celebrating (plate 41). The crowds feast, the sadhus dance and sing, the maharaja is back in his Fort, Rama has triumphed. Through fire, the flames streaking scores of feet into the night sky, Ravana is liberated and ascends to Vishnu (plate 42). The war is over.

Environments, Mise-en-Scène, and Directionality

Just as there was a Troy and a Trojan War, so there were occurrences that underlie the *Ramayana*. These events probably took place in northern and central India, from Ayodhya on the river Sarayu, south to Allahabad (Prayag), west to Chitrakut, and southwest to what was a forested area north of the river Narmada. But as the telling of the *Ramayana* spread southward along with, as part of, Sanskritization, so did its field of geographical refer- ences (see figure 4.1). "The gradual spread, first of the *Mahabharata* and then of the *Ramayana* into the Deccan, Karnataka, and Tamil Nadu, shows the slow absorption by society, high and low, of certain ethical values. . . . Simul- taneously places all over India came to be associated with episodes in the *Ramayana*" (Sankalia 1973, 55).

As the *Ramayana* stories spread—were carried person-to-person south and east—they were identified with local deities and sacred places. Indian culture, like Japanese, does not reject its past when something new comes along. Rather, the culture remembers everything and displays it in a palimp- sest. Thus, in many events, Ramlila among them, one can detect pre-Hindu, Hindu, Muslim, and English elements. Certainly the Hindu coloring is domi- nant, but it is not alone. The sacred rivers and crossings are surely pre-Hindu; the pomp of the maharaja and his very dress owe as much to Mogul influ- ences as to the Hindu ideas of kingship; the maharaja's marching band, his Cadillac, the Petromax lanterns that are "old-fashioned" in the minds of most spectators, and traditional, are all of Euro-American origins. These are just a few examples of many that could be cited to demonstrate the multicultural dimensions of Ramlila. But this multiculturality is natural in India (as elsewhere).

The very geography of Ramlila of Ramnagar echoes with very ancient pre-Hindu and Hindu references. And the geography of Ramlila—its hilltops, rivers and river junctions, cities, temples, caves, trees, wells, and paths—are models of actual places that carry and emit bundles of significance. "The number of Hindu sanctuaries in India is so large and the practice of pilgrimage so ubiquitous that the whole of India can be regarded as a vast sacred space organized into a system of pilgrimage centers and their fields" (Bhardwaj 1973, 7). The centers indicate stasis, and the fields motion: this is the pattern of Ramlila, from intense activity to the stillness of the murtis during arati. The *Ramcharitmanas* tells the story of Rama's adventures as they were retold by a great sixteenth-century religious poet. These adventures differ somewhat from the *Ramayana*. In *Ramcharitmanas* Rama knows he is god; he knows the outcome of his adventures. Thus the whole drama becomes a kind of conscious and reflexive display: a watching in the mirror. This makes it very natural to the story that a crowd of spectators should follow Rama wherever he goes. Rama is twice-born, his story twice-told. And Rama's adventures are actually his journeys; and his journeys are the spectator's pilgrimages. Without exile there would be no kidnapping, and without kidnapping no flight to Lanka, and without flight to Lanka no great war—a war that is prepared for by a long march south and east from Panchavati to Rameshwaram and across the great stone bridge to Lanka. Many Ramlilas are staged in environments that are spread over distances that make the spectators move from place to place, literally imitating Rama by following him in order to attend to his story. This kind of processional performance is very common around the world. But, in my experience at least, nowhere is it so highly developed, so sophisticated and full of levels of meaning, as at Ramnagar Ramlila.

Seen spatially, in terms of cultural geography, the Ramlila moves between two poles: Ayodhya = home = Ramnagar = the maharaja's Fort = rightful authority versus Lanka = away = beyond the city = Ravana = unlawful authority (see figures 4.4 and 4.5). In between is a no-man's-land of demons and rishis, friendly monkeys and bears, hostile and friendly tribes, rivers, jungle. Between the just order of Ayodhya (where promises are kept, even while ethical Bharat refuses to rule in Rama's absence) and the unjust order of Lanka is the adventurous unknown domain of chaotic mountains and jungle. This is a mythopoetic map of India as drawn by its Hindus from the time of their first invasions more than three thousand years ago. The jungle and mountains are appealing because here reside the greatest saints and ascetics, the folk heroes of India. Extraordinarily, these geocultural categories have remained more or less constant from Valmiki's time (fourth century B.C.–second century A.D.). The categories are seen today not only in the deep respect for ascetics and renouncers but also in continuing tensions between India's "scheduled castes and tribes," its *harijans* (literally, "children of god"; operatively, "untouchables") and tribal peoples, and other Indians whose ritual-social status is more acceptable; and in the interplay between the relatively few cities and the vast rural population. The environment at Ayodhya is modeled on the interior courtyards of the maharaja's Fort—which are very much like palaces and great homes all over North India. The vast field of Lanka is a self-contained otherworld far to the southeast of Ayodhya. Lanka contains several structures, including Ravana's Fort, which looks like a primitive battlement. Old photographs show that it was once more impressive and even more primitive looking. From one perspective Ravana is a "great king"; from another, he is a savage. Between Lanka and Ayodhya are rivers, forests, hermitages, and other less extravagantly worked-out environments. There are two exceptions. Janakpur is several kilometers to the northeast of Ayodhya and is a very intricately worked-out environment of several buildings, a pleasure garden, small temples, and auxiliary structures (see figure 4.6). Janakpur is more developed than Ayodhya, probably because Ayodhya is hard by the maharaja's Fort and is identified with it. Ayodhya is also not allowed to be in competition with the maharaja's palace complex. The other fully worked-out environment is Rambagh, once actually the "pleasure garden" of the maharajas of Benares. The marble latticework gazebo in the center of the large, four-gated, walled-in garden is a good piece of work. Only at the very end of the Ramlila is Rambagh part of the drama—as the site for Rama's teachings, at the moment of Ramraj when all of Ramnagar has been transformed in Ayodhya. But, earlier, Rambagh figures in the Ramlila both as the workshop of technical director Atmaram and as a dharamsala where the swarups spend a number of days living and rehearsing. And the imposing outer walls of Rambagh form a backdrop for the very first lila when Ravana ravages the world; and for the lila depicting Visnu's awakening from his cosmic nap on the *kshir sagar*, the ocean of milk. Chitrakut is placed close to Rambagh, and Rama's route from Chitrakut to Panchavati takes him around Rambagh. So Rambagh—though used in the drama only once—figures very strongly in the theater of Ramlila (see Schechner 1977 for the distinction between drama and theater). It, along with the Fort and Lanka, forms a triangle-boundary of the whole Ramlila environment.

Ramlila is environmental theater on the grand scale. The environment as a whole and individual environments for each lila are at the core of the narrative, from the level of the *Ramayana* and the *Ramcharitmanas* to the level of the maharaja of Benares. That is, all of the various themes of Ramlila from

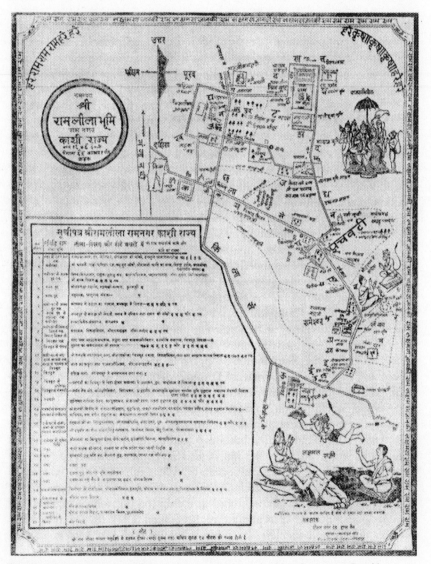

Figure 4.4. *Program-map distributed to spectators at the 1946 Ramnagar Ramlila*

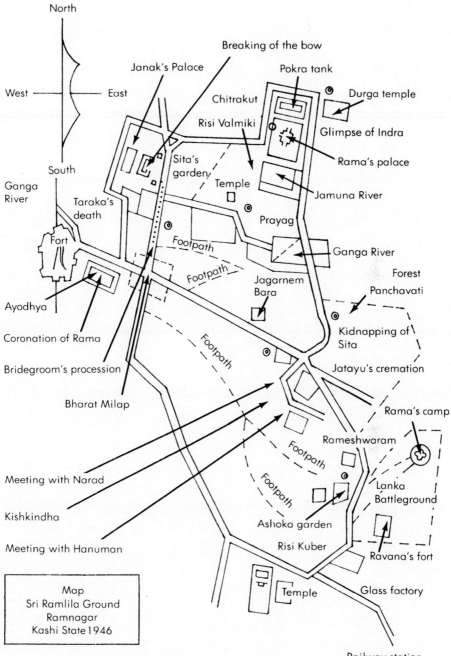

North

West —— East

South

Ganga
River

Janak's Palace

Breaking of the bow

Pokra tank

Chitrakut

Durga temple

Risi Valmiki

Glimpse of Indra

Sita's
garden

Rama's palace

Temple

Jamuna River

Taraka's
death

Prayag

Footpath

Ganga River

Footpath

Forest
Panchavati

Fort

Jagarnem
Bara

Ayodhya

Kidnapping of
Sita

Coronation of Rama

Footpath

Jatayu's cremation

Bridegroom's procession

Bharat Milap

Rama's camp

Rameshwaram

Meeting with Narad

Footpath

Lanka
Battleground

Kishkindha

Footpath

Meeting with Hanuman

Ashoka garden

Risi Kuber

Ravana's fort

Glass factory

Map
Sri Ramlila Ground
Ramnagar
Kashi State 1946

Railway station

Figure 4.5. *This program was used in 1946. At present map-programs are not used, though a program giving a synopsis of each day's lila is distributed. The 1946 map-program is reasonably accurate in terms of location and scale. There is more text in the Hindi original (figure 4.4) than has been translated. This is because the original measures 11 × 14 inches.*

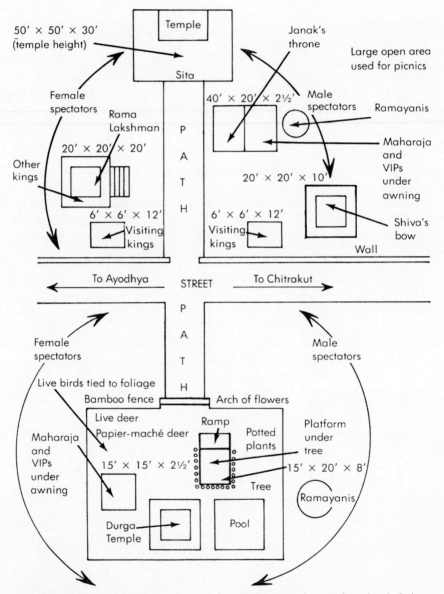

50' × 50' × 30'
(temple height)

Temple

Sita

Janak's
throne

Large open area
used for picnics

Female
spectators

Rama
Lakshman

40' × 20' × 2½'

Male
spectators

Ramayanis

20' × 20' × 20'

P
A
T
H

Maharaja
and
VIPs
under
awning

Other
kings

20' × 20' × 10'

6' × 6' × 12'

Visiting
kings

6' × 6' × 12'

Visiting
kings

Shiva's
bow

Wall

To Ayodhya   STREET   To Chitrakut

P
A
T
H

Female
spectators

Male
spectators

Live birds tied to foliage

Bamboo fence   Arch of flowers

Live deer

Papier-maché deer

Ramp

Potted
plants

Platform
under
tree

Maharaja
and
VIPs
under
awning

15' × 15' × 2½'

15' × 20' × 8'

Tree

Ramayanis

Durga
Temple

Pool

Figure 4.6 *Environments at Janakpur: Side with Sita's garden used on day 3. Side
with Shiva's bow used on day 4.*

epic literature to contemporary politics are stated spatially. The environments not only set things in the theatrical sense, they iconoize in the mythic-religious sense: the struggle of the incarnated king Rama versus the demon king Ravana—a struggle publicly observed by the present king Vibhuti Narain Singh; the maharaja and his city versus the not-yet-civilized countryside; the love for the sophisticated palace life versus the simple life of the peasants, the tribals, and the renouncers. In fact, Rama's life as shown in Ramlila is nearly evenly divided into three parts that represent an ancient ideal: one-third as king, one-third as warrior, one-third as renouncer-wanderer. Except that in Rama the sequence is reversed.

But why organize the cycle here at Ramnagar on such a vast scale? Induja Awasthi suggests: "Ramnagar was predominantly a Muslim population, and the Maharaja, in the 19th century, in a bid to restore the lost glory to the Hindus and to win them over, might have decided to accord state recognition to the Ramlila" (n.d., 2). The maharaja discounts Awasthi's idea, saying that his forebears copied the older Krishnalila of Vrindaban, which is staged environmentally. But Hess and I think Awasthi's explanation, though by no means the whole story, has merit. Until Independence in 1947, the maharajas of Benares were rulers of their realm, and their endorsement of Ramlila, their deployment of its settings across a large territory (larger-seeming in the mid-nineteenth century than now), can be regarded as a political act. Rama is that incarnation of Vishnu who rules as a king, who defends his honor as a soldier, who conquers a whole subcontinent. Rama's reign is known as Ramraj, a golden age. The Ramnagar Ramlila developed during the early period of modern Hindu nationalism and is doubtlessly associated with it, a main expression of it.

The audience at Ramlila takes naturally to a performance that includes procession (see figure 4.7): the crossing by Rama of an imitation Ganga and Jamuna, the long journey of Hanuman from Lanka northward to the Himalayas in search of the herb that will restore Lakshman after he has been wounded by Meghnad's shakti weapon, the magnificently slow two-day return journey from Lanka to the boxing-ring-like square where the Bharat Milap is staged, the regal procession on elephant from Rambagh to the Fort the night after Rama's coronation when the maharaja feeds Rama, Sita, and the other swarups—or, on a more modest scale, the thin line of followers behind Rama and Lakshman as they wind through the back pathways of Ramnagar on Rama's first adventure, his encounter with the demon Taraka on his way from Ayodhya to Janakpur.

The Ramnagar Ramlila cycle condenses much of the Indian subcontinent into a comprehensible single sacred space with nine main stations: Ayodhya, Janakpur, Chitrakut, Panchavati, Rameshwaram, Lanka, Bharat Milap

Square, Rambagh, and the Fort. Add to these the ponds that serve as the Ganga and Jamuna and you have a map of sacred India according to *Ramcharitmanas*. Remember that most of the spectators at Ramlila will not travel, even as pilgrims, far from where they were born. Their experience at Ramlila—during a month out from ordinary time—is an actual/metaphorical moving through Rama's India. Their experience of following Rama is somewhere between "going to a play," an entertainment, and some kind of ritual procession through a space that has become what it represents in much the same way as the boys who play swarups have become murtis, the gods incarnate. Without suggesting any disrespect, one might say that the feeling is parallel to what happens to Americans when they go to Disneyland and enter the "Magic Kingdom" or visit any one of the hundreds of "restored villages" that mark the American landscape. These places create, or re-create, or actualize, American history and imagination. The stations of Ramlila are anchor points of a very carefully organized system of movements and directional significations.

Ramnagar literally means "town of Rama." I'm not sure whether the town name or the Ramlila performance came first. But like so much that is part of the Ramnagar Ramlila, the doing of a thing—literally (in the Greek sense) a drama—is tied in with the name of the thing done; thus Ramnagar, the boatman Ramdas, the technical director Atmaram. Others have been absorbed into their roles. Narad is called Narad in his ordinary life, and his authority and wealth have considerably increased because of his reputation as a powerful performer in Ramlila. Brahma was played in 1976 and 1978

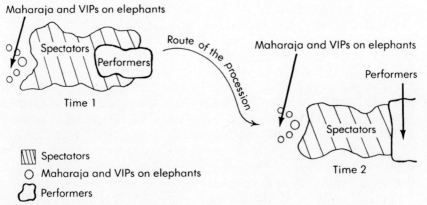

Figure 4.7. Procession. *During several lilas the performance moves from one place to another. Sometimes there is simply the move and sometimes action occurs on the road.*

by a man who had performed the role for decades, a man said in 1978 to be ninety-six years old, and looking it: his feeble voice, gentleness, and very distant-looking eyes becoming, for me at least, an incarnation as well as a representation of the god Brahma. He is now dead. Other performers are more ordinary in their theatrical identities. There is nothing Hanuman-like about the man who plays Hanuman, and a number of other roles too. But there was "old Hanuman," who died in 1981 in his eighties. In 1978 he still had a booming voice but was not strong enough to carry both Rama and Lakshman on his shoulders simultaneously, a requirement of Hanuman. Old Hanuman attended the swarups wherever they were: in their dharamsalas resting, playing, eating, or rehearsing; or onstage where old Hanuman fanned them with a fly whisk, held their feet, and saw to their immediate needs. Thus this person who performed Hanuman in Ramlila for more than thirty years played his role's essence as a stagehand and personal attendant.

As with the characters, so with the town of Ramnagar (see figure 4.5). During the first half of the nineteenth century, under the supervision of the maharajas of that time, numerous stage settings were built throughout the town in order to provide places for the various Ramlila events. Some places, like Chitrakut, were raised platforms over which for Ramlila a giant canopy could be thrown. Others, like Janakpur, combined several raised platforms of various heights with small temples and gardens covering several acres. Existing ponds were brought into the Ramlila or modified to serve as the rivers Ganga and Jamuna. And, as noted, some environments, like the Fort, are used as is—neatly superimposing mythopoetic place over actual contemporary place in a palimpsest that owes its special power over the crowds to the confluence of significances. In the old days, according to the maharaja, some Ramlila locations—Janakpur, Rambagh, Panchavati—had their own plots of land attached where crops were grown. The proceeds from these crops were used to maintain the location. Now these arable lands are gone. It is much harder to get the money to keep up the environments.

So there are theatrical environments of all types: those built from scratch, those adapted from what is already in use, and those used as is, "found spaces." This layering of the types of environments gives Ramnagar Ramlila an impressive reality of its own. It seems to properly belong to and in Ramnagar, and the special environments—Ayodhya, Janakpur, Lanka— emerge naturally from adapted and found spaces.

Once more, and very significantly, the actual orientation of these spaces, as well as their positions relative to each other, is a reasonably accurate model not only of India and Sri Lanka but also of Rama's movements through the countryside. Lanka is far to the southeast of Ayodhya (which is next to the Fort); Janakpur is to the north; Chitrakut and Panchavati are to the northeast.

Rambagh is also to the northeast, and this is where Ramlila begins and where Ramraj is celebrated with Rama's teachings. The northeast, I'm told, is an auspicious direction.

The action of Ramlila is thus both physical and narrative. The actual movement of the characters is itself a decisive part of the story. The first night of the performance, when the gods implore Vishnu to incarnate himself and rescue the world, takes place on and around the kshir sagar (the Pokra tank of the Durga temple), in the good-luck northeast. When Rama goes into exile, he crosses make-believe Ganga and Jamuna as he heads from Ayodhya in the northwest back toward Chitrakut in the northeast. After Sita is captured, Rama's army moves steadily southeastward. This move is analogous to the historical movement through India of the Sanskritic culture the Aryan invaders of India brought with them. And it's no accident that in parts of South India Ravana is regarded as a hero, for at one level of the *Ramayana* story he represents the original culture of the area. Among the poems the Aryans brought with them was the *Ramayana*—or at least an ur-*Ramayana*. The Aryan story merged with Dravidian tales and other native traditions. This merging included absorption of sacred places and routes. And it is this movement and absorption of sacred action and place that the Ramlila reenacts.

After climactic battles at Lanka, battles that have looked more or less the same for 150 years, Rama victorious and his party are loaded into the pushpaka, which flies in *Ramcharitmanas* but is pulled with great vigor through the mud and over the roads by the people of Ramnagar in Ramlila. The return trip is a recapitulation narratively and spatially of Rama's adventures. As Rama says in the *Ramcharitmanas*,

"Sita," said Raghubir, "look at the battlefield; that is where Lakshman slew Indrajit, and those huge demons lying on the field were slain by Hanuman and Angad; and here was killed Kumbhakarna and Ravana, the two brothers who discomfitted gods and sages. Here I had the bridge built and set up the image of Shiva, abode of bliss." The gracious lord and Sita did obeisance to Shambhu. Where the Lord of grace had encamped or rested in the forest, he pointed out every place to Janaki and told her the name of each.

Swiftly the car travelled on to the most beautiful forest of Dandaka, where dwelt Agastya and many other high sages; and Rama visited the homes of them all. After receiving the blessing of all the seers, the Lord of the world came to Chitrakut, there he gladdened the hermits, and the car sped swiftly on. Next, Rama pointed out to Janaki the Jamuna . . . then they beheld the holy Ganga. . . . "Next," he said, "behold Prayag . . . and now behold the city of Ayodhya." [Tulasi Das 1952, 429]

For theatrical reasons, in Ramlila the return trip is much more direct, though it does take two days. But there is no retrogressive crossing of rivers, no visit to Chitrakut. Rama describes and recounts but does not repeat the outward journey. The pushpaka rests one night near a sacred tree (sacred to residents of Ramnagar but not mentioned in the *Ramcharitmanas*) and another at Bharadwaj's ashram. During the day kids play on the pushpaka. And on the third night the reunion, the Bharat Milap, takes place in the main town square of Ramnagar.

Once Rama enters Ayodhya to be crowned, a marvelous conflation of time and space takes place. All the Ramlila places become part of Rama's kingdom, and the whole of Ramnagar becomes Ayodhya. Thus Rama goes to his Rambagh to preach, he travels through the streets of his Ayodhya-Ramnagar on his elephant as a king would proceed through his own capital, and finally he is welcomed by the maharaja at the Fort: one king receiving another. There, assisted by the royal family, Rama and his family have their feet washed, are garlanded, and fed a sumptuous meal. This feeding takes a very long time, hours, and I mused that the boys who were enacting nearly their last scene as swarups were prolonging it and deeply enjoying a unique situation where they were being honored, worshiped, and fed by the maharaja of Benares. Thousands of townspeople crowd into the courtyard of the Fort to watch.

Something very powerful theatrically and religiously takes place, creating a unique social, even political, situation. This situation climaxes during the meeting of kings at the Fort, but it has been present and building through the month of Ramlila. In 1949, two years after India won its independence through a long and bitter revolutionary struggle, the principalities were abolished. After all, not only were Gandhi's and Nehru's ideals those of democracy, but also some of India's maharajas were on the British side, less than lukewarm to Gandhi's populism and Nehru's secularism. The privy purses were discontinued (though the All-India Kashiraj Trust, the maharaja's foundation, receives government money to produce Ramlila). Despite all this, everyone calls Vibhuti Narain Singh "Maharaja." And this title is not honorific or nostalgic, though it has elements of both. It is operational: it works in the world of today. Why is this so? The answer, in no small way, is to be found in Ramlila. For the Ramlila season, especially during the celebration of the arati ritual that concludes each evening's show, the murtis (literally "images" of the gods)—the boys playing Rama, Sita, Lakshman, Bharat, Shatrughna—are thought by many in the audience to actually be the gods they otherwise represent. It is a miracle analogous to transubstantiation in Catholicism.

The presence of the murtis bestows on their patron, host, and theatrical producer a royalty that might by now be much eclipsed (as it is with many other former maharajas). But it's not quite that simple. There is something more like a symbiotic, syncretic feedback going on—a circumstance tied up with the whole physical setting of Ramnagar Ramlila, its function as a pilgrimage center, the particular sanctity of Kashi, and the role in that sacred complex of the maharaja. For a month, in a whole town, Rama lives and moves throughout the town. The maharaja of Benares is the only person with enough religious-traditional force to sponsor a great Ramlila—to sponsor it and participate in it as one of the principal figures/characters. For the Ramlila he sponsors validates his maharajadom: it gives him a chance to appear on his elephant, displays him before the crowds in a darshan of regal splendor; it allows him to manage a great religious and devotional event, confirming in the popular imagination his own authenticity as a ruler-manager. And, through his daily practice of sandhya puja—when the performance stops, and everyone but the maharaja rests, eats, strolls—the maharaja publicly and yet secretly displays his religiosity. For often a temporary enclosure is set up, into which the maharaja retreats for puja: everyone can see where he is going, and everyone presumes to know what he is doing; yet he does it privately. Ultimately, the climactic visit of mythic-theatrical Rama to the Fort of the actual-mythic-theatrical maharaja is an intersection of ancient and modern, mythic and theatrical, actual and transformative, extraordinary and ordinary—a historical circumstance that would please Pirandello and Genet.

The details of the performance of Ramlila also underline the great importance of the environments, of movement, of directionality. More than half of the lilas include journeys, processions, or pilgrimages. Movement from place to place is the most salient theatrical action of Ramlila. The permanent environments for Ayodhya, Janakpur, Chitrakut, Panchavati, the rivers Ganga and Jamuna, Rameshwaram, and Lanka are linked by processions that trace the outline of the story. Instead of ending one day's show in place *A* and beginning the next day in place *B,* often the movement from *A* to *B* is the start of or even most of the performance. A very short scene in one place will begin a lila, and then comes a long procession to a new performance area. Some of these processions are great events: Rama's and Sita's marriage procession returning from Janakpur to Ayodhya; the start of Rama's exile when many spectators, weeping, follow him into the forest; the procession of elephants on Dashahara day when the maharaja rides among the 100,000 spectators who line the way and follow him from the Fort to Lanka (plate 43). Especially tumultuous is the two-day return from Lanka of victorious Rama, culminating in the Bharat Milap.

For the performances of 1976 these were my notes:

Day 27, 7:30 P.M. After Sita passes her fire ordeal, she takes her place on a huge, 20-foot-high cart next to Rama and Lakshman. Dozens of male spectators tug on the two

43. Lanka on Dashahara, 1976. A crowd that some estimate at 100,000 gathers to celebrate Rama's victory over Ravana. Ravana's huge effigy, which will be cremated in the evening, is seen in the upper right. Photo by Richard Schechner.

ropes moving the four-wheeled carriage out of Lanka and down the long road toward Ayodhya. Many in the crowd of 100,000 follow, and many go on ahead: the road is all people. After a few hundred yards the cart stops—it is Bharadwaj's ashram, where Rama will spend the night. Arati is performed. The lila is over.

The performers do not actually spend the night on the set. They are carried back to their residence near the Fort. But, interestingly enough, partly as a practical consideration and partly to help the boys who play the murtis to experience their roles, their place of residence changes during the Ramlila. They begin living near the Fort; then, during the days in Chitrakut and Panchavati, they live at Rambagh; during the days of war in Lanka, they live in Lanka; and during the final days of celebration, they live, once more, near the Fort. So the performers, too, make a ritual journey that is a model of the narrative. At the end of each night's performance, the swarups are carried back to where they will sleep, eat, and rehearse. On that twenty-seventh day in 1976 I recorded this scene:

One of the last images of the night: five men trotting down the street with the five boys, the swarups, on their shoulders. These actors' feet do not touch the ground while they are in costume, while they wear the crowns that confer on them their status as swarups, unless they are also playing their roles. And then it is presumed that the ground they walk on is holy. So they are carried to and from the performance grounds—either on men's shoulders or in bullock-drawn carts, or by some other conveyance. But this time as they go by, still in the costumes of their gods-characters but no longer in the lila, which is finished for the night, there are no shouts of "Jai Ram!" from the crowd: the swarups are noticed, the people fall back and make room for their passing, but they are not actively adored. Like temple icons they are being put away for the night.

The twenty-eighth day's lila begins with several scenes happening simultaneously in different parts of Ramnagar. All these scenes will converge at the Bharat Milap staged in the town's center. At Nandigram near the Fort, Bharat and Shatrughna sit under a bower waiting for the word of when Rama, who is close at hand, will meet them. In the Fort, the maharaja and his court are mounting elephants for a grand procession to Ramnagar's main intersection where the Bharat Milap will take place. A mile or so away at Bharadwaj's ashram, Rama and his court begin their very slow progression toward the Bharat Milap square. Sitting in their big wagon, looking very much like a big extended family, are Rama, Sita, Lakshman, Hanuman, Jambavan, the bear general, Sugriva and his nephew Angad, the forest chief, Guha, the head vyas, several assistant vyases, the old vyas whose job it was to shout, "Keep quiet! Pay attention!" before each recitation of samvad, and others who have found their way onto the pushpaka: friends, small children, relatives. I don't know exactly what the rules are for riding on the pushpaka. As the wagon rolls over ground covered before, Rama points out the sights to Sita to all: "This lovely city is the place where I was born" (Tulasi Das, 1952, 433).

8:30 P.M. Bharat gets the news from Hanuman that Rama is approaching. Bharat and Shatrughna set out for the high stage near the arch, the site of the Bharat Milap. Meanwhile, the maharaja and his party on elephants ride out to greet Rama. As the maharaja proceeds down the street from the gate of the Fort to the Bharat Milap square, flares are lit to illuminate him more brightly. People look up at him from the street, down at him from the roofs, across at him from windows. The maharaja greets Rama, takes darshan, and then positions himself at the square to await the reunion of the brothers.

9:00 P.M. Rama continues his slow advance. It reminds me of a Robert Wilson performance. Everyone knows what is going to happen and can trace out in advance the map of the action; but it takes forever for it to actually physically happen, and in that space of waiting, a certain meditation occurs. At many temples and at many displays of sacred murtis, Rama's pushpaka halts, he gives darshan, and the white flare of arati is ignited. Much could be made of the continuing importance, from perhaps pre-Vedic days, of fire, the sun, illumination, in Indian worship. Rama himself is scion of the Solar Race, a Sun King, a king of fire.

Up and down the street from the Fort to the arch several blocks beyond Bharat Milap square are colored lights, puppet shows, small temples with groups of people chanting bhajans. Vendors sell tea, sweets, snacks, temple beads, ocher and yellow powders for making holy marks, betel nuts, cigarettes. The sights, sounds, smells, sense of the whole thing are a perfect mixture, blending, of the sacred and the profane:

to such a degree that the distinction is no longer viable. There is the experience. It is whole, total.

Some displays are traditional images rigged with contemporary engineering, like the electrically powered figure of Hanuman who opens his own chest to reveal his heart, on which is engraved an image of Rama and Sita. Some displays are of old-fashioned painted clay figures.

10:30 P.M. The wagon meets the square stage where the Bharat Milap will take place. Rama and Lakshman step from the wagon onto the stage. Bharat and Shatrughna have been standing there for a few minutes. The four boys rush across the stage and embrace; they kiss each other's feet. The flares burn. The crowd roars. The maharaja watches in what I suppose is full and joyous approval.

But the maharaja maintains his mask perfectly. It is not possible to get inside or behind that mask. He is what he performs. Once I asked him:

RS: Do you believe that the boys are gods?

MR: If you see a Christian movie, like *The Robe*, what do you feel?

RS: I feel it's a representation, done with devotion maybe, but still a great distance from being God.

MR: The same, I feel the same.

But now, writing this some seven years after that interview and having watched the maharaja through one entire Ramlila (1978), I think he misrepresented his feelings—insofar as those feelings are manifest in his actions. His actions speak devotion—and a seeing through the swarups to whatever it is that he feels is divine. In the Hindu context the divine is not a simple thing to define, nor is it radically separable from ordinary human existence. As with so much else in Indian culture, the divine exists as a palimpsest: it is there in ordinary life, it manifests itself in incarnations and less forceful presences such as rishis, sadhus, devout individuals; and it is present in an essential, highly refined, substance as the Ramlila murtis who are, and represent, at the same time what they are presumed to be (plates 44–45).

But not everyone feels—or acts during Ramlila—this way. Many are not watching arati but munching snacks; many come for the show alone or do not attend at all—even people of great authority. Ramesh Chandra De, now dead but longtime personal secretary to the maharaja, said in 1978 when Hess and I asked him why he didn't attend Ramlila anymore: "My views on Ramlila have not changed. It is all playacting. Can you take street urchins and make them gods?" De's opinion is definitely in the minority. His characterization of the swarups as "street urchins" reflected his ironic sense of things. He knew as well as anyone the care with which the boys who perform

44. *From left to right:* Lakshman, Rama, and Sita. This photo dates from the 1920s. Photo courtesy of the Maharaja of Benares.

45. A devotee of Rama in about 1920. He is touching Rama's feet as Rama prepares to cross the Ganga during his exile. Apparently in past times the actual Ganga was used in the Ramlila. Nowadays the scene is played on a small pond near Rambagh that signifies the Ganga. Photo courtesy of the Maharaja of Benares.

in Ramlila are selected. The vyases search for candidates who must be Brahmans, well-behaved, with "good looks" (itself a complicated criterion) and strong voices. Their families must agree to their participation in Ramlila, which means giving up school for three months. Finally, when the number of possible swarups has been reduced to the top candidates, the maharaja himself auditions them. He talks to them, listens to them recite, looks them over. He makes the final selection. They move to a dharamsala near the Fort in July and begin rehearsals. They are paid for their work, and the method of payment signals a return to the non-Ramlila world after the cycle of performances is ended. The day after Ramlila ends, the swarups and major characters come to the Fort, where the maharaja thanks them for their efforts. In 1976 each swarup got 440 rupees, a considerable sum but no fortune, especially considering the work they did over more than three months. Other principal participants—actors, vyases, technical director—are paid too. Many confided in us that the pay was inadequate. And the maharaja complained that the funds available to him for Ramlila were inadequate. Wealth, which used to flow as from a limitless treasury of a great maharaja, is increasingly scarce. The maharaja knows that this lack of funds threatens the Ramlila. He wonders how his "industries" will do, whether or not his son will be as devoted to Ramlila as he is, what the future of the whole enterprise will be.

There is, on the day before the full payment made in private, a public ritual payment of one rupee to each swarup during the Kot Vidai, or Farewell, at the Fort. Nowhere is the special place of the maharaja demonstrated more clearly than on this last day of Ramlila, a ceremony unique to Ramnagar. Although a portion of the *Ramcharitmanas* remains to be chanted, the events of the "thirty-first day" are outside the Rama story. Late in the afternoon (or at night, as in 1978, when an eclipse of the moon on the second day of Ramlila skewed the whole schedule),[5] riding two magnificent elephants, the five swarups arrive at the Fort. The maharaja, dressed simply, barefoot, greets them as if they were visiting royalty. They are seated on a platform, and their feet are washed by the maharaja, who also applies tilak to their foreheads and garlands them. He performs arati to them as if he were a temple priest (he is a Brahman) and they gods. Then the swarups are served a sumptuous meal. The Ramayanis chant the final portions of the *Ramcharitmanas*. As the swarups eat, the maharaja is handed a one-rupee coin by one of his attendants, and he hands this coin to a vyas who gives it to Hanuman who gives it to Rama: in this way each of the five swarups is paid. Then each of the Ramayanis and the other principal performers take one rupee from the maharaja via the vyas. I believe this public gesture of paying the performers is an affirmation, at the end of Ramlila, of the order of the non-Ramlila world: it shows who's king. A nemi (a devout and knowledgeable Ramlila-goer) disagrees: "It is the dharma [duty] of a king to give money to the Brahmans." As with so much in Ramlila, the two interpretations do not cancel each other out. After the swarups have eaten—it takes them more than an hour—the maharaja performs arati again. Then each of the swarups takes off his garland the puts it on the maharaja. This gesture is repeated with members of the royal family, each of whom gives and receives garlands from the swarups. During Ramlila is the only time when the females of the royal family are out of purdah. (Purdah is the system of concealing all of the female body, including the face, whenever a woman goes into a public place. It was adopted by some Hindus from the Muslims.) Then elephants arrive to take the swarups back to Ayodhya where they give darshan, and the royal family retires inside the Fort.

The ceremony of the thirty-first day is trivalent: the maharaja is paying his performers, he and his family are welcoming visiting royalty, and he is worshiping gods. All three events take place simultaneously, being accomplished by the same set of gestures—the meanings radiate outward through three frames, that of Ramnagar where Vibhuti Narain Singh is king, that of the mythic narrative where Rama and the others are legendary figures, that of the cosmic-religious Hindu system of reality where gods are incarnate and manifest themselves (figure 4.8). The largest event cosmically is contained within a mythic event, which in turn is contained within the social order of Ramnagar. And through this ceremony of multivocal reduction, of the lesser reality containing the larger, and the private payment that takes place within the Fort the next day, a month of extraordinary happenings is ended; things are returned to the ordinary. In Turner's language, a reintegration has occurred.

Maharaja, Ramayanis, Rama, Sadhus

The maharaja and Rama are mirror images of each other, the twin heroes of the Ramnagar Ramlila. The maharaja is as much a mythic figure as Rama.

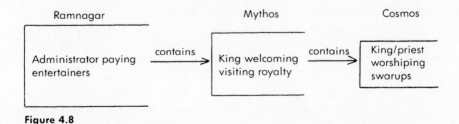

Figure 4.8

His real political power is gone, relegated to history along with the British raj. But throughout the Ramlila, his maharaja-ness is displayed, more than at any other time in the year. He appears on his elephant, raised far above the masses of people; or he rides in his horse-drawn carriage. Occasionally he is seated in the plush of his elegant 1928 Cadillac. Always he is accompanied by a dignified elderly man, the maharaja's companion—"someone to talk to," the maharaja told me, though in all the hours of observing them riding together I have never seen a word pass between them. Also, the maharaja at Ramlila appears in many different guises: for the wedding of Rama and Sita he is dressed in full turban and glorious silks; for Dashahara he is similarly dressed but with some royal details added; on other days he may wear plainer clothes; at coronation dawn arati he has on a military-style overseas cap. Among the people—and we spoke to many, all of whom confirmed our observations—the maharaja is honored as an upholder of religion, a repository of tradition and authority. His job as sponsor of the Ramlila is recognized as a difficult one. Several people spoke affectionately of the "poor maharaja" who was doing his best to keep up the old traditions in the face of myriad difficulties. In Varanasi the maharaja's reputation is based on something more than nostalgia: the rulers there are known for their support of the arts and learning, as well as for their piety. And Vibhuti Narain Singh has been on the throne since 1936, reaching majority in 1947.

The maharaja is the representative of Shiva, who is considered the lord of ancient, holy Kashi. The identification with Shiva is so complete that everywhere the maharaja goes he is hailed by great rolling roars of "Hara, Hara, Mahadev!," a greeting for Shiva. And while the maharaja is cheered as a god in the Ramlila, Rama is cheered as a king. The traditional shout that goes up whenever Rama speaks is "Bol Ramchandra ki jai!" ("Victory to King Ramchandra!"). This inverse link between the two kings/deities is a helix at the heart of Ramnagar Ramlila.

The maharaja himself recognizes this situation but denies his personal enhancement of it:

RS: The people call you "Mahadev."

MR: It's not personally for me. It is for my whole family. My ancestor who started the dynasty also began a renaissance of Hinduism.

RS: The Ramlila is part of the renaissance?

MR: The Ramlila was started by Tulsidas. My family gave it a push.

RS: For the people, the eternal realm of Rama is mirrored in the role of your family?

MR: Not quite.

RS: But Ramlila is the only drama I know of that can't begin until a certain spectator arrives. What happens if you are sick?

MR: Some member of my family must represent me.

RS: That means?

MR: It is really an administrative aspect. Someone must be in control. From the audience point of view, my presence does give some prestige. Someone has to take the lead. It is also spiritual: in the *Ramayana,* Shiva tells the story to Parvati. So the representative of Shiva must be there.

This last comment is extremely revealing. In a sense, the whole Ramlila is the maharaja's-Shiva's story: he is telling it while Parvati (in the maharaja's case, a woman still in purdah, often barely visible behind a curtain) and the vast audiences listen.

Usually the maharaja, positioned on his elephant, alongside several other elephants bearing various VIPs, forms one of the spatial limits of a scene, with Rama forming the other (see figure 4.9). Both maharaja and Rama are elevated, though the maharaja is usually the higher of the two. The audience is on ground level, except at Ayodhya where women and children sit on the walls and roof of the palace. In some scenes, the gods are represented by large effigies fixed atop very tall bamboo poles, forty-five to fifty feet high, overlooking the whole spectacle. These gods are the ultimate spectators.

The maharaja is often very far from the action. But he is scrupulously aware of the specific gestures necessary for his role:

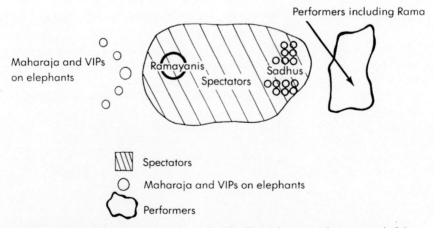

Figure 4.9. *Spectators, Rama, and the maharaja. The maharaja anchors one end of the performance space, Rama the other. During those few lilas when Rama is not present some other commanding figure is anchor. The ramayanis station themselves near the maharaja, the sadhus near Rama. In between these two poles are the spectators.*

RS: Sitting so far away on your elephant, you can't see the scene very clearly, or hear.

MR: My father used to use opera glasses. I don't. There is a practical reason for my sitting at the back. My presence establishes control. The crowd is in front of me.

RS: What do people think when you sleep during the performance? [Occasionally I saw the maharaja doze.]

MR: I don't know what they think. But I am aware of the way I watch. I keep a serenity, a dignity. I don't talk.

The environment of every scene—both processional and fixed—features the maharaja as strongly as any other character, including Rama. There are a number of scenes where Rama is not present; but the maharaja is there for almost the whole Ramlila.

RS: You leave the Ramlila twice: at Sita's kidnapping and at Ravana's death. Why?

MR: And a third time, too: during the confrontation between Dasharatha and Kaikeyi. My great-grandfather did not leave, but my grandfather did because of the tragic scenes. Dasharatha weeping, the emotional power of that my grandfather didn't like to witness. And also the kidnapping of a queen, the killing of a king, he did not want to see these. But it is only a rule, not a tradition, so I sometimes break the rule.

The maharaja also misses a lila at Ramnagar when he goes to Benares to see the Bharat Milap of the Nati Imli Ramlila. That visit brings out the largest crowds of the season—it seems as if all Benares is leaning out windows, crowded onto roofs, packed into the small area where the Bharat Milap takes place. I don't know how many Ramlilas are staged in Benares—many. Also, sometimes parts of a Ramnagar lila continue even while the maharaja is doing his sandhya puja (evening prayer). When the weather has been bad it is necessary to make up some lilas and squeeze others together. Usually, however, there is a regular rhythm to the day's performance. The sandhya puja provides a break of one to three hours. The maharaja's arrival at five o'clock starts the day's lila, his departure for puja at around six marks an intermission (and an opportunity for the sadhus to take center stage). The lila resumes at seven-thirty as twilight arrives. Usually the lila ends by nine-thirty or ten, except on a few special nights, and on Coronation Day, when it goes all night until dawn. During the sandhya puja break, which is also the time of twilight, neither day nor night, the strict drama of the Ramlila is relaxed into a mela: a great fair mingling the sacred and the secular. The sadhus celebrate wildly, dancing and singing, sometimes even, especially at Chitrakut where a large temporary stage has been erected, going onto the stage itself to dance and sing. Performers in costume mingle with spectators: I took tea with Hanuman and chatted about his performing. Families picnic, food stalls do a brisk business, trinkets and powdered colors and toys are sold. There's a festive feeling in the air quite distinct from the more solemn attention paid to the lila itself. During the puja break, while the maharaja prays, the people play—all except the swarups, who remain in place, their crowns off but their demeanor serious. Often spectators will approach them and touch their feet. A person may snack, gossip, and then change mood and come to the swarups for darshan. The swarups sitting for darshan during puja break give a sense of the timelessness of Ramlila: during the drama they perform the actions of ancient, mythic days; during the puja break they are deities present here and now.

The open structure provided by the sandhya puja break is at no time more meaningful than on Dashahara day. The action is set in Lanka, a huge square plain almost a half-mile across in all directions. To the south is Ravana's four-gated Fort and, next to it, his throne. To the north, on a hill, is Rama's camp. To the west is the Ashoka Garden with Sita sitting kidnapped, surrounded by adoring women spectators. In the center of Lanka is the small rectangular battleground. During the afternoon's lila Ravana has surrendered to Rama. A great seventy-five-foot high bamboo and papier-maché effigy of the demon king is set atop his Fort. A crowd of perhaps 100,000 has gathered. The maharaja has come and gone. His procession from his Fort had been magnificent: elephant after elephant, each hung with cloaks of purple and gold brocade, adorned with jewels and silver; the maharaja, like Rama, in gold, wearing a turban adorned with feathers, symbols of his royal authority. He arrives but does not stay long. After the maharaja's departure, Ravana surrenders to Rama and disappears amidst the huge crowd. Then ensues an extra long puja break.

At this climax of the story opens a time/space where the many themes of the Ramlila are in suspension: good versus evil, the ever-present versus the evanescent, gods versus demons, people versus superhumans, commoners versus rulers, the outer circle of the mela with its commercialism versus the inner circle of the lila with its devotion. For a few hours, as it gets dark, all is in suspended balance, the great struggles neutralized, the principles of the cosmos revealed: Ravana = evil, insatiable appetite, is dead but not cremated; Rama and Lakshman = good, absolute, but sportive, sit on their temporary thrones, victorious but still in exile; Sita = mother of the world, sheer devotion, waits patiently under the ashoka trees. The population of this world, the audience in attendance at Ramlila, circulates among and between these great figures that triangulate Lanka. Of the gods they take darshan; but they also peer up at Ravana's giant effigy. The great figures are immobile, but lesser performers, in costume, drink tea, chat: a demon next to a monkey next to a sadhu next to a businessman next to a beggar next to Schechner next to a one-armed vendor selling roasted peanuts next to Hess next to a crying child next to a blind man next to a tourist next to an itinerant singer next to a student next to a mother nursing her infant next to three men on solitary camels. "Where do you come from?" I ask them, imagining a very long, dusty journey from Rajasthan. "We are the men who come on camels," one answers. "Each year we come, for this day only." That is all they speak. Nearby, sadhus are dancing so energetically that sweat soaks one's saffron shirt from shoulder to hips. Their drumming and singing pierce the evening air. In no other theater does the audience as such emerge so clearly as part of the performance. Nowhere else is there time/space allotted for the audience to so clearly, easily, and fully play their various roles. At Ramlila spectators watch, drop out, say their prayers, eat, join small groups singing bhajans, sleep, press in close for scenes of high drama—all within the scene of a performance with a story to tell, a score to follow. Dashahara night at Lanka was one of those great Brueghel paintings with no center yet full of harmony—thousands of people organized by their interdependent activities. And above them, overlooking it all, the three poles of the world on the last night of their conflict and captivity.

Thinking about this suspension/balance at the climax of the epic cycle, I recognized that Ramnagar Ramlila combines the feel of big events/environments like world's fairs, Olympic games, Disneyland, and great religious gatherings and political assemblies with their endorsement of ideology and enactment of patterns of behavior through audience participation with relatively tighter dramas such as the processions of the Bread and Puppet Theatre, Robert Wilson's spectacles, Peter Brook's *Orghast*, and Grotowski's paratheatrical experiments. These smaller events have stories and/or themes, but they can't match the scale, both theatrical and conceptual, of Ramnagar Ramlila. They fall within the aesthetic-critical range: they can be "enjoyed" and "evaluated." They need not be "entered into," as Ramlila demands. Even as Hess and I tried to keep our distance in order to analyze Ramlila, we felt ourselves, happily, caught in its cosmic, social, religious, and theatrical web.

Ramesh Chandra De was not so enmeshed or hopeful:

Because people have more money, they come to see the show only. Religious belief is fading. The Ramlila hasn't changed because the maharaja is a conservative. After him? Elsewhere Ramlila has changed. Today people come to see friends, relations, make purchases. Before they had to walk, had no money to waste or spend. Now with good income they travel by train and bus, they visit the city and buy. Some leave before arati.

But I'm not certain the deterioration De speaks of is occurring. In India people have the habit of saying the old times were better—at least when talking about religion. I think that Ramlila—like other great gatherings I attended (for example, the Kumbh Mela at Prayag in 1977)—always combined the sacred and the secular.

The maharaja is not alone at his end of the playing space. Near him, always, are the Ramayanis, the twelve men who chant the *Ramcharitmanas* (plate 46). Because the maharaja is at the back and not in their midst, spectators must turn away from the stage action if they wish to see him. Attention is on the maharaja mostly when he arrives, while his elephants or carriage are maneuvered into place. Then, among the crowd, the closer one is to the stage the less clearly can the *Ramcharitmanas* be heard; conversely, the closer one is to the maharaja and the Ramayanis the less clearly can one see the stage and hear the samvads. Intentionally or not, a situation has been set up that makes spectators choose whether they will gravitate toward the maharaja or toward Rama.

The Ramayanis focus attention on the maharaja as well as give him a special experience of the performance. The chanting of the Ramayanis is a counterpoint of the samvads. The *Ramcharitmanas* is a sacred text, a beautiful poetic text. The performance of Ramlila alternates between the chanting of that text and the stage action. The Ramayanis form their oval close to the maharaja: he hears every word of the *Ramcharitmanas* but only some of the samvads. When he is separated from Rama by a great distance, and an immense noisy crowd, it is as if there were two performances going on, the link between them stretched almost to the breaking point. At one end of the performance field is the bright, Petromax-lit stage, its well-composed arrangements of figures in gaudy costumes; at the other end is the maharaja, either visible in daylight or barely visible after dark, and the Ramayanis with their manuscripts of Tulsidas illuminated only by the burning of mustardseed-dipped torches. At night especially, the performance seems stretched in two directions. The stage is for the eye; the Ramayanis for the ear. And if you turn to follow your ears, you perceive the ever-present maharaja high on his elephant. On clear nights he sits in an open box; on rainy ones, in a closed cabin strapped to the giant elephant's back, like some weird boat floating atop a sea of people. When the maharaja moves into the action on the final days of the cycle, the Ramayanis move with him, resolving the duality of the drama into its ultimate unity.

Just as the maharaja has his Ramayanis, so Rama has his sadhus (plate 47). These holy men crowd to the front of every scene—they are devotees of Rama and want to get as close to him as they can. They are different from the rest of the audience. Some are naked or nearly so, many wear only loincloths, most are bare-chested. Some of them dust their bodies with ashes, turning their dark brown skin gray-blue. Their hair is very long, uncut, matted, sometimes wound into high buns or done in braids. They look very

46. The Ramayanis, always assembled near the maharaja, chant Tulsidas's *Ramcharitmanas*, 1978. Photo by Richard Schechner.

47. A group of sadhus. Standing is the "150-year-old man" as he was in 1978. Photo by Richard Schechner.

much like the holy recluses of the mountains and forests described in the ancient Sanskrit literature. They sing, chant, dance, laugh, smoke, shout— sitting or standing in circles of from 15 to 250. For them the Ramnagar Ramlila is a great annual reunion.

In 1976, eighteen thousand rupees were spent on feeding them. The maharaja gives them rations and places to sleep. The free food and lodging attract a number of sadhus to Ramnagar Ramlila—but it would be wrong to leave it at that. Sadhus traditionally exist by begging; a month's free food and lodging are not only welcome but part of their traditional way of living. And they are very devoted to Rama. They show this devotion by singing and dancing, and by simply crowding close: taking continuous darshan of the swarups. (In 1976, fewer sadhus than usual attended because of a rumor that the Indira Gandhi government was sterilizing men found traveling on trains without tickets—and sadhus routinely travel without tickets. That they are supposed to be celibate did not encourage them to seek sterilization.) There are actually two sadhu populations at Ramnagar Ramlila: the two to three hundred staying at the maharaja's dharamsalas (pilgrimage dormitories) and regularly accepting his food, and the many more in attendance at certain lilas. Among the sadhus are many regulars who have come to Ramnagar for as long as people can remember. These sadhus are theatrical performers in their own right. Their presence is expected; their gestures are fixed not by text or through rehearsals but by habit, tradition, and the expectations of the spectators. One very old man, clad only in a strip of banana leaf and called by everyone the "150-year-old man," was something of a trickster. When other sadhus begged, he gave out money; in the rains while everyone crowded under any available shelter, he pranced in the wet. The maharaja considers him a very holy man—and remembers him even from his own childhood, more than fifty years ago. He is gone now.

The sadhus attend Rama. They lead each other and the crowd in chanting bhajans—especially the one whose whole text is "Sita Ram, Sita Ram, Sita Ram jai, Sita Ram!" On and on, over and over, this chant goes until I found myself singing it too, even in my dreams. The maharaja and his Ramayanis (their leader is the maharaja's chief domestic priest) express the formality, order, and classical text of Ramlila. The group of sadhus surrounding Rama and utterly devoted to him (the living Hanumans of today), express a wide range of sacred actions: enactment of the serious narrative, ebullient devotion to Rama during the month when "god is on earth," sacred clowning, singing, and a wide range of actions that are part of the informal but deep texts of the oral tradition.

The presence of the maharaja and the sadhus makes a difference in the kind of performance obtained. Certainly Ramnagar Ramlila is different than others. Hess and I attended the Ramlila that legend says Tulsidas himself is said to have begun, the one sponsored by the Sankat Mochan temple of Varanasi, a temple holy to Hanuman. This Ramlila is performed over ten days at several sites: near Tulsi's house on the banks of the Ganga; at Sankat Mochan temple; and in a triangular field called Lanka near the temple. We went to the coronation of Rama in 1976. Here is what I recorded in my notebook:

9:30 P.M. This is like a home movie while the Ramnagar is a Hollywood epic. There is authenticity here, a lack of big resources, and therefore the clear impact of modernization: men and women spectators less rigidly segregated; the stage is an elevated square platform at one end of the space under a shamiana [brightly colored cloth ceiling] with a painted backdrop—just like many other modern Indian folk theaters I've seen [Yakshagana, Raslila, Jatra]. The pronunciation of Hindi is not standardized here—it is the way people talk, so I get the feeling of a small town with its own particular dialect. The Ramayanis are very strong, they use a drum and shehanai [clarinetlike instrument], which adds to their power. Only one sadhu in attendance—not a naked baba but a jolly man in saffron. We don't feel sneaky photographing; we don't feel intrusive, like we're violating anything. This event does not demand, command, and get the kind of attention common at Ramnagar.

The difference is in the attitude of the spectators, and this attitude is controlled by extratheatrical factors: (1) no maharaja here; (2) no sadhus; (3) no police with their big sticks beating back the surging crowd; (4) no uniformed guard as the maharaja has who, along with the police, give Ramnagar Ramlila the feel of an event where an important public person, like a prime minister, is making an appearance. At Ramnagar the sadhus give the event religious significance, the police and honor guard give it secular significance, and the maharaja combines these. Also, at Ramnagar the sheer size of the audience is awesome. Here it is small, less than 1,000, and homey. At Ramnagar, when the coronation was over, spectators fought to have darshan, and the police with their sticks beat them back to keep order. Here all who want darshan may have it for the asking. The swarups themselves are not so formal or formidable looking. Deities they may be, boys they certainly are.

About 85 percent of the close-up spectators are children, mostly under ten years of age. They laugh a lot. Their attention wanders. What a contrast to the nemis and sadhus at Ramnagar. And there is no one comparable to the maharaja on his elephant, or in his Cadillac or horse-drawn carriage, to set an example of disciplined attention. Except for Rama and Sita, even the swarups here are very casual; even during the performance itself they sometimes snack and talk.

In Ramnagar a world is created with six circles of attention—drawing people toward a very hot center. At Tulsighat a neighborhood performs a play with four circles of attention—actually leading people away from a cool center:

Ramnagar: Centripetal	Tulsi: Centrifugal
1. Maharaja-Rama	1. Performers
2. Ramayanis-sadhus	2. Ramayanis

3. Male spectators
4. Female and child spectators
5. Fringe spectators
6. Vendors who are kept out except during puja break

3. Child spectators
4. Other spectators, vendors, all with wandering attention

Significantly, the most skilled performers at Tulsighat are the Ramayanis, while at Ramnagar, the maharaja, Rama (and other principals), Ramayanis, sadhus, and nemis all play their roles beautifully. The absence of maharaja, sadhus, and attentive male spectators undercuts the effectiveness of the Tulsighat Ramlila: there is no model of how to experience the performance.

Performing Styles, Roles, Rehearsals, Directors, Staging, Iconography

Earlier, I quoted a spectator who thought that everything at Ramlila was "natural." This just shows what a slippery culture-bound concept "natural" is. From my Western perspective, the acting styles and staging are anything but natural. More: they are not analogous to what is current in mainstream American acting or staging. The use of Ramnagar itself—both the constructed environments and the found spaces (streets, forests, streams, fields)—has more in common with American experimental theater than with anything in the mainstream. Ramlila, like the movies, is staged "on location," using nonactors iconographically.

The acting is flat for most of the time. Words are spoken or declaimed in a singsong fashion and shouted so that the vast crowds can hear. Only rarely—when Rama laments the wounding of Lakshman, when Parashuram storms in angry that Shiva's bow has been broken, when Sita complains of her imprisonment in Lanka, when Angad taunts Ravana in an often humorous dialogue, when Narad sings his haunting song about Panchavati— does the acting carry emotional weight. Much of the dialogue recited by the more than thirty characters of Ramlila is mumbled, inaudible beyond the first few rows. Sometimes the performers actually appear embarrassed by who they are or what they have to say, as when several teenaged boys enact the young women of Janakpur reciting long speeches in admiration of the beauty of Rama and Lakshman. (All roles are played by males.)

The gestures of the actors are the same scene after scene, regardless of the situation. The most typical gesture is a sweeping motion of the right arm from the shoulder, with the hand and arm moving away from the chest making a broad semicircle that arcs over and includes the audience. The actors look mostly at the audience and not at the person to whom they are speaking.

Many big moments are nonacted—for example, the contest for Sita's hand. Many princes have come to compete for Sita, who will be given to the man who can lift Shiva's great bow. Several princes try; all fail. In their attempts no effort is made to indicate how heavy the bow is, how massive its size. Each prince perfunctorily stoops over the bow, pretends to tug at it, and fails. Then Rama steps up and effortlessly, without hesitation or doubt, lifts the bow, snaps his wrists, and breaks the bow in three. Instead of this gesture revealing Rama's incredible strength, it underlines the fact that the bow is made of papier-maché, designed to break at the slightest touch. As Rama breaks the bow, the white arati flare burns, a cannon goes off representing the thunder crack as Shiva's bow snaps, and the crowd roars. This impressive staging is not matched by the acting, which remains flat. Yet, for me at least, the nonacting fit perfectly with the iconography and meaning of the scene. Rama's playful, even ironic, omnipotence is shown by the way he not only breaks Shiva's bow but exposes it as a stage prop. In Rama's—Vishnu's—lila the great bow is a toy. Then Parashuram storms into Janakpur, yanking the mood back to that of conventional and effective drama. Often these two kinds of style succeed each other, giving Ramlila a special tension—a sense of existing in two worlds at once—that of ritual and that of theater.

The Bharat Milap also conveys several levels and kinds of performance simultaneously. On an elevated square stage, something like a boxing ring, set up in the intersection of the two main Ramnagar roads, the brothers enact their reunion after Rama's fourteen-year exile. After embracing and then lying prostrate on the ground and touching each other's feet, the swarups stand up in a straight line and face the crowd eight separate times, slowly rotating clockwise. Each time they face a direction, the white flares associated with arati are lit and the crowd goes crazy. It is simple, abstract, extended, and moving: a sheer display of the five divine figures united at last, showing themselves to all the assembled people. Thus the narrative drama is transformed at this moment into darshan.

So it is also, if less spectacularly, at the end of each night's lila when arati is performed. Whoever among the swarups has been present for the night's lila is the object of the arati: mostly Rama; Sita from the time of marriage to her kidnapping, and then again after her rescue; Lakshman with Rama and Sita during the time of exile . . . and so on. At the end of each night's lila there is the arati temple service with the focus on divine-human "icons." Different characters have the honor of waving the camphor lamp; Hanuman usually wields the fly whisk. During arati red and then white flares are lit, illuminating the scene and flattening the perspective so that it appears that temple murtis, not living performers, are there. The swarups are carefully instructed in the poses they take. During the red flare, their bodies are stiff and still, their faces frozen. During the white flare, the bodies remain as before but their faces smile. At arati spectators surge to take darshan: to get a look at the gods. On one occasion, at the start of his exile after crossing the make-believe Ganga, Rama performs the temple service to a Shiva lingam. This service is particularly exciting to the crowd, which mercilessly presses inward to catch a glimpse of the action that brings together these two most powerful gods.

The samvads that the characters recite are dialogues in modern nineteenth-century Hindi, but they are far from colloquial in either tone or meaning. The samvads repeat or elaborate what is chanted in the classical Hindi of the *Ramcharitmanas*. Classical Hindi stands in roughly the same relationship to today's Hindi as Chaucer's English does to today's English. Thus, as in several Asian traditional theaters, some of the language chanted is not understood by most of the audience. And, as in Noh where the kyogen tells the story in a more accessible Japanese, the samvads in a sense translate the *Ramcharitmanas*. But often the samvads do much more than translate; they elaborate. The story of how King Janak got hold of Shiva's bow is not in the *Ramcharitmanas*, but it is in the samvads; the episode between Kaikeyi and Manthara is drawn out extensively in the samvads.

The samvads are rehearsed in two different ways. The swarups change from year to year, though boys are encouraged to stay with the Ramlila for several years and move up the ladder of roles so that frequently enough a boy who plays Shatrughna or Bharat one year will "graduate" to Lakshman or Rama in a year or two. Still, there is much turnover, and extensive rehearsal. Training begins three months before Ramlila for up to ten hours a day (including a two- to four-hour siesta). For the first month the boys work just on memorizing the dialogue. Then they learn how to speak and move. This practice is sheer imitation. One vyas works only with the swarups. He says a line, they repeat; he shows a gesture, they do it exactly the same. Everything is learned by imitating the vyas: pronunciation, intonation, projection, rhythm, gestures, movement. During the performance itself the vyas, samvad book in hand, stands behind the swarups making sure that all the words are said correctly, all the gestures acted precisely (plate 48). In fact, if you are close enough to the action, you can hear the vyas pronounce every word quietly into the swarups' ears; in an actual sense, the dialogues are twice-done. Rehearsals are not over when performances begin. Each day the swarups practice for several hours. Then another hour or two is spent in putting on costumes and makeup. All the boys attend all the rehearsals. In 1976 the father of the boy playing Lakshman died in the middle of Ramlila month. It was not possible for the performer to continue to play Lakshman because the death in his family polluted him. The boy playing Shatrughna took over the role. "I was at all the rehearsals, I knew what to say." The training pays off.

Within the conventions of flatness and iconographic rather than naturalistic staging, the overall effect of Ramlila at Ramnagar is very powerful. I remember from the 1976 Ramlila especially Sita's lament on day 25. After Rama fails to defeat Ravana, the whole vast crowd moved to where Sita sat imprisoned under the ashoka trees. There, in the clearest voice of the Ramlila, Sita spoke and moaned, a formalized moaning that extended certain final vowels, their sound diminishing slowly, vanishing like smoke in the air. Her voice was clear, her moans moving without being sentimental. Still, the swarup vyas thinks the quality of acting has gone down: "In the past more rupees were spent. They get the same amount now, but it buys less. If they do a good job, it is out of faith and love, and if that is lacking, the performance gets worse."

Hess and I spoke to another vyas who played Sita when he was young:

RS: When you played Sita were you possessed by her, or was it "just a role"?

Vyas: I get the feeling in my heart that I am Sita. It is written: Whoever is a true devotee becomes absorbed in god. When you're absorbed you behave as that person. If you cry it is real crying. When the actor believes "I am the character," then he really cries.

This is very much the same kind of reply Jane Belo got when interviewing people in a Balinese village about their experience of being in a trance and performing various beings (animals, gods, household things like brooms).[6] We asked the same question of the swarup vyas and of the boy playing Rama:

Chief vyas: If in the play it says "It's raining," and you look into a clear sky, still it is raining.

RS (to Rama): When people come and touch your feet, what do you feel?

Rama: The feeling of god is in me.

RS: Why did you audition for Ramlila?

Rama: I have the desire, the respect for all the important people involved, and my faith. If you come from a poor family, it is a good chance, and if you come from a rich family, it gives you a good reputation.

Earlier I asked the maharaja how the swarups are selected early in July. The chief vyas—a temple priest at the Fort—has searched the neighborhood communities for candidates; about fifty boys are invited to the Fort to meet the maharaja.

RS: How do you choose the performers?

MR: Voice, good looks, family bringing-up.

RS: What happens to the boys after their experience in Ramlila?

48. A vyas holds the book containing all the samvads and stage directions, 1978. To his left is Ravana, played by Narayan Pathak. For more strenuous scenes, his son Kaushal Prasad Pathak plays Ravana—the fourth generation of Pathaks to perform the role. Photo by Richard Schechner.

MR: Some become sadhus, one became a vyas and gives discourses on the *Ramayana*. This particular vyas played all four roles [except Sita]. For many years his voice didn't change so he could continue to perform.

I suspect there is some romanticizing here in regard to the lives former swarups live. Hess and I tried to track down a few. One man was a journalist, and he said that his experience as Lakshman, his work "in the theater," opened up for him the possibility of a career in "communications." Another young man had played Rama in the early seventies and had earned a great reputation for his sincerity in performance. It was said that he shed real tears when Lakshman was wounded. In itself this was not unusual; many of the performers get deep into their roles. But this Rama seemed to have had a very special feel for the role. In meeting him, and his mother, I sensed his continued sincerity. He was very poor, yet attending a religious school his mother could hardly find the money to pay for. His ambition was to become a scholar. Most ex-swarups vanished into the population.

There are more performers in Ramlila than the swarups. Some roles are hereditary. Ravana has been in the Pathak family since the time of Ishwari Prasad Narain Singh, who ruled from 1835 to 1889, the time that Ramnagar Ramlila developed its present form. At present Ravana is played by both father and son (plate 48). The scenes that are not physically demanding are played by the frail father, the rest by his more vigorous son. The son tells how Ravana came to be in his family:

Kaushal: The story is, people were being selected there in Ramnagar [the Ravana family, called "Ravan-raj" by all the neighbors, live in Surauli village about ten miles from Ramnagar]. My baba reached there in Ishwari Narain Singh's time. His name was Ayodhya Pathak, and the king's minister was Bhau Bhatt. My baba reached the place where they were choosing among eighteen men. Yes, an open selection. My baba's age was thirty-five to forty then. So they heard the voices of all eighteen men. My grandfather's voice pleased Ishwari Narain Singh. He asked Bhau Bhatt, and Bhatt said, "Your Highness, he is Maharavana [Super Ravana]." The other people around said that for the other candidates you could have hopes—they were all younger and lived nearby. You may hope for them, but this one has fulfilled all hopes. The maharaja gave the order. That was it. They gave my baba the book to study. He memorized it. Since then the part of Ravana has remained in our family. By now it's been about four generations. Ayodhya Pathak, Jogeshwar Pathak, Narayan Pathak—he's the one you see here—and his son, me, Kaushal Prasad Pathak.

RS: So Shri Naryanji has played Ravana for a long time?

Narayan: I have said the role for fifty-eight years.

The man playing Parashuram has performed it for thirty-four years. He says the role is already being passed on to his son.

Some people literally grow into their roles so that their physical being appears to be a reflection of their Ramlila identities. The man playing Brahma in 1978 was ninety-six years old, with a feeble voice and very delicate gestures. He had played Brahma more years than he could remember. Other performers play several roles. The man who plays Hanuman also plays Valmiki, Atri-muni, Agastya, and Lomas-rishi. Some of the best actors, such as the man who plays Angad, are young—and they came into Ramlila by accident. The family of the vyas who rehearses the roles other than the swarups, and who is in charge of all technical arrangements, had come into possession of a number of key roles, including Hanuman, Angad, Sugriva, and others: a total of eleven roles. Then, in 1977, a death occurred in this family during Ramlila season. This meant that a number of key roles had to be replaced immediately, causing a great strain on the performance and perhaps even a decline in its quality. Through this crisis, the maharaja recognized that too many roles had been centralized in one family. It was during the rush to find replacements that the man who now plays Angad was brought into the Ramlila.

In one case at least, a Ramlila role has had a deep effect on the performer's non-Ramlila life. The man who plays Narad with great force is the mahant of two temples in Mirzapur, about fifty miles from Ramnagar (plates 27–28). He is a relatively wealthy man. He moved to Mirzapur in 1957. But he was not always a mahant. He's been in the Ramlila for thirty years, since 1948. When he lived in Ramnagar he was "in the service of the maharaja." He did various jobs: "I used to be the priest of the salagrama for the rani in her palace. I did all kinds of work. I did puja-path [a general term for priest's work]." But with Independence "many people had to be let go, that was in 1952." I asked Narad—he is known by that name in or out of Ramlila—how he got involved.

Narad: My own story is this. When I was first at the maharaja's, I was just a child, thirteen years old. During the time of Ramlila my job was to stay with Ramji. Every year I was sent there, and since there was never any complaint about me, there was no objection. From 1929 to 1951 I stayed with Ramji for a month and looked after all the arrangements. I was in charge of all their studying, training, teaching. You know the Ramlila books? Well, besides me, you won't find anybody who has them.

RS: You have the whole samvad?

Narad: The whole samvad. If you come to my place I can show it all to you, the dialogues of all four swarups. Then, from 1951 to 1958, I was the vyas for the swarups. There was a baba there too, Baba Kamala Saran. He was very old. So I said to him, "You just sit there, I'll do all the work, but you'll get the credit, don't worry." He, poor thing, was eighty years old. It was then that the maharaja gave me a copy of the samvads. It took my brother three years, working half-an-hour every day, to make a copy. I gave the copy to the maharaja and he showed it to a German lady and she ran away with it. Now I'm helpless. He asks me for another copy. I say, "Look, I live in Robertsganj. My brother is old and sick. How can he write it?"

RS: After 1958, when Raghunath Datta took over the vyas work, what did you do?

Narad: I became a projectionist in the cinema in Benares. I went to Calcutta to pass an exam to be a projectionist. I was a projectionist for eleven months and worked in the Ramlila for one.

RS: And since when have you played Naradji?

Narad: Always, for thirty years.

RS: So you played Narad all the time you were doing these other things?

Narad: Yes. Narad's part comes only for five or six days. The other days I spent with the swarups.

RS: Who played Narad before you?

Narad: He also stayed with the maharaja. When he played I used to stay near him. Nobody explained anything to me. I just listened to him and did it the way he did it. One day he said to me, "Listen, you do this work now." He went to the maharaja and said, "I won't do this now, my body has reached the state, my age, where I can't." The maharaja asked who should do it. I was a vyas at the time, so he said to me, "You do it."

RS: We like your acting very much. How do you do it so well?

Narad: My experience is this. When I put on my crown and am before Ramji, then I feel sure that I am really before him, only before him. I don't see him as a man. I see him as a bhagwan. At that time, if anybody tries to talk to me, I don't want to talk. At that time, everything appears extraordinary. What people call *tanmaya* [completely merging, losing a sense of the self]. It's like when you're in love. Whatever exists, it's only Ramji, only he.

RS: Could the same feeling come to any good actor playing any role? As a projectionist you've seen lots of actors.

Narad: No, the same feeling couldn't come. Acting is done for money. When anybody works for money he just says, "All right, let me do my duty." But for him who works in a feeling of love, there is no question of money. Didn't I tell you before that the maharaja can't make me work for money? It is my love, and only because of that, that I've reached this condition. By god's grace I've arrived here.

RS: What do you mean?

Narad: Imagine. I used to live with the maharaja like an ordinary man. I got fifty rupees a month. Now I have reached a high position. Everyone in the city respects me. A mahant is like a king. I get a thousand a month.

RS: When did you become mahant?

Narad: In 1970 my guruji passed away. And this is 1978. In 1970 it all came into my hands.

RS: Have Narad's words and personality influenced your life and your work as a mahant?

Narad: There is a proverb: "Whatever anybody does, it's only Ram. Man can do nothing by himself. The doer is only Ram."

Very few people know Narad by his actual name, Mahant Baba Omkar Das. The role of Narad he has played in Ramlila has come to define his ordinary actuality. And this, I'm sure, is due largely to the quality of his acting—his projection of deep sincerity, his demeanor, which is imposing and authoritative, and his gifts as a singer. Ironically, Narad did not perform in the 1983 Ramlila because he was involved in legal matters concerning his Mirzapur temple properties. He was afraid that if he left Mirzapur he would lose some or all of his wealth.

Thus, in Ramlila we are presented with an incredibly complicated aesthetics. At one extreme is the flat acting, at the other a role so powerfully performed that the player is absorbed into it; his whole present life is defined by it. The iconography of key scenes, along with the nightly arati, projects Ramlila into the realm of the Hindu temple service with its manifestations of divine presence. Hereditary actors perform side by side with those who audition for roles on a yearly basis. Certain roles are not hereditary but still are controlled by families. The maharaja, as producer, oversees the whole thing, but it is too vast for him to know everything that's going on. This is in keeping with what seems to me to be perhaps an unconscious but still all-pervasive intention of Ramnagar Ramlila: to be more than any single human being can take in. As I wrote in my notebook after Dashahara 1978,

No one, not even the most knowledgeable, not even the maharaja, the vyases, Atmaram the carpenter, the most diligent scholars, the most faithful nemis—no one knows it all. Even at the most basic level of what's being done day by day by everyone involved. No one even knows how many are involved. Where do you stop counting? With the direct participants? With the man who takes a month out of every year from his work to fashion with his own hands the garlands that the swarups wear each night for arati? With the nemis or sadhus who travel great distances to attend? With the spectators who attend irregularly? With the operators of the tea and chat [snacks] stalls who never see any lila at all but who keep the mela going night after night? No one can see every scene because many are simultaneous and occur far removed from each other in space.

Thus Ramnagar Ramlila creates its own model of the universe.

The Future of the Ramlila of Ramnagar

There's no doubt that Ramlila will continue to be celebrated all across Hindi-speaking northern India. Thousands of Ramlilas are performed annually, in every village, town, and city. But about Ramnagar Ramlila—the longest, largest, and to many the most holy—there are some problems which I can only touch on. Money is getting tighter all the time, and tradition is wearing thin. Even given the fact that it is normal for people in India to speak of the "old days" as having more splendor, more piety, more devotional intensity (paralleling in everyday discourse the devolution predicted in the yuga theory of history), it seems that Ramlila of Ramnagar really is less opulent and less lavishly produced than earlier (plates 38 and 40). A large part of this is a question of budget. Subsidy is given to the maharaja by the government of Uttar Pradesh, but it is not enough. Since 1949, when the privy purse along with the maharaja's political power was abolished, Uttar Pradesh gave, first, Rs 100,000 and, more recently, Rs 115,000 annually to support the Ramlila. This money cannot simply be translated into dollar equivalents to give Americans a sense of its worth. In terms of buying power, think of a grant of about $150,000. This is still very little compared to the scope of Ramlila, its grounds, costumes, props, and other items of expense including salaries of performers, vyases, Ramayanis, guards, musicians, and so on. A budget accounting from 8 February 1977 showed the following items as major expenses:

Feeding of sadhus	Rs 18,000
Contractor for effigies	3,500
Pay for swarups	2,200
Rental of Petromax lamps, payment to their bearers	2,160
General labor (grounds, porters, etc.)	1,700
Arati flares	1,375
Other actors	1,350
Bullock cart rental (to transport swarups)	1,295

Items ranged down to Rs 20 paid for fifteen days' service of a washerwoman. Lots of things are not budgeted but kept from year to year, such as costumes and the basic environments. The costumes are getting threadbare; those at the Sankat Mochan Ramlila, new in 1978 at a cost of more than Rs 20,000, are out of reach for Ramnagar. Other items are collected over the year, when they can be gotten most cheaply. For example, bamboo is collected in February. Also many persons on the maharaja's staff spend much of their time organizing the Ramlila. The four vyases are temple priests in Ramnagar. Their budgeted salaries for eighty-five days' work total Rs 576, but they also receive support from their temples and from the maharaja's temple trusts. All in all, 231 persons spent 1,441 workdays preparing for and performing the 1976 Ramlila. A detailed analysis of the budget shows that in 1955 Rs 103,763 was spent on Ramlila; in 1975 it was Rs 125,360. According to information supplied by the maharaja's staff, "there has not been any change in the amounts paid to performers over the past fifty years or so." Which means, simply, that the amount has gone down drastically as inflation eats up the value of money.

Make no mistake: Ramlila is a big production by any measurement. In it are employed ninety-five performers, more than a hundred workmen, and four persons from the maharaja's temples. Thirteen temples connected with the Ramlila are maintained by the All-India Kashiraj Trust at a cost, in 1977–78, of Rs 51,262. It is difficult to put all the information together, but Hess and I estimate that the total actual cost for each year's Ramlila, as of 1976 or 1978, was about Rs 350,000—or a buying power equivalent to about $500,000.

The maharaja is not a poor man, but neither is he in command of fabled wealth, unlimited resources. As maharaja of Benares, he is in a somewhat difficult situation, economically speaking. Because of the particular religious significance of his position, he cannot turn the Fort into a tourist hotel or become a full-scale industrialist the way some former maharajas have done. To do this would be to sacrifice the authority earned by virtue of his apparent "disinterest" in the economic affairs of this world. The maharaja exists at least to some degree as a figure of religious mystery—mystery in the medieval European sense: a person who draws on forces that can't be itemized in a budget or reduced to a flow chart. The maharaja is the causer of the Ramnagar Ramlila, but he is caused, or kept in his special existence, by the Ramlila. The Ramlila and the maharaja are in a symbiotic relationship.

On the other hand, if some economically productive plan is not developed, the sheer production elements of the Ramlila—the effigies, the environments, the costumes, the flares—will get shoddier and shoddier. A look at old photos and etchings makes it apparent that much decay has already occurred. The maharaja is trapped: he can't be the kind of maharaja he is and make a lot of money; without a lot of money he can't maintain the Ramlila. The unique situation of Varanasi-Kashi-Ramnagar precludes this double role. Thus the maharaja faces the contradiction of supporting a ritual superstructure by means of a modern infrastructure that undermines the very thing it purports to support. I spoke briefly to the Raj Kumar, the heir to the throne. He wants to be an industrialist; he wants to keep up the Ramlila.

The maharaja of Benares is special because the Ganga and Kashi are special. Even as India has become a modern secular state, or is in the process of becoming such on its own terms, the ritual aspects of its culture, especially in the villages and in the villagelike neighborhoods of many cities, remain resilient, living, very active. The maharaja of Benares sustains his identity as maharaja solely on the basis of ritual: tradition, pomp, parades, public religious devotion, Ramlila—theatrical activities.

In Ramnagar Ramlila we have what is fundamentally a folk art perfected during the colonial phase of India's history, arising in a "princely state," continuing to exist in the modern era, reflecting the very special qualities of Benares. This theatrical-religious-political-social event is of great interest to me as a theater person, and I recommend it to Indian theater persons. If Kathakali and like forms have developed meaningful and powerful aesthetics based on classical norms (reinterpreted to be sure), then Ramnagar Ramlila has developed its own aesthetics based on folk norms. These are even more appealing to me than the classical dance and drama. Ramlila uses myth, audience participation, political allusion, constructed and found environments, performers at all levels of skill and involvement, and even the existing sociopolitical circumstances to develop a performance of great diversity and power. Ramlila cannot be imitated, but it can be learned from.

NOTES TO CHAPTER 4

[1]Research on Ramlila of Ramnagar was carried out by Linda Hess and me in 1976, 1977, and 1978. I attended portions of the Ramlila in 1976 and all of it in 1978. Hess lived in Varanasi and attended most of the lilas for those three years. Portions of this chapter are adapted from our

coauthored article, "The Ramlila of Ramnagar" (1977). For comparisons of Ramlila to an American folk theater, see my "Ramlila of Ramnagar and America's Oberammergau" (1982c) and my "Performance Spaces: Ramlila and Yaqui Easter," in *Performative Circumstances* (1983).

[2] Periodically, the samvads are revised. According to the maharaja, the last revision was undertaken by scholars/poets gathered by his grandfather, Maharaja Prabhu Narain Singh in 1927–28.

[3] The distinction between "Great" and "Little" traditions was first made, I believe, by anthropologist Robert Redfield. I am using Milton Singer's elaboration of that distinction as expressed by Singer in *When a Great Tradition Modernizes* (1972).

[4] I use the term "station" as it applies to "stations of the Cross" or the stations used by performers of some medieval cycle plays in Europe. This pattern of movement and stopping punctuated by ritual and/or performances is typical also of Ramlila. I do not think there is any direct link between medieval drama, Catholic ritual, and Ramlila—just parallel solutions to analogous narrative situations.

[5] The Ramlila must start on the fourteenth day of the month—as the moon is waning. Dashahara must be in the middle time of a waxing moon, on the tenth day of the lunar month. Ramlila must end on a full moon. These requirements can cause some peculiar adjustments to be made. In 1982, for example, because of the insertion of an extra half-month in the lunar year, the Ramlila had to be calculated backward from the full moon, and so it did not begin on the fourteenth day.

[6] See Schechner and Schuman, eds., 1976, 150–61. Or see Belo's book-length study of Balinese trance (1960). As trance-dancer Darja said: "When I've already gone into trance, my thoughts are delicious, but I do not remember it. . . . I feel just like a puppy, I feel happy to run along the ground. I am very pleased, just like a puppy running on the ground. As long as I can run on the ground, I'm happy" (Schechner and Schuman, eds., 1976, 156). This identification with the actions of the character portrayed is what Stanislavski and his interpreter Lee Strasberg wanted of the Euro-American actor.

5

PERFORMER TRAINING
INTERCULTURALLY

At the Kathakali Kalamandalam in Kerala, southwest India, where, apparently, an old and traditional way of training is followed, the boys who will become Kathakali performers get up before dawn during the rainy season to begin eight hours of training embedded in a thirteen-hour day (plate 49). I never trained as a Kathakali performer, as some Americans have, but I followed the training routine for several weeks in June and July 1976. All references are to notes I made at that time.

This "new" Kalamandalam is of institutional design—not like "traditional" Kerala. The Kalamandalam covers the crest of a treeless hill; its several buildings and brand new theater (built in conformity with ancient formulas laid down in the *Natyasastra*) hold to that pebbly hilltop. The buildings are mostly small concrete-block houses with cement floors (scandalizing Western dancers, who say the body needs wood, or something giving, to run, jump, stamp against). The training rooms are about 15' by 30' each, and in them boys from eight to about twenty years old sweat through the training.

The training during the rainy season consists of a variety of lessons for the feet, hands, face and eyes, and torso. These exercises are, with the exception of an extraordinary full-body massage and some moves based on Kalarippayatt (a martial art), all derived from the actual performances of Kathakali.

Training in Kathakali—as in Noh, classical Western ballet, and so many forms that own a living repertory—is fundamentally a repetition of whatever it is that the training is training for, a very logical preparation but one fundamentally different than that used for contemporary Euro-American theater, mainstream or experimental.

Imitation is the core of Kathakali training—imitation at all levels. A performer is free from imitating only relatively late in his life, and then only under special circumstances. This is different from what Stanislavski saw as the essence of theatrical art (and training)—and from Stanislavski through to almost every nook and cranny of the Western theater world: Meyerhold, Brecht, Strasberg, Spolin, Chaikin, Benedetti, Schechner, Grotowski . . . just about everybody. Stanislavski:

Let us now return to the definition of the creative road of the actor. Are there any generally accepted and recognized rules which can teach you how "to act"? If I have just told you that an actor can be said to have embarked on the road of creative art only when he finds in himself the never changing, unshakable, unquenchable love of art which thrives on difficulties, and failures, and which always burns with a steady flame, then will you please tell me this: do you think it is possible to lay down generally accepted rules, according to which every actor can learn "to act," that is, to express *his* feelings, in the same way as any other actor? Every man discovers for himself *his own* germ and his own love of art and sets them free for his creative work by a special and unique method, which constitutes his individual uniqueness and his own secret. For this reason the secret of the creative work of one man is of no earthly good to another and cannot be handed to anyone as a model for imitation. For imitation is the most deadly sin of all. It is something that is completely devoid of any creative principle. And by imitation I mean teaching someone to imitate someone else's voice, or manner, or results, or to give an exact copy of the deportment of a well-known actor. That is not the road of individual creative work, that is to say, it is not the way to awaken in an actor an ever new perception of life and its problems, but the choking up of the purely organic thought by an accidental mode of expression which has become the established manner of one actor. [1962, 162]

Following Stanislavski's dictum, few Euro-Americans imitate Stanislavski, his way or his exercises; but many use his ideas as "jumping-off places."

Stanislavski did have a method. Or "system," as some prefer to call it, wanting to distance themselves from the particular interpretation of Stanislavski's training procedures developed by Lee Strasberg of the Actors' Studio. Again Stanislavski:

But how are we to find something of a general nature that is applicable to *all* as the road to the achievement of the final goal of creative art by everyone individually? Let us see if we cannot find in the nature of the human feelings themselves steps that are common to all and on which, as on the rungs of a ladder, everyone can climb up so as to attain the desired end of becoming a creative artist on the stage. [1962, 163]

Before looking at these steps—and comparing them to what goes on in Kathakali training—let me say that Zeami, one of the founders of Noh drama as it is today performed, said things back in the fifteenth century that sound very Stanislavski-like. Though almost certainly using a method of strict imitation (still in force when learning Noh today) and extolling the system of learning the "secrets" of a particular great performer—passing these on in the body of the disciple—Zeami in the matter of "general principles" sounds a lot like Stanislavski. In his *Kyui* Zeami outlines nine levels of acting and suggests a sequence that actors ought to follow in achieving each of these levels. Actors are, surprisingly, to start not at the bottom but in the middle, with roles and techniques that are more "naturalistic" and neither extremely heroic nor coarse. And it is only after mastering the natural and next the heroic and godly that the actor turns to the coarse, the demonic, the "dangerous." For to attempt these roles without the "flower" of a mature skill is to do them coarsely. But when demonic roles are performed by old masters "they too become harmonious." Zeami puts it this way in *Kyui:*

Yet once [the actor] has reached the flowers of the upper three [levels] from the middle three levels and gained a level of ease and the Miraculous Flower, then he comes back and even performs in the manner of the lower three levels. And when he creates such performances they too become a harmonious [synthesis] of Media and Principles. [Nearman 1978, 329]

Nearman explicates Zeami thus:

The actor begins his formal training with a study of voice and body techniques, as Zeami comments later in the text. Following carefully the teacher's demonstrations, the student-actor works on bits and pieces from the repertory. The student's attempts to mimic the teacher develop his powers of observation and his ability to reproduce behavior while he absorbs elements of stage decorum. For Zeami, this superficial mimicry is the usual way in which humans learn and is therefore the path that the student is to follow if he is to develop as an actor. However, it is not the ultimate path, but is only the first gateway to the art of acting. [1978, 314]

Zeami's writings are elliptical and often difficult to follow for two reasons. First, they are part of the "secrets" kept within the Kanze family and passed on from generation to generation. "Zeami stipulated that the treatises be passed on only to one whose achievements and understanding in the art were clearly attested and who was capable of accepting the responsibility for training others" (Nearman 1978, 300). Second, anyone receiving the writings would have also received the body-to-body training prerequisite to becoming a master shite (lead performer). The writings, in other words, are the conceptual core, and maybe even a reification, of a total system that is present and transmitted in the doing. Zeami's training, like that of modern Noh and Kathakali, is based on "imitation," but imitation of a very special kind.

For this doing-as-training is a kind of plunge into direct experience. Students learn to perform (in Kathakali, in Noh) very much the way infants learn language. They are surrounded by what they are learning, which is "broken down" not into abstract grammar but into graspable units of movement and sound. Only a few masters will ever learn the "grammar" of Kathakali, and many masters will never learn it; they will simply get better and better at doing it. Certainly Zeami knew the "grammar" of Noh—his writings are reconstructions based on well-thought-out deconstructions—but he never implies that others need to follow him in this deconstruction/reconstruction process. One does not explain grammar to an infant. You talk to the baby, you try to elicit responses from the baby, and you might even adjust your way of speaking to the baby's: substituting vocables for words, slowing down the speed of talking, raising the pitch of the voice an octave, gesturing broadly to illustrate the meaning of the words. It doesn't matter, at this beginner's level, whether or not the neophyte knows anything about the "grammar" of what's being learned. Grammar, history, and philology come later, if at all. At the first level, doing is learning, learning is doing. When my son, Sam, was two years old and wanted to be carried, he'd say, "Pick *you* up." This was because people called him "you" and he thought "you" meant "Sam." When I corrected him and said, "No, pick *me* up," he'd get angry. "Not *me*, daddy, *you!*" Then I'd laugh and play according to his logic. Finally, after much repeating and the passing of some weeks, he said, "Pick *me* up." It was still later that he got the difference between "me" and "you"—a difference that depends entirely on usage within context. Well, this is a model of learning by direct experience, the kind of learning done at the Kalamandalam and in Noh. Only after repeated use—and only from the inside-by-experience—can the learning performer know what a technique "means." Long before that illumination happens, he knows how to use the technique. To demand to "know" before one can "do" often retards the learning process. It locates the learning in the head before it gets into the body. Too often, when I conduct a workshop, I am barraged by "why" questions when at the first stages of work the questions should all be "what" and "how."

Back to the Kathakali training in the summer of 1976: I was very taken by the "hands-on" method of training, and by the full use of imitation. On 21 June I watched the first-year class, the absolute beginning of the training. This class contained seven boys ranging from about ten to eighteen years of age. The bigger boys took the lead. At the start of their session, at 4:25 A.M., no teacher was in sight. The practice began with each boy applying gingelly (sesame) oil to his whole body but especially generously to the thighs and upper legs. Then they did a series of moves and jumps with the knees flexed, froglike. The better jumpers kept their arms outstretched too, and the knees were brought up to the chest (if possible). There was a lot of difference between the "better" and the "worse" jumpers, but nothing was made of the difference. Training was a game of follow-the-leader with lots of repetition but no corrections.

Over the next sixty-five minutes the boys went through a series of exercises, sometimes one at a time, more frequently in groups, and often with two lines of boys facing each other. These exercises included stamping, footwork, head rolls, body rolls, stretches (plate 49). "All this done," my notes say, "with no supervision or attention to detail. The method is repetition and letting it seep in." Somewhere during the first half-hour the teacher arrived. "Teacher stands and watches but makes only a few corrections, given individually by summoning a student to him. The teacher appears sleepy." About halfway through the hour the students begin to chant the *tal* (rhythm) in unison: "Da da da di da da. . . ." Two older boys lead this. They stand facing the others. Later I understood that this tal was carried by the Kathakali drums and that it spoke directly to the feet. The "better" boys worked with double-time tal, the "worse" with half-time.

The boys' bodies gleam in the lamplight. There is an early morning breeze. It is very pleasant. The sound of different work goes on, coming from several of the sheds. The teacher takes his stick and beats the tal. Sometimes he beats it directly at the feet of the students. The sound of the wood hitting the concrete floor makes a ringing-pinging that pierces the air of the room.

The exercises are continuous with not too much time spent on any one exercise—except for the footwork with the chanted tal. This goes on for twenty or more minutes. Earlier work brought out a slight sheen of sweat; this brings out rivulets. And the unison chanting and beating of the tal stick makes the whole sequence build from scattered individual beginnings to a unified, and satisfying, work with a whole group.

I was very much reminded of the warm-ups practiced by The Performance Group (which I directed from 1967 to 1980). There also we would start with individual work, proceed through teamwork, and conclude with sound-and-movement exercises involving everyone (see Schechner 1973*b*). This work—like that beginning Kathakali training—was both to give individuals a sense of belonging to a group and to summarize, in a physical way, the performance-to-be. Often part of TPG warm-up included individuals or subgroups running through portions of the performance we were working on. This gave

49. Early-morning training at the Kathakali Kalamandalam. Photo courtesy of the Sangeet Natak Akademi, New Delhi.

50. The Kathakali massage at the Kalamandalam. Photo by Richard Schechner.

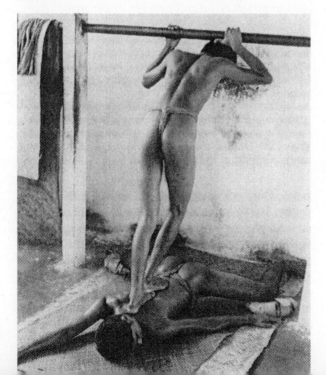

a kind of crazy-house sense of things: people rushing around the Performing Garage reciting lines, singing songs—not trying to be in synchrony with the whole group but refreshing/revising their own individual or subgroup scores. Of course, the similarity between Kathakali training and TPG training is not just coincidence. Some of the basic Grotowski exercises were taken directly from Kathakali; and these same exercises were transferred from Grotowski to me and from me to TPG (see Schechner 1977, 83–84).

Taken as a whole, the Kathakali early-morning class followed a structure of individual and scattered starts, slowly building to unified chanting of tal linked to footwork, then breaking into pairs for the massage. This period of sixty-five minutes was marked by no formality at the start or finish except for the *namaskaram* (ritual bow) that each boy did to the ritual lamp (which also provided basic illumination until dawn, though other sheds, I discovered, were lit by electric bulbs—retaining the oil lamp too, however). The basic structure of this early morning work is shown in figure 5.1.

The sense of tightening group work coming about halfway through, followed by a loosening up at the end, is not unlike the structure of an all-night Kathakali performance, which at the very end does not conclude climactically (that scene usually occurs just before dawn, a big fight full of roaring and excitement) but rather quietly dissipates. This is true because Kathakali performances often consist not of complete plays but of episodes—albeit episodes that follow one another from 9:00 P.M. till daylight.

The point is, even at the very start of training what is being incorporated (literally, put into the bodies of the neophytes) is both the details and the overall structure of Kathakali.

A few words about the massage (plate 50). The technique is simple. The massager stands and regulates his weight—the pressure is applied by the feet to the massaged—by holding onto a bar. Most of the massage is done with

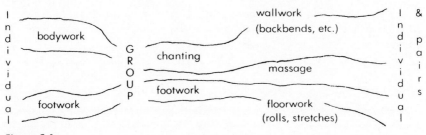

Figure 5.1

the ball of the foot, though some deep work is done with the heel and sometimes the whole foot slides on or slaps the body. The intention of the massage, it seems to me, is at least twofold: literally to re-form the young body so that it "accepts" as "natural" the severe turnout required by Kathakali, as well as adjustments needed in the spine; and to sensitize extremely the feet of the massager, for Kathakali is a dance-drama where the feet "speak." My reaction to having the massage done to me follows:

It might get sensual—the feel of the foot is very firm and good. But there is also a great deal of pain in the inside of the leg tendons where they meet the crotch—so there is little invitation to eroticize, at least on the part of the boy being massaged. It is hard for me to let go into the massage because of the pain. But, I am told, after a little while the pain goes away. And I do experience, along with pain, a very relaxed sensation—a real stretching out of my back and legs. The massage seems definitely aimed at making the "Kathakali body"—turned-out legs, arched back, strong shoulders. The working with the feet is good for both partners: it involves the feet as living, knowing body instruments, not as the mute "ends of the body." It gives the feet a very particular and highly skilled task, directly educating the feet in pressure, rhythm, and control (all of which is useful to the Kathakali performer). For the person being massaged, the use of the feet means that what is happening to his body is controlled by the other's release of weight, not by pressure or sheer strength. The massager releases weight into the massaged and the massaged senses a great easy reservoir of force which is lovingly but powerfully applied. The massage is not a great strain to give, physically speaking—but it is difficult from the point of view of control. The depth of the massage is not probing, as in Shiatsu, but elongating, stretching, spreading out. The final two gestures—the massage of the face and head by the hands and the reciprocal give-back of the massaged, who ends by kneeling in front of the massager rubbing his feet and calves (a physical thank-you)—make an excellent finish to the whole twenty-minute experience.

After, I felt full, released, relaxed.

On subsequent days I observed the classes of more advanced boys and the rehearsals of the professional Kathakali company. The patterns that I saw in the beginners' class were reinforced. My sense was that at the Kalamandalam there was not only training to be learned but specific roles, already scored in great detail, to be absorbed. The school is a place where the concrete integers of a tradition are taught in detail. The actual roles are transmitted to the next generation of performers.

In the American theater students learn techniques appropriate to "approaching" roles, "preparing" roles, "building" characters—all done in school "as practice." But what is being practiced is not what will be performed later in life. The students may or may not play the same roles after they finish school. But they certainly will not play those roles as practiced: the whole intent of rehearsals is to find new ways, surprising ways, original ways of playing roles and staging plays. In Kathakali, as in Noh, there is only a little chance that a performer will play in a new work; and even less chance that this new work will be well received and find a permanent place in the repertory. But a large part of the American actor's work is in new plays; the health of the theater is largely determined, still, by the availability of new plays. In my essay, "Decline and Fall of the (American) Avantgarde" (Schechner 1982*b*), I discuss in some detail how experimental theater in America has suffered because no way was developed to transmit "performance knowledge." In other words, the theater of the 1960s and 1970s was not a theater of new plays, or literary texts interpreted at all, but a theater of new mise-en-scènes—a theater of whole performance texts consisting of movements, stage placement and tableaux, music (and other sonic elements), visuals including settings, environments, costumes, projections, and a number of nonactor performers: masks, puppets, projections, films. The dream of "total theater" envisioned in Euro-American culture by Wagner was realized by artists as diverse as Grotowski, Laurie Anderson, Richard Foreman, Robert Wilson, Mabou Mines (Lee Breuer, JoAnn Akalaitis), Elizabeth LeCompte, and others. But there was no system akin to that developed for Kathakali to keep this repertory alive.

And not even the Kathakali system can cope with bringing new total theater into existence. In a little while I will return briefly to the Stanislavski system and some of its offshoots. This system is almost entirely concerned with creating roles within the frame of the literary theater—the theater where playwrights first write plays and then directors, actors, and designers "produce" those plays. The experimental theater of the sixties and seventies was not literary, though it did use texts (just as Kathakali and Noh use texts) as part of a total fabric, a weave, of performative elements; for this performance theater the Stanislavskian means were not adequate.

But neither ought anyone to romanticize or idealize the Kathakali Kalamandalam method. Still there are many things to be admired, especially the nonjudgmental way the training went along and the luxury of having many hours a day and six years to complete a full course. As I observed in 1976:

Excellence is strived for but not "professionalism" in the Euro-American sense of slickness, polish, finish, or even stage presence. Just do what's asked for. If it is rough, it shows as rough. With repetition, and maturity, the professionalism will come in, the polish will shine not through intense hard work over the short haul but through repeated additions of patina over years of working. There is time here to "let it happen" rather than, as in Euro-American training, "making it happen." The focus is on the work being done here right now, not on the audience to be.

This slow organic growing leads to the artist's sense that he is working on an objective task. And this objectivity yields not "mechanical acting" but, often enough, truly illuminated performing. Having mastered a concrete physical score, the artist is free inside this "second nature"—a second nature that has even reconstructed the way he stands, walks, moves, gestures, uses his eyes. And, under the immense costumes and ornate makeup of Kathakali, the artist is doubly transformed, first through training and massage in his basic physical being and then through makeup and costuming in his appearance. Yet this double transformation does not weigh him down, rendering him psychically or artistically immobile. On the contrary, he is free within the objective world of Kathakali. At least, the best actors are free. As I watched the professional company rehearse, I realized that

The individual performer is nonconscious and free; he is absolutely "controlled" in all his gestures from the most gross to a tiny blink of the eye, a gesture of the small finger, a turn-up of the big toe. Psychologically he "feels" free. Socioaesthetically he is in the web of a transindividual matrix: part of what he is has entered him through his training and repetitive performing. But at the same time he is free from thinking about the performances, he is free of himself and from himself when he is performing. He is not "in trance," but he may as well be. He is responsible for expressing the socioaesthetic matrix that his performance actually manufactures on the spot. But he is "in flow" in regard to that matrix; he lets go into it, and in that way he is personally free. Free even, if he is up to it, to invent.

I spoke to some of the best performers. They improvise. But there is no training for improvisation. Improvisation is something that an actor tries relatively late in his career: it is an earned privilege. And, if an improvisation is impressive enough, one might pass it on to a younger student as a piece of business. That's that way Kathakali slowly, but very steadily, changes. I interviewed V. M. Govindan whom everyone calls Gopi, among the best of the "younger" performers (in his forties); he said that "Improvisation cannot be taught. One can learn [its principles] by watching the teachers and the elders." Thus the creative aspect of Kathakali—if by "creative" is meant the addition of something new—is the right of the most mature performers; and it is something they themselves learn to do after mastering their roles, not something they are taught to do. This is very different than in the Euro-American tradition, where improvisation is mostly the work of the young and where improvisations are used early in the rehearsal process as a means of exploring the various possibilities of a role and/or mise-en-scène.

There is a theory of acting implicit in the Kathakali Kalamandalam method. As I see it, this theory is based on the following:

1. Learn the details of specific roles in their most concrete, physical sense: gestures, rhythms, footwork, eyework, etc.

2. Repeat these drills until they are mastered and they enter the body and become "second nature."

3. From the beginning, performers learn "performance sequences"—that is, elements of Kathakali that will actually be used in performances. These elements are not made into a logical grammar of movements (though such a grammar could be constructed from them) but are taught as drills. Thus, from the beginning the student learns actual parts of the performance—whether or not he "understands" these parts is irrelevant.

4. These bits of performance are accumulated into longer and longer sequences until enough has been accumulated to make a role and enough roles have been accumulated to make a performance. Accumulation of bits and absorption of whole roles by new performers go along together.

5. Early in a new performer's career—even while a beginning student—master teachers (and directors) identify neophytes with specific roles and role-types. According to bone structure, body size, gracefulness and other criteria students are typecast for life. This both freezes and frees them. Their range of roles is severely limited, but as their career develops they can experiment within their roles.

6. Younger performers are put in actual professional productions as soon as practicable. The repertory contains enough simple, basic roles to accommodate beginners. As performers mature they progress through a series of roles suited to their age and skills.

7. Over time students develop into young performers, young performers into mature ones, and a few mature ones into masters. There is a lifelong progression envisioned and provided for. As the performer matures, a sense of "character" is experienced by the performer. This sense of character is not specifically sought after, as in Euro-America. It may first present itself as a sense of a whole class of characters. Individuation, like "creativity," occurs later in an artist's life. The feelings that go with becoming a character follow automatically as an actor matures and keeps playing the same characters over and over. Of course, there is the danger that the performing will become mechanical. But for outstanding performers a sense of authentic depth comes with deep familiarity and identification with a role or set of roles. Thus Gopi particularly enjoyed the Pacha roles of Nala and Bhima.

As basic work becomes second nature, subtleties emerge that reflect very precisely the personality of the performer. It is not as an American might think: creativity has not been stifled by all the apparently mechanical training. Rather, when the time comes for individuality to be expressed it emerges from a wholly mastered technique that no longer feels "technical" either to the performer or to the audience. Masters contribute from themselves—even if they are not always conscious that they are doing so. From their point of view, they are doing what they know how to do, pouring themselves into the vessels of their scores. But these vessels are not stone-hard, they are surprisingly malleable, not only during the times of allowed improvisation but even in the details of the scores themselves. Watching Gopi dance, with his thin, athletic body (during rehearsals costumes are not worn), was an altogether different experience than watching one of his more portly colleagues doing exactly the same role. This goes without saying. But I would suppose that even two actors of exactly the same physique would bring, or could bring, very different tones to their roles. The parallel in Western art that I think of is that two ballerinas or two symphony orchestras performing the exact same scores can yield wildly different occasions.

I watched Gopi rehearse Bhima's killing of Duhsasana from the *Mahabharata*. Duhsasana had humiliated Bhima's wife, Draupadi.

Gopi stabs, cuts open Duhsasana's stomach, drinks blood, pulls out the intestines, bites them off, whirls them around over his head, and gallops away on a horse (he does the galloping himself). He goes to Draupadi and sprinkles Duhsasana's blood on her. Gopi has spectacular body and facial control, including his eyes. His technique is the best I've seen. When finished with this riff, he is slightly out of breath. This solo took ten minutes, and in it he discharged tremendous energy. All through, the drums were pounding and the clanging cymbals drove Gopi forward. At the end of this fabulous riff, the director talks a little to the musicians, not a word to Gopi. Actually the praise ethic (so popular among us) can be destructive because it focuses the performer outside himself, undercuts his self-reliance and assurance. The directing to strive for is to speak technically, analytically, correctively, and descriptively. But not in terms of praise or blame.

Gopi's dancing is luminous. Very precise, with finely tuned eye and face gestures. His body is slim, well-tuned. He moves with irony and grace, his eyes twinkling. It is a delight to watch him move because he does it so clearly with no extraneous flutters—no circles where there should be square corners. Also he works effortlessly—like the gods, he doesn't seem to sweat, his eyes are always open, unblinking (except where blinking is called for in the score), and he seems always a few inches off the ground, so lightfooted is he.

Even after this extremely strenuous sequence, Gopi is not out of breath. He finishes with a slow faint after a very long athletic sequence. The music stops, he gets up at once, and walks out of the room. His partner is heaving breaths.

As I talked with Gopi, it became apparent to me that his training had blended into his performing and that the achievement of the two taken together was to permit Gopi *not* to feel the feelings he is showing. There is nothing "pumped up" in his performing; as with the great athlete, admiration is given as much for the effortlessness of the achievement as for the thing done (Willie Mays chasing down a fly ball). The feeling is evoked in the spectator (rasa theory; see chapter 3). The performance score is so deep in his body that Gopi simply relaxes into doing what he is doing. At his best, such a performer is nescient: blank. Then, as the score dances him (not the other way around anymore), his emotions are released. His performance may be illuminated by this flow of feelings generated here and now by the particular moments of the performance. Nescience is not ignorance but abandonment of the pursuit of a specific goal—because the mastery of what is needed to achieve that goal has been attained. Just as any person can walk and think at the same time—the gentle rhythm of walking is often a tonic for thought— so a Kathakali master performer like Gopi can perform and think at the same time. His thinking is not meandering, however, but connected to the performance being performed. "When I do any role," says Gopi, "I think I am that particular character. I don't allow my concentration to waver. So it might be due to this I am so good."

The work method is not to begin from a set of abstractions, characterologically speaking, emotionally speaking, but from very specific routines, bodily speaking: mudras, footwork, eyework, talas, et cetera. The performer emerges as an individual "I," a "star," only at the height of his career—only after achieving nescience. The goal of training is to lead the performer to this nescience. The mudras (hand gestures) are and are not a language. It is possible to make something new with the mudras. Some of the boys told me that at their dormitories they play with the mudras as a kind of sign language. But that door is tightly shut in Kathakali itself. Mudras are taught not as morphemes and workable grammar but as established formulations: whole phrases, sentences, narratives. Like yoga asanas—or like boys chanting the Vedas in a Sanskrit they did not understand but which they memorized letter-perfect—these total items become part of the body. They are not "thought about" but "incorporated." Apparently nothing changes. But then, every several generations, maybe, an innovator, not in the guise of a rebel but almost always as one who has mastered the whole vocabulary, who is fully in control of the traditional formulations, revises what is given, rearranges it, makes changes. Then this new way becomes part of the accepted tradition, even to the degree that the innovation is "forgotten"; it heals seamlessly into the ongoing flow (see chapter 2). There are three styles of Kathakali in Kerala, evidence of the outcome of divergent evolutions of the basic genre. And new plays are composed for Kathakali, but few find a permanent place in the repertory of the Kalamandalam. From the perspective of the Euro-American theater, Kathakali is conservative and traditional, more like Noh than American experimental or even mainstream performance. Kathakali could, perhaps, be compared in its methods and development to classical ballet.

The practices I've described imply four theorems that apply not only to Kathakali but, I think, to almost all "traditional" performing arts:

1. The inner and the outer are manifestations of a One, and therefore training either inner or outer is training both. Since the outer is more easily trained, it is the object of training. And the chief method is repetition based on imitation.

2. Training consists of repeating concrete sequences of behavior. These sequences are taken as integers from the finished form.

3. A limited repertory exists—and a limited history, a limited cosmos. All that is will ultimately repeat itself.

4. The whole is greater than its parts: by repeating the parts the whole will be grasped; by repeating the whole the form of the whole will (or may) ultimately reveal itself. This is the mantra theory of knowing. Illumination occurs, if at all, only when the performer no longer thinks about "doing the part" or doing anything but just blankly does.

Such an approach to art, to life, is extremely conservative. In this way the training at the Kathakali Kalamandalam is consistent with old-style Indian thought. If this kind of training is not done with careful attention to the particular relationship between teacher and student (what the Indians call the guru-shishya relationship)—which must be one of mutual respect, even love—the whole thing can quickly become brutal, authoritarian, mechanical, and deadening. To a certain degree, even at the Kalamandalam, it has become just that.

On 12 July, a few days before leaving the Kalamandalam, I noted some of the negative aspects of the training: "The discipline is slack; no one really makes corrections of exercises; the senior students, instead of setting examples—or staying outside so they can correct the younger students—halfheartedly participate, often displaying sloppy footwork, incomplete exercises." The exercises have become mechanical. They are done over such a long period of time, six years, that they are absorbed as dogma and then slighted—the way a Roman Catholic priest might mumble the Mass. I saw only two or three of the older boys go at the basic exercises with precision and dedication. When I spoke to members of the professional company, Gopi included, I was told that of course the mature performers "wanted to do" the exercises but there was never enough time. A definite kind of "school attitude" was apparent: people do what they are supposed to do, required to do, but that's all. Occasionally, for official visits and for the benefit of note-taking outsiders like me, the discipline is polished up.

What's missing is the old-fashioned guru-shishya relationship. Boys used to study with their fathers or with teachers to whom they owed an almost absolute allegiance. They studied the specific roles of their guru; furthermore, the guru instilled in the shishya a sense of social responsibility. The relationship was hedged by obligatory exchanges of gifts; students were knitted into the household of their teacher. At the Kalamandalam, founded in 1930, a somewhat "modernized" situation exists. The school has many qualities associated with Western-style education: dormitories, classrooms, class periods, teachers who are assigned to specific classes (the students change). The whole feeling of the Kalamandalam is ambivalent: between traditional Indian and modern Western methods.

Still, when all is said and done, I came away from the Kalamandalam able to list a considerable number of "good points" as well as some "bad points."

Good points
• The dance goes into the body.
• Ultimately, there is a freedom from within: when the routines of the performance are in the body the mind is free, and finally the body is free too: masters of Kathakali improvise.
• A very beautiful dance-drama is maintained and transmitted more or less intact.
• The training is a model for an intensive and deep body training needed in the Euro-American tradition (where it exists in ballet and modern dance but not in theater).

Bad points
• Except for a very few persons, individual initiative is stunted.
• At the Kalamandalam, at least, there is very little experimentation.
• The "language" of Kathakali is more or less closed: a museum.
• As the guru-shishya relationship is put aside but some of its external rigor kept, students and teachers are alienated from each other.
• The result is a dogmatic authoritarianism.

The Kalamandalam system does not generate new work so much as it preserves a specific style of Kathakali. There are groups in Kerala who do experiment with the form—introducing new stories, bringing Kathakali up to date. And teachers, from the Kalamandalam and elsewhere, have gone to Delhi and beyond, where Kathakali training and mise-en-scène have been used by innovators within and outside of India.

Some of the basic elements of the Kalamandalam system were brought to Grotowski in the early 1960s and were used by him as an important part of his "poor theater" training (plate 51). Eugenio Barba visited the Kalamandalam in 1963. In the school's guest book Barba wrote: "My visit to Kalamandalam has greatly helped me in my studies and the research material I have collected will surely be of the greatest assistance to those people working at the Theatre Laboratory in Poland." In *Towards a Poor Theatre* (Grotowski 1968, 133–215), the training methods used in Grotowski's theater during the early to middle sixties are recorded in detail. Many of these methods—head rolls, body rolls, eye and face exercises—seem influenced by the Kathakali training. Other aspects of Grotowski's training—the emphasis on breath, the

51. Training at Grotowski's Polish Laboratory Theatre in 1964. Some of this training was modeled after Kathakali training. Photo by Fredi Graedel.

headstands and shoulderstands, the process of concentration—are based on hatha yoga. Grotowski notes that much of the training process between 1959 and 1962 was "recorded by Eugenio Barba during the period he spent at the Theatre Laboratory" (1968, 133). In 1963 Barba went to the Kalamandalam. The training at Grotowski's theater changed after Barba's return from India. As Barba himself noted in *Towards a Poor Theatre* (which he edited), "On comparing the exercises [of 1966] with those of the 1959–62 period, a definite change is noticeable" (1968, 175). Grotowski used a more "hands-on" method, touching and manipulating the students; there was a greater integration of movement and voice; animal exercises played a very important role. There was even a suggestion of adapting the idea of mudras: "The hands are, in a sense, a substitute for the voice. They are used to accentuate the body's objective" (1968, 191–92).

When I studied with Grotowski in November 1967 I had not yet been to India. I made no links between what Grotowski and performer Ryszard Cieslak taught and Kathakali. Now, in retrospect, I see lots of connections. But there are decisive differences too, for Grotowski's training methods owe much to Stanislavski's emphasis on an "inner technique" (self-analysis, psychologizing) and to Meyerhold's "biomechanics" (rigorous body training adapted, somewhat, from the time-and-motion studies of the American, Frederick Winslow Taylor).

What impressed me most about the methods at the Kalamandalam was the insistence—not spoken or theorized but omnipresent nevertheless—that the body comes first, that performance knowledge enters a person by means of rigorous, continuous, rhythmical bodywork. On 6 July I joined the class of young boys. Immediately after, I noted:

Felt very good. Much easier to do when there are others doing it too. Much easier both mentally and physically. But at the same time the work is harder—more strenuous—than when I was doing it alone, or with only my teacher. This morning sweat rivered my face and torso. Instead of asking "What's next?" I just went with the others. My eyes saw, my body did. No translation; just eyes to muscles. Later, my teacher [M. P. Sankaran Nambudirir] explained: "Some get it easy, some hard. But sooner or later they all do it without thinking."

ə

What are the functions of training? Are these the same in all cultures? I can think of six functions. These do not exist separately but overlap. These functions are:

1. Interpretation of a dramatic text or performance text
2. Transmission of a performance text
3. Transmission of performance "secrets" (as in Noh)
4. Self-expression
5. Mastery of a specific technique
6. Group formation

In the Euro-American tradition especially, "creativity" and "originality" are prized; "new" interpretations of plays (dramatic texts) or mise-en-scènes (whether of theater or dance) are sought. Critics go out of their way to praise performers who can "find something new" in classic texts; and little praise is reserved for those who, for example, do Shakespeare just the way the last group of actors did it. This craze for new interpretations is not so different than its sister craze for "new plays" or "new dances." There is a sense that art, like everything else of value, ought to be progressive: always moving on to "what's next." Thus a new interpretation is a way of uncovering the progressive tendencies in an apparently old (= outdated, of no more use) text. But there are limits. When I deconstructed classic texts like Euripides' *Bacchae* (to make *Dionysus in 69*) and Shakespeare's *Macbeth* (to make *Makbeth*), more than one critic anxiously urged me to make my own plays rather than take apart someone else's. My response is that I want to work with both new and old material: to explore the mythic qualities of classics whose stories and characters are ingrained in the culture; and yet to use postmodern and intercultural techniques of preparation and staging.

Many other directors and choreographers in recent years felt this same double tug. Grotowski, Peter Brook, Joseph Chaikin, Elizabeth LeCompte, JoAnn Akalaitis, Lee Breuer—and many others—neither interpret old texts nor compose wholly new ones but practice a kind of theatrical *bricolage,* deconstructing/reconstructing texts and mises-en-scènes from a variety of sources, including the lives of the performers (see Schechner 1982*b*). But mainstream Euro-American theater still works from literary texts, and therefore depends on actors who can portray any number of different characters in different performance styles. Actors are trained to play Hamlet one day, Gogo the next, a character in a soap opera the next, and "something from the Restoration" on weekends. The regional theater builds seasons based on a formula that mixes classic, nineteenth-century, contemporary, and experimental (at least new) plays. The same actors are expected to excel in all these modes. In practice, the various modes are reduced to versions of naturalism; and naturalism as it applies to acting is usually trained for by using Stanislavski's methods. Stanislavski emphasized flexibility. He was proud of his own ability to play many different kinds of characters. The actor's function in this kind of theater is to be the recipient of both the author's and the director's instructions and ideas. A difficult task, that, to be both passive (receptive to the ideas of others) and active or "creative" (able to make these ideas one's own, and to broadcast them boldly to an audience). Meyerhold, in his "theory of the straight line," summarized the process of such a theater:

The actor reveals his soul freely to the spectator, having assimilated the creation of the director, who, in his turn, has assimilated the creation of the author

Author → Director → Actor → ← Spectator [Braun 1969, 50]

But it's not only Euro-American modern theater that demands of its performers extraordinary flexibility. There are genres that emphasize story-telling—with the narrator enacting many roles, even animals, stones, and weapons. Instead of playing different roles on different nights in different plays, the Sanskrit tradition as it has continued from the tenth century to the present day in Kutiyattam gives the master performer the opportunity to transform himself during one scene into many different characters and characterizations. On 13 July 1976, at the Kalamandalam where he was teaching Kutiyattam (having brought the art out of the temple, its traditional home), I enjoyed the late master Ramchakyar (plate 52) playing a scene where Hanuman, the monkey-god, tells the story of Ravana's war against Indra. Hanuman has penetrated Ravana's guard and is in Ravana's garden in Lanka. He admires the beautiful trees of the garden. These trees remind him of the trees Ravana took from Indra's heavenly domain. This, in turn, reminds him of the war between Ravana and Indra. The sequence is taken from act 6 of the Sanskrit play, *Anguliyangam*. Frequently in Kutiyattam only a portion of a play is performed on a given occasion. Also stories within stories within stories are a hallmark of Hindu literature and dramaturgy (see O'Flaherty 1982). These "nests" of narrative, as O'Flaherty calls them, form a system wherein all reality is expressed relatively. Touch one part of the webbed system and other parts vibrate responsively. In less than one hour Ramchakyar as Hanuman became Ravana, Ravana's general, six musicians, Ravana's army marching, a bow and arrow, a sword and shield, and a spear. All in all, Ramchakyar showed fourteen characters and/or characterizations. Ramchakyar's achievement is shown in figures 5.2 and 5.3. In Kutiyattam "a role" = "what one performer does during a performance." This is different than in mainstream Euro-American theater where "a role" = "a character." Kutiyattam is closer to Brecht's Verfremdungseffekt or to what Michael Kirby described as "non-matrixed performing" common in experimental theater and performance art (see Kirby 1965 and 1972). Brecht's ideas about acting were greatly influenced by his understanding of Chinese classical theater, Peking Opera especially, where the performer is more than an actor—acting a single role is only one of the performer's tasks. Others may include story-

52. Ramchakyar as Shurpanakha. Photo by Richard Schechner.

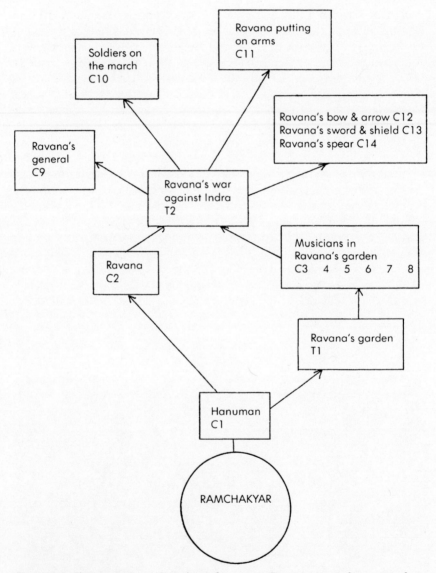

Figure 5.2. *Characterizations (C) and transformations (T) in a sequence from act 6 of Anguliyangam as performed by Ramchakyar in July 1976.*

telling, commenting on the actions of the character or characters one is playing, rearranging scenery, dealing directly with the audience. Experimental theater from the 1960s into the 1980s carried these ideas still further (see Schechner, ed., 1970, Schechner 1973*a*, 1973*b*, and Loeffler, ed., 1980).

The second function of training—one very common in Asian theater but found in the West mostly in dance—is to transmit a performance text. Kathakali cannot be contained in its written text, nor can Kutiyattam, Noh, or Balinese topeng (to name just four genres out of many). Ballet and the dances of Martha Graham and Doris Humphrey can be "notated" but are not

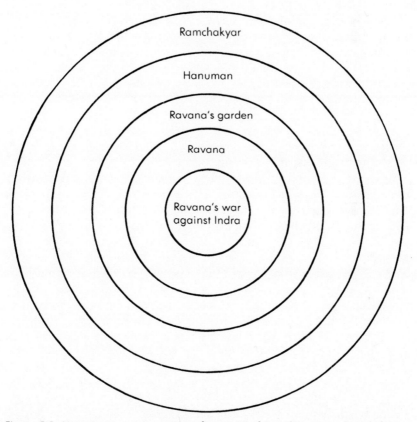

Figure 5.3. *Narrative nests in a sequence from act 6 of Anguliyangam. Ramchakyar as Hanuman describes Ravana's garden (into which he has come as an enemy of Ravana). In the garden (Ramchakyar-Hanuman) Ravana tells the story of his war against Indra. Ramchakyar as Hanuman as Ravana tells the story of the war and in doing so enacts six more characters.*

based on a literary text in the same way as a production of *Hamlet* by the Royal Shakespeare Company is based on Shakespeare's playtext. The movement is the dance, and only a limited amount of interpretation is possible. To transmit the "text" of the dance, as in the Asian genres, is to transmit the dance itself. This dance itself (or a specific Noh, Kathakali, Kutiyattam, etc.) is a "performance text." Unlike the plays of Shakespeare, Ibsen, Beckett, or Kalidasa, the scores of these dance-dramas and dances are identical with specific mises-en-scènes. The words of Shakespeare have been used as the armature, or pretext, for any number of enactments, each of which may differ strongly from the others without tampering with any of Shakespeare's words. But Balanchine's *Agon* is the *Agon*—a whole and complete score including movement, music, costumes—just as the Kalamandalam's *Daksha Yagam* is itself and no other. It is different to train a performer to make new interpretations of a dramatic text—even to deconstruct the literary text and use it as the basis for a new text—than it is to train a performer to preserve specific performance texts. The performance text is put into the body of the performer through a training whose bases are integral parts of the performance text itself. Once in the body of the performer, the performance text is manifest during performances and passed on to younger performers in turn. This process of training, which is also a process of preservation and transmission, is most of what goes on at the Kalamandalam.

In an even more radical way it is the process of transmission still used by the masters of Noh drama in Japan. The "secrets" of Noh remain within certain families. Not even all members of the family know the secrets. They are passed on from father to son or from senior company member to designated successor. The means of transmission always include body-to-body training but may also include written notes and treatises (as with Zeami's writings). The passing on of secrets is only the most severe form of transmission in a carefully organized hierarchy. At the lowest level, in today's Japan, several million people study Noh as a hobby. Some of these persons become very skilled, and audiences at Noh performances contain many such aficionados. Company members receive intense training from early childhood from elder members of the family. And, finally, specially designated persons receive the family's guarded secrets concerning performing.

The preservation of performance secrets is quite the opposite of what has been going on in Euro-American theater for the past eighty or more years. Here the emphasis has been on telling all—through writings, open classes, demonstrations, workshops. The success of the Stanislavski method is founded on its adherents' fervent wish to proselytize. In a similar way, and each for his own method, Brecht, Meyerhold, Grotowski, Brook, Chaikin—almost everyone who trains theater people in the West—have tried very hard to get the word out. Brecht, of course, was mostly interested in an acting style that would suit his dramaturgy. And his work has survived more in his plays than in a particular method of acting. Stanislavski, on the other hand, was a great actor whose whole life's energy went into developing methods of systematizing what he felt were the "subconscious" means of creativity employed by great actors. In his three powerful books about actor training— *An Actor Prepares* (1946), *Building a Character* (1949), and *Creating a Role* (1961)—Stanislavski laid out his methods in detail. The methods were not frozen; over more than thirty years they changed considerably. The changes are noteworthy in that the tendency was to leave behind subjective/psychologistic interior training and move toward what Stanislavski called his "method of physical action." This method combined elements of concrete physical work familiar to those who know the Asian techniques with standard "find-the-motivation" work from Stanislavski's earlier periods. What Stanislavski wanted to do, ultimately, was to physicalize the psychological work, to make the interior states of mind (intentions, motivations, "through lines" or "spines") clear by developing for each role a specific physical score. This goal of physicalizing interior mental states is shared by many Euro-American theater artists. It is what joins people like Richard Foreman, Robert Wilson, and Lee Breuer to such unlikely comrades as Joseph Chaikin, Robert L. Benedetti (author of two widely used books on actor training [1970, 1976]), and Viola Spolin, whose *Improvisation for the Theater* (1963) bridges some of the differences between Brecht and Stanislavski. Next to Lee Strasberg and his Actors' Studio, Spolin through her work on improvisations and theater games has been the most influential American actor trainer.

A few more words on the third function of training, transmission of performance secrets: To keep secrets about performing assumes that performance knowledge is powerful. It says that performing is something more than entertainment. For a person to have access to performance knowledge is both a privilege and a risk. This attitude toward performance knowledge is a clear link between performance and shamanism. There is evidence connecting the origins of theater with shamanism. E. R. Dodds (1951) links elements of early Greek religion and theater to shamanism. E. T. Kirby (1974) finds the origins of many popular entertainments—clowning, acrobatics, rope tricks, juggling, sword swallowing, fire tricks, and so on—in shamanism. As Dodds says, shamanism is characterized by a "belief in a detachable soul or self, which by suitable techniques can be withdrawn from the body even during life, a self which is older than the body and will outlast it" (1951, 146–47). As I have pointed out in "Towards a Poetics of Performance" (1977, 127–32), it's a short step from shamanism understood in Dodd's way to the practices of Balinese trance, Noh, and "characterization" in modern theater.

It is an equally short step from shamanism to believing performances to be efficacious, either on behalf of the individual, as in curing ceremonies, exorcisms, or "simple" Aristotelian catharsis, or on behalf of the community, as in political theater, satire, or obligatory rites. Thinking of training as the transmission of performance secrets maintains in force a high seriousness concerning performance, a respect for its traditional functions both personally and collectively.

The fourth function of training is to give the performer a means of self-expression. This is important in both the West and the Orient, but it is achieved in very different ways. Since Stanislavski, and especially since Grotowski, self-expression has become a main function not only of training but of theatrical performance itself. In some significant ways—workshops, "paratheater," the "human potential movement"—procedures that previously were part of training, that were done before, and in preparation for, public performance, have become the performances themselves. Sometimes, as in Grotowski's work since the midseventies, public performances have been abandoned. All that remains are techniques of self-expression, group interaction, intercultural exchange. The focus of theatrical activity has shifted from the "finished work" to the "process of working," and this process has become a thing in itself. In this way, theatrical workshops have augmented, or replaced, certain kinds of religious experiences. It is a phenomenon that anthropologist Ronald Grimes calls "parashamanism."

Like shamanism proper, parashamanism is not a sect, movement, or ecclesiastical institution. Rather, it is an individualistic, ritualistic practice which is presently taking shape in the margins of culture. . . . Parashamanism is characteristic of the Polish Lab [Grotowski], Actor's Lab [of Toronto], and Welfare State [England], as well as a number of individuals . . . and institutes. . . . The social locus of parashamanism is in the interstices among university, church/synagogue, theater, and therapy groups. [1982, 255]

But even before such radical departures from mainstream modern Euro-American theater, training was used to help performers "find" and express themselves. Such a function is based on the belief that there is a self within yearning to be free. As Benedetti writes of Stanislavski:

In his search for *being,* Stanislavski developed ways of heightening the personal involvement of the actor in his own performance. The most famous aspect of his training was his "psycho-technique," a set of exercises and principles designed to help the actor involve his own personal feelings and experiences in the creation of his role. Through self-discipline, life observation and the development of total concentration, Stanislavski's actor learned to "recall" particular emotional sensations from his own life which were analogous to those experienced by the character. Armed with his disciplined memory for sensation and emotion, the actor then opened himself to experience what the character experienced *as if* it were actually happening to him. By thus putting himself totally in the place of the character, the actor was able to construct a performance which became a *real* experience for him, not merely a re-enactment or representation of a fiction. Although Stanislavski's actor always worked from the basis of his own personal self ("always be yourself on stage," he taught), the actor's self was metamorphosed into a new self by the power of the experiences of the character, the experiences were happening *as if* to the actor himself. Just as we are formed by the experiences and conditions of our lives, so Stanislavski's actor allowed himself to be re-formed by the experiences of his character-as-if-himself, permitting him to truly *be* in the reality of his character. [1976, 42]

There's a lot to unpack in Benedetti's gloss on Stanislavski.

First, Stanislavski's "as if" is very close to Turner's "subjunctive mood" and Bateson's "play frame." These are all ways of saying that humans have various spheres of reality, each of which involves persons intensely, wholly; but some of them—the "as if," the "subjunctive," the "playful"—do so in a way that detaches actions from consequences. To murder a wife "in life" has consequences very different than Othello's smothering of Desdemona. And yet the smothering of Desdemona as a theatrical act, in play, "as if," has very definite theatrical consequences and involves—at least in Stanislavski's system—the engagement of feelings, intentions, and expressions analogous to what "goes on in life." These references are in quotation marks because those marks signal in writing the framing that is signaled by means of theatrical convention in the theater. And the arousal of one mood, the subjunctive, invariably puts into question (or quotation marks) the other, the indicative.

Next, Stanislavski's work in helping the actor to express his own feelings within the "given circumstances" (the life conditions) of the character was the first step in a process that has led by now to a number of performers building whole shows around expression of their own personal lives (see Schechner 1982*b*). This is traditional in poetry, even the novel; but it's new for mainstream theater. Where it has been theatrically more common is in popular entertainments: singers, storytellers, stand-up comics. The performance of the self in theater has also been strongly influenced by the movement from visual art to environments to happenings. The confluence of these tendencies has created a new genre, Performance Art.[1]

Third, in its own way, Stanislavski's system of training is not so different from what goes on at the Kalamandalam. The techniques are different, but the underlying assumption of Stanislavski—that a theatrical character is an actual person—guides these techniques toward an ever more precise apprehension of that "second person" who is the character. Just as the neophyte Kathakali performer imitates the concrete score of a dance-drama and finds his way toward acting by such imitation, so the neophyte Stanislavski actor tries to locate in his own life strict analogies to what he supposes has happened to the character. In lining up analogies—particular "given circumstances," in Stanislavski's jargon—the actor discovers precise physical actions, associations, and feelings appropriate to the role he is preparing. The difference is—and it is a very great difference—that right from the beginning of training and from the start of his career the Stanislavski actor will be "creative," will invent his very own interpretation of each character he plays.

In this placement of creativity—where it occurs in the rehearsal process and where in a career that lasts a lifetime—the Euro-American and the Asian methods diverge absolutely. José Quintero, whose credits as a director include renowned productions of O'Neill's *The Iceman Cometh* and *Long Day's Journey into Night*, put his finger on the two most important reasons that today's American theater suffers from a lack of first-rate young directors: the dissolution of groups and the failure of American society to grant creative freedom to its senior theater artists.

> The young director has no recourse but to initiate a fearful journey inward, an exploration of the world within him, where he begins to find the materials of his real identity. Daily he comes to rehearsals; filled with shame and terror at first, he reveals a raw piece of himself, whose texture matches, and therefore illuminates, a patch of the reality of the play [he is directing].
>
> This most frightening and miraculous process can only happen within a group where mutual dependency and loyalty to a common goal create a feeling of solidarity against the pressure of outside forces. Now that inflated costs and union rules have made even Off Broadway production terribly expensive, there are far fewer producing groups than when I started out [in the forties]. And today, these producing groups have no programs. They put on unrelated plays with outside casts, instead of using people from the group.
>
> I cannot help but wonder, therefore, where a young director of today goes to meet his greatest allies—the actors and actresses of his generation—to begin braiding that all-important relationship through the seemingly unimportant and everyday rituals of eating together, dancing together, exchanging confidences. Most crucial, director and actors have to work together over and over again until they find that they have developed a private language, a connection unmarred by fears. . . .
>
> At a memorial service after Harold [Clurman's] death, Arthur Miller talked about the frustration Harold must have felt during his last years, for here was a man who had come to the full maturing of his art, and found he had no place to go. For this country has no national theater, where the great works of dramatic art (which Broadway—and now even Off Broadway—cannot afford to do) can be performed by the most mature talent in the land. . . . A theater which not only ignores, but accepts such waste [of its mature talent] must tend to rein in a novice director's urge to concentrate on mastering the disciplines of his art. [Quintero 1982, 23]

On both ends of the creative life there is a horrendous gap. But Quintero misses part of the problem, which is actually the paradox of encouraging a kind of chaotic, willy-nilly creativity early on, while preventing mature artists (and Clurman is only one example among dozens) from fully exploring the creative opportunities of performing arts, as either directors, actors, scenographers, or what-have-you.

In the kind of training most common in Euro-America—training for the interpretation of dramatic texts—creativity is encouraged early in the program. Improvisations "loosen up" the young actor/director; during rehearsals everyone is encouraged during the first weeks to "try things out." The invention of something new happens most frequently early in training, early in the rehearsal process, and early in an artist's career. The avant-garde is almost synonymous with youth, with *les enfants terribles*. Euro-Americans think that a person can afford to experiment while young. The Puritan hatred of theater underlying such "affording" is not often recognized: Fool around while you still have time enough ahead of you to recoup and "get serious." Getting serious means getting down to business, means satisfying the tastes (at the box office) of the upper middle class. A director says to an actor, "You want to try something new? Go ahead," but not at dress rehearsal. A producer says to a director, "You want to try something new? Go ahead," but not with a show capitalized at $1.5 million.

The process of Asian theater is different, as is the nature of what is thought of as new or experimental. First, know that in Asia there is a modern theater roughly equivalent to what goes on in Euro-America. Shingeki in Japan, the "new" theater in India, the "modern" theater in Indonesia—all the large Asian cities, at least, have theaters that perform a repertory mixing Ibsen with Rakesh, Miller with Kishida, and beyond to a world of experimental theater that although it has local peculiarities is fundamentally intercultural and postmodern. I mean the work, in Asia, of Sircar, Rendra, Ikranagara, Suzuki, Terryama, and many others. But outside of this world of modern and experimental performance, and much larger than it, is the world of traditional performance.

At the start of training in an Asian traditional form the students do nothing but imitate. They are plunged directly into the work; there is no creativity allowed. In the method of direct acquisition the beginners begin by learning parts of actual performances. Words are not separated from actions; actions are not broken into "alphabets" of basic "grammars" to be learned abstractly. Everything is specific, concrete, drawn from actual performances. Learning this way is extremely personal. The methods—even when written down, as Zeami wrote down his ideas about acting—are not textbook-ridden. No one outside of Zeami's school would use his writings as a textbook of acting the way *An Actor Prepares* by Stanislavski and many another book by Western masters are used. As Chaikin comments:

In books which document exercises, I feel that I am reading a book of recipes, whether they are exercises by Stanislavski, Viola Spolin, or the Open Theatre. The reason they cannot be [authentically] documented is because it is internal territory. If the actor could explain it, the exercise would be unnecessary. The exercise is an agreed-upon structure. The structure can be explained yet it is empty of content. An exercise is untranslatable. [1972, 134–35]

Many actor trainers disagree with Chaikin. I disagree with him. There is value in writing out the recipes. But the danger is obvious: alienated training. Books have a way of justifying themselves, of explaining why they are instructing. And the "classics" of training are surrounded by other writings that explicate, analyze, and add. The teacher using such books becomes a retailer of someone else's methods. This is different than when a method is passed on from teacher to student, who later becomes a teacher in his own right. At the start, the Stanislavski method had this quality of known direct links: Stanislavski to Meyerhold, Vakhtangov, Michael Chekhov (to name three of Stanislavski's students), who then instructed others while changing the techniques they acquired. But soon enough the methods were learned mostly from books, or by using books as recipes. Teachers got away from direct acquisition—and it was not so important to know the way a particular teacher taught as to ask what method he was teaching. But the way a particular teacher passes on what is learned, modified by his/her own experiences, is the way oral traditions conserve and modify their substance simultaneously. Teaching by direct acquisition means teaching only what one has actually, physically, concretely learned or invented, and that means sharing and transmitting a particular style.

In this way, the "self-expression" of a particular artist is bound up as much in how and what he teaches as it is in his performing. And often enough, in Asia at least, this self-expression, this style, is a way of living just as it is a way of performing. It incorporates an outlook on the world—the Noh way, the Kathakali way—so that it is not only an aesthetics but a sociology, a cosmology, and a religion. These values are transmitted directly as part of performance knowledge. It is there in how the student—who often shares a home with his teacher—eats, sleeps, carries out daily tasks, shows respect for his guru. Such teachers can't use Stanislavski's books, or Grotowski's, or Chaikin's, or Schechner's. This kind of teacher has only his own experiences, and what he has learned directly from his teacher. And he passes on, as directly as possible, as intact as he chooses to, what he knows. He does this because a living tradition embodied in his students is the only means he has of telling the next generation what his life has been. He truly has a "life in art," and that life only.

In Euro-American culture teaching is often looked down on. "Those who can't do, teach." But in India, Japan, Bali—elsewhere too—"Those who do it best, teach." Teaching is the crowning achievement of the artist. The great Ramchakyar came out of the temple not in search of new places to perform but in search of students: he knew that without them Kutiyattam was doomed. To many artists of traditional forms in Asia, their students are as important as their biological children. The two, often enough, are the same: the chief student is one's own child. And if an artist has no children, or none who chooses to go into the art, he seeks someone as a surrogate inheritor, and the line of the art is passed on through that person. The "publications" of a great guru are his/her students.

One reason that this kind of system has not made too much headway in the West (except in dance where it is widely followed, though modified by Euro-American styles of social interaction) is that we are taught to think abstractly from the start of our lives. We value "the best" even if we can only lay our hands on it in reified form. Many feel it is better to have a mediocre teacher-performer use a great text by a great master—a Stanislavski, a Spolin, a Grotowski—than to have the teacher fiddle around with his own (second-rate) stuff. Many believe that a mediocre teacher-artist can become better if he has the right material at hand: the best exercises, the great texts, the most up-to-date equipment. American universities are loaded with students living such pathetic illusions.

Another line of this tendency is the belief that artistic styles can be mass-produced and exported, the way fashions are premiered in Paris or New York and shipped to the hinterlands. So theater workers flock to theater centers hoping not only to see the best that's being done but to pick up a quick fix. Or workshops are organized, importing whoever is hottest. But these practices don't build the sustained groups that Quintero laments we have lost. Nor do such practices develop mature artists—like Harold Clurman—who have somewhere to go with their abilities.

The Euro-American obsession with the new, with what's next, has cut short many a creative life, relegating senior theater artists to a kind of limbo: honored but not employed—or employed the way some movie stars are, to do again and again that for which they are famous. Certainly this is a rigidity far beyond what I saw in Asia. For there it is the senior artists who have earned the right to make changes in the tradition; and these changes are regarded as the high points of an artistic career. They are what give both the individual and the tradition a sense of personal expression.

Earlier I noted Zeami's specification that the Noh shite move through nine levels of training and performing. As the shite's career develops he both ascends and descends the nine levels until he has played roles of all types. Training in Noh is linked to the performance of specific roles. And the repertory is so arranged that a great actor may expect to find new roles challenging him at every stage of his life. The roles—and kinds of roles: gods, warriors, women, demons—change; the performer is always facing problems demanding new solutions. The most respected performers are allowed more improvisation, more tampering with the rules, than younger actors. The relative liberty of an older artist compared to a younger was brought home to me in September 1982 when I studied Noh for a few days with "living national treasure" Izumi Yoshio and his younger colleague (from another Noh school/family), Takabayashi Koji. In my opinion, both were master performers, but Izumi had reached a status that Takabayashi had not yet achieved. They each spoke about how they prepared for a role.

Takabayashi: As soon as I hear that I am going to play a role—whether this is one year, six months, or one day beforehand—I take out my notes on the play and keep these in my mind. I study the mask before performing [plate 53]. If I know six months ahead of time that I am going to perform a given mask I can look at it every day—I can see what the mask is, what it gives me. Or, on the other hand, if I receive a mask but don't know what to use it in, I will study the mask every day till it suggests a play for me to use it in. The mask influences my state of mind, my body. At noon on the day before my performance I refrain from all defiling activities. No contact with death,

53. A Noh actor contemplating his mask prior to entering the stage. Photo by Kaneko Hiroshi.

none with women, menstruating women especially, no food prepared by women, no alcohol. Sometimes these taboos are not followed—in Ithaca [where the Noh workshop was held at Cornell University] I ate a full meal before performing *Okina*. But if I defile myself I think of the pine, the tortoise, the crane to purify myself. It is only *Okina* [a ritual role that initiates the Noh season] that I perform over and over. Once a shite performs *Okina*, that role is present within you—the world of *Okina* has been built within. *Okina* is the only role that should be performed repeatedly. Otherwise I know 170 roles. I am constantly being refreshed in them by teaching them, by playing the roles of stage attendant and chorus.

Izumi: I'm not as serious or conscientious as Takabayashi. I let it all go until the day before. [The seminar participants all laughed at this—Izumi was mixing some truth with a great deal of the noblesse oblige a national treasure has earned.] When I know I am going to play a role I reread the text and my notes—and maybe other commentaries on the role. I let it all sit in my mind. During spare moments, when I am alone with myself, I imagine the play and try to see the stage figure in my mind. I perform the movements in my mind. But I do very little physical practice. I think over all the masks I have, or that are available. I try to find the mask that I want, and then I sit with it and study it.

Takabayashi: You think not only when you're sitting and thinking—but when you're walking. Suddenly I want to practice. I pull out a sword. In Edo once a Noh actor, deep in his inner practice while taking a walk, drew his sword suddenly—a passing Samurai was confronted and what followed was a little misunderstanding.

Takabayashi, in his forties, is a very well respected performer, and a person most concerned with Noh traditions. Izumi, in his sixties, has achieved a higher status. There are differences in their personalities, but these alone do not explain their different approaches. The older artist has earned his right to be more relaxed and personally expressive, to modify tradition as well as follow it. Takabayashi was accompanied by his son Shinji. Shinji taught at the Cornell workshop, and he also performed. He was eighteen, still deep in the relatively early phases of his training and apprenticeship. He displayed even less freedom than his father. To observe the three shites—boy, man, senior artist—was to be witness to the developmental stages central to Noh.

Zeami in his *Kadensho* speaks of his father Kanami when he was past the age of fifty (very old in fourteenth-century Japan).

From this age, as a rule, one had better do nothing. An old saying has it that a live dog is better than a dead lion. But if he is a really accomplished master, who has acquired the true spirit of this path, this flower of his will be visible on the stage, though many kinds of plays will become difficult for him to perform, and the numbers of his audience will become less in any case. My father Kanami died on the nineteenth day of May, at the age of fifty-two. On the fourth day of the same month he gave a dedicatory performance in front of Sengen Shrine in the province of Suruga. His own performance on this program was especially brilliant, and the audience, both high and low, all applauded. He had ceded many showy plays to uninitiated shite, and he himself performed easy ones, in a subdued way; but, with this additional color to it, his flower looked better than ever. As his was *shin-no-hana* [the artistry a shite acquires by severe training and which lasts to the end of his life] it survived until he became old without leaving him, like an old leafless tree which still blossoms. [1968, 23–24]

There is something miraculous—the quintessential creativity—about a great performance by a very old person: it is so "antinatural" that it represents the triumph of pure culture. It is what I felt while watching Ramchakyar play with comic ribaldry the role of Shurpanakha, the demon sister of ten-headed Ravana. In blackface, aiming his wooden milk bottles that were breasts as if they were cannons, roaring with laughter and curses, this old, potbellied man rocked around the stage expressing joy, energy, and a total mastery of Kuti-yattam. Or watch Nakamura Utaemon—another "living national treasure" of Japan—playing the Kabuki role for which he is most famous, Hanjo, the old grieving woman of *Sumidagawa*. As Carol Martin and I noted in our review of the Grand Kabuki,

Utaemon is elegant in her/his perfectly placed gestures of grief and madness; her dishevelled hair is messy in a precise way with a few black wisps straggling across her white-as-paper face. Her bony fingers play the empty air as if it were full of harp strings.

Hanjo meets a compassionate boatman who tells her of a sick child who was nursed by villagers until he died, his mother's name on his lips. In that instant, both Hanjo and the boatman know the boy was her son. Utaemon strikes a silent pose of grief, and lets escape a thin, shrill cry. More than Helene Weigel's silent scream for her dead Swiss Cheese, less than Melina Mercouri's roars for her murdered children. Utaemon's pose and cry are both male (the actor) and female (the character). He/she is resplendent and pitiful in silk brocade and nearly voiceless despair.

Yet, and this is the art of Kabuki, such "unnaturalness" evokes in us responses of genuine emotion. More deep, even, than what we feel watching the real tragedies of the six o'clock news from which *Sumidagawa* could have been extracted. Why? In Hanjo's quiet scream and in the boatman's responsive pause we, the audience, are given what the six o'clock news can't afford to give: time. Time for the eye to take in the scene; time for the ear to hear both the sound and the silence. Time to let Hanjo's unspeakable emotions press against the glass of the boatman's words. And at the Metropolitan Opera House in New York, as at the Kabuki-za in Kyoto, there was additionally the contradiction between the glittering theatre, the elegantly dressed audience, and this old woman in frozen, yet frantic, grief. [1982, 40]

In India and Japan, at least, being old does not mean being worn-out, being without creativity. In fact, old age is associated not only with the masterful performances—marked by control and precision—of Kanami and Utaemon but also with the wildness of Ramchakyar. And more: old age is associated with the traditions of the wandering yamabushi, the ascetic world-renouncing sanyasin, the wilderness domain of shaman-demon Yamamba.

Yeats had a touch of all this, refracted in his last poems, his monologues attributed to "Crazy Jane." But our theater, and our culture, more often pulls the teeth of the old and junks them along with eight-year-old cars.

The fifth function of training is the "mastery of a specific technique." I think I've made clear how this works in Kathakali. It works in analogous ways in Noh, Kabuki, and other forms where there is a hands-on, body-to-body system of transmission. In Euro-America, dance more than theater uses such specific techniques. The existence of these techniques goes a long way in explaining the stability and continuity of the line from ballet to modern dance on to a variety of postmodern dance styles. Examples of just one or two lines of transmission should make my point. From 1915 on Ruth St. Denis and Ted Shawn pioneered a dance company called Denishawn. Although they rejected the particular format of ballet, they instituted their own eclectic technique, and they passed this technique on to members of their company. Among these were Martha Graham and Doris Humphrey. Humphrey passed her technique on to José Limon, whose company still performs dances choreographed by Humphrey. Among the members of Graham's company was Merce Cunningham, who, through his dancing, teaching, and longtime association with musician John Cage, has exerted a great influence on postmodern dance. As dance historian Sally Banes writes:

Merce Cunningham, a soloist in Martha Graham's company from 1939 to 1945, offered a fresh approach to dance in his own work. Beginning in 1944, he gave dance concerts that departed radically from the by-then traditional modern dance. His innovations in dance paralleled those of his friend and colleague John Cage in music. Essentially, he made the following claims: 1) any movement can be material for a dance; 2) any procedure can be a valid compositional method; 3) any part or parts of the body can be used (subject to nature's limitations); 4) music, costume, decor, lighting, and dancing have their own separate logics and identities; 5) any dancer in the company might be a soloist; 6) any space might be danced in; 7) dancing can be about anything, but is fundamentally and primarily about the human body and its movements, beginning with walking. [1980, 6]

In 1960 Cunningham invited Robert Dunn to teach a composition class. Dunn was at the time married to Cunningham company member Judith Dunn. He was also a friend of James Waring, who in the late fifties gave composition classes and staged performances involving many who were later to be leaders of the postmodern movement, Lucinda Childs, David Gordon, Deborah Hay, Yvonne Rainer among them. Among the students in Dunn's classes were Steve Paxton, Simone Forti, and Rainer. And it was from Dunn's classes that the seminal concerts at the Judson Church in New York in 1962 and 1963 were given.

Over the decades the techniques of Denishawn, Graham, Cunningham,

54. A young Balinese sanghyang dancer in trance. Photo by Werner Hahn and Hans Hoefer.

and the postmoderns (some of whom categorically reject technique) both remained steady and spawned divergent, even opposing, works. The point is that the master techniques were there, being passed on body-to-body. It is still possible today to see not only the most contemporary postmodern dances of Carol Martin and Johanna Boyce but also the "classical" work of Humphrey and Graham. Such lines of descent—and the preservation of concrete mises-en-scènes—are very rare occurrences in Euro-American theater. At the Moscow Art Theater Stanislavski's works, and at the Berlin Ensemble Brecht's, are performed. The Comédie Française displays examples of the neoclassical tradition in France. But these theaters, as generators of living styles, appear sterile compared to what's happened in dance. Maybe it is because dance is a body art and Euro-American theater remains, despite the upheavals and new ideas of the sixties, a literary art.

But what about performances demonstrating a mastery of technique without any prior training? The performance of sanghyang dedari trance dancers in Bali is very instructive regarding this problem. In the sanghyang two prepubescent girls are possessed by the spirits of the dedari, divine nymphs. The dedari chase away leyaks (demons) and insure the well-being of the village. It is said that these girls dance without previous training (plate 54). The Balinese say this; foreigners say this. I have seen sanghyang dedaris dance, their eyes closed, their prehensile feet clutching the shoulders of the men carrying them. From the waist up the dancers sway their bodies, sometimes precariously, and they move their arms, fingers, necks, heads in ways prescribed by Balinese dance. An extraordinary spectacle, and one likely to make an audience believe that these children are indeed possessed by dedari who are dancing through the bodies of young girls. But Covarrubias tells us:

Two little girls, trained to go into a trance, are chosen from all the girls of the village for their psychic aptitudes by the temple priest. . . . Choruses of men and women are formed and the training begins. Every night, for weeks, they all go to the temple, where the women sing traditional songs while the men chant strange rhythms and harmonies made up of meaningless syllables, producing a syncopated accompaniment for the dance that the little girls, the *sanghyangs*, will perform. By degrees the little girls become more and more subject to the ecstasy produced by the intoxicating songs, by the incense, and by the hypnotic power of the *pemangku* [priest]. The training goes on until the girls are able to fall into a deep trance, and a formal performance can be given. It is extraordinary that although the little girls have never received dancing lessons, once in a trance they are able to dance in any style, all of which would require ordinary dancers months and years of training to learn. But the Balinese ask how it could be otherwise, since it is the goddesses who dance in the bodies of the little girls. [1937, 335–36]

As sanghyangs, the little girls do many kinds of performative actions. They dance on the shoulders of men; they dance "unconcerned in and out of fire, scattering the glowing coals in all directions with their bare feet"; they chase leyaks out of the temples. "The temperamental girls may suddenly decide that the dance is over. Then they must be taken out of trance with more songs; and the sanghyangs become ordinary girls again" (1937, 338). Ordinary?

In ordinary life the little girls are normal children. However, they are forbidden to creep under the bed, to eat the remains of another person's food or the food from offerings, and must be refined in manners and speech. Their parents are exempt from certain village duties and are regarded highly by the rest of the community. [1937, 339]

The sanghyang dedari actually undergo training and preparation; and after their performance they are "cooled down," systematically brought out of trance. What they don't do is rehearse. But every person in a Balinese village has seen sanghyang dedari dancing. By the time a girl is eight or nine she has seen many, many performances. When she is selected by the pemangku she knows what she is expected to do. The period of training in the temple is not training about how to dance but actually an extended period of preparation or warm-up for the dancing. The "how to" has been absorbed through the eyes over the years. In watching sanghyang dedari myself, I, like many others including the Balinese themselves, am moved by their grace, simplicity, and naiveté and by their feats of balance and fire walking achieved while in trance. But their skill as dancers, measured against what fully trained Balinese dancers do, is nothing special. What is spectacular is the sanghyang dedari performance taken as a totality: trances, feats, dancing, intensity of participation by the whole village. It is this participation that makes people exaggerate the dancing skills per se of the little girls. Everyone knows they've had no formal training, so what they do appears all the more incredible. But they've been specially selected, isolated, prepared, warmed up for weeks. The girls know what sanghyang dancers are supposed to do. And they do it with grace and naiveté, because they also know that they are in trance, not responsible for their own actions, that they are the vessels for and the puppets of the dedari gods.

The sanghyang dancers have what Zeami called a natural hana, or flower. "Their youthfulness being attractive, their performances are very graceful in any kind of drama," Zeami wrote of young boy performers. "But," he adds, "the hana of these ages is not shin-no-hana. It can only be the flower that rises spontaneously from youth" (1968, 17–18). Zeami's editor comments that shin-no-hana is "the hana which a player acquires by severe training and which will last to the end of his life" (1968, 100). Sanghyang dancers have hana but not shin-no-hana. But, whether or not their skills endure, their performances don't just happen. Sanghyang performances belong to the world of twice-behaved behavior, but their technique is absorbed rather than learned through training.

There are also performance genres that militantly oppose any kind of technical training. There was a period in the development of postmodern dance where untrained performers were preferred. Punk bands celebrated their lack of musical knowledge and technique. Dancer Johanna Boyce and Happener Allan Kaprow, both leaders in their fields, look for untrained people to work with. Squat Theatre never rehearses. In 1965 John Cage said:

I try to make definitions that won't exclude. I would say simply that theatre is something which engages both the eye and the ear. . . . The reason I want to make my definition of theatre that simple is so one could view everyday life itself as theatre. [1965, 50]

If "everyday life" is theater, then people doing ordinary things are performers. According to Cage, theater is made by using one of two frames: either by the viewer looking at a subject "as theater" or by performers "intending to make" theater. Usually these two are joined, as when people go to a theater to watch a play. But Cage says the two can function independently of each other, and that the presence of either one is enough to make theater happen. So theater that is truly "in the mind of" the observer can occur without any training, rehearsal, preparation—or even knowledge on the part of the "performers" that they are performing.

In my 1965 interview with Cage I tried to challenge this definition. At the time I found it too inclusive. Cage had been talking about watching simply what was happening on a beach as theater.

Schechner: Isn't the difference between the beach and the theatre that the beach is not rehearsed and the theatre is? The thing that bothers me about the happenings I've seen is that they were obviously rehearsed but badly done. Either they shouldn't have been rehearsed, or they shouldn't have gone half way. . . .

Cage: I couldn't be in greater agreement. If there are intentions then there should be every effort made to realize those intentions. Otherwise carelessness takes over. However, if one is able to act in a way that doesn't have intention in it, then there is no need for rehearsal. This is what I'm working on now: to do something without benefit of measurement, without benefit of the sense that now that this is finished we can go on to the next thing. [Cage 1965, 56]

Cage's thinking is somewhat out of style in the eighties. But it keeps, for me, its importance. He reminds us that there is no such thing as structureless behavior: rhythm, sequence, intensity, progression do not depend on intentions. Cage's influence on theater, dance, and music has been immense. His presence is felt in theater mostly in Performance Art where untrained performers, real-time events, and "conceptual art" (= the frame is set by someone telling the viewer, "This is performance") abound. A look at Loeffler's *Performance Anthology* (1980), a "sourcebook for a decade of California performance art," details much of this post-Cage work combining film, video, live performance, painting, and sculpting, a range so wide that it's not possible to categorize it. The "technique" of this work is a "way of thinking," a "frame of mind."

The sixth and last function of training is group formation. Noh drama exists as the art of several families, very close-knit groups who admit outsiders only rarely. The Kathakali Kalamandalam would not make much sense without the professional company attached to it. This company does the teaching and provides the model for the students. There are many more students than can be accommodated in the Kalamandalam company or any other company in Kerala. Kathakali performers are exported to other parts of India, and abroad, to give a little Kathakali flavor to the entertainment menus of tourist hotels or to spice up a non-Kathakali show. This overproduction of trained artists is actually the result of a school somewhat modeled on Western lines: once geared up to produce graduates, it is very difficult to scale down the quantity to fit the replacement needs of existing companies or the needs of new companies in formation.

In Euro-America, theater has long been considered a composite art. The theatrical occasion is the coming together of the actor, the writer, the director, the designer, the musician, the painter, and so on. The rehearsal process is designed to transform these separate elements into a powerful whole. Because participants need different skills, and enter training at different levels of achievement, each skill is taught separately. Acting, directing, playwriting, designing, management are taught in separate classes. And each subject is divided into more parts—until the whole of our art lies fragmented at our feet. Then critics, artists, and audiences alike complain that productions lack unity. The only practice students get at unity is when productions are in rehearsal. And too often rehearsal is frantic patchwork. By rehearsal time it is too late; nothing whole can be made from so many ill-fitting pieces. The professional theater, with its separate unions, keeps actors, writers, designers, directors, technicians, and managers apart, even antagonistic to each other.

It was in reaction to these deep structural faults that so many groups formed over the past century, especially during the past thirty years. But the faults are ancient, going back to Greek theater where the great festivals were based on competitive contests among actors and writers (see chapter 3). To the Greeks the competition was more important than the establishment of an ensemble. They took pains to make sure that if a great writer teamed up with a great actor it was only by chance, for actors were assigned to writers by lot.

Noh drama is also composed of people who work separately. The shite and chorus train together, and the waki, the kyogen, the hip drummer, the shoulder drummer, and the flutist each trains separately, making a total of six components. But rigorous scoring of performances controlled by the shite and the playing of a fixed repertory that can be practiced in training—training that beings as early as age five—help bring about unity. The Zen tradition that has been incorporated into Noh—emphasizing mental preparation, taking aim, and shooting with an "empty mind" (nescience again)—makes many Noh performances models of professional cooperation, not competition. The fact that Noh plays, ideally, are to be performed by a shite only once in his lifetime leads to an intense concentration when the opportunity to play a role arises. Takabayashi said that he sometimes repeats a role but never with the same colleagues. In this way, the performance text grows and changes. It belongs not to individual Noh shites but to families; and these groups, represented by individual artists, meet to make programs of Noh. During the actual performance of Noh—as in Kathakali—the shite can signal that he is going to add, subtract, or vary elements. He can repeat a portion of a dance; he can speed up; he can slow down. Every member of the ensemble pays careful attention. There have been no rehearsals; as with a jazz group, the moment of the performance is the moment when things come together or fail. If a particular variation is successful it may be passed on. The tradition is not frozen, but it usually changes by means of details, not by the invention of whole new performances.

Euro-American artists have felt the problem of unity. When I directed The Performance Group (1967–80), I wanted always to maintain a steady system of training that would form the basis of our individual and collective style (see Schechner 1973*b*). Other groups did likewise. Both Brecht and Meyerhold devoted much energy toward developing training that would give their theaters a distinct identity. More recently, Richard Foreman's works were unified because Foreman is author, director, and scenographer; and he tells performers who work with him precisely how to behave (see Davy 1974 for a description of Foreman's rehearsal procedures). But not everyone who makes theater, or who works in theater, owns Foreman's diverse talents. There must be other avenues opened that will lead to creative, unified productions.

℘

Finally, it is as Eugenio Barba says. "The numerous and complex rules which seem to enclose the actors and dancers of India, Bali, China, and Japan in an armour of pre-established signs are in reality ways of modelling energy in order to transform it into communication" (1982, 20). All training—Euro-American, Oriental, any kind—attempts to transform energy into communication; and different methods indicate different kinds of energy, different messages communicated. The actor—sometimes that more expansive being, the performer—can be creative in at least three ways. One way is according to the Stanislavski method and its derivatives, the method of "creating a role." A written text is assumed to contain living human beings called characters. The actor's task is to find analogies in his own life that suit the "given circumstances" of the play's characters. But let me emphasize that the "reality" of the characters is just a convention, and one that does not include the other arts. I don't pick apples from a landscape painting or assume that a portrait is a person. Rather, I am always clear that the "artwork" is a "picture of." The energy of the Stanislavski actor is put strictly in the service of a rigorous humanism. And that is the message communicated: theatrical art is the art of the actions of human beings.

The second way a performer can be creative is what happens in Kathakali, Noh, or ballet. A performance text, a fixed score, is there to be learned and presented by the performer. There is no research into motivations, throughlines of action, or given circumstances. All the information of the role is there in the performance text which, paradoxically, is complete in itself and complete only when performed. The energy of the performers goes into mastering the score; and the message of these scores is their insistence on their own automony. Only the greatest artists have sufficient force to make changes in the scores. The scores are passed down the generations more or less intact—and in this way they achieve their status as "classics," which means "to endure." They hold in their persistence and totality the values of specific cultures. Yet historical research reveals that each of these "fixed forms" was at one time something else—and that they were suddenly transformed into what they are. The suggestion is that they await, at some future moment, new transformations. Thus, before Kanami and Zeami, there was Sarugaku Noh, a rougher, more rural popular entertainment; before Vallathol and his colleagues at the Kalamandalam, there was a less systematized Kathakali, still performed today by non-Kalamandalam-trained performers in Kerala. To take a lead from evolutionary theory, a pattern of "punctuated evolution" seems to describe the development of performance genres.

The third kind of performer creativity is the method very much in use between 1960 and 1975 by masters of the "experimental theater" in Europe, America, Latin America, Asia, and Africa, for experimental theater was a worldwide phenomenon. This method is still being used in America by such surviving groups as the Wooster Group and Mabou Mines. Here the performer—working with a director who serves as an "outside eye"—finds, invents, and/or constructs a performance score from scratch. The words, gestures, and music are developed during a long workshop-rehearsal process that may take months or even years. The playwright is no longer the originator of a dramatic text that serves as the armature for the performance text. Words may be used—taken from plays, novels, letters, journals, newspapers, the improvisations of performers, anywhere—and a playwright may be asked to assemble a playable text from various sources, as Jean-Claude van Itallie did for the Open Theatre's production of *The Serpent.* But the core creativity belongs to the performers. In *The Serpent* at least, three kinds of texts were used: the Bible both as literature and narrative; the Zapruder film of the actual assassination of President John F. Kennedy; and improvisations by members of the Open Theatre. These improvisations yielded words, music, gestures, relationships. Working with all these texts, van Itallie made a verbal text and director Chaikin made a mise-en-scène: a performance text. The performance text included texts that were literary, pictorial, oral, musical, and gestural. Some were public and mythic, like the assassination of JFK and the murder of Abel by Cain; some were private and intimate, their roots known only to members of the Open. This process of constructing a performance text that the performers both make (postmodern technique) and fit themselves to (traditional technique) is well put by Karen Malpede, talking about Shami Chaikin's work in the Open's *Terminal:*

Self-realization becomes possible as a theatre activity only insofar as the actors have felt it in their own lives. Perhaps Shami's singing of the Jewish prayer for the dead in *Terminal* is the first solo moment of self-abandonment reached by any of the four actors who were with the company the longest. The song takes us beyond character and its attendant neuroses to the awful impersonality of grief. "The song fills the woman. It uses her voice to sing itself." The stage direction, written after the fact, is an accurate description of what happened. [1974, 27]

Creativity is the ability to introduce change, whether that change is collective or personal or sudden or gradual. In Euro-American theater, creativity has been identified with radical change, and radical change has been thought of as the privilege, maybe the indulgence, of the young. But what if the most creative period of an artist's life comes not early—not early in training, not early in living, not early in rehearsal? The Asian examples I've discussed— and I'm certain examples from other traditional cultures abound in Africa, Native America, everywhere—suggest a different kind of training, one more suited to the transmission of performance texts. And since experimental theater has become a theater of performance texts its leaders have naturally turned to methods of training used in traditional cultures. This goes a long way toward explaining Grotowski's Theatre of Sources and Barba's Theatre Anthropology.

Around 1969 Grotowski moved away from making performances for the public. He moved into a phase of "paratheatrical" experiments that ranged widely from encounters that were close to what goes on at Esalen or "outward bound" weekends in the wilderness to bringing together masters of various performance disciplines from different cultures for project Grotowski called Theatre of Sources. The Theatre of Sources did not involve training per se. But it did put Western theater people (and some nontheater people) in direct contact with performers from Haiti, India, and other non-Western cultures. The work with these people was not "training" in the usual sense.

Action is, perhaps, an abstract, awkward way of referring to the things we did [during the summer of 1980]. But Grotowski and his [international] staff deliberately refrained from labelling them "events," "exercises," "rituals," and so on. . . . One action consisted of long walks, during which we paused at transitions in terrain or foliage, honored the sounds of animals, clung to trees, lay on the earth, crawled under dense pines, watched fish, ran through thickly entangled forest at night, and walked under waterfalls. The ethics of participation required silence, lightfootedness, non-pollution, careful imitation of the guide, and no movements disruptive of forest life or the group. [Grimes 1982, 183]

Earlier in this phase of working, Grotowski and other members of his Polish Laboratory Theatre developed a number of workshops and/or events without audiences but with participants called (for instance) "meditations aloud," "acting therapy," "song of myself," "vigil," "special project," and so on. (For descriptions of this work, see Burzynski and Osinski 1979; Mennen 1975; Kolankiewicz, ed., 1978; and Grimes 1982.) This work attracted to it leaders of Western theater who stayed a few days or made repeated visits over several years. I participated in one such adventure in 1978. Others who participated include Peter Brook, Joseph Chaikin, Jean-Louis Barrault, André Gregory, Luca Ronconi, Eugenio Barba, "and over 5,000 persons from all continents" (Burzynski and Osinski 1979, 128).

Grotowski has never written extensively about his work, either before or during the paratheatrical or active culture phases. He prefers the transcribed "meeting," lecture, or interview. In 1975 he said:

Passing to what I define as leaving theatre behind, at the outset I knew very little, that is to say, no stories, no plot, no talk about anything or anyone—that was one thing I knew; the other was that the selection of those who enter it had to be mutual. For the press one could say that this is a training period which required suitable predispositions and not skill. Moreover, I knew that what ought to happen was something utterly simple, elementary, trustful between human beings; that it is based on phases, gradations, but cannot be a rite—in the sense that it would be like a structured ritual—because it must be simpler than rite. It must be based on such things as recognizing someone, sharing substances, sharing elements—even in the archaic meaning—as space is shared, as water is shared, as fire is shared, as running is shared, as earth is shared, as touch is shared. . . . How to become oneself, having rejected games and everyday pretence? How to go beyond professionalism? How is it possible to be spontaneous between the routine of professionalism and the temptation of chaos? What are man's capacities in action when confronted face to face with another man? What is creative in man in the face of the living presence of others, in a mutual communion? How is it possible—while respecting differences between people—to achieve human understanding above the differences of nationality, race, culture, tradition, upbringing, language? In what conditions is it possible to achieve interhuman fullness? Is it possible to create a form of art other than those hitherto known—outside the division into the one who watches and the one who acts, man and his product, the recipient and the creator? [Burzynski and Osinski 1979, 109]

Grotowski's program—or is it better to call it a utopian wish?—is to transcend culture. To go "above the differences of nationality," and so on, is to create transcultural experiences. Jung felt that in archetypes, and the collective unconscious, such transculturation was manifest; and perhaps postmodern information theory and practice is reaching for another kind of transculturalism (see "The Crash of Performative Circumstances," in *The End of Humanism* [Schechner 1982b]). Certainly it's necessary to find ways out of the impasse created by the destructive aspects of human technological achievement. Nuclear war and the poisoning of the environment threaten human life on a global level as never before. Maybe Grotowski's work signals still another development in the sequence progressing from cultural to intercultural to transcultural performances.

Grotowski's "road to active culture" (as one of the pamphlets describing his transcultural work is titled) is a road away from a theater of works performed for an audience, of training meant to develop the skills of a professional, toward a kind of whole-life training focused through specific face-to-face encounters. This road is not fundamentally different than what Grotowski achieved during his "poor theater" phase, but through "active culture" he wants to assist many nonprofessional people in achieving the kind of "penetration of self" characteristic of the "holy actor." Grotowski's paratheatrical work has been often described experientially. This is so because one of its purposes is to accomplish personal transformations, and therefore its "results" are not theatrical productions but quasi-religious testimonies.

What troubles me about Grotowski's work in this area is that it has become very cultish. People are not really being trained in this or that technique; rather, they are drawn into a kind of cult of personality (or personalities, because some of Grotowski's longtime associates share his charisma or have developed their own). People are drawn very deeply into highly personal work—into the "breakdown" phase of workshop, or the "separation/ordeal" phase of initiation—but they are not then "reconstructed," either by being integrated into a society or by being given specific roles to play in a performance. Rather, they are returned to their cultures of origin—or wherever (because a few of Grotowski's devotees are wanderers)—"disenabled." These graduates of Grotowski's University of Explorations (as a 1975 project was called) are really left with reduced options: they have been detached from the ordinary theater, but they have not been integrated into the theater of Grotowski; they have been "prepared for living" but not in any specific way, in the terms of any particular culture. Training needs to be a fully realized three-stage process: separation, deconstruction, reconstruction. Grotowski's paratheatrical work is all separation and deconstruction. It is a brave vision of human capabilities that supposes individuals able to reconstruct themselves; or that proposes to individuals that they live lives of sanyasins or yamabushis: wanderers in the service of truth.

Grotowski's latest project—objective drama—answers some of these questions in a concrete, constructive way. Due to the political circumstances in Poland following the crushing of Solidarity and the imposition of martial law, Grotowski left Poland on what may be an extended or even permanent exile. He is currently in America, where at the University of California, Irvine, he began in 1983 an Objective Drama Institute. This institute would be a "theater laboratory."

The work of the laboratory is designed to facilitate the transmission of specific, objective techniques of performance. These techniques of the master teachers [from Haiti, India, and elsewhere: people Grotowski worked with in the Theatre of Sources], who are in residence for periods of up to six months, are transmitted to the team of [four] instructors and to [varying numbers] of students. . . . The techniques of the master teachers are not all "known" beforehand. They are not all items that have been previously identified and isolated as performables.

Part of the work of the laboratory is to transform various liturgical/performative modes and items into technical/performative modes and items. This work includes a rigorous investigation of various liturgical and ritual genres—an investigation whose purpose it is to identify in performative terms—that is, in ways that can be taught, repeated, and creatively varied—sequences of "objective drama."

Step-by-step these sequences will be built by Grotowski into "fragments" or models of a total, intercultural work. . . . As Grotowski has explained it, his long-term intention is analogous to Bach's making a Mass, except that Grotowski's work is intercultural, drawing on techniques whose performative/psycho-physiological basis is shared among many, if not all, cultures. Grotowski's work codes may be religious by origin, but they are in the process of being isolated into technical codes by means of the work of the laboratory.[2]

Grotowski believes there are certain sounds, rhythms, gestures, and movements whose effects are "objective"—that is, based on physiological and/or archetypal systems. Heartbeat, breathing patterns, certain pitches and precise progressions of sound, certain facial displays, body and hand positions, and movements constitute for Grotowski an intercultural or universal performative system. These elements of objective drama are mainly preserved in the world's various liturgical performances. Grotowski wants to identify, isolate, and then teach performers these elements separate from their religious/ideological content. According to Grotowski the objective drama project will take at least five years. It is a continuation of his earlier work:

The work of the Institute will be cross-cultural and interdisciplinary, representing the fourth stage of Grotowski's research into the elemental and archetypal aspects of human behavior. The Objective Drama Institute represents a continuation of Grotowski's explorations of the "theatre of performance" (the so-called "poor theatre" 1959–1969), the "theatre of participation" (1969–1976), and the "theatre of sources" (a broad and vigorous program of transcultural research both in Europe as well as throughout the world, including extensive field work in India, West Africa, Haiti, and Mexico, 1976–1982). With the Objective Drama Institute, this ongoing process enters into its fourth phase. It is highly defined work, not random experimentation, the culmination of a widely-heralded and influential *oeuvre* begun in Poland in 1959.[3]

Whether or not Grotowski achieves his goals over five years, his intention is clear. Objective drama is Grotowski's integration of theater and paratheater. One might even see a classic dialectical process: poor theater as hypothesis led to paratheater as antithesis. Objective drama is the synthesis. And from the perspective of ritual process objective drama attempts exactly what the paratheatrical experiments avoided: the use of various ritual techniques in the development of definite "fragments" or "models" or "works." Objective drama supplies the constructive reintegrative phase of the process.

Barba in his work at Odin Teatret has been more down-to-earth than Grotowski. He has kept his theater intact as a theater; and he has initiated and sponsored many tours and workshops. For twenty years Barba's work has been closely related to Grotowski's. Barba studied with Grotowski in the 1960s, and he proudly refers to Grotowski as his teacher. Barba's "Theatre Anthropology" grows directly from Grotowski's Theatre of Sources. Possibly Barba's emphasis on isolating technical principles useful to actors has influenced Grotowski's objective drama project.

At his International School of Theatre Anthropology (ISTA), Barba has sought to find basic connections in the actor's craft between East and West— more precisely, to identify what the Euro-American actor can learn from Asian performers. In this Barba is making real what Artaud theorized a half-century ago. To ISTA Barba brings performers from different cultures, both to exchange specific techniques and to search for underlying performative principles. The goals of ISTA are put this way by Barba:

Where can an Occidental actor turn in order to find out how to construct the material bases of his art? This is the question which theatre anthropology attempts to answer. . . . Theatre anthropology does not seek principles which are universally *true*, but rather directions which are *useful*. . . . Originally, the term anthropology was understood as the study of man's behavior not only on the socio-cultural level, but also on the physiological level. Theatre anthropology consequently studies the socio-cultural and physiological behavior of man in a performance situation. [1982*b*, 5]

In 1982 a session of ISTA had as teachers performers from Japan, Bali, India, France, Italy, China, Peru. Their genres ranged from Noh and Kabuki to Odissi dance, political theater, Beijing opera, Topeng, Kyogen, and mime. Such mixing, in Barba's view, is meant to lead not to a potpourri but to basic principles.

A theatre can . . . open itself to the experiences of other theatres not in order to mix together different ways of making performances, but in order to seek out the basic principles which it has in common with other theatres, and to transmit these principles through its own experience. In this case, opening to diversity does not necessarily mean falling into syncretism and into a confusion of languages. . . . Theatre anthropology seeks to study these principles: not the profound and hypothetical reasons which might explain why they resemble each other, but their possible uses. In doing so, it will render a service both to the person of the Occidental theatre and to one of the Oriental theatre, to he who has a tradition as well as to he who suffers from the lack of one. [1982*b*, 6]

For a long time, maybe since the start of human cultures, contact among humans has meant mutual influencing: syncretism. But the works of Grotowski, Barba, Peter Brook,[4] and some others are the first fully conscious attempts in theater to establish, analyze, and promote intercultural exchange. What kind of training and, from that, what kind of performances will eventuate it is too early to say. But clearly the intercultural movement is strong in theater, and it is growing also in anthropology proper.[5]

Not all the mixing has been originated by Euro-Americans who import "masters" from Asia (or Africa, or elsewhere in the formerly colonial world). Suzuki Tadashi in Japan is attempting a unique synthesis of classical Japanese, modern intercultural, and ancient Greek elements. Suzuki's training methods are extremely exacting. The "disciplines" involve group movements and chants that demand of each Waseda Shogekijo member absolute attention, physical exertion, and obedience.

The system is very Japanese. No one speaks a word except Suzuki. No one asks a question. No one makes a suggestion. The acknowledged star of the group, Kayoko Shiraishi, an actress of terrifying force on the stage, is indistinguishable among the other performers. There is an electric alertness, a quiet tension in the room. They accept shouted criticism, slaps on the head, calls of "damned fool" (*baka yaro*). Suzuki is their teacher, their *sensei*. In this respect the Waseda Little Theatre is following attitudes toward learning a "way" (*do*) and the strict master-pupil relationship that is typical of traditional arts of all kinds in Japan. It should be added that after the disciplines are over this hierarchical relationship is set aside and Suzuki is warm and informal. [Brandon 1978, 30–31]

Suzuki says he has come to his current way of working through trying, and then rejecting, the Stanislavski system. "Using realistic styles of performance made it impossible to accommodate the entire range of human experience" (Suzuki 1982, 88). He began to experiment in developing a training method combining elements from Noh and Kabuki with his own interests in shamanism, theatrical experimentation, and narratives from Greek tragedy.

But, like Barba, Suzuki is interested in intercultural performer training. In a rural area of Japan, at Togamura, he has built a center.

I want the Togamura complex to be a center for exchange among theatre groups on a world-wide basis. We have built a dormitory that will accommodate about thirty persons, and we hope to bring many groups together for varying periods. I am also considering a formal school with fifteen American and fifteen Japanese students at a time. Many kinds of training can be pursued in this kind of center—music, art, even anthropology. [1982, 92]

Suzuki's production of Euripides' *Bacchae* used a company consisting of Japanese and American performers.

My experiences in Asia have helped me grasp the creative process differently than I had when I knew only Euro-American theater. I have come to know the body as the source of theatrical thought as well as a means of expression. I experienced a confluence of theater, dance, and music: they became transformed into the consciousness of action, movement, and sound. I felt, as Suzuki does, that "the word is an act of the body" (1982, 89). And I know what Phillip Zarrilli means when he reflects upon changes wrought in his being through training in Kalarippayatt, a Kerala martial art closely related to Kathakali training.

In the course of these six years of nearly daily practice of a highly disciplined form of Indian movement, my initial ineptitude, my initially sore muscles, and my total ignorance of the important implications of all I'd been learning gave way to an experience of such movement forms [as Kalarippayatt and Kathakali] which is totally the opposite: "flow," "release," "psycho-physical integration," are but a few of the terms I use to describe my present experience of Kalarippayatt. . . . Visitors would come [to Minneapolis] where I was teaching at the time to observe and talk. [Musician-dancer] Meredith Monk said: "you suddenly *became* a warrior-hero, right before my eyes." I hadn't expected her comment. In fact, I had only been "doing the exercises," or "manipulating the weapon," exactly as taught. I hadn't consciously tried to "act" the warrior-hero. . . . There had been no pretence or artifice, no "playing at." [Zarrilli 1982, 3–4]

Through surrendering to a total discipline a transformation takes place—a transformation that is unpretended and therefore unpretentious. This state of performed actuality is very appealing to people who want to perform their passions precisely but without the phoniness associated with "acting." As choreographer Carol Martin remarked: "I really don't like acting—it's such an incredibly old-fashioned thing to do."

Even more "old-fashioned" is the state of free mind/body flowing from the Asian techniques of performer training—old-fashioned and postmodern too. These techniques of training lay the groundwork for individual and group creativity that comes late in the trajectory of an artistic career: the final, great work of a Ramchakyar, the shin-no-hana performance of a Kanami. Neither is art limited to aesthetics: in oral cultures especially, a performance is an art, an entertainment, a ritual, an education, a political manifesto, a social corrective (through satire and parody), a repository of folklore, history, and culture. In this context, originality is not measured by sheer energy or even by beauty. We expect the young to be energetic and beautiful; that is nature's gift. But originality—the ability to affect culture at its deepest levels—is, as Zeami said five hundred years ago, "like an old leafless tree which still blossoms." Creativity in art is the appearance—sudden and unexpected, yet prepared for by a lifetime's devotion to discipline—of sheer knowledge, wisdom hard-won by experience, precipitated into a gesture, a song, a look: a performance.

NOTES TO CHAPTER 5

[1]Performance Art comes out of the meeting of popular entertainment (especially rock, punk, and new-wave music), happenings (with their sources in visual arts, the music of John Cage, and theories of indeterminancy), theater, and dance. The movement is particularly vital these days in California (see Loeffler 1980). Ongoing work in Performance Art is chronicled in several journals, most notably *High Performance, Live* (stopped publication in 1982), and *Alive* (successor to *Live*). See also Kaprow 1966 and Goldberg 1979.

[2]Descriptions of the objective drama project are taken from a grant proposal prepared by Grotowski in consultation with several people (including me) and submitted by the New York University Tisch School of the Arts in June 1983. NYU was not able to raise or supply the necessary money. Work on objective drama began at UC, Irvine, in August 1983.

[3]From the NYU grant proposal.

[4]At his International Center for Theatre Research in Paris—and on tours to Africa, Latin America, the Middle East—Brook has also long been interested in intercultural performance exchange. Presently he is working on a production of the *Mahabharata*. He has performed works based on Iranian and African sources. Brook's company is composed of people from different cultures, though most members are Euro-American (see chapter 1).

[5]Victor Turner was foremost among anthropologists working this vein. His *From Ritual to Theatre* (1982*a*) deals extensively with the intersections of anthropology and theater. See also Turner and Turner, 1982.

6

PLAYING WITH GENET'S *BALCONY:* LOOKING BACK ON A 1979/1980 PRODUCTION

The poison of the commercial theater has so soaked into our ways of thinking that even an experimental production is regarded as a success or a failure. The show either makes it at the box office, with critics, by word of mouth, or it is sent away defeated. "Forget about it," people say, "and go on to the next thing." This is a stupid way of advancing theatrical thought, for why can't a work be neither a success nor a failure but a step along the way, an event that yields some interesting data? In other words, though entertainment values are truly important in the theater, they are not the only values. And those devoted to experimentation need to be particularly rigorous in separating out from each work what is useful, regardless of the overall "success" of the project.

I don't think that this is a fancy rationalization for my production of *The Balcony* in 1979/80. This production was the last I did with the The Performance Group, and there were many problems with the show, some of them relating to the fact that my relationship with members of TPG was strained. The production went through several phases. First, there were audition workshops in February/March 1979. These were necessary because only a fraction of the people in TPG wanted to work on *The Balcony*. Many people were involved with Elizabeth LeCompte and Spalding Gray in their work on *Point Judith;* other longtime members of The Group had left and were trying their skills elsewhere; I myself was ambivalent about whether to stay in TPG, quit directing for a while, or start another theater group.

Anyway, I decided to audition new people, thinking I would work independently with them, later either integrating them into TPG or starting a new group. At worst, they would be fun to work with on a single production. Performance Group members Ron Vawter, Spalding Gray, Willem Dafoe, and Libby Howes—most are still active in The Group—wanted to work on *The Balcony.* But—and this is a decisive *but*—they wanted to work with LeCompte on *Point Judith* too. Directors, like the Old Testament God, are jealous and want no other directors before them: thus, conflict, tension, and unhappiness. Besides, TPG members did not participate in the workshops, except sporadically, during the spring of 1979. And TPG member Stephen Borst—who was not working with LeCompte and who played the Police Chief in *The Balcony*—also participated only occasionally in the workshops.

So I found myself becoming more and more deeply involved with seven new people. Throughout several months of intense workshops, we investigated together sexual and power fantasies, psychophysical exercises (the core of "traditional" TPG training; see Schechner 1973*b*), vocal work emphasizing breathing, and yoga taught by a man who had studied in India with the son of my yoga teacher. This kind of work went on from March through May 1979. Then I went away to Connecticut College, where I ran a student workshop. Assisting me were Borst, Vawter, and Carol Martin (a dancer-choreographer specializing in ideokinesis, a body imaging and movement technique). With the students we built a version of *The Balcony* that included much double casting; for example, four different people played Irma, depending on the scene. The summer work was successful insofar as it finalized the text: I had been working with Jean-Jacques Thomas and Alexander Alland in retranslating it, collating the several French versions Genet had published. The Connecticut College production also gave me a handle on how I wanted the production in New York to be.

But then, in the fall of 1979 during actual rehearsals in the Performing Garage, all the problems implicit in the split way of working became manifest. Saskia Noordhoek-Hegt, an extraordinarily powerful performer, joined the company to play the Judge; Gray came in to do the Bishop; Vawter worked during the summer and fall on Irma but still had to divide his time between LeCompte and me (as did Gray, as well as Dafoe, who played Arthur, and Howes, who played Carmen). Tensions rose on all fronts. The people I'd worked with during the spring approached their roles through living inside a complicated set of improvisations, some of which I'll describe shortly. But

TPG people, by and large, jobbed in: they arrived, learned their lines and blocking, and performed the play. This was especially true of Gray, a performer I admire and a friend I love. I am not attacking him but recognizing the absurdity of the situation; how demoralizing it was to see him play a role with only a part of his being. TPG people had little chance to sink deeply into roles that, after all, are as much about intense living through fantasy as anything.

More mundane matters intruded too. Scheduling continued to make waves. LeCompte wanted to rehearse *Judith* in the Envelope Theatre next-door to the Garage. People often were late for one rehearsal or the other or, even worse, distracted when they did arrive. And finally money—the lack thereof—caused unhappiness. Everyone was paid very little, Group members and newcomers. But in a crunch Group members received preference, as was their right. Too often meetings called to discuss *The Balcony* focused on the bank account. And what was missing in cash was made up in bitterness.

All of these circumstances meant that *The Balcony*, as it was performed in New York from December 1979 into January 1980, did not cohere. It never developed the power inherent in the concepts, the performers, the text. A director can't shrug off his responsibilities in these matters. A director is the Harry Truman of his productions: the buck stops here. But if *The Balcony* was not a success, neither was it a failure. On conceptual grounds especially—in what the production suggested but could not entirely realize—I am proud of the work.

In planning the environment for *The Balcony* I looked a lot at Brassai's *Secret Paris of the Thirties* (1976) and Bellocq's *Storyville Portraits* (1970): bored whores, some pretty, some not so; shady characters; always the sharp ring of the cash register. Irma's place is run-down and cheap. After all, her prices range from fifty to seventy-five dollars (1980 money), and that's Korvette's, not Bergdorf's. Irma promotes her studios, but in fact they are small rooms, whose mattresses are stained with body-juices and punctured by cigarette burns. Before the start of the General's scene, Carmen polices beer cans, soggy towels, crumpled Kleenex. Irma's fuckery, as she calls it, stinks with the sour smell of stale liquids not quite mopped dry. On a busy night the whores have their hands full. One lady plays both the General's horse, Dove, and the Bishop's Penitent. She runs back and forth between her clients, making quick costume changes, sometimes mixing up her lines or cracking a smile in the wrong place (plate 55). She's bored, sometimes very angry, but still she must service these obsessive clients. While indulging her tricks, she dreams of being a real actress in a real theater. The elegance of Irma's place is in the minds of the clients—and, ultimately, the audience: the elegance of fantasy.

Were I to stage the play again, I'd have Carmen perform the Thief so that

55. The Bishop, played by Spalding Gray, blesses the Penitent. Joan Evans, who plays the Penitent, also plays the General's horse, Dove. She must run back and forth between these two scenes played at opposite ends of the theater. Photo by David Behl.

her long dialogue with Irma in scene 5 would be interrupted by the sado-masochistic scene with the Judge. This would underline the small-business aspect of Irma's house: tight on staff, stingy with cash for special effects. And it would give Carmen a chance to act out what she says she likes: some nightly duty in the trenches. Despite its tawdriness, Irma's house is managed with panache. This whorehouse thrives on fantasy (i.e., imagination). But it is also a capitalist, cost-efficient business. That combination makes it so like the kind of theaters I've spent my life in: small experimental houses whose enterprise it was to make and share fantasies.

One change I made for the 1979 production was to put the revolution on sound-effects records. The promising tumult of the 1960s has been reduced to a series of replays. Prominent in Irma's room—which she shares with Carmen, and which is at one and the same time living room, green room, tech booth, and office—is a phonograph and microphone. Carmen is hooked up to the studios by intercom. She can talk to the girls, listen to the action. Muzak is broadcast over the system, and so is the revolution. Like Colonial Williamsburg or Plimoth Plantation (see chapter 2) or like Disneyland, Irma's place runs on "themes." And tonight it's the "revolution." A very nostalgic myth, that of revolution. Carmen's sound-effects record pipes into the studios (and theater) bursts of machine guns, rifles, artillery: whatever is needed to make the revolution real within the confines of the whorehouse. What's "really" outside we don't know. Thus, when the famous parade on the balcony happens, it's staged inside the house, with the General in boots and jacket but sans pants, the Bishop naked under his cope, the Judge in disarray. Irma and the Police Chief pose à la the Perons on a platform overlooking the audience. Their positions and gestures imitate what people have seen in the movies, on TV, and in the theater: the Perons, Mussolini, Mao, Brezhnev, Reagan—how the public people make "appearances." Next to them, and slightly behind, are their clients, still propped up by the whores. I was not able to pull it off, but if I were to do *The Balcony* again, and I want to, there would be sex on the balcony along with the public appearances: the total mix of eroticism and power, the underlying lust/fantasy of the modern epoch.

Cross-gender casting was another aspect of this production. Since Genet's play is about fantasy and how it motors so-called ordinary life ("so-called" because even ordinary life is soaked in fantasy), I felt that a slavish meticu-lousness about gender would deprive performers and spectators alike of a full investigation of *The Balcony*'s underlying themes. So, to begin with, Ron Vawter played Irma. The audience sees him first as a man in jeans but shirtless, like so many advertisements in magazines and on TV: the "Jordache look." Then he strips naked. Next, step by step, scene by scene, he makes himself up into a queen in both senses: royalty-in-drag. He puts on a silk robe, the kind of housecoat suitable for both men and women. Then he begins to apply makeup, which occupies him during much of the long scene with Carmen. He puts on a real-hair wig, some lipstick. But during the scene with the Police Chief, when they fight, the Chief rips off Irma's wig, smears her lipstick, revealing her, for one pathetic moment, as an early-middle-aged drag queen. Also, the relationship between the Chief and Irma was seen, from this perspective, as a gay one—but only for that moment, for I was trying not to make a definitive statement about Irma's "sexual preference" but rather to insist that within the context of *The Balcony* gender is flexible, chosen, wished-into-being. I was also making the point that, at least for the night of this performance, Irma had chosen to be a man-as-a-woman, or maybe more precisely, a man-and-a-woman. I say this because I did not ask Vawter to play Irma with any feminine gestures or characteristics. I wanted a man in woman's clothing, a version of that proverbial wolf in sheep's clothing; I wanted him to be one gender biopersonally and another socioculturally.

Additionally, I played with the genders of two other characters. The Judge was purely and simply a woman client. Why shouldn't women go to whore-houses? Don't they? So Noordhoek-Hegt played a mousy lady from West-chester who wants to be a judge sadomasochistically entertained by a man and a woman: a classic example of troilism. Arthur, played by a muscular, punk-looking Dafoe, greased himself with baby oil before entering the studio; the whore Ruby, the Thief (who would be Carmen, as I said, if I did *The Balcony* again) was basically bored by this routine. Not so Arthur, whom another scene reveals as a cream puff disguised in muscles: this Judge's scene is his chance to act tough. Irma and the streets scare Arthur. When he plays his muscleman role in the studio, he's all whip and cock. The case of the General is much more complicated and arose very directly from the spring workshops (I'll discuss these later); in brief, the General was a young woman performer playing an adolescent boy in drag as a thirty-year-old lady.

One other matter should be mentioned before I discuss some of the work in more detail: the scenic environment. I wanted to have the audience "in" the house and yet able to keep some distance from it; I wanted to underline the Pirandello-like theatricality of *The Balcony* by suggesting a theater-in-the-theater; and I needed to solve the problem of where Roger's castration, the mausoleum scene, would take place. This scene dramaturgically breaks the fantasy frame of the play and therefore must in some sense physically violate the conventions of the production.

Figure 6.1 shows how the space was arranged. I wanted the spectators to feel the performance taking place all around them: over, under, to the sides, in front of, behind. I wanted spectators to experience a kind of voyeurism—

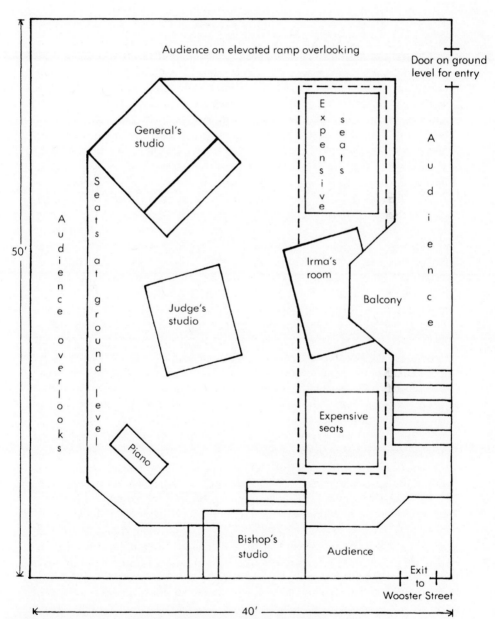

Figure 6.1. *Ground plan, Performing Garage, The Balcony, 1979/80.*
Dimensions: 50' × 40' × 20' height.
− − − − = outline of pit, on top of which are expensive seats and Irma's
room. For castration scene, Irma's room and expensive seats slide left, exposing the
whole pit.

as was very much present in the Connecticut College production. The "world" of *The Balcony* is very labile, capable of transforming itself, of expanding and contracting, of shifting focus suddenly, precipitously. At the conceptual center of this world is Irma's room, which I placed along the north wall of the Garage. The balcony where the Great Figures make their appearance in scene 8 is directly over Irma's room. Under her room is the mausoleum, the thirty-five-foot-long, eight-foot-deep pit that is an architectural feature of the Garage. Facing Irma's rooms on two sides were rows of formal theater seats. These expensive seats were also over the mausoleum. We sold these seats for a higher price than the general admission tickets. In the front row of these sat the clients: the would-be Bishop, General, and Judge. These high-priced seats were more comfortable than the wooden scaffolding and platforms arranged in different configurations and elevations around the rest of the room. But from the perspective of the rest of the room and through lighting, the customers in the expensive seats seemed almost part of the production. The studios themselves were platforms of different elevations. When these were not in use, spectators were allowed to sit on them, though generally they shied away from using them. (Conventions die hard, and most spectators don't like to put themselves in an ambivalent situation regarding whether or not they are performing.) Chantal and her piano were on a movable platform. Between scenes, and during some of them, the professor played and sang songs she composed, a tradition I happily took from New Orleans's Storyville, though it was not in Genet's *Balcony*. Irma's room and two of the studios were framed so that spectators could imagine looking into rooms without walls. The scaffolding with its seating and walk-arounds rose to a level of more than twelve feet, providing a panoramic view into Irma's house—"Brothel, whorehouse, cathouse, fuckery!" she cries at one moment.

Near the end of this play Roger, the revolutionary but also a plumber who is frequently needed at Irma's, castrates himself. He is in love with Chantal, who symbolizes the revolution. But Roger realizes that Chantal, too, is part of the house of illusions, that the revolution itself is canned. He shoots Chantal and comes to Irma demanding that he be allowed to play the role of the Police Chief, the one Great Figure that no one, to that point, has asked to enact. In Genet's text, the Envoy describes the mausoleum studio as if it were Franco's architectural exercise of Fascist hubris, "The Valley of the Fallen." In my production it was the old grease pit along the north wall of the Garage. For the mausoleum scene the whole north side of the theater—Irma's room and the two sections of expensive seats—slid out to the center of the theater, exposing the full length of the pit. The audience moved from all parts of the theater and surrounded the pit; two hundred people sat at its edges, or

56. For the mausoleum scene at the end of the play, Irma's room slides into the center of the Performing Garage, uncovering a 35-foot-long pit near the north wall. Down in that 8-foot-deep trench, the Police Chief, played by Stephen Borst, sips coffee as he keeps vigil over Roger's castrated corpse. The audience crowds around and peers down into the pit. Photo by David Behl.

hovered over it, peering down into its eight-foot depth. Down there Roger abuses a Slave and then castrates himself. The Police Chief jumps into the pit to wait the "2,000 years" necessary for his being to become the equivalent of the Bishop, Judge, and General (plate 56). Carmen hands him a tuna sandwich and a Coors—then the floor slides back over him and Roger's bloody corpse.

A last note on the space: The audience entered the *Balcony* environment from the building next-door to the Garage. They passed through the Envelope Theatre—empty at the time of performances of *The Balcony*—and through a side door connecting the Envelope to the Garage. It had the feel of being let into a speakeasy. (In several of my productions the way in and out—the crossing of the limen—was symbolically significant. In *Makbeth* the audience went upstairs, over the performing space, into a maze and descended into Makbeth's hell, all painted white. In *Dionysus* I stood at the entrance, allowing people through a small door one at a time, separating groups and couples. But at the end of the performance the large central Garage door was raised and the audience followed Dionysus out into Wooster Street. For *Mother Courage* I again stood just inside the theater and worked a cash register, making change for tickets that cost $1.99 or $3.98 or $5.97, amounts that meant money would have to pass back and forth. There were no advance sales, so the line was long and the cash register's bell rang frequently. Throughout the performance each time a transaction took place the cash register was rung.) At the end of *The Balcony* Irma sends the audience home through a different door than the one they came in. They exit directly onto Wooster Street. "You must go home now, where everything—you can be sure—is phonier than here. Go now, leave by that door, through the alley. It's morning already." One of the ideas I wasn't able to realize was to have a disco-cabaret called "De/Basement" in the cellar of the Envelope. There spectators, a few at a time and for lots of extra money, would be taken from the Garage to spend some minutes in an "actual" whorehouse. The improvisation from workshop of fulfilling some secret fantasy would be offered to theatergoers.

Having chosen to do a "modern classic," I had to deal with the written text. In Genet's case this meant confronting several texts and sorting among them. It meant also finding a proper English idiom to manifest Genet's combination of almost classic French—replete with *tirades* by Irma and Carmen—with the sudden use of slang, expletives, and obscenity. It also meant, for me at least, a way of cracking open Genet's scenic progression, a progression that slows the play down, grows very talky, and works against what I wanted to do.

This is not the place to describe in detail what Thomas, Alland, and I did to the text word by word. I'll say only that the available translation by Bernard Frechtman expresses the impediments of the 1950s, and we corrected as many of those as we could. (I expect that our version will need another revision some years from now.) I wanted to play *The Balcony* not as a period piece but as an action taking place in today's world. At the same time, I wished to be faithful to Genet's French.

Even deeper than the word-by-word work were the rearrangements I made scenically, because Genet's progression of scenes disturbed me dramaturgically. The first three or four scenes—those in the studios—arrest an audience's attention with their satire, fantasy, irony, playfulness, and action. They are also, some of them, erotic. It's hard to say which are erotic, since taste in sexual matters varies greatly and whorehouses cater to these variations, working from the same principles and carrying out some of the same functions as restaurants. Scene 5 is a problem because it is almost all talk, and it is very long, nearly one-third of the whole text. In the midst of this scene—Irma and Carmen expounding on the history of their whorehouse and the nature of illusion—Genet inserts the action of Irma spying on the studio with the Legionnaire in the desert. This studio obviously was popular during the Algerian war of independence. I cut the reference to the Legionnaire and played scene 2—the Judge-Thief scene—in its place. This encounter broke up the talkiness of scene 5 and extended some of the excitement of the opening scenes deeper into the production.

Also, I began the play differently from Genet. All three of the clients are sitting in the expensive seats close to Irma's room as the audience enters. When almost everyone is settled a song is heard. It is Chantal singing her theme (all the music for my production was composed and performed by Phoebe Legere). Taking a cue from New Orleans whorehouses, I made Chantal into a "lady professor"—simultaneously the symbol of both Irma's brothel and the revolution. During Chantal's first song, Carmen goes to the man who plays the Bishop and whispers to him that his studio is ready. That scene begins. Before it is over, Carmen tells the person playing the General that his/her studio is ready. These scenes overlap. The woman playing both Penitent and Horse has to make a quick change as she runs from the Bishop's studio to the General's. If I were to stage *The Balcony* again, I would fragment these two scenes even more, making it necessary for the whore to change costume and personality several times in quick succession as she runs back and forth between two demanding clients.

Also, I would not cut scene 4, the Bum scene, but would save it for late in the action, playing it during scene 7 or scene 10, when the other clients are living through their fantasies of actually becoming the characters they are playing. So, even as the Police Chief is brutally suppressing the Bishop,

General, and Judge, the Bum—who offers no threat to established authority—would be permitted to live his fantasy out to the fullest, lice and all.

These rearrangements corrected what I still feel is a fault in Genet's dramaturgy. He lets the business of the whorehouse fade away as the fantasy-political issues emerge. Although epistemological questions, and political ones, are at the heart of *The Balcony*, the action of the play is, and ought to continue to be, the business of running a whorehouse.

In working on the text, I did not take Genet's own thoughts and interpretations as anything more than his intention concerning how the play ought to be staged. In other words, stage directions are not really part of the text, which consists of dialogue, but are part of the mise-en-scène which, finally, belongs to those staging the play. Thus, in regard to what a play might be onstage, and how its most powerful contemporary insignia might appear, the author is not in a privileged position. As a result, much of a director's most important work is deconstructing both the text itself and the author's own vision of it. I would go so far as to say that we must not only avoid slavishly following the author's "intentions" but also work hard to get completely free of them. If after our own researches—researches suited to the theater, carried out in workshop and rehearsals, done on the stage itself—we arrive at the same staging as that which the author suggests, all is well. But, as in the course of interpreting one's own dreams, when the dreamer may not have the best, sole, or most decisive insights—the dreamer needs the help of the dream interpreter—so with the staging of a play. This analogy holds especially true for an author like Genet, whose work is so oneiric, so full of private references, codes, and cover-ups. In particular, I felt that the homoerotic basis of *The Balcony* needed to be brought out into the open—thus, some of the gender-free, or cross-gender, casting, and the gay love affair between Irma and the Police Chief. I needed to make public what was not public in the text; and the production of a play—especially a "classic" that has gathered around its hulk all the seaweed of criticism, interpretation, and scholarship—is an event that can only benefit from stringent scrubbing down. In brief, my colleagues and I deconstructed a literary text and reconstructed it as a performance text.

Dramaturgically, the biggest problem for me was scene 6, the revolutionaries' scene. At first I was determined to keep it intact. Wasn't I a "radical," and couldn't I sympathize with political action raised to the level of armed struggle? But even as I worked on it in Connecticut, I began to sense that scene 6 was as much a fantasy as what was going on in any of the studios. The scene is laced with Genet's own love of muscular boys, his fierce attachment to the insignia of power: Chantal's metamorphosis into an emblem. The scene has little to do with guerrilla warfare anywhere, or even with the romantic terrorism of Europe. At Connecticut College the scene was played twice: first, before the play began, as the audience assembled in a cafeteria-lobby; and then during an intermission after scene 5 that also featured songs and acts cabaret-style back in the cafeteria. This was my way of trying out not only scene 6 but the notion of "De/Basement." But once rehearsals began in New York, the creakiness of scene 6 became plain. The streets of Manhattan gave the lie to Genet's vision of revolutionary action. And although the scene is dramaturgically necessary to establish Roger's fanaticism and his love for Chantal, it is theatrically silly. In trying to find a way to make the scene work, I came face to face with the question of armed revolution in America: the whole thing was a fantasy, an extension of what was going on in Irma's studios. It was then that I decided to put the revolution on record, to make it part of the whorehouse's apparatus: an additional kick for the customers. I cut scene 6 to a few lines of heated exchange between Roger and the man who later plays the Slave in the castration scene. The dialogue makes it clear that Roger still believes in revolution and that he's fallen hopelessly in love with Chantal, the whore-singer. He sees her as part of the revolution, but she sees herself as part of the whorehouse. He shoots her.

He shoots her as she is singing the praises of Irma, the Queen, in scene 8. The development of the role of Chantal gives an insight into how I work with performers and how the workshop-rehearsal process does more than "interpret" a given text. During the audition workshops in February 1979, Legere showed her talents as a singer, composer, and piano player. Her style was high punk; she sometimes looked wasted, only to burst forth with an incredibly powerful, deep, almost gutteral, belting voice. Her own songs were brutal, sexual, feminist; a few were lyrical and sad, even romantic. She participated in the workshops and developed as an actress, but her life was music. She composed a score for *The Balcony* that took the revolution seriously, except that it was not a military revolution, organized and fought mostly by men according to rules of combat that are culturally masculine, but a revolution of consciousness and song led by women. In other words, Legere involved herself deeply in Chantal: a Chantal who was not a symbol for someone else's revolution but the main actor in her own.

Legere's music, and her presence at the piano during and between scenes, became integral to *The Balcony*. She also stirred my memories of New Orleans, where I lived from 1960 to 1967. Legere sang as the audience entered the theater; she played between and behind some scenes; she sang again after scene 5, when there was an interlude, including the pared-down scene 6; and she sang when Irma, the Queen, appeared on the balcony accompanied by the Great Figures. As Chantal sang in celebration of Irma, the Queen, Roger gunned her down. The Slave laid Chantal out on the piano and threw an American flag over her body.

The music was integral to the production, but it wouldn't have been there

57. The Judge's scene at Connecticut College. Spectators peer over and around the "walls." Two versions of this scene were performed simultaneously. Photo by Richard Schechner.

58. The Bishop and Penitent at Connecticut College. Photo by Richard Schechner.

59. Anne Z., as the client who wants to play the General, talks with Irma in the Connecticut College production. Photo by Richard Schechner.

60. Close-up of Anne Z. as the General underneath his horse, Dove, during a rehearsal for the New York production. Photo by David Behl.

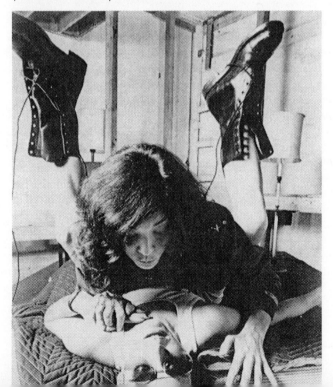

at all if Legere hadn't auditioned in February. I took an opportunity that walked in the door. A good policy, that.

In August 1979 I staged a student production of *The Balcony* at Connecticut College (plates 57–59). I had previously been invited to the college to work with about twenty students ranging in age from fifteen to fifty, but most in their twenties. I thought this would be a fine chance for me to step back from the pressures of New York theater and to try out some ideas concerning *The Balcony*. Vawter and Borst from TPG, and Anne Z. and Phillip Murphy from the spring workshops at the Garage joined the work, with Vawter and Borst assisting me in teaching. In addition, Carol Martin taught the group techniques of ideokinesis. Vawter and Borst not only taught basic psychophysical exercises but helped rehearse and stage some scenes. Martin staged scene 4 and helped work on other scenes, too. It was a collaborative effort in which I functioned as overall director but not as the only creative source.

The play was staged scene by scene. We were concerned more with allowing individual students to find means that would advance their training than in staging *The Balcony* as a whole work. Each scene had a new cast, so that every member of the workshop had significant roles to play. Some scenes were staged twice, such as the Judge-Thief scene. In retrospect, I realize that this multiple casting and double playing constituted but one element in what became a systematic deconstruction of Genet's play, a deconstruction that was necessary if the work was to find, in New York or anywhere, a distinct shape of its own. I needed to get far enough inside *The Balcony* so that it would evoke my own fantasies and not serve only as a conduit for Genet's. All this holds true as well for the others working on the project. Today I regret only that I didn't go further with this deconstruction, make *The Balcony* even more my own. By my own I mean not only Schechner's but everyone's participating in the project.

But even in Connecticut the production had its problems. Vawter was working that summer on *Point Judith*. LeCompte arrived with other members of TPG to film a sequence in nearby Waterford. Gray was on campus working on his monologues and performing some of them. The tension in The Group, which I had sought to escape by coming to Connecticut, followed me. Also, the fragmentation of *The Balcony*—especially as carried out by students at many different levels of skill, experience, and understanding—was only partly consistent with creative notions of deconstruction. Often fragmentation of energy and amateur skills prevented a deep look at this or that scene: too much time and effort had to be spent just on getting it up—for, although the summer was devoted mostly to workshopping, I had decided to stage a version of the play in August. Inevitably, people's energy focused on this public showing.

The strongest scenes in the student production were the Judge-Thief, the General, and the final scene. The Judge-Thief was double staged, two versions of the same scene going on simultaneously in a small room. Temporary walls of gym mats were erected so that the audience had to peep around and through cracks to see what was going on (plate 57). In one area a young woman, and in the other a fifteen-year-old boy, played the Thief; one of the Arthurs was a man, the other a woman; one of the Judges was a man, the other a woman. So, the ideas of private fantasy and gender inversion were tried. The General's scene was also played by two casts but ran sequentially rather than simultaneously. This was very interesting on two counts. First, it showed that any playtext can be given more than one authentic playing, because both General scenes worked; and second, it gave Anne Z., who played the role in New York, a chance to explore. She built her characterization from memories of her own childhood, both real and fantasy. She is the daughter of an Air Force colonel; she had often dreamed of growing up to be a pilot. These dreams sometimes led her to imagine that she was a male. Sometimes she would stand in her father's closet and just smell his uniforms. As a client at Irma's, she arrived dressed in a black, sequined sheath dress, a bright, rust-colored wig, and high heels (plate 59). Her voice was low, urgent. The whore asked her to strip. When she did, the audience saw that under the wig was short hair combed in a masculine style; and she was wearing boxer shorts and sleeveless underwear. This person appeared very much like an adolescent boy (plate 60). Gender ambivalence gave the General's scene a particular kick. And for Anne Z. she had the chance to play at being the young man she supposed her father had wished her to be: a young man with a spectacularly successful military career. In an almost archaeological way, she was a woman (gender fact) as a boy (daughter's fantasy of father's wish) as a woman (what Anne Z. "turned out" to be). *The Balcony* allowed Anne Z. to "strip down" to her boyness and become for the audience what she imagined her father wanted her to be. In this way, the audience was her father. Actually, her father saw Anne Z. play the General. He told me he enjoyed the performance.

I took advantage of Connecticut College's physical environment for the last scene. The workshops took place in an elementary school on campus. Most of the play was staged in a medium-sized lounge; scene 6 was played in the "lobby," the cafeteria. Behind the lounge is the gymnasium. This gym had a balcony at one end. Roger's castration and Irma's farewell to the audience were played in the gym with the audience on the balcony. Roger was lit so that his body cast three huge shadows on the far wall; Carmen's voice was amplified—she whispered, yet her voice boomed off the gym's cinder-block walls. We created the feel of a mausoleum. The audience was more than fifty feet from the scene. Then Irma appeared at the farthest reach of the gym. Slowly, she made her way until she stood just under the audience. Speaking very quietly, she sent them home.

Another effect that worked in Connecticut, but which I couldn't bring to New York, was that of the revolution as something going on outside. Anne Z. trained a squad of performers—always changing because it used everyone who wasn't in a particular scene—in military cadence counting. For no particular reason, the number sixteen was chosen. All the cadences were counts from one to sixteen, at various speeds, intensities, and rhythms. The squad stationed itself outside the lounge, in the gym, in the hallways of the school, and in the street near the school building. The audience could hear these soldiers running, marching, shouting—sometimes close and sometimes far. They were a continuous military presence. After the final scene, as the audience left through the school's front doors, they passed the squad lined up at parade rest but dressed as punks, whispering in cadence the numbers one through sixteen.

Returning from Connecticut, I had three distinct subgroups in need of finding unity: TPG members, some of whom had worked on the production and some who hadn't; people from the spring workshops, two of whom had worked at Connecticut; and persons brought into the production for the first time in the fall, including Noordhoek-Hegt and the designers of the New York environment, costumes, and lights. To make a long story short, the production never did find its center. The environmentalist dropped out, and I did the design myself, assisted by Jim Clayburgh and Bruce Rayvid. The costumer did a good job, but of the off-Broadway kind: she jobbed in, worked with us between her other jobs. Noordhoek-Hegt was superb.

As the last weeks of rehearsals came upon us in November, everyone made an effort to agree on a single style. Performers are finally marvelous people when faced with the stupendous problem of getting a show up. But a unified style just couldn't be found. Yet, for all this, a number of things about TPG's *Balcony* worked: especially the reconstruction of Genet's text, ways of staging the show environmentally, experimentation with cross-gender role playing.

The deconstruction of a text involves not only an analysis of what the author has written—that's just the first step—but an analysis-through-action; that is, work in the theater at both the "molecular" and the personal levels of the text. By "molecular," I mean the level at which the actions of the playtext are broken down so that they no longer are what they were when in the context of the whole flow of the play. Then these discrete actions are allowed to play themselves out according to their own logic—or rather, to be more precise, according to the relationships found between these actions and the performers acting them. At this level personalization comes in. Thus, the molecular constituents of a text may be of the same length and complexity as a bit or even a scene, but they are not tied to the internal logic of the text. For example, in *The Balcony*, asking a whore to fulfill "my fantasy of . . ." is a molecule of action, and a key one. If the performer is not forced to reply according to the text, namely, "I want to be a Bishop, Judge, General . . . ," then new answers can be given that will—in being acted out—help the performer to experience, not just understand, what some of *The Balcony* is. Many directors use this kind of technique. I try to carry what's found out directly into the public performance itself.

Only in the case of Anne Z.'s General and Legere's Chantal was this approach wholly successful. In retrospect, of course, I find that my mistakes are obvious. TPG members and the others didn't mix; what was good for one group was bad for the other—but I was the director of both Group and play: Good-bye, peace. The summer production at Connecticut College, no matter how interesting and even important to my own ideas about the play, broke the rhythm of the work coming out of the spring workshops. Thus, the fall rehearsals were not exploratory enough but were a rush to get the show up. It got up, but it never got going. So it closed a bare six weeks after opening. Audiences were there; not packed houses, but enough. What was lacking was the spirit to go on. In December 1979 I left for Japan and Korea. When I returned early in January 1980, *The Balcony* was closed. I couldn't make it live. I didn't see it die.

The most important conceptual-scenic lesson of the production concerns the frames of actuality with which *The Balcony* plays. There are five of these frames (figure 6.2), each containing the others. At the heart of the play's action are the fantasies of the clients. The revolution is an extension of these fantasies: the revolution turns the tawdry role playing into something exciting, actual, contingent, important; through revolution the clients become Great Figures. Surrounding this core is the workaday apparatus of the whorehouse, stage-managed by Carmen. Here we have overworked whores, intrigues among Arthur, Carmen, Irma, and the Chief of Police. Is he "really" a police chief? As I see it, he's in the force, paid off by Irma, but pretty low on the scale of things. He plays the role of Chief but probably is a sergeant. Beyond this frame, things grow more "real." That is, Roger is supposed actually to believe in the revolution—not the one on the phonograph controlled by Carmen but the one of the sixties that didn't work. Seeing "his revolution" parodied and commercialized in the whorehouse, he performs one authentic act, his castration—authentic, that is, theatrically, as deep play. And outside this frame—that of Roger's action and the Chief's commentary on it, his sitting with the corpse, probably waiting for other police to arrive—

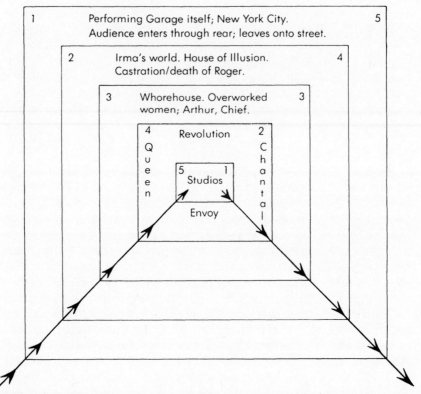

Figure 6.2. The Balcony as a five-frame structure. Movement can be from the center out or from the edge in. Each larger frame contains within itself all smaller frames; each smaller frame projects out into all larger frames.

the audience resides, the only genuine representatives of a reality outside the theater.

Of course, as Irma reminds us, it's all playacting, all "false." But I believe one can use these five frames—working either from the outside in, as a spectator would, or from the inside out, as a performer would—to explore the complicated world of *The Balcony*.

Joined to this system of frames, or boxes within boxes, is a set of characters who dissolve the usual categorical boundaries familiar to us in modern Western theater. Thus, for example:

- Irma, a "female" character in Genet, was played by a male who throughout the performance progressively put on drag; this male was playing a homosexual having an affair with the Police Chief (= "raw" power expressed through authority) but also "in love with" Arthur (= "raw" beauty expressed as sheer physicality). Irma's underlying situation is analogous to Genet's own: Genet, who celebrates his attraction to muscular boys and his attachment to the symbols of power.

- The Client Who Wants to Be General, a "male" character in Genet, was played by a female disguised as an adolescent male disguised as a female.

- The Client Who Wants to Be a Judge, a "male" character in Genet, was played by a female (plate 61). Here there was no layering of genders but simply a change from the Genet text to my production.

- The Whore who is the General's Horse is also the Bishop's Penitent. Here the audience had a chance to see the mechanism by which the fantasies are manufactured and manipulated. Usually, in productions of *The Balcony*, the spectators are also taken in: the Horse and the Penitent are "beautifully" played; their "whoreness" is swallowed up by their "actressness." I kept the signal of whoreness very clear by showing the operation by which one woman alternately plays two roles; and I demonstrated the fact that the "sumptuousness" and "actuality" of Irma's whorehouse are mostly in the minds—that is, the fantasies—of the clients (and by extension, the audience) and not in the place itself. Thus, I made clear in what ways a theater is a "house of illusion," sister to the whorehouse. After all, one of the root meanings of prostitute is substitute: someone who stands for someone else (in the mind/body of the client).

- Carmen who, if I were to do it again, would play two roles. She would play herself, the whore who has been promoted out of floorwork to administration but who still recalls the thrills, risks, and glories of frontline action (where she was the Bank Clerk's Virgin in Blue)—all this is in Genet's text. And I would emphasize Carmen's nostalgia for the front line by having her play the Judge's Thief.

- The Client who wants to be a Bishop is a "male" character who covertly likes to dress as a female and therefore chose as his "figure" a male who is covered in silks, satins, lace, and brocades.

- Chantal, a mysterious symbol in Genet, was transformed in my production into the whorehouse's resident piano player, a person who played her own compositions, many of them avant-garde music, angry and feminist. But for all that, she was attached deeply to the apparatus of the whorehouse, an attachement Roger couldn't understand. To Roger the whorehouse was a job or ought to have been; but to Chantal it was a community or ought to have been.

About Irma I need to add a few remarks. In my staging, Irma-Queen was sexually true—a man in drag—but politically false, not even the figurehead most royalty has become by now. Underlying this was my insistence that the audience have their noses rubbed in ambiguity. Genet intended, I think, to sweep the audience away with the pageantry mustered by the Great Figures and their Queen, as sometimes people are swept away by the pageantry of the Nation. With the Brecht in me still urgent, I wanted to undercut all this. I wanted the audience to ask but not be able to answer: "Is this performer,

61. Arthur fixes the bed as the Judge, played by Saskia Noordhoek-Hegt, watches. Spectators surround this movable platform. When the scene is over, they sit on it to watch other scenes. Photo by David Behl.

this Ron Vawter, really a drag queen?" At the same time, I wanted the audience to know that neither I nor Irma intended for them to think that the Queen on the balcony was meant to be some "real" queen of some "real" nation. And, ultimately, I wanted the audience to know that the distinction doesn't matter, because "real" queens are actually people in drag—in political rather than sexual drag. Thus, the layerings:

False political queen	in life and the play
True drag queen	in life and the play
Ron Vawter	in life and the play

Instead of making the levels airtight, as in much orthodox theater, or allowing the personal life to show clearly through, as in much experimental theater, I opened up gaps, wishing to confound the inquiries of those who wanted to find out "what was really going on." In this way, I detected a strong affinity between Genet and Pirandello. But Pirandello operates at the level of plot, producing ambiguity "between" himself and his audience, with the actual performers as mere messengers; Genet works at the level of characterization, making the performers true participants in the ambiguities of the play (through the production). Whoever we may suppose Pirandello's "six characters" are, we know they are actual actors in a play. We don't have this assurance with Genet—or at least my intention was to remove some of this assurance. With the General and Irma, I may have come close to succeeding. Or was it with Anne Z. and Ron Vawter? That's the question I insist must be kept open.

Thus the boxes or frames in figure 6.2 are really permeable, full of holes and leaks. This condition is what makes a production of *The Balcony* risky, and it also encourages two-way movement. There is movement from the center, the smallest of boxes, the tightest of the frames, Irma's studios; it continues out through the frames of revolution, Carmen's stage-managed world, Roger's castration (which takes place in Irma's world), and finally to the experience of the spectators in the theater place, the Performing Garage transformed for this production. Two-way movement: not only out from the center, as I've just outlined, but in from the edges toward the center.

I start with a hypothesis: The text as literature is fundamentally and irreconcilably separate from the text as material (to be) used in a performance. There are great—that is, significant, poetic, radiant, paradigmatic—literary texts, but there is no necessary correlation between a great literary text and a great performance. Otherwise, theater would be easy: limit the repertory to *Lear* and fifty plays of like stature and sail away. Unhappily, the use of great literature does not insure interesting or even tolerable performances—such an obvious truth, but with such powerful consequences for performance theory.

Not all productions of *Hamlet* are superior as experiences to all productions of *Barefoot in the Park;* moreover, a great performance—that is, a significant, poetic, radiant, and paradigmatic performance—can be built using a rotten text. For example, *American Buffalo* by David Mamet on Broadway or any number of films (those of Bergman, Kurosawa, and Scorsese come to mind) have texts, screenplays, or stagetexts that as literature are not significant. These texts are not worth studying aside from their use as part of a performance. To put this point another way: there really is a difference between "literariness" and "theatricality." They can serve each other or hinder; relate or pull in opposite directions.

Having said all this, I should add that the selection of a text deeply affects the production of which it becomes a part, whether the text is chosen before rehearsals begin or during workshops or sometime during the performative process (as it was when I chose *The Bacchae* to do after three months of work with The Performance Group in 1967/68 and, from that work and Euripides' text, ultimately made *Dionysus in 69*, which cannot be evaluated on the basis of its text alone). But to emphasize the obvious again: the text does not determine either the significance or the triviality of the production.

Nevertheless, the question remains: Is the great staging of a great text superior to the great staging of a rotten text? First, I want to distinguish between those stagings that stop at the limits of interpretation, leaving the text intact, at least trying to find the sources of the stage action within the text, and those stagings that treat the text as material to be used in the making of a new and different art work, using but not necessarily following the text. In the first case, it's clear that interpreting a text depends on that text and its qualities as ideas, actions, meanings. Thus, Brecht's *Mother Courage* in the author's own productions or Brook's interpretations of Weiss's *Marat/Sade* are exemplary interpretive productions that illuminate but don't destroy the texts on which the performances were founded. But in work not done from an interpretive basis—such as Grotowski's *Faustus*, my *Dionysus*, Brook's *Ik*—the important element in selecting a text, as in selecting performers, is that a "click" or connection be viscerally felt between the director (or whoever the principal creator is) and the words, scenes, and actions.

Looking back at my own work over the past fifteen years, I detect a pattern of clicks regarding certain thematic material; and in relation to this I see in my own performance texts certain recurring images. My productions often center on violent power struggles between males, one of whom ultimately turns out to be passive. So macho Hoss in *The Tooth of Crime* is actually narcissistic and childlike; Pentheus begins ranting against Dionysus but ends softly compliant. And Dionysus is something like Crow in *Tooth:* polymorphous, bisexual. Characters, especially female characters, have a way of doubling in my productions; so there were two Agaves in *Dionysus*, two Marilyns in *Marilyn Project*. Neither Euripides nor David Gaard foresaw this doubling. I have also played a lot with gender shifting and confusion. In *Richard's Lear*, Lear is played by a woman who at one point takes off her mask, sticks her fingers through its eyeholes, and asks the spectators: "Does any here know me? This is not Lear." Then she puts the mask back on and resumes the character of Lear. But her text denying Lear is Lear's: she is Lear and is not him simultaneously. On some nights a female performed Dionysus;

the Judge and General in *The Balcony* were played by females, as was Banquo in *Makbeth*. Irma is Vawter getting into drag and finally becoming a Queen in *The Balcony*. I could go on showing how I have made performance texts that do not conform to the intentions of the playwrights' dramatic texts—and how the performance texts I've constructed allow me to "play with" themes that obsess me. I could also interpret those themes, in the same way that dramatic critics have examined dramatic texts, discovering in them a variety of meanings: psychological, social, political, religious. It is of course not so clear in looking at performance texts, because these are usually collective (even if a principal creator organizes them) and need techniques drawn not so much from dramatic criticism as from semiotics, folklore, and the interpretation of oral literatures. What I want to show here is that when a dramatic text is not accepted ready-made but used as material, the obsessions or, if you prefer a neutral word, the concerns of the primary creators of the work—creators other than the author of the words—will be obvious to those who want to see what's there. That more hasn't been written in this vein—thematic criticism of performative work, a criticism parallel to what is classically written about literary texts—shows only the backwardness of critics. A good dose of semiotics purged of its jargon would remedy the matter.

In examining the development of the role of the General in more detail, I can say a few things concretely about the deconstruction-reconstruction process, the function of workshop in making this kind of theater, and the relationship between play and performance. This last is of great theoretical importance. Just as all art making has a ritual dimension or quality, so it also has a playful aspect. Art combines the impulse to "make belief" (ritual) with that of "make-believe" (play).

Work on *The Balcony* began in the early spring of 1979 when I placed an ad in the *Village Voice* announcing an audition-workshop. Sixty-one persons showed up. Instead of auditioning them one at a time, I asked everyone to stay for the whole audition; I said that I would see everyone that night even if it took all night. About three hours later around forty-five people remained. I then began an exercise designed to get people moving and to explore one of the basic themes of *The Balcony*. I asked the men to stand on one side of the room and the women on the other. "Look each other over," I said. "Don't move until I give you the signal. But if any of you feel inside yourselves, at this moment, that you belong on the other side of the room—that even though your gender is male or female your sense of yourself, at this instant, is that you belong on the other side of the room, then: Move." About four men went to the women's side, and nine women went to the men's side. Then I said: "How many of you feel that this sharp division according to 'men' and 'women' doesn't suit you? That there is an alternative that's not 'male' or 'female' or even 'bisexual' but something more elusive, harder to define?" I waited thirty seconds. Then I said, "Move." This time there was a great rush up the bleachers to a place I designated as "the neither male nor female place."

Unfortunately, but probably not altogether accidently, a young woman rushing to that liminal place struck her head against a steel ceiling beam. The exercise stopped; she was taken to a hospital where her wound was repaired with four stitches. Later she joined the workshop at Connecticut College. The accident didn't end the auditions, which continued until past 7:00 A.M. Sometime during the night Anne Z. auditioned. She showed up in a khaki Eisenhower jacket. She was wearing women's high leather boots. Her audition consisted of marching and speaking in a barking, masculinized way. When given the chance, she chose to be among those up on the bleachers in the not male, not female place.

I invited Anne and nineteen other people from that night's audition into a special workshop I ran during the spring in preparation for *The Balcony*. Workshops can fulfill any number of functions. They can be used for personal growth or for acquiring skills or for therapy or as a means of active research for a performance. These functions overlap, but usually the emphasis is on one or another. The spring 1979 workshop was designed to find material to use in *The Balcony*, and to mold a disparate collection of people into a group. At the start of March I cut the original group down to eight, including Anne Z. One of the eight left during the spring workshops. The remaining seven were joined from time to time by members of TPG and Noordhoek-Hegt.

The spring workshop sometimes took us very far from the narrative of *The Balcony* but never far from its themes. For example, people were sent from the Garage to walk the Soho neighborhood, visit bars and restaurants, and return after thinking about a "secret desire." This secret was shared with only one other person: the subject's own private Irma. This Irma then arranged, insofar as possible, the fulfillment of the secret desire. That spring in the Garage we saw a combination marriage-funeral, a massage given to an individual by a group of admirers, an ornate procession, much cross-gender dressing and undressing. Soon we combined several "secret desire" scenarios so that these were performed simultaneously: we were making a *Balcony* of our own. Images that I could not keep in the production still haunt me: several of the whores quietly playing cards, waiting for customers, joking with each other, and stroking each other gently; Arthur at target practice with the pistol he is afraid to carry out into the streets; Irma staring at herself in a mirror for a very long time. Once, each performer chose one of the characters from *The Balcony* and told the story of the play from this character's point of view, detailing what that character did that night. Or, shouting and speaking very quickly, each performer recited the story of the play as "objectively" as possible as if it were being reported to someone standing on the other side of a noisy waterfall.

What happens at workshops like this is not only a deconstruction of the text and narrative of the play being done (if one is doing a literary text) but also a parallel deconstruction of the lives of the performers. The four-phase "social drama" process developed by Turner (working from Van Gennep) applies to the workshop-rehearsal-performance sequence. Turner says that social dramas follow a sequence of breach, crisis, redressive action, and reintegration or schism. Applying this model to the theatrical process, the breach is the separation from ordinary ways of behaving that signals the start of the workshop phase. In *The Balcony* this separation happened from the first night of auditions through to the time in March when I cut the group back to eight persons. Crisis and redressive action are the stuff of workshops. Each meeting intentionally provokes crisis and demands redressive actions. The purpose of this core work is to deconstruct all the elements that will later be reassembled in a new way to make the production. Reintegration is what happens during rehearsals. Reintegration is completed when the work is ready for the public: the mise-en-scène, the whole performance text, is a return to the social sphere of elements that had previously been withdrawn from it. If the rehearsals fail to make a unified production, a schism occurs: the play closes and everyone goes their separate ways, or the group attempts another project. The first work to be done on a performance is not making the production but unmaking all the ready-mades that stand in the way of creating a new work. If one rushes too early into the reintegration phase, the work is bound to be full of unintentional clichés, as most theater is. Most productions are not allowed enough time—nor do their leaders and workers have the conceptual grasp of the process I'm talking about—to separate the deconstruction phase from the reconstruction. People are too soon doing the work of rehearsal, reconstructing what they've never had the chance to deconstruct. The full process is shown in figures 6.3 and 6.4. By "history" I mean that texts, people, space—everything—enters workshop already full of various pasts. Workshop is the place where those pasts are, as much as possible, put aside: an authentic liminoid time-place is created. All who participate in the workshop strive for "now," what Turner calls moments of spontaneous communitas: a situation where impulses flow freely, associations are made across time and space without regard to previous hierarchies or obligations. The reconstruction phase makes a new historical circumstance, one that is a dialectical reconciliation of "history" and "now."

It was during the spring workshops that I learned about Anne's past. I never inquire during workshop whether what is being presented is a "real"

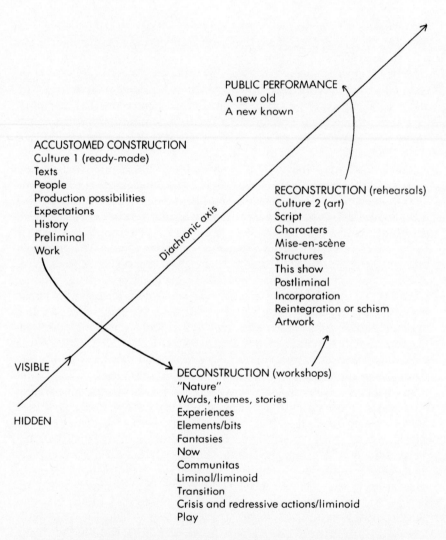

PUBLIC PERFORMANCE
A new old
A new known

ACCUSTOMED CONSTRUCTION
Culture 1 (ready-made)
Texts
People
Production possibilities
Expectations
History
Preliminal
Work

Diachronic axis

RECONSTRUCTION (rehearsals)
Culture 2 (art)
Script
Characters
Mise-en-scène
Structures
This show
Postliminal
Incorporation
Reintegration or schism
Artwork

VISIBLE

HIDDEN

DECONSTRUCTION (workshops)
"Nature"
Words, themes, stories
Experiences
Elements/bits
Fantasies
Now
Communitas
Liminal/liminoid
Transition
Crisis and redressive actions/liminoid
Play

Figure 6.3. *Once a performance is "made" it tends to "slow up" in relation to the diachronic axis. That is, it doesn't change much as time goes on. But while in the deconstruction/reconstruction phases it changes relatively rapidly. Absolutely traditional performances would be "vertical" relative to the diachronic axis: that is, frozen in time.*

past or something made up. The telling must be convincing within the context of workshop. Through exercises in storytelling, through movement work that included acting out childhood memories, through meetings just between Anne and me, we shared details of her "history." From the very beginning she wanted to play the General. She'd come to the audition dressed for the role. During workshop she led the group in military drills; she played out the time she stood in her father's closet smelling his uniforms and touching his medals. Anne Z. is a poet and actress; she felt her father had wanted her to be a male military person. She was painfully ambivalent about her father. She wanted him to be a hero, but he was in the wrong war (Vietnam); she wanted him to be a peace lover, but he was a combat pilot. These conflicts are not unusual; the point is that all this information surfaced during workshops and was presented in such a way that it could be used in *The Balcony*.

It turned out that Anne Z. was the one person who participated in all phases of *The Balcony:* spring workshop, summer production at Connecticut College, and winter production in New York. In assimilating her relationship to her father, she deconstructed her own history and reconstructed it in terms that both suited Genet's script and was in dialectical opposition to it. Some details were taken directly from her past life. The medals she wore in the play included some of her father's own, and she also wore his hat. It was Anne Z.'s idea to have the General enter the theater with the audience, dressed in high heels, a black, sequined dress, and a bright, rust-colored wig. She looked like a parody of a hooker. When, during the General's scene, she undresses, the audience expressed surprise: underneath the hooker was an adolescent boy. She had her hair cut very short; her breasts were bound flat; she wore a man's sleeveless undershirt and underpants. Her voice was that of a boy's. The personal dimensions of these identities were unknown to the audience but clear to those who had gone through workshop with Anne Z. There she had a chance to play with becoming the boy she felt her father wanted her to

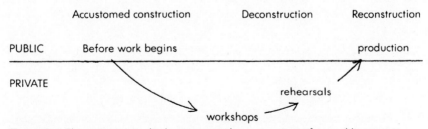

Figure 6.4. *This process can also be represented as a movement from public space to private space and back into public space.*

be. And this boy could play at becoming a General (one rank beyond her father's colonel). But this becoming was a play within a play: for it was a scene in *The Balcony*.

The work of workshop is play. And the opposing tendencies and various functions of play are fulfilled by workshop. These tendencies and functions can be summarized in two ways, as a list and as a set of oppositions.

List
1. To detach consequences from actions so that the actions can be "played out" safely, under "controlled" circumstances, in a nurturing environment, a permissive environment
2. To try combinations of behavior that in ordinary circumstances would not be tried
3. To reduce anxiety
4. To express aggression safely and harmlessly
5. To gain experience
6. To develop group solidarity
7. To integrate personality
8. To experience flow—autotelic pleasure

Set of Oppositions
1. ritual rigidity
   freedom and voluntariness
2. rules
   free flow
3. pain and anxiety
   pleasure and relaxation
4. test of skills, competitive
   just for fun, collaborative
5. serious, totally absorbing
   counts for nothing, "I was only playing"
6. public display
   private fantasy
7. reflexive
   self-absorbed

To be playing seems to need these contradictions. Playing is neither just the top half or the lower half of the set of oppositions. But the oppositions suggest classic dichotomies such as social versus private, conscious versus unconscious. Workshop fulfills all the functions of the list while emphasizing the lower half of the oppositions. The top half is brought back during rehearsals. That's not to say there is no anxiety or no rules in workshop, but these are deemphasized; things are done and said that within the context of the project at hand "count for nothing." In workshop much more is "thrown away" than "kept" for the later public performance. In rehearsals, the tendency is to keep more and more until the later rehearsals resemble absolutely the performance. A dress rehearsal is a performance by another name.

A performance is basically a communication between the performers and the audience. A rehearsal is the place where a technique is developed that will make the performative communication effective. Workshop is the place where raw material is researched, discovered, and examined. Workshop operates at the level of play, rehearsals at the level of technique, and performances at the level of narrative (or other "finished" communicative systems). These three levels interface each other. Usually they are kept separate, but in some cases, and for some performances, intentional up-wellings from the level of workshop through to the level of performance occur. This is what happened in Anne Z.'s case when she played the General.

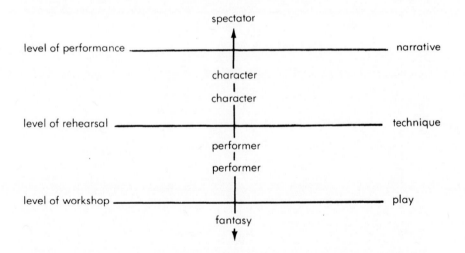

The fantasies of workshop help the performer in rehearsal "find" the character who during performance "presents" the narrative to the spectator. When Anne Z. took off her dress and wig, the character the audience thought it was seeing dissolved into another it did not expect: an adolescent boy. When the boy put on his Eisenhower jacket with its sixteen medals, the audience thought it was seeing another aspect of this character, the General. But the jacket is Anne Z.'s, some of the medals her father's. This boy in military drag—a boy who is actually (in workshop, in life) a woman—

knocking off a piece at the whorehouse is a vision from Anne Z.'s fantasy of what she imagined her father might have wished her to become. Genet helps by having the whore pretend to be the General's Horse, who not only satisfies him sexually but leads his funeral cortege. The General dies (comes) with his boots on, a hero. At this point images and actions from the play level of workshop erupt into a display at the narrative level of the public performance.

The Balcony—like many productions in experimental theater based on workshops—followed over time a wavelike pattern of development (see

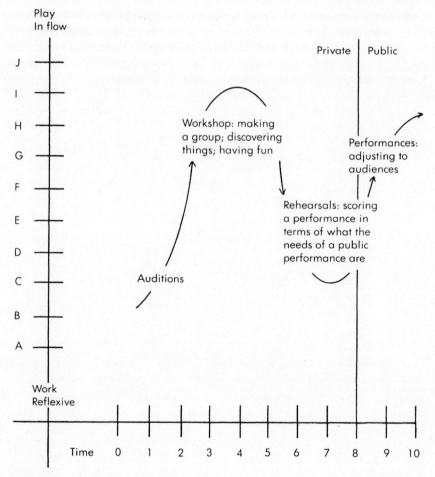

Figure 6.5

figure 6.5). Workshops were playful. But as the time for public performances approached, workshops were replaced by the serious business of rehearsals. *The Balcony* process was unusual in that the student production at Connecticut College came between the workshops of the spring and the rehearsals of the fall. The Connecticut production was liminoid, combining the playfulness of workshop (my professional reputation wasn't at stake, I felt I could "fool around") with the serious work of getting a production up. The promised arrival of an audience concentrates the mind.

When I returned to New York in the fall, new problems arose concerning my ability to integrate the phases of the work. Turner's scheme describing social dramas applies. The breach within TPG and between TPG members and the others who were working on *The Balcony* overwhelmed the energies wanting to incorporate the spring workshop and summer production into the New York rehearsals. Only Anne Z. in a full way, and some others partially, was able to use what was uncovered in workshop and tested at Connecticut. In December, when the play opened at the Performing Garage, the forces of schism were too powerful. Neither the redressive actions of workshops and rehearsals nor many group meetings among members of TPG were able to effect a reintegration. The production closed. Shortly thereafter I left The Performance Group. Within a year those who remained renamed it the Wooster Group.

7

NEWS, SEX, AND
PERFORMANCE THEORY

It's as hard to write about performance, theory or practice, as it is to put ideas, as such, onstage, for the writing is always indirect, representative, the map not the territory. And the stage always is there, physical first, a gaping territory only vaguely pointing elsewhere. But both writing and performing create negativity. Emily Dickinson: "Wonder is not precisely knowing, / And not precisely knowing not, / A beautiful but bleak condition."

Performance theory, when well done, takes into account both the beauty and the bleak condition—as well as the negativity, full of the Japanese Mu, pregnant pause, full emptiness, that the stage so totally is. As Artaud said, the stage is first a physical space waiting to be filled. But when the stage is full, it is filled with propositional emptiness. All effective performances share this "not–not not" quality (see chapters 2 and 3). Performer training and workshops focus their techniques not on making one person into another but on encouraging the performer to act in-between identities; in this sense, performing is a paradigm of liminality. And what is liminality but literally the "threshold," the space that both separates and joins spaces: the essence of in-betweenness?

This in-betweenness, thresholdness, also is emphasized by poets as having something to do with performance, with the flow and evanescence of human life (as consciousness of itself). "But tell me," Rilke asks, "who *are* they, these acrobats, even a little more fleeting than ourselves?" Rilke has no answer until, maybe, the Ninth Elegy:

Threshold: what does it mean
to a pair of lovers, that they should be wearing their own
worn threshold a little, they too, after the many before,
before the many to come, . . . as a matter of course!

Here is the time for the Tellable, *here* is its home.
Speak and proclaim. More than ever
things we can live with are falling away, for that
which is oustingly taking their place is an imageless act.

Act under crusts, that will readily split as soon
as the doing within outgrows them and takes a new outline.

[Rilke 1952, 85]

I feel that way: the threater I know, for all its activity and visual splendor, has become an imageless act. But also my seismograph detects that Mu stirring beneath—the tilted jugs under the Noh stage, reverberating with the stamping that summons the ghosts.

Thus the theme of this writing: in-betweenness, thresholds—the creative negativity, the double negative that when multiplied yields only positive sums.

There are two main realms of performance theory: (1) looking at human behavior—individual and social—as a genre of performance; (2) looking at performances—of theater, dance, and other "art forms"—as a kind of personal or social interaction. These two realms, or spheres, can be metaphorically figured as interfacing at a double two-way mirror. From one face of the mirror persons interested in aesthetic genres peep through at "life." From the other side, persons interested in the "social sciences" peep through at "art." Everything is in quotations marks because the categories are not settled. The very activity of peeping through unsettles the categories. Or, as Erving Goffman slyly remarked in 1959, "All the world is not, of course, a stage, but the crucial ways in which it isn't are not easy to specify" (1959, 72).

Sometimes—I would say almost always—people peeping through see not only what's on the other side but their own image too. The interface between realms is a mirror. Only by willingly disregarding that image of themselves are they able to "see through" to the other side. But this willing suspension has grown too costly. Many prefer to see things stained by the consciousness that one is seeing. Thus the reality of the perceived event—as art, as life—is of both what is seen and the seeing of it. So much has this experience of seeing myself even as I see the event I am looking at become central, even obsessional, that I run back and forth from one side of the mirror to the other, looking first at art from the life side and then at life from the art side, always seeing myself from either side.

This activity—trying to see all there is to be seen, including oneself seeing; trying not to use conventions to block out what is there—leads to the development of "meta" theories: theories that take into account not only what people experience on each side of the mirror—within the sphere of art or of life—but also what they experience moving back and forth from side to side.

The reports of those dealing with meta—performance theorists all—are complicated, even confused, because so many levels or modes of seeing, or experiencing, are present simultaneously. A person sees the event; he sees himself; he sees himself seeing the event; he sees himself seeing others who are seeing the event and who, maybe, see themselves seeing the event. Thus there is the performance, the performers, the spectators; and the spectator of spectators; and the self-seeing-self that can be performer or spectator or spectator of spectators.

It is this *layering* of seeings that radically distinguishes animal play, animal art, animal ritual, animal symbolism, animal communication, animal thought, from their human counterparts.

This layering can also be called playing. It is not all that playing is, but it is a very strong part.

Bateson got at the relationship between play and theater:

We might expect threat, play, and histrionics to be three independent phenomena. . . . But it seems that this would be wrong, at least so far as mammalian communication is concerned. Very brief analysis of childhood behavior shows that such combinations as histrionic play, bluff, playful threat, teasing play in response to threat, histrionic threat, and so on form together a single total complex of phenomena. And such adult phenomena as gambling and playing with risk have their roots in the combination of threat and play. It is evident also that not only threat but the reciprocal of threat—the behavior of the threatened individual—are part of this complex. It is probable that not only histrionics but also spectatorship should be included within this field. [1976, 70]

But what is play?

Now this phenomenon, play, could only occur if the participant organisms were capable of some degree of metacommunication, i.e., of exchanging signals which would carry the message "this is play." [1976, 68]

This message is transmitted by means of the play-face, the play-mood, the eyebrow flash, the slack lower jaw: signals given in milliseconds. Such signals can be transformed and socially encoded; they may even be faked. Once they are socially encoded—understood as conventions belonging to this or that specific culture—they can be used to signal "this is play" across a broad spectrum of activities.

Buying tickets is one such signal in our culture. When I reserve seats at Madison Square Garden to see the Rangers play hockey, I am prepared to witness mayhem but within a controlling play frame. When I go to that same Garden for the circus, I am prepared to see danger but also to be tricked about what is dangerous. And if I go to the theater, on Broadway or off, I may even see feigned death. If I were a Roman attending the Circus Maximus I would see real death but death still bounded by the play frame. It is a matter not simply of consequences (Does the actor die or not?) but of context. The gladiatorial combatants need not be enemies of each other, any more than the player performing Hamlet need hate the person who performs Claudius. But the conventions of the Circus Maximus dictated, usually, death for the loser, while the conventions of Shakespeare's theater asked only that, in Hamlet's own words, the mirror be held up to nature "to show virtue her own feature, scorn her own image, and the very age and body of the time his form and pressure." The difference between the Circus Maximus and the Globe is the difference between Spanish and Portuguese bullfighting. Surely the difference speaks of nontheatrical differences within the societies, and I prefer peaceable to blood-letting drama. Still I tune into professional football each Sunday afternoon. So if I announce for peace I nonetheless enjoy, if not the death of entertainers, a sport that has its fill of broken bones.

And even in New York today there is some theater—not sport, not licensed combat like boxing, but authentic theater—where the "real" is mixed in with the fantasy. This theater includes live acts and episodes on television. Before this chapter is over, I will be saying a good deal about television reality. For the moment, let me speak of Belle de Jour, a sadomasochistic theater on West Nineteenth Street in Manhattan. It costs thirty dollars for men, five dollars for women, to attend Belle's. Belle herself welcomes the audience and takes them on a tour of the place. Before the theatrical presentation begins, we see a woman stretched on a rack (obviously pretending to be hurt), a man burned by a candle, a woman urinating into a man's mouth. Then the audience is seated on bridge chairs opposite a small raised stage of gloriously polished wood. It reminded me of a Noh stage. As part of several skits, some of them comic, some meant to be scary, a variety of sadomasochistic actions take place: whipping, breast pinching with pliers, testicle tying, dripping of molten wax on a woman's breasts and body. One of the climaxes of the performance comes when Belle herself drives a three-inch nail through the penis of her "toilet slave." This is no Grand Guignol trick. In fact, nothing at Belle's is like the Grand Guignol where we, as spectators, expect to be tricked. Belle thrives on giving her audiences the real thing.

After the skits Belle invites spectators onto the stage to spank or be spanked. About fifteen of the audience of fifty respond. It usually takes some coaxing to get people onstage. More men than women accept Belle's invitation. The participants spank or get spanked (plate 62). One or two of them are given a heavier workout. I saw a man stripped, hung upside down by his ankles, and spanked until his buttocks were very red. Participating spectators usually don't work on each other. They work over Belle's people, or her people work them over. It's all very carefully controlled. Most people are new for each performance; a few are regulars. When the participation segment is over, Belle announces that "private sessions" will be offered until 2:00 A.M. These sessions actually occupy Belle and her staff most of the week. The big money is in private sessions, where clients propose scenarios that are acted out with/for them. Belle's theater is actually doing very much what Genet proposed in *The Balcony*. I asked Belle: she never heard of Genet or his play.

62. A spectator getting spanked by another spectator as Belle (whip in hand) and her assistant look on. Photo by Catherine Burgheart.

Talking with Belle, I found out that much of her artistry, theatrically speaking, came accidentally. She was the owner of a clothes boutique specializing in the kind of garments sadomasochists like to wear. She designed the clothes herself. She describes herself as a "dominant." One day she moved into a loft on Nineteenth Street. It had a stage in it. "I didn't know what to do with that in the middle of my living space," she said. After about a year it dawned on her: stage = theater. And so she started Belle de Jour. It's been very successful. She talked to me about a new idea she has: opening a small dinner theater specializing in S&M acts and featuring a cutesy menu with items like "humble pie" for dessert.

Belle wants to take acting lessons. I wouldn't advise it. Her stage presence is strong just because it is so unstudied. She mumbles, she looks spectators straight in the eye, she actually gets angry when something goes wrong. In her fifties, with straight gray hair cut short, Belle is very convincing in her black leather miniskirt, high heels, net stockings, and riding whip. An original. Hers is an authentic folk theater.

Is it decadent? If decadence means what happens when cultures "decline" (itself a shady concept), I caution against labeling Belle de Jour. I'd guess that activities like hers have been around a long time, in many different circumstances and cultures. And compared to what I've seen in gay bars, bathhouses, and at punk clubs, the audience at Belle's is very bourgeois, dressed mostly in conservative suits and ties, or sweaters. I wouldn't label the bars, bathhouses, or clubs decadent either.

The people at Belle's—players, spectators, and spectator-participants—are playing and they are not playing. Or, if you prefer, their play takes on an intensity, a concentration, a seriousness that we do not often see in the "real theater" where we have been accustomed to a flabby pretense. The concentration I felt at Belle's was like what I've seen in professional sports, or at a black church I attended in Harlem, or with my own family celebrating Passover seder.

Intensity, passion, concentration, commitment: these are all part of the play mood. But this alone is not what makes play play. There is also the quality of acting out, of becoming another, of displaying a normally hidden part of yourself—and of becoming this other without worrying about consequences. Play implies getting away with it. Or, as Bateson put it, "These actions, in which we now engage, do not denote what would be denoted by those actions which these actions denote. The playful nip denotes the bite, but it does not denote what would be denoted by the bite" (1976, 69). Or, as Belle put it, if someone really hurts someone in her theater she knows something is wrong. Nips are "pretend" bites, and even if they hurt they are forgiven (usually) if framed in play. But even these pretend bites remind us

NEWS, SEX, AND PERFORMANCE THEORY

that nips are a "kind of" bite and can, if the play frame is destroyed, become "real" biting.

Where does this leave the bleeding gladiator or even the authentic sado-masochist at Belle's? Their conditions, theatrically speaking, are very different. The gladiator doesn't want to play. He is not playing. He is a spectacle for the spectators. He is one with the animals, brought in under guard to be used as entertainment. The spectators are "at play," but the gladiator is a slave given only the choice of death now or death later. But still, his own situation, which is not play, is presented within the play frame. If this seems strange, even obscene, it is not too different from what NBC presents each night on its local nightly news, the "Six o'Clock Report" on channel 4 in New York.

As for the man who gets his penis nailed at Belle's, he is in "real life" a mechanic. He likes getting his cock nailed. He is not paid for it. He also likes Belle urinating into his mouth. It is a matter of psychological opinion whether or not this man is more or less free than the ordinary actor who also likes his work, which may involve simulation of some pretty gruesome situations. One fact is clear: the man at Belle's is not physically coerced as the gladiator is.

But are the foregoing actions—which I pick as extremes to test Bateson's propositions concerning the play frame—mere nips denoting the bite but not denoting what would be denoted by the bite? In other words, is the death of the gladiator any sure indication of enmity between him and his opponent, or even between him and a wild animal? Is the man at Belle's being "hurt" by the nail? Is she punishing or torturing him?

However these questions are answered, it is certain that Belle de Jour is a "liminoid" theater. Its performances are advertised not (yet) on the theater pages of the *Village Voice* but in a quasi-classified section near the back entitled "Adult Entertainment." There a number of "fantasy" entertainments are listed. Many of these are thin masks for prostitution; others, like Belle's, comprise a genre of performance of the "not–not not" category. Places like Fantasy Manor, where, the ad promises, a person can "experience decadence & delight in a new unique concept of sensual, bizarre, & unusual partying—plus all facilities of an on-premise swing club for singles & couples." On Thursday at Fantasy Manor there are "live onstage 'unusual' performances."

Although this kind of stuff is not reviewed in the *Voice* or the *New York Times*, it has been written about in the *Drama Review*, the nation's leading scholarly theater journal. The March 1981 issue was devoted to "Sex and Performance." Most of the articles concerned legitimate theaters, both mainstream and experimental, that have used sex or sexual themes. Obviously, this can include a lot of items since sexuality has been one of the major preoccupations of theater throughout history and in many cultures. But one article was specifically about the kind of theater presented at Belle de Jour's. Catherine Burgheart's article begins:

One need only open a copy of the *Village Voice* to become familiar with the wide variety of sexual performance available today. Along with the peep shows on 42nd Street and the private "on-the-premises" clubs, there exists a little-known network of four or five establishments in lower Manhattan offering sexual entertainment in the form of theatre. Sex theatre deals almost exclusively with sado/masochism (S&M), bondage and discipline, and dominance and submission. [1981, 69]

Burgheart's article goes on to detail the "network of sex theatres" which, she claims, "form a small and intimate community." In other words, these theaters—and the people who run them as well as the audience that attends—are not yet part of the entertainment world, competing with each other, but they are "not not" part of that world either. Just as the activities inside the theaters—what happens on the stage, in the "private sessions," with the participating audience—cannot be strictly categorized as belonging to either theater, prostitution, ritual, economic exploitation, community sharing activity, or any other single category, so the theaters themselves are also "in-between."

But liminality is not only a quality that is found in performances that stand between the "legitimate" and the "illegitimate" theater but also something that experimenters in the theater have been playing with. (Is there anything comparable in literature? Or in so-called pornographic writing?) In experimental theater, the limen is between "life" and "art" and, relatedly, between "chance" and "fixed" structures. Because much of this work dates back to the surrealists and includes, more recently, the work of John Cage and is therefore well known, I won't linger on it. Instead, I shall present a more recent example from a theater still working in New York, a theater whose very history is liminal.

I am talking about Squat, a performance group residing and performing on Twenty-third Street, just west of the Chelsea Hotel. This group has received a lot of attention in New York and is considered one of the city's leading experimental theaters. Squat, as the name implies, is a theater of exiles, a bunch of squatters, people of several families who began work in Hungary, were forced to leave, worked in other places in Europe for a few years, and then came to America in 1977. They first performed here at the New Theater Festival in Baltimore in 1977. Shortly thereafter they moved to New York. The ground floor of their rented building is a storefront theater with room for about sixty-five spectators sitting on risers facing the window. On the other three floors are small performing spaces (sometimes used, sometimes not), a lobby, and living quarters.

63. Two audiences watch Squat's *Andy Warhol's Last Love*. One audience is in the theater; the other is on the sidewalk peering in. Photo by Roe DiBona.

Almost all of Squat's shows exploit the window fronting on Twenty-third Street. This window actually is a model of that two-way mirror I was talking about at the beginning of this chapter. On the Twenty-third Street side there is "life"; on the inside there is "art." And Squat plays with moving back and forth from one side to the other (plate 63). Let me give examples from *Pig, Child, Fire!* (1977) and *Mr. Dead and Mrs. Free* (1981). For much of *Pig* the street is a backdrop offering some gags: passersby doing double takes as they see something strange going on behind the window, like a goat eating vegetable scraps as a family sits at table or a little girl parading around in falsies; and the audience laughs at passersby, as they would at "Candid Camera." That's because the audience inside knows that *Pig* is a "play" (however offbeat) while the passersby can't decide what they are seeing. So the audience sees people who are unable to find a proper frame to contain and locate what they are seeing, and the audience inside enjoys watching the confusions of the incidental audience outside. Later in *Pig*, a TV camera is focused on the audience inside the theater. At that point the paying spectators can watch themselves watching.

It even happens that some knowing persons, having seen *Pig* from inside the theater, return later to watch it from outside. At that point there are three audiences: insiders, outsiders, insiders who are outside. Sometimes the street is used to stage coups de théâtre, as when a man strolls by, his arm ablaze.

(He wears a special kind of plastic coating that flames at relatively low temperatures.) I won't discuss the overall flow of actions of the five parts of *Pig*. These are not coherent as drama, narrative, or social commentary. (That itself is a problem, the problem of meaning or content.) The actions of *Pig* evoke and illuminate the system of transformations relating the "art" side of the performance to the "life" side. Again and again, Squat points up the differences of these realms and then questions those differences. Examples:

1. A large puppet hangs upside down. From out of its anus protrudes the head of a man whose face is identical to that of the puppet. Around this man's neck is a noose. For twenty minutes or so this man stares unblinking at the audience. The large puppet is removed so that the man appears to be born from the puppet's asshole; and as he is born, so is he hung. Then, slowly, he removes his "face" (a very cunning mask that conforms precisely to his own features). The mask = both his own face and the face of the puppet. The face under the mask is identical to the mask. This confounds the audience's expectations concerning the mask. For what is a mask if it is not a concealment of, or at least different from, the face? One might say that this performer was wearing a mask that had been drained of its maskness. Or, to apply the categories I began with, the puppet is art in reference to the man who is coming out of its anus; but the face of the man = his own mask and cannot be categorized as either "art" or "life." I cannot "place" either the mask or the face on either side of my "life"/"art" double mirror. For some time I thought the unblinking mask I was looking at was actually a face. That's because I checked it out against the face of the puppet, which was more "art," less "life," than the mask. Squat gave me a proper lesson in relativity.

2. A taxicab drives up outside the theater. A man gets out of the cab and draws a gun. Across Twenty-third Street another man, a pedestrian, stops, kneels by a streetlight, and draws a gun. Between them flows the actual traffic of a busy Manhattan street. A few drivers and passengers duck as they see men with drawn guns on either side of the street. In typical New York fashion most cars don't stop but drive through this battle zone. Inside the theater, a woman performer draws a gun and takes aim at the gunman who had arrived by taxi. She shoots, he falls, but the glass between them is not shattered. Again a system is revealed. The taxi = "life" and belongs to Twenty-third Street. The gunmen in the street are ambivalent. They belong both to the realm of art and to what we have increasingly become accustomed to as life in the streets. To passing pedestrians and motorists, the gunmen are "life." Then the woman drawing her pistol and shooting from inside the theater makes clear that the two gunmen outside are "art." The

blank shot that drops a person proves the point. But to whom does it prove it? The people just passing by on Twenty-third Street see a man with a gun fall. Maybe they think they didn't hear the shot. Or maybe they assume a movie is being shot. Or maybe they don't think anything but just move through minding their own business.

3. In *Mr. Dead and Mrs. Free,* a jeep drives up on the sidewalk and stops close to the glass door adjoining the storefront window. Two soldiers in battle dress unload a bloody passenger from the back seat and carry him through the door into the theater. They put him in a hammock. A priest and nurse attend him. Spectators gather outside the theater, peering in and staring at the jeep on the sidewalk. Soon a police car arrives. It is an actual New York City police car. Why did it arrive? Did someone in the theater call for it? Or did a passerby? Do the police come every night? Don't they know that a "play" is going on? *Dead/Free* had been running more than a month when I saw it. Does Squat have permission to use Twenty-third Street? To drive a jeep onto the sidewalk? Two cops get out of the car and talk to the performers next to the jeep. Then the cops enter the theater through the glass door. The audience laughs. They laugh some more, and gasp, when a city ambulance, with all its lights flashing, drives up nose to nose with the police car. The cops confer with the performers in the theater; one cop writes in his notebook. They leave. The ambulance leaves. The cop car drives off. Then the jeep drives away. The cops and the ambulance are "life"—but when the cops enter the theater they are also "art." The jeep on the sidewalk is "art," but to some passersby it is "life."

Squat intentionally confounds these categories. Squat makes me ask: What's the difference? Enjoy what is. The performances of *Pig* and *Dead/Free* expose these categories as not being dynamic or flexible enough to handle today's experiences. The audience inside is not shocked. Neither are the passersby. Somehow popular aesthetic sensitivity is better able to handle the situation than orthodox aesthetic theory. Audiences and passersby, even the cops, can cope. But there's no performance theory to explain their being able to cope.

A closer examination of the spheres of space used for *Dead/Free* (and *Pig* too) reveals five separate areas (figure 7.1). There's a lot of communication among these five. Between each area is something that both separates and connects spheres. The jeep is of the street but driven onto the sidewalk. The cops come from their car in the street, cross the sidewalk, and walk into the theater. The glass door and the window both separate the indoor from the outdoor spaces and unite the two because of the see-through quality of glass. The movie screen and curtain (a film is shown as the first part of *Dead/Free*) mark off and connect the spectator and stage spaces. On several occasions the

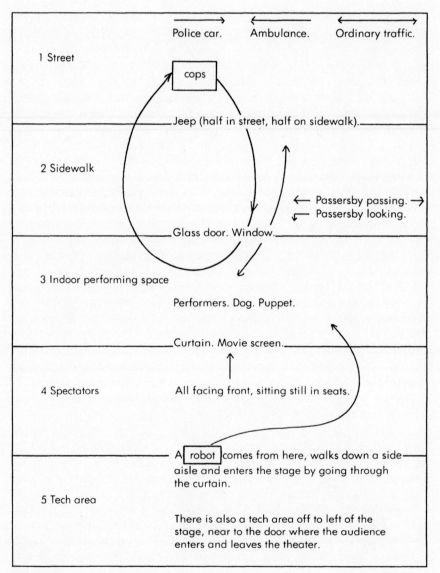

Police car. Ambulance. Ordinary traffic.

1 Street

cops

Jeep (half in street, half on sidewalk).

2 Sidewalk

← Passersby passing. →
Passersby looking.

Glass door. Window.

3 Indoor performing space

Performers. Dog. Puppet.

Curtain. Movie screen.

4 Spectators

All facing front, sitting still in seats.

A robot comes from here, walks down a side aisle and enters the stage by going through the curtain.

5 Tech area

There is also a tech area off to left of the stage, near to the door where the audience enters and leaves the theater.

Figure 7.1

curtain is used not just as a barrier or as a mask for the stage but as the link between the stage and audience spheres. Near the end of the performance a robot emerges from the tech area behind the audience and makes its way down a side aisle, turns in front of the audience, and disappears through the place where the two halves of the curtain meet. Just after that a man with a violin and a female singer emerge from behind the curtain. She sings, he accompanies. It's like an entr'acte, except that nothing is being prepared behind the curtain. When it opens the play is over.

Such back-and-forth movement—police, spectators, performers, robots—and inversions—the police entering the theater as part of the performance, the final curtain opening to signal the end of the play rather than closing to signal it (or opening to signal the beginning)—draw attention to boundaries, frames, the interfacing of the various performative realms. Also they invite an investigation of the rules, formal and categorical as well as experimental and pragmatic, that govern the relationships among the realms. In other words, Squat's performances are an invitation to make performance theory.

What remains questionable at Squat, what doesn't yield easily to interpretation, is meaning, content. The performers of Squat do what they do extremely well, but what are they doing? Or rather, what does it mean, these things they do? In August 1982 I arranged a special performance of *Dead/Free* for participants of an International Symposium on Ritual and Theatre. This symposium brought together performers, performance theorists, anthropologists, and theatre scholars from several cultures. Part of the program included performances of Noh from Japan, Korean shamanism, *A Chorus Line* on Broadway, a Sunday morning gospel service at Brooklyn's Institutional Church of God in Christ, and Kutiyattam, a Sanskrit theater form from Kerala, India—very wide-ranging stuff. The anthropologists and scholars had in their lives experienced many genres of performance—initiation rites, exorcisms, trance dancing—as well as familiar things within the Western modes. But for some Squat was outside the pale. Several scholars and visiting performers left before the performance was over. The only way out was across the stage and through the front door. On the morrow they claimed illness or unpostponable previous engagements. But, from what I saw, it was clearly a case of not being able to stomach what they were experiencing.

It wasn't the violence, or even the nakedness (which was tame compared to some of the stuff seen around town), but the confusion of categories: the apparent "meaninglessness" of it all. The cruelty and sexuality of some of the images (shootings, fellatio administered by a priest to a dying soldier), the unusual iconography (a great naked female baby doll with TV screens for eyes, screen-eyes full of Esther Williams's water ballets): this stuff taken together did not seem to make sense; there was no semantic system into which it could be absorbed. No one played Clifford Geertz and read it like art. I am not about to do that now. I will say that *Dead/Free* is thematic and iconographic rather than narrative and characterological. It associates patterns of stereotyped fictive action with leitmotifs from New York street life. The shootings, the war scenes, the singing of a cabaret song whose most discernible words are "sex machine" as the penislike robot makes its way from the back of the theater, down the aisle, and onto the stage, the film of two women walking, one of them apparently a young teenager speaking as a man might the most graphic yet clichéd pornography: all of this evokes, in me at least, a mood of ironic despair. Is this the way it really is in New York? I flash on the last days of Weimar—and wonder where America's Hitler will come from. *Dead/Free,* with its backdrop of Twenty-third Street, a street invited into the theater, just as the theater—the audience—can literally see into the street (a street we, supposedly, came into the theater to get out of), insists that the spectators experience the infiltration of street life into every aspect of living. There's no getting away from banal violence. "This is the way ordinary life is in New York these days," the Squat production "says." It's much the same message that local news on television reiterates day after day.

Whatever the meanings of *Dead/Free*—and the question of content is again very important, as it has not been since the first burst of performance experimentation in the midfifties—the artists of Squat intentionally confound orthodox aesthetic categories. They delight in doing that. This is what so provoked the participants in the symposium, many of whom make their livings defining categories. Although the audience at Squat sits immobile, facing front, in the most conventional of the Euro-American orientations, what that audience witnesses (and I use the word advisedly) is a systematic subversion of Western theatrical conventions. By introducing Twenty-third Street onto the stage, Squat goes beyond Pirandello and the Living Theatre. Yet, by framing Twenty-third Street as part of *Dead/Free,* Squat ironically reimposes on the very street itself the placidity of aesthetics. It is ironic because the Squat(ters) know very well how fragile and labile aesthetic order is. The violent contingencies of everyday life can sweep away all aesthetic categories with the ease of a woman whisking away flies.[1]

The question that Squat's performance puts to its audiences is the same one that Goffman asked in 1959: How can you distinguish between performance and nonperformance, between art and life? I'm not sure that it's an important question as such. The artists of Squat assert that what is "art" depends on the frame surrounding the actions. When the cops walk into Squat's stage they have positioned themselves "as art," regardless of what they may intend to be doing or how they themselves feel about it. In an epoch of information media—I mean TV, movies, radio, the microchip, the satellite hookup—when "authenticity" is often a highly edited, refined, idealized (or brutalized) version of "raw" experience, people wonder exactly what is "raw" and what is "cooked." Is there any such thing as "human nature" understood as unmediated, direct, unrehearsed experience? And if there isn't (there isn't), how can understanding the whole theatrical process—rehearsals, training, warm-ups, preparations, cool-down, aftermath as well as the show itself—help us grasp social process: how lives are lived ordinarily and in crises?

These questions have a "content" and "value" dimension. Cooking the news is preparing it in such a way as to support particular social and political positions. There is no neutral information.

Geertz, anthropologist, "reads" behavior as if it were literature. He says of the Balinese cockfight:

Like any art form—for that, finally, is what we are dealing with—the cockfight renders ordinary, everyday experience comprehensible by presenting it in terms of acts and objects which have had their practical consequences removed and been reduced (or, if you prefer, raised) to the level of sheer appearances, where their meaning can be more powerfully articulated and more exactly perceived. . . . What it [the cockfight] does is what, for other peoples with other temperaments and other conventions, *Lear* and *Crime and Punishment* do; it catches up themes—death, masculinity, rage, pride, loss, beneficence, chance—and, ordering them into an encompassing structure, presents them in such a way as to throw into relief a particular view of their essential nature. [1973, 443]

To interpret a Balinese cockfight "as if" it were a conscious art form is to treat the cockfight the way Squat treats Twenty-third Street. Such a treatment by Geertz tells us more, probably, about the emerging way of looking at experience typical of "postmodern consciousness" than of how the Balinese themselves think of cockfighting.[2]

Granted that the Balinese "use" the cockfight the way Geertz says they do (and not all those who have lived in Bali and experienced cockfighting there agree with Geertz), do they "interpret" the cockfight the way he does? That is, even if the cockfight is like *Lear*, do the Balinese believe it is like *Lear?* And if they do not, how much attention should we pay to the Balinese interpretation and how much to Geertz's? And is this question any different from wondering who knows more about my dreams, I the dreamer or a skilled dream interpreter? Pharaoh preferred Joseph. But Geertz has not written his interpretation at the request of the baffled Balinese driven to understand their cockfights. The Balinese are perfectly happy with things as they were ante Geertz. Also, he is writing in what is, to them, a foreign language. His interpretation is addressed to people who cherish *Lear*, not the topeng pajegan play, *Jelantic Goes to Blambangan*.[3] So, even though I might agree with Geertz that the Balinese cockfight functions "as if" it were *Lear* in Bali, "catching up themes" of great importance to the Balinese, Geertz's perception that this is so finds no native place in Bali.

Ought Geertz, therefore, abandon his project? His position is liminal, in between Bali (where his "raw" material is) and Euro-America (where his "cooked" or "manufactured" product is distributed). Is his work leading to a better understanding among peoples, or is it a further imposition of alien categories on Third World cultures?

Victor Turner goes even further than Geertz. Turner sees as the motor driving all kinds of social conflict everywhere a four-phase dramatic sequence: breach, crisis, redressive action, reintegration (or schism). Geertz himself has summarized Turner's scheme:

> For Turner, social dramas occur on all levels of social organization from state to family. They arise out of conflict situations—a village falls into factions, a husband beats a wife, a region rises against the state—and proceed to their denouements through publicly performed conventionalized behavior. As the conflict swells to crises and the excited fluidity of heightened emotion, where people feel at once more enclosed in a common mood and loosened from their social moorings, ritualized forms of authority—litigation, feud, sacrifice, prayer—are invoked to contain it and render it orderly. If they succeed, the breach is healed and the status quo, or something resembling it, is restored; if they do not, it is accepted as incapable of remedy and things fall apart into various sorts of unhappy endings: migrations, divorces, or murders in the cathedral. With differing degrees of strictness and detail, Turner and his followers have applied this scheme to tribal passage rites, curing ceremonies, and judicial processes; to Mexican insurrections, Icelandic sagas, and Thomas Becket's difficulties with Henry II; to picaresque narrative, millenarian movements, Caribbean carnivals, and Indian peyote hunts; and to the political upheaval of the sixties. [1980, 172–73]

This is what Turner calls a "social drama." It works itself out the way a dramatic plot works and is strictly analogous to classical and modern Western drama. Again, the problem is whether or not Turner is projecting onto a number of social and aesthetic genres the shape of one particular form. Or, as Geertz says, "This hospitableness in the face of cases is at once the major strength of the ritual theory version of the drama analogy and its most prominent weakness. It can expose some of the profoundest features of the social process, but at the expense of making vividly disparate matter look drably homogenous" (1980, 173). But lest we fall with Geertz into the fallacy of heterogeneity, it is not necessarily a mistake to find some rather simple universal processes underlying all the elaborations and diversity of human social behavior. Turner's four-phase sequence conforms nicely to mainstream Western dramatic convention. It doesn't suit what happens at Squat or, for that matter, Aeschylus's *Seven against Thebes*. And some social processes, at least, seem to emphasize not the resolution of crises but their prolongation and their segmentation. Social life may be as much like a soap opera as it is like Ibsen.

So there is theater in the theater; theater in ordinary life; events in ordinary life that can be interpreted as theater; events from ordinary life that can be brought into the theater where they exist both as theater and as continuations of ordinary life (the cops at Squat). For some, drama is the motor underlying social processes and crisis management. For others, like Goffman, all human behavior has a strong performative quality.

A theatrical performance or a staged confidence game requires a thorough scripting of the spoken content of the routine, but the vast part involving "expression given off" is often determined by meager stage directions. It is expected that the performer of illusions will already know a good deal about how to manage his voice, his face, and his body, although he—as well as any person who directs him—may find it difficult indeed to provide a detailed verbal statement of this kind of knowledge. And in this, of course, we approach the situation of the straight-forward man in the street. Socialization may not so much involve a learning of the many specific details of a single concrete part—often there could not be enough time or energy to do this. What does seem to be required of the individual is that he learn enough pieces of expression to be able to "fill in" and manage, more or less, any part that he is likely to be given. The legitimate performances of everyday life are not "acted" or "put on" in the sense that the performer knows in advance just what he is going to do, and does this solely because of the effect it is likely to have. The expressions it is felt he is giving off will be especially "inaccessible" to him. But as in the case of less legitimate performers, the incapacity of the ordinary individual to formulate in advance the movements of his eyes and body does not mean that he will not express himself through these devices in a way that is dramatized and preformed in his repertoire of actions. In short, we all act better than we know how. [Goffman 1959, 73–74]

As Goffman explains, "the details of the expressions and movement used do not come from a script but from a command of an idiom, a command that is exercised from moment to moment with little calculation or forethought" (1959, 74). What then formally separates acting in the strictly theatrical sense from behaving in the ordinary sense? From Goffman's point of view—like that of John Cage—nothing. The theatrical event is theater only because it is framed as theater, presented as theater, received as theater. Just as the message "this is play" identifies play behavior, so the message "this is theater" identifies theatrical behavior. Inside the frame "this is theater," every conceivable kind of behavior—from the most calm and mundane to the most intense and exciting—is presented. And some genres of theater—performance art, happenings—even specialize in the undramatic, while some kinds of presentations of ordinary life (framed as "not theater but real life") specialize in the dramatic. Newspapers and magazines have long done this with their photographs and headlines. But TV news has made the theater of ordinary life its special province.

TV news seems to me to be a paradigm of that peculiar kind of in-between or liminoid performance genre we are getting more and more of. It illustrates the theories of Goffman, Turner, and Geertz while offering a kind of performance akin to that of Squat. Despite its apparent frame of "this is real life," TV news presents a format that proclaims "life is theater, and this is it."

There are two kinds of regular TV news ("specials" are something else again): the local and the national network news. Some items usually overlap; and the late local news usually repeats a lot of the early evening news. Thus there is, at the outset, some kind of ritual repetition of items. (In this, the news coverage itself is like the commercials; both rely on repetition, a form of incantation, to get their message across.)

Just as there are two kinds of news, so are there two kinds of performers on the news. There are the regulars whose presence reassures viewers about the stability of the world; these regulars find, report on, and narrate the news. Some of the regulars usually stay in the studio; these are the "anchors." Others go out on location. The second kind of performers are the dramatic players themselves, and these fall into two categories also. First, there are ordinary people caught up in this or that event, sometimes as participants, sometimes as witnesses. Just being on a plane coming in from Warsaw the week after the imposition of martial law in December 1981 made some people "newsworthy." Other ordinary people are involved in "life's tragedies" like fires, murders, muggings, or diseases, poverty, and unemployment. The news broadcasts never put these into an overt ideological perspective. They take the form of either detached Greek or Ibsenian episodes. There are heroes and villains, but these are not seen as agents of larger social forces or even of "destiny" as such. Then there are the stars of the political, sports, and entertainment worlds. Between these figures and TV a symbiotic feedback situation exists. The stars would not be stars except for "exposure"; yet being a star guarantees exposure, at least for a while. These stars keep appearing as long as they are high in the sky. They vanish quickly when their star sets. How often is Jimmy Carter on TV these days? Not surprisingly, the most durable figures belong to the entertainment world. People like Orson Welles, Bob Hope, and Lauren Bacall keep popping up. And, slippery tricksters that they are, they manifest themselves one day as actor, another as figure in a commercial, another as themselves on a talk show. And, through the feature of rebroadcasting old movies, some stars never set: John Wayne, Marilyn

Monroe, and Humphrey Bogart (to name just three of many) are as eminent today as twenty or more years ago.

Recently I've been keeping a log of TV news. For example, on 24 December 1981, on the six o'clock local news program of channel 4, NBC, in New York, there were eighteen news items, and twenty-five commercials. The commercials took up about 20 percent of the broadcast time. The news items began with two reports of fires—almost always, when they occur, a top item. In both fires children were burned fatally. The second news item was about a nun beaten up in front of a Bronx church; the church was broken into and items were stolen. The third story—leading into the first commercial break—was about Christmas in Israel. The commercials were from American Express, Harvey's Bristol Cream sherry, *Annie* on Broadway, and the New York Health and Racquet Club. Over the hour, commercials centered on luxury items: American Express appeared again; there were three for fur coats; two more for shows on Broadway; several for perfumes, watches, and wine. Other news stories concerned travelers trying to get away for Christmas, the events in Poland (reported in item 6, about twenty-five minutes into the program), Haitian refugees locked up in a Brooklyn detention center since July and now beginning a hunger strike, the wedding of the leader of the subway vigilante group, the Guardian Angels; and some regular items like sports, weather, and consumer reports. The twelfth item of news reported that Ford and GM were about to lay off 300,000 more workers. This report was immediately remedied by cheerful news from Wall Street where the Dow rose a few points. A block of commercials followed featuring *Dancin'* on Broadway, Flemington Furs, Honda cars, and, again, American Express. No question that the news is carefully designed. And that the commercials are aimed not at everyone but at a small slice of the citizenry. The implication is that anyone can get into the news—be murdered, bombed or burned out, or something—but that only a relatively few rich people are the decisive spectators of the news, patrons of the news. Much research is done locating who watches what when.

I haven't kept my log long enough to make too many generalizations. Instead, I want to concentrate on a few specific items. A fire has burned out a home in Staten Island, and two children have died, the rest of the family made homeless. Arson is a possibility. Several firemen have been injured. As the camera pans the burned-out wreckage, still smoldering, the narrator describes the "tragic situation." It's a morning-after shot. Next, the reporter is talking to the mother of the children. She wasn't home when the fire broke out. She is bereaved but restrained, not hysterical. On camera she breaks into held-back sobs and is comforted by a neighbor. She is talking about how the landlord refused to repair the electrical system. Neighbors crowd into the camera's eye and confirm that the mother is speaking the truth. Next, the narrator describes how the fire spread so quickly that despite "heroic efforts" by the firemen, the children could not be rescued from the "inferno." Familiar words, almost liturgical. Finally, there is a quick cut to the landlord, who has been located and defends himself by saying that everything in his houses is safe. Back in the studio the anchor promises that the news staff will investigate the charges made against the landlord. A quick cut to an ad for *Evita*, the award-winning musical in its third year on Broadway. (The ad, incidentally, features performers no longer in *Evita*.)

This video *tranche de vie*, one of the commonest items on New York nightly news, is both authentically moving and patently manipulative. I shudder when I see, and participate in, the exploitation of the mother. Sometimes, especially when little children are victims, I cry. Then I despise myself for crying and ridding myself of guilt through that cheap catharsis. At the same time I wonder: Why shouldn't the mother be given the chance to ventilate her grief and rage publicly, broadcasting to all of the polis tuned in, much in the mode of the *Trojan Women?* And why shouldn't I cry for "real-life" drama? Or is feeling to be restricted to fictional events? And if Geertz can write so eloquently of the Balinese cockfight, isn't this item an American way of public acting out—even including the quick cut to a promise of escapist entertainment, available at a price?

Also I can't hide my admiration for the skill with which the news department has put together a minidrama: event, heroine, victims (unseen except for something wrapped in black plastic on a stretcher being carried from the burned-out house), villain, chorus, and storyteller. And, yes, the storyteller promises a *deus ex machina*, an investigation. It is all framed as "news," and while apparently satisfying our society's demand for facticity, it actually is (soap opera) tragedy.

It is said that too much of this kind of thing deadens public responsivity. I don't know about that. What I do know is that the framing of TV news is very sophisticated. Two messages, "this is theater" and "this is life," are broadcast simultaneously. All those quick cuts, edited to the second, mixing news and commercials, appearances of regulars who often achieve star status, the juxtaposition of items that are specifically new but categorically familiar (wars, fires, regular features where everything is the same, like sports and weather): together this format is one that makes of news programs a ritual theater. Playwright Jack Richardson noted some years ago:

To be bound at a prescribed time to millions of others, to share with them an identical image and text, to be shown again and again the same polished day divided into the same neat sections of significance, to be assured by the traditional sign-off of the on-the-spot network subaltern who gives his name as testimony to the truth of what we've witnessed, to be convinced by immediate and portentous comment that we have participated in a day of deep and novel events and fully understood their meaning—what more could one ask for in the way of ritual than all of this? [1975, 38]

The ritual is in the format, in the programming, not in the content as such. The format insures that certain contents, certain classes of events, will be repeated; and repetition is a main quality of ritual. The facticity of the reports and the excitement associated with items that are "new" (not reported before) tell viewers that the program is "real life." The sense of "real life" is nested in the ritual format. Each facticity is part of a sequence of similar events: this fire is followed by the next and the next; this international crisis by the next and the next. Thus, if I were to diagram the frames of TV news, they would look like figure 7.2. This scheme is like nothing so much as a Hindu theory of maya-lila where all experience is both authentic and theatricalized (illusion, ludic) and where the whole of existence is an unending ritual cycle.

The differences between local and network news are worth examining. Local news is made mostly of the kind of domestic tragedies just described, spliced into a known format that includes comfortable, familiar items like sports, weather, consumer reports. All this is seasoned with details aimed at a genuinely local market and audience. In Wisconsin there is farming news; in New York the subways come in for a lot of attention. The national news

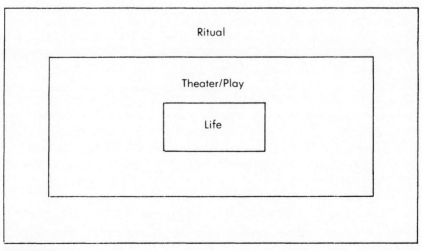

Figure 7.2

eschews both the directly personal and patently sensationalized items on the one hand and the strictly local items on the other. But all news originates somewhere, is local to some place. Or is it? A visit to the home studios of NBC news, the actual physical sets where "Nightly News," "Today," and "News Overnight" (the best of the news programs, now canceled) originate, reveals very modest domains, theatrically speaking. Close up, the sets are ordinary, even shabby. It's the camera, the splicing in of tape clips, the closeness and charisma of the reporters and, especially, the anchors that give the news a feeling of expansiveness/expensiveness. The format of national news—which means international news as well—makes it seem to originate everywhere/nowhere: in these make-believe studios, on the road, wherever the anchorman is. There's a kind of Mephistophelian conceit to national TV news. "News is where I am" = anchored in the home studio, editing stuff sent in from all over. It takes a big event—Sadat's assassination, the launching of the *Columbia*, the marriage of Prince Charles and Lady Di—to pull the anchor off base; and the presence of the anchor on location endorses the event, marks it as important: thus there is a mutual reinforcing of event and anchor.

When an item is obviously both extremely local and of international importance—such as the Iranian hostage crisis, the imposition of martial law in Poland, the great Italian earthquake of 1980—a definite kind of multilocality wash is applied, draining away the particular local character of the events and transforming them into something worldwide. The very flexibility of the global information net makes this possible. Thus we see armored cars in Warsaw, hear a report from Washington concerning the crisis, meet some travelers who have just arrived in London from Poland, and witness a protest parade in Chicago by Polish Americans—all this within four or five minutes. Just where is the news taking place? Also, the events from all these places are narrated by familiar voices, or at least voices with familiar standardized accents. Dialect is something anchors and reporters rarely give voice to. The anchors, the reporters, the government spokespeople tend to spread out and homogenize even the most piercingly local events. By definition, an item that goes national is of interest "to the nation" and will have responses and repercussions in many different areas. The exception to this is an item or two of "local color," usually given near the end of the news. But these items are almost always not news—not something pressing against anyone's consciousness—but an offbeat item of uplift, piquancy, poignancy, or humor.

The importance of speaking—the tone of voice, whose voice it is, what kind of message is being spoken—in generalizing the national news cannot be overemphasized. Local news usually has a large proportion of "native speakers"—like the mother on Staten Island. But in national news most of the speaking is official: by reporters or by official "spokespeople." The visual images may be local (although these too are frequently the anterooms of government offices, which look just about alike all over the world), but the cognitive information, spoken in English, homogenizes the news. National news all takes place in NBC-land, where Tom Brokaw, Andrea Mitchell, and Bernard Kalb live.

What's dealt with on national news is often more threatening than anything seen on the local program. Nuclear weapons, invasions of nations, mass starvation, refugees, great natural disasters—these items are framed calmly, presented reassuringly. The domestic tragedy on Staten Island may affect me, but it doesn't directly threaten me. The subways of New York may be unsafe, but I can choose not to ride them. But a nuclear war? Local news is close, hot, forcefully dramatized and personalized. The national news is cool, under control, rationalized. What's interesting from the point of view of performance theory is that these different kinds of news follow particular formats based on theatrical conventions. The local news is a kind of modern, Ibsenian naturalistic drama contained in a burlesque or variety-show format surrounded by certain ritual formulas. The national news is more directly cinematic, connected to those weekly newsreels of the thirties and forties and to the kind of documentary film that overlays the visuals with soothing narration.

Whatever lip service there may be about TV news as news, the way the programs are pushed in newspaper ads and on billboards, the means of hooking an audience, is sheer showbiz. For example, in 1982 when Tom Snyder joined the "Eyewitness News Team" (ABC's local in New York), his face looked straight out—just as he would on camera—at passersby as they descended into the purgatory of the New York subway system. One saw Snyder's face and read that

He's Charming
He's Exciting
He's Caustic
He's Outrageous
He's Influential
He's Controversial
He's Involved
He's Emotional
He's New York

HE'S TOM SNYDER. EYEWITNESS NEWS 7
Tonight at 11

Channel 2, CBS in New York, is supposed to be a little more reserved. But ads in the *New York Times* for its "Newsbreakers" local news at six o'clock pushed the following items in the spring of 1982: "You're single and 40. Should you pack it all in? . . . Life on tranquilizers . . . tranquil or tragic?" Remember this is CBS news, not a soap opera, and the medium is the *New York Times,* not the *National Enquirer.*

Promotion of the national news followed an apparently more "mature" line. Take the ad in the *Times* for ABC's "World News Tonight" Special Assignment (sounds like James Bond, doesn't it?):

COULD DEFENDING AMERICA DESTROY AMERICA?
The allocation for defense in President Reagan's new budget is huge. So huge that many economists have questioned the effect it could have on the Nation's economy for years to come.
    Some have gone so far as to predict disaster.
    Tonight and tomorrow night, Special Assignment takes a hard look at the battle over defense spending—a battle whose outcome will affect you and your family.

True enough, but written like a soap opera.

I'm not saying it could be much different. TV is a visual medium. To give it a heavy talk format would go against its grain. But there are ways of using longer segments of time, and appropriate visuals, to go effectively into a story: to make journalistic as well as intellectual sense. It's not happening that way because the public and those who exploit the public both want increased theatricalization, which means simplification, quick arousal, and satisfactory resolution of the excitement. (The dragging on of the Iranian hostage "crisis" made it difficult for TV; luckily for the media, the hostages' release coincided with the Reagan inauguration, making for one stupendous television day.)

The real battles concerning TV news at the level of network executive suites are, as everywhere in videoland, about ratings. When Roone Arledge, head of ABC sports, took over the news and jazzed it up, the other networks jumped. Tony Schwartz reported in the 1 March 1982 *New York Times:*

When William J. Small was forced to resign as president of NBC News last week, it was just the latest upheaval in the fastest growing, fastest changing, and most hotly debated area of television. . . .
    What gives?
    The answer, as one veteran CBS newsman bluntly sums it up, is "the Roone Arledge factor." Mr. Arledge is the ABC News president whose aggressive approach to news gathering and instinct for showmanship helped transform ABC News from an also-ran into an upstart trend setter in the last five years. . . . Ironically, perhaps, top executives at CBS and ABC News privately accuse each other of the same sins— slickness at the expense of substance. . . . But if technique is so important, how does one explain the phenomenon of "The NBC Nightly News"? Throughout all the

upheaval NBC has stuck with both its traditional format and its longtime anchor, Mr. [John] Chancellor, and the broadcast remains in a close ratings race with both competitors. [1982, C-15]

Well, shortly after Schwartz's story, Chancellor got booted, and "NBC Nightly News" added sparks, and Tom Brokaw, to its format. Also, the networks scheduled early-morning and late-night broadcasts: News is getting to be as exciting as football. The point is that news as TV fare is not news, not simply information, but theater. It's theater that makes it in the marketplace, not information as such. Facticity needs a push from drama; and a liminal form, not art—not journalism, emerges.

Much has been made of the connection between violence on TV and violence in society. Links that were once thought to be just possible are now recognized as proven. The *New York Times* reported on 6 May 1982 that

A federal analysis of a decade's research on the behavioral effects of television viewing has concluded that there is now "overwhelming" scientific evidence that "excessive" violence on television leads directly to aggression and violent behavior among children and teen-agers. [Reinhold 1982, C-27]

The report, prepared by the National Institute of Mental Health (NIMH), "focused on entertainment programming rather than news." But the report still holds for news: we all know the quotient of violence on the news; and violence in the news is presented as real. The NIMH report described "four theories to explain the purported violence link." These were "observational learning," "attitude change," "arousal process," and "justification process." This last means that a person who has aggressive tendencies is reinforced by what is seen on the tube.

A fifteen-year study made by a team led by George Gerbner of the University of Pennsylvania's Annenberg School of Communications shows that people who watch prime-time TV a lot have a different view of social reality than light viewers. The heavy TV viewers' sense of what living in America is like conforms to what they see on TV, not to what social statistics reveal. According to a report on the Gerbner study written by Harry F. Waters for *Newsweek:*

In every survey, the Annenberg team discovered that heavy viewers of television (those watching more than four hours a day), who account for more than 30 percent of the population, almost invariably chose the TV-influenced answers, while light viewers (less than two hours a day) selected the answers corresponding more closely to actual life. [1982, 136]

The warping of reality affects perceptions about sex and sex roles, age, race, work, and crime—especially violent crime. Heavy TV viewers think, for example, that "women should take care of running their homes and leave the running of the country to men" (136–37), that the elderly "make up a smaller proportion of the population today than they did 20 years ago" and that "old people are less healthy than they were two decades ago" when the opposite is true (137), that racial stereotypes are true and that blacks are taught on the tube "to accept minority status as naturally inevitable and even deserved" (137); and "heavy viewers greatly overestimated the proportion of Americans employed as physicians, lawyers, athletes, and entertainers, all of whom inhabit prime-time in hordes" (137). Finally:

On the small screen crime rages about 10 times more often than in real life. But while other researchers concentrate on the propensity of TV mayhem to incite aggression, the Annenberg team has studied the hidden side of its imprint: fear of victimization. On television, 55 percent of prime-time characters are involved in violent confrontation once a week; in reality, the figure is less than 1 percent. In all demographic groups in every class of neighborhood [surveyed] heavy viewers overestimated the statistical chance of violence in their own lives and harbored an exaggerated mistrust of strangers—creating what Gerbner called a "mean-world syndrome." Forty-six percent of heavy viewers who live in cities rated their fear of crime "very serious" as opposed to 26 percent for light viewers. Such paranoia is especially acute among TV entertainment's most common victims: women, the elderly, non-whites, foreigners, and lower-class citizens.

Video violence, proposes Gerbner, is primarily responsible for imparting lessons in social power: it demostrates who can do what to whom and get away with it. "Television is saying that those at the bottom of the power scale cannot get away with the same things that a white, middle-class American male can," he says.

At a quick glance, Gerbner's findings seem to contain a cause-and effect, chicken-or-the-egg question. Does television make heavy viewers view the world the way they do or do heavy viewers come from the poorer, less experienced segment of the populace that regards the world that way to begin with? In other words, does the tube create or simply confirm the unenlightened attitudes of its most loyal audience? Gerbner, however, was savvy enough to construct a methodology largely immune to such criticism. His samples of heavy viewers cut across all ages, incomes, education levels and ethnic background—ethnic backgrounds—and every category displayed the same tube-induced misconceptions of the world outside. [138]

One correction can be suggested. Those living in the inner cities do live in the more violent, dangerous neighborhoods: their views of life with regard to violence may not be as skewed as those people living in safer environments. In which case, we may have a kind of "video gladiatorial games" syndrome: the wealthier, safer people are being entertained by violence done to the poorer citizens. In a democratic society members of the poorer classes can also watch this kind of entertainment, of course.

Naturally there is a feedback system too. Violence in society at large is the basis of entertainment and news, which in turn exaggerates, dramatizes, and focuses this violence back into the society. Gerbner's study shows how the television world exaggerates, distorts, displaces, and transforms ordinary actuality. (I dare not say "reality" because the television world, like all of maya's illusions, is also real—and, as Gerbner's study shows, can create more realities.) This process is identical to the ritual process, ethologically speaking. One could say that violence on TV—news and/or entertainment—ritualizes a certain dimension of American mythology. For America has a long, and very deep, tradition of violence: it's how the West was won; our most celebrated historical moments are wars civil and foreign; the gangster, like the gun-toting cowboy, is a resilient folk-hero.

TV news sends three messages at once: its content is violent, the delivery of that content is silky smooth, and the commercials literally supporting it all sell viewers with money (from a few pennies to alleviate pain up to thousands to get away from it all on a Caribbean island) an America where dentures don't slip, bowels work reliably overnight, skies are friendly, and Sheratons have style. Where does this leave Belle de Jour and Squat—sex, violence, the streets, and the refracted realities derived from and fed back onto those streets? Some people just don't get the connection. "Saxon violins? I didn't even know they made any." But Belle, rather than dissociating sex and violence—as TV news tries to do, on the surface at least—builds her whole show on bringing them together. At Squat also, sex and violence as a single package supply most of the imagery—but with the ironic double take that more of the same is there for the looking on Twenty-third Street, just on the other side of the windows that make up Squat Theatre's upstage wall.

It's this "Twenty-third Street reality" that the local news on TV confirms. The sexuality is present in the flirtatious behavior of the newscasters: they joke with each other and ogle the viewer through the camera. On local news at least, "attractive" men and women abound. The Offbeat Character on the "team" is usually the weatherman. The segregation of explicit sexuality from violence on TV news is not fundamental: implicit in the news is that where there's one there will also be the other. The "news" is grief, the "newscasting" is sexy. And when a good sexy murder trial comes along—like the shooting of the Scarsdale Diet Doctor by his lover—it's played up for all it's worth.

National news slicks over the connection between sex and violence. The dominant personalities there have been the Old Uncle (Cronkite) and the Wise Brother (Brinkley). But that's changing with the arrival of Tom Brokaw and other sexy youths. And there's loads of sex in the commercials which, I emphasize, must be seen not separate from but occupying the same time/space as the rest of the news show. Interestingly, women newscasters on national news are likely to be desexualized—possibly because Americans still believe that a sexy woman can't be telling the truth.

Everywhere it's "personality" that counts. Very little separates newsman Tom Snyder from entertainer Johnny Carson from interviewer Phil Donahue. The anchor is a star—and his longevity on the job depends on his ratings, his continuing to be a star. When the locals flirt with each other they also wink at the camera, telling the viewers that it's all "in fun," all "playacting." But it's a special kind of playacting that says news (= facticity) is fun, news is exciting.

TV has now entered a period where it is a private as well as a public instrument. TV games, home computers, cassette systems, cable networks, public access channels, feedback systems that allow subscribers to communicate with each other or with a hub in order to vote, buy, or in other ways interact—all these, and more, are common. Programming has gone way beyond what the networks offer: everything from going to the supermarket at home to pornography, from sports all day to the latest prices for farm animals and grains. What we have now—and will increasingly get more of— is a very wide spectrum of videonics. (See figure 7.3.) Live theater occupies a rather small middle ground between two great video realms: that of private communications–home electronic theaters and games and that of the more or less mass programming of cable, UHF, and VHF (the twelve most familiar channels, from 2 to 13). "News" as information moves through all of this complicated system. Maybe it's that the local and national news served up by the networks and their affiliates has whetted everyone's appetite for information. Maybe it's always been that the really important news of our lives— births, deaths, business transactions—have mostly been very local. Maybe the popular imagination is way ahead of theory, and there is no significant difference between news and entertainment. From gossip to local catastrophe to world events, what "happens" or is "staged as happening" is fun to find out about. Whatever: increasingly, the same equipment is used to communicate, educate, inform, buy and sell, vote; and a conceptual spillover is taking place, blurring categories that until recently seemed locked away from each other. A world that was securely positional is becoming dizzyingly relational.

There will be more "in-between" performative genres. In-between is becoming the norm: between literature and recitation; between religion and entertainment; between ritual and theater. Also, the in-between of cultures: events that can't easily be said to originate in, or belong to, this or that culture but that extend into several cultures—like the nightly news, which is neither nightly nor news.

The future will not deny mass communication but will also include intense uses of TV as a private instrument. Does this mean that mass media

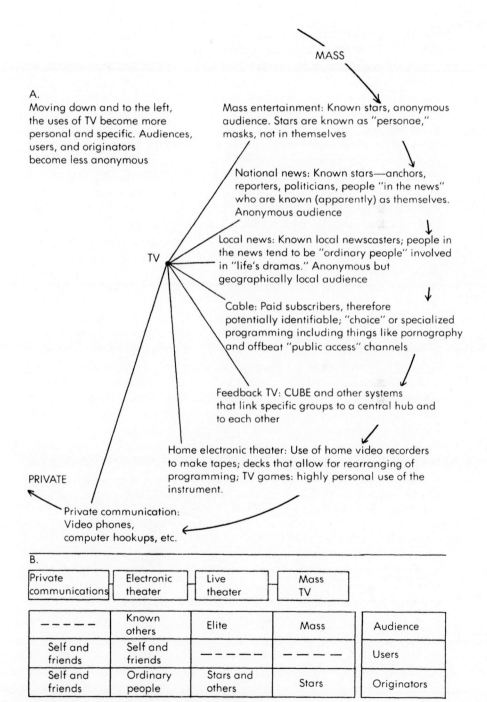

A.
Moving down and to the left, the uses of TV become more personal and specific. Audiences, users, and originators become less anonymous

MASS

Mass entertainment: Known stars, anonymous audience. Stars are known as "personae," masks, not in themselves

National news: Known stars—anchors, reporters, politicians, people "in the news" who are known (apparently) as themselves. Anonymous audience

Local news: Known local newscasters; people in the news tend to be "ordinary people" involved in "life's dramas." Anonymous but geographically local audience

Cable: Paid subscribers, therefore potentially identifiable; "choice" or specialized programming including things like pornography and offbeat "public access" channels

Feedback TV: CUBE and other systems that link specific groups to a central hub and to each other

Home electronic theater: Use of home video recorders to make tapes; decks that allow for rearranging of programming; TV games: highly personal use of the instrument.

TV

PRIVATE

Private communication: Video phones, computer hookups, etc.

B.

Private communications	Electronic theater	Live theater	Mass TV	
– – – – –	Known others	Elite	Mass	Audience
Self and friends	Self and friends	– – – – –	– – – – –	Users
Self and friends	Ordinary people	Stars and others	Stars	Originators

Figure 7.3. A: Video wheel. B: Video and live theater

will become more private or that private interactions, even the most intimate (getting medical advice, finding mates), will use the equipment of mass communication? Probably some of both. The blurring of categories separating different ways of being with, and relating to, others continues. Both the "rugged individual" and the "mass man" are dying off. A much more ironic, skeptical, and not so easily manipulatable public—or diverse set of publics—is coming into existence. The political process is changing, with more emphasis on interactions among smallish local groups, even consortiums of groups. The "national interest" isn't so easy to identify. As in medieval times, the interests of various "guilds" do not cohere into a single "national interest." To serve these multiple publics new genres of information/entertainment—genres that don't segregate information from entertainment—are being developed. There really isn't any right name to describe people who use a wide range of videonics: multiple collective private persons. And I don't know to what degree I'm excited by these possibilities and to what degree I'm depressed by their unfamiliarity.

I suppose it is necessary, and positive, to reaccumulate our disparate society into some kinds of collective entities; and that this reaccumulation will have to be under the aegis of videonics. "Have to be" always disturbs me. Yet I have no humanist alternative to suggest—which brings me back to Emily Dickinson and her "beautiful but bleak condition" of not knowing and not knowing not. I come to where I know what I would not know had I the choice. Performances that exist "between" "art" and "life" make all those quotation marks necessary, for these performances throw into question the very categories they represent. TV news says clearly that it is "life," but it isn't; Belle urges her participating audiences to make pain while the sun shines; Squat ironically frames its own performances in ways that make identification of any reliable "reality" just silly. These kinds of performances—and there are many more examples that I didn't cite—undermine not only classic Euro-American aesthetics but the social reality these aesthetics were constructed to reflect and support.

NOTES TO CHAPTER 7

[1]For more on Squat, see Squat 1978, Shank and Shank 1978, Shank 1982, Schechner 1982*b* ,and Dasgupta 1983.

[2]Lots has been written about postmodernism, most of it not very good. I do recommend some of the essays in Benamou and Caramello, eds., 1977; Davis 1981; and my own two essays on the subject in Schecher 1982*b*.

[3]For anyone interested, this topeng play is translated and published in *Drama Review* 23, 2 (June 1979): 37–48.

REFERENCES

Anderson, Michelle
  1982 "Authentic Voodoo Is Synthetic." *Drama Review* 26, 2: 89–110.
Andrews, Edward Deming
  1948 "The Dance in Shaker Ritual." In *Chronicles of American Dance*, ed. P. D. Magriel. New York: Henry Holt.
  1963 *People Called Shakers*. New York: Dover.
  1967 *The Gift to Be Simple: Songs, Dances, and Rituals of the American Shakers*. New York: Dover.
Ashton, Martha Bush, and Christie, Bruce
  1977 *Yaksagana*. New Delhi: Abhinav Publications.
Awasthi, Induja
  n.d. "Dialogue-based Ram Lilas in Traditional Style." Manuscript.
Banes, Sally
  1980 *Terpsichore in Sneakers*. Boston: Houghton Mifflin.
Barba, Eugenio
  1979 *The Floating Islands*. Holstebro, Denmark: Thomsens Bogtrykkeri.
  1980 "Theatre Anthropology: First Hypothesis." Transcript of a talk given in Warsaw. Privately distributed in typescript.
  1981 Flyer distributed to participants in the second session of the International School of Theatre Anthropology, Odin Teatret, Holstebro, Denmark.
  1982 "The Way of Opposites." *Canadian Theatre Review* 35 (summer): 12–37.
  1982a "Theatre Anthropology." *Drama Review* 94, 2:5–32.
Bateson, Gregory
  1972 *Steps to an Ecology of Mind*. New York: Ballantine Books.
  1976 "A Theory of Play and Fantasy." In *Ritual, Play, and Performance*, ed. Richard Schechner and Mady Schuman. New York: Seabury Press.
Beeman, William O.
  1982 "Tadashi Suzuki's Universal Vision." *Performing Arts Journal* 17: 77–87.
Bellocq, E. J.
  1970 *Storyville Portraits*. New York: Museum of Modern Art.
Belo, Jane
  1960 *Trance in Bali*. New York: Columbia University Press.
Benamou, Michel, and Caramello, Charles, eds.
  1977 *Performance in Postmodern Culture*. Madison: Coda Press.

Benedetti, Robert L.
1970   *The Actor at Work.* Englewood Cliffs, N.J.: Prentice-Hall.
1976   *Seeming, Being, and Becoming.* New York: Drama Book Specialists.
Benjamin, Walter
1936   "The Work of Art in the Age of Mechanical Reproduction." In *Illuminations*, trans. Harry Zohn. Translated and reprinted, 1973. London: Collins/Fontana.
Bharat-Muni
1967   *The Natyasastra*, trans. Manomohan Ghosh. Calcutta: Granthalaya.
Bhardwaj, Surinder Mohan
1973   *Hindu Places of Pilgrimage in India.* Berkeley: University of California Press.
Bhattacharyya, Asutosh
1972   *Chhau Dance of Purulia.* Calcutta: Rabindra Bharat University Press.
1975   Program for Chhau dancers used at the University of Michigan, Ann Arbor.
Bierman, James H.
1979   "Disneyland and the 'Los Angelization' of the Arts." In *American Popular Entertainment*, ed. Myron Matlaw. Westport, Conn.: Greenwood Press.
Birdwhistell, Ray L.
1964   "Communication without Words." Manuscript supplied by Eastern Pennsylvania Psychiatric Institute, Philadelphia.
Bouissac, Paul
1982   "System versus Process in the Understanding of Performances." In *Multimedia Communication, Volume II: Theatre Semiotics*, ed. Ernest W. B. Hess-Lutich. Tübingen: Gunter Narr Verlag.
Brandon, James R.
1978   "Training at the Waseda Little Theatre." *Drama Review* 22, 4: 29–42.
Brassai [Gyula Halasz]
1976   *The Secret Paris of the 30's.* New York: Pantheon Books.
Braun, Edward, ed.
1969   *Meyerhold on Theatre.* New York: Hill and Wang.
Brecht, Bertolt
1964   *Brecht on Theatre*, ed. John Willett. New York: Hill and Wang.
Brook, Peter
1973   "On Africa (an Interview)." *Drama Review* 17, 3: 37–51.
Brown, Trisha
1975   "Three Pieces." *Drama Review* 19, 1: 26–32.
Burgheart, Catherine
1981   "Sex Theatre." *Drama Review* 25, 1: 69–78.
Burzynski, Tadeusz, and Osinski, Zbigniew
1979   *Grotowski's Laboratory.* Warsaw: Interpress.
Byrski, M. Christopher
1973   *Concept of Ancient India Theatre.* New Delhi: Munshiram Manorharlal Publishers.
Cage, John
1965   "An Interview." *Tulane Drama Review* 10, 2: 50–72.
Chaikin, Joseph
1972   *The Presence of the Actor.* New York: Atheneum.
Chelkowski, Peter, ed.
1979   *Ta'ziyeh: Ritual and Drama in Iran.* New York: New York University Press.

Covarrubias, Miguel
   1937   *Island of Bali.* Kuala Lumpur: Oxford University Press. Reprinted, 1972.
Csikszentmihalyi, Mihaly
   1975   *Beyond Boredom and Anxiety.* San Francisco: Jossey-Bass.
Dasgupta, Gautam
   1983   "Squat: Nature Theatre of New York." *Performing Arts Journal* 7, 1: 7–20.
Davis, Douglas
   1981   "Post Performancism." *Artforum,* October, pp. 31–39.
Davy, Kate
   1974   "Foreman's *Vertical Mobility* and *PAIN(T).*" *Drama Review* 18, 2: 26–37.
Dodds, E. R.
   1951   *The Greeks and the Irrational.* Berkeley: University of California Press.
Drama Review
   1981   Sex and Performance issue, 25, 1.
Ekman, Paul; Friesen, Wallace V.; and Ellsworth, Phoebe
   1972   *Emotion in the Human Face.* New York: Pergamon Press.
Eliade, Mircea
   1965   *Rites and Symbols of Initiation.* New York: Harper.
   1970   *Shamanism: Archaic Techniques of Ecstasy.* Princeton: Princeton University
         Press.
Evanchuk, Robin
   1977–78   "Problems in Reconstructing a Shaker Religious Dance Ritual." *Journal
            of the Association of Graduate Dance Ethnologists* 1 (UCLA).
Foreman, Richard
   1976   *Plays and Manifestos,* ed. Kate Davy. New York: New York University Press.
Gardner, Robert
   1975   Presumed author of the shooting script used in the filming of the
         agnicayana of 1975. Script titled *Atiratra Agnicayana.* Undated photocopy
         of typescript.
Garner, Nathan C., and Turnbull, Colin M.
   1979   *Anthropology, Drama, and the Human Experience.* Washington, D.C.: George
         Washington University, Division of Experimental Programs.
Geertz, Clifford
   1973   *The Interpretation of Cultures.* New York: Basic Books.
   1980   "Blurred Genres." *American Scholar* 49, 2: 165–182.
Goffman, Erving
   1959   *The Presentation of Self in Everyday Life.* Garden City, N.Y.: Doubleday/
         Anchor.
   1974   *Frame Analysis.* New York: Harper Colophon Books.
Goldberg, RoseLee
   1979   *Performance.* New York: Harry N. Abrams.
Grimes, Ronald L.
   1981   "The Theatre of Sources." *Drama Review* 25, 3: 67–74.
   1982   *Beginnings in Ritual Studies.* Washington, D.C.: University Press of America.
Grotowski, Jerzy
   1968   *Towards a Poor Theatre.* Holstebro, Denmark: Odin Teatret Forlag.
   1973   "Holiday." *Drama Review* 17, 2: 113–35.
Haas, Irwin
   1974   *America's Historic Villages and Restorations.* Secaucus, N.J.: Citadel Press.

Hawley, John Stratton
   1981   *At Play with Krishna.* Princeton: Princeton University Press.
Hein, N.
   1972   *The Miracle Plays of Mathura.* New Haven: Yale University Press.
Ishii, Tatsuro
   1982   "An Examination into the Mature Thought and Conceptual Framework Presented in the Later Treatises of Zeami." Manuscript.
International Theatre Information
   1978   "Theatre of Sources," winter, pp. 2–3. Paris: UNESCO.
Kafka, Franz
   1954   *Wedding Preparations in the Country and Other Posthumous Prose Writings.* London: Secker and Warburg.
Kaprow, Allan
   1966   *Assemblages, Environments, and Happenings.* New York: Harry N. Abrams.
Khokar, Mohan
   1983   "The Greatest Step in Bharatanatyam." *New Delhi Sunday Statesman,* 16 January, p. 4–1.
Kirby, E. T.
   1974   "The Shamanistic Origins of Popular Entertainments." *Drama Review* 18, 1: 5–15.
Kirby, Michael
   1965   *Happenings.* New York: E. P. Dutton.
   1972   "On Acting and Non-Acting." *Drama Review* 16, 1: 3–15.
Kolankiewicz, Leszek, ed.
   1978   *On the Road to Active Culture.* Wroclaw: Theatre Laboratory. (The pamphlet notes that it is not for publication. It was prepared for use by participants in a symposium on 4–5 June organized by Jerzy Grotowski.)
Kott, Jan
   1980   "After Grotowski: The End of the Impossible Theatre." *Theatre Quarterly* 38: 27–32.
Kriazi, Gary
   1976   *The Great American Amusement Park.* Secaucus, N.J.: Citadel Press.
Lannoy, Richard
   1971   *The Speaking Tree.* London: Oxford University Press.
Levi-Strauss, Claude
   1963   "The Sorcerer and His Magic." In *Structural Anthropology.* New York: Basic Books.
Lex, Barbara W.
   1979   "The Neurobiology of Ritual Trance." In *The Spectrum of Ritual* by Eugene G. d'Aquili, Charles D. Laughlin, Jr., and John McManus. New York: Columbia University Press.
Loeffler, Carl E., ed.
   1980   *Performance Anthology.* San Francisco: Contemporary Arts Press.
Lomax, Alan
   1973   "Cinema Science and Cultural Renewal." *Current Anthropology* 14, 4: 480.
Mackay, Patricia
   1977   "Theme Parks." *Theatre Crafts,* September, pp. 27 ff.

Malpede, Karen, ed.
1974   *Three Works by the Open Theatre.* New York: Drama Book Specialists.
Marriott, McKim
1982   Letter to Richard Schechner, manuscript.
Martin, Carol
1979   *"The Shakers:* Sources and Restoration." Manuscript.
Martin, Carol, and Schechner, Richard
1982   "Grand Kabuki." *Alive* 1, 2: 40–41.
1983   "Seminars/Workshops at the Padatik/ITI Calcutta Meetings, January 1983."
        Quarterly Journal of the National Centre for the Performing Arts (Bombay).
McNamara, Brooks
1974   "The Scenography of Popular Entertainments." *Drama Review* 18, 1: 16–24.
1977   "Come on Over: The Rise and Fall of the American Amusement Park."
        Theatre Crafts 11: 86 ff.
Mead, Margaret
1970   "Presenting: The Very Recent Past." *New York Times Sunday Magazine,* 15
        March, pp. 29–32.
Mennen, Richard
1975   "Grotowski's Paratheatrical Projects." *Drama Review* 19, 4: 58–69.
Miller, Tim
1981   Article describing how roles are cast and prepared at Plimoth Plantation. *Old
        Colony Memorial* (Plymouth, Mass.), 2 April.
Moore, Alexander
1980   "Walt Disney World: Bounded Ritual Space and the Playful Pilgrimage
        Center." *Anthropological Quarterly* 53, 4: 207–18.
Moran, Maurice J., Jr.
1978   "Living Museums: Coney Islands of the Mind." Master's thesis, New York
        University, Department of Performance Studies.
Myerhoff, Barbara
1976   "Balancing between Worlds: The Shaman's Calling." *Parabola* 1, 2: 6–13.
1978   *Number Our Days.* New York: E. P. Dutton.
Nearman, Mark J.
1978   "Zeami's *Kyui." Monumenta Nipponica* 33, 3: 299–331.
O'Flaherty, Wendy Doniger
1982   "The Dream Narrative and the Indian Doctrine of Illusion." *Daedalus* 111,
        3: 93–114.
Paul, Robert A.
1978   Review of *Altar of Fire. American Anthropologist* 80: 197–199.
Pavis, Patrice
1982   *Languages of the Stage.* New York: Performing Arts Journal Publications.
Plimoth Plantation
1980   "2/80." Information sheet distributed by the Plantation.
Princep, James
1830   *Benares Illustrated in a Series of Drawings.* Calcutta: Baptist Mission Press.
Quintero, José
1982   "Where Are the New Directors? *New York Times,* Arts and Leisure Section,
        28 November, 1–23.
Rassers, W. H.
1959   *Panji, the Culture Hero.* The Hague: Martinus Nijhoff.

Read, Kenneth E.
  1965   *The High Valley.* New York: Charles Scribner's Sons.
Reilly, Tom
  1981   Article in the *Sippican Sentinel,* Marion, Mass., 19 April, concerning Plimoth
          Plantation.
Reinhold, Robert
  1982   "An 'Overwhelming' Violence-TV Tie." *New York Times,* 6 May, C-27.
Richardson, Jack
  1975   "Six o'Clock Prays: TV News as Pop Religion." *Harper's,* December, p. 38.
Rilke, Rainer Maria
  1952   *Duino Elegies,* trans. J. B. Leishman and Stephen Spender. London: Hogarth
          Press.
Rubin, Dorothy
  1982   "Historical Authenticity? The Process of Reconstruction." Manuscript, New
          York University, Department of Performance Studies.
Sankalia, H. D.
  1973   *Ramayana—Myth or Reality?* New Delhi: People's Publishing House.
Schechner, Richard
  1969   *Public Domain.* New York: Bobbs-Merrill.
  1973*a* "Drama, Script, Theatre, and Performance." *Drama Review* 17, 3: 5–36.
  1973*b* *Environmental Theater.* New York: Hawthorn.
  1974   "Letter from Calcutta." *Salmugundi,* no. 25: 47–76.
  1976   "The Performance Group in India." *Quarterly Journal of the National Centre
          for the Performing Arts* (Bombay) 5, 2: 9–28.
  1977   *Essays on Performance Theory.* New York: Drama Book Specialists.
  1978   "Anthropological Analysis." *Drama Review* 22, 3: 23–32.
  1982*a* "Ramlila of Ramnagar: An Introduction." *Quarterly Journal of the National
          Centre for the Performing Arts* (Bombay) 11, 3 and 4: 66–98.
  1982*b* *The End of Humanism.* New York: Performing Arts Journal Publications.
  1982*c* "Ramlila of Ramnagar and America's Oberammergau: Two Celebratory
          Ritual Dramas." In *Celebration,* ed. Victor Turner. Washington, D.C.: Smith-
          sonian Institution Press.
  1983   *Performative Circumstances from the Avant Garde to Ramlila.* Calcutta: Seagull
          Books.
Schechner, Richard, ed.
  1970   *Dionysus in 69.* New York: Farrar, Straus, and Giroux.
  1982   Intercultural Performance Issue. *Drama Review* 94.
Schechner, Richard, and Hess, Linda
  1977   "The Ramlila of Ramnagar." *Drama Review,* 21, 3: 51–82.
Schechner, Richard, and Schuman, Mady, eds.
  1976   *Ritual, Play, and Performance.* New York: Seabury Press.
Schwartz, Tony
  1982   "The Tumult in TV News." *New York Times,* 1 March, C-15.
Shank, Adele Edling, and Shank, Theodore
  1978   "Squat Theatre's *Andy Warhol's Last Love.*" *Drama Review* 22, 3: 11–22.
Shank, Theodore
  1982   *American Alternative Theatre.* New York: Grove Press.
Singer, Milton
  1972   *When a Great Tradition Modernizes.* London: Pall Mall Press.

Spicer, Edward H.
  1980   *The Yaquis.* Tucson: University of Arizona Press.
Spolin, Viola
  1963   *Improvisation for the Theater.* Evanston, Ill.: Northwestern University Press.
Squat Theatre
  1978   "Answers: Making a Point." *Drama Review* 22, 3: 3–10.
Staal, Frits
  1978   "The Meaninglessness of Ritual." Manuscript.
  1979   "Comment: *Altar of Fire,*" a response to Robert A. Paul. *American Anthropologist* 81: 346–47.
  1983   *Agni: The Vedic Ritual of the Fire Altar.* Berkeley: Asian Humanities Press.
Stanislavski, Konstantin
  1946   *An Actor Prepares.* New York: Theatre Arts Books.
  1949   *Building a Character.* New York: Theatre Arts Books.
  1961   *Creating a Role.* New York: Theatre Arts Books.
  1962   *Stanislavsky on the Art of the Stage,* trans. and with an introductory essay by David Magarshack. New York: Hill and Wang.
Suzuki, Tadashi
  1982   "The Word Is an Act of the Body." *Performing Arts Journal* 17: 88–92.
Tarlekar, G. H.
  1975   *Studies in the Natyasastra.* Delhi: Motilal Banarsidass.
Tulasi Das (Tulsidas)
  1952   Translation of the *Ramcaritamanasa* [*Ramcharitmanas*] by W. D. P. Hill. Bombay: Oxford University Press.
Turnbull, Colin
  1972   *The Mountain People.* New York: Simon and Schuster.
  1976   "Turnbull Replies." *Royal Anthropological Institute News,* no. 16.
Turner, Victor
  1969   *The Ritual Process.* Chicago: Aldine.
  1974   *Dramas, Fields, and Metaphors.* Ithaca, N.Y.: Cornell University Press.
  1979a "The Anthropology of Performance." In *Process, Performance, and Pilgrimage.* New Delhi: Concept Publishing Company.
  1979b "Dramatic Ritual/Ritual Drama: Performative and Reflexive Anthropology." *Kenyon Review,* n. s., 1, 3: 80–93.
  1982a *From Ritual to Theatre: The Human Seriousness of Play.* New York: Performing Arts Journal Press.
  1982b "Are There Universals of Performance?" Paper prepared for Wenner-Gren Foundation for Anthropological Research, Symposium no. 89: "Theatre and Ritual," 23 August–1 September.
Turner, Victor, and Turner, Edith
  1982   "Performing Ethnography." *Drama Review* 26, 2: 33–50.
Valencia, Anselmo
  1981   Transcript of remarks made to a Conference on Yaqui Deer Dance and Pascola Dance sponsored by the Wenner-Gren Foundation for Anthropological Research, Oracle, Ariz., November.
Van Gennep, Arnold
  1960   *The Rites of Passage* (originally published in 1908). Chicago: University of Chicago Press.

Vatsayan, Kapila
  1968   *Classical Indian Dance in Literature and the Arts.* New Delhi: Sangeet Natak Akademi.
  1974   *Indian Classical Dance.* New Delhi: Publications Division, Ministry of Education and Broadcasting.
Waters, Harry F.
  1982   "Life According to TV." *Newsweek,* 6 December, pp. 136–40.
Wilmeth, Don B.
  1982   *Variety Entertainment and Outdoor Amusements: A Reference Guide.* Westport, Conn.: Greenwood Press.
Winnicott, D. W.
  1971   *Playing and Reality.* London: Tavistock.
Youngerman, Suzanne
  1978   "The Translation of Culture into Choreography." In *Essays in Dance Research,* ed. Dianne L. Woodruff. Dance Research Annual, vol. 9. New York: CORD.
Zarrilli, Phillip B.
  1982   "Body Work: The Physical Shape and Experience of Culture." Manuscript.
Zeami
  1968   *Kadensho* (originally written in 1405?) Kyoto: Sumiya-Shinobe Publishing Institute.

INDEX